Enfield Voices

The Birth of the People's Universities

Edited by Tom Bourner and Tony Crilly

Enfield Voices

Enfield Voices

'… the essential feature of the polytechnic as an urban community university, as a people's university, must be its responsibility and responsiveness to the democracy rather than its insulation from it.'
Eric Robinson, *The New Polytechnics* (1968).

Much of life changed in Britain in the 1960s. The tiredness induced by the war effort gave way to a new energy, and this manifested itself in a drive to make higher education more accessible. The liveliest evidence of this occurred in lowly colleges in the further education sector where arose courses of study leading to vocational degrees of a very high standard. Enfield College of Technology was a leading player in this movement. Its story is told here.

Enfield Voices

ISBN: 9781717559715

All feedback is welcome.

tom.bourner@ntlworld.com or tonycrilly42@gmail.com

This book is available through Amazon

Contents

PART TWO
MID-TIME ARRIVALS
1966-1968

PART THREE
LATER COMERS
1969-72

Abbreviations

ATTI	Association of Teachers in Technical Institutions
AUT	Association of University Teachers
BABS	BA Business Studies
BAEBA	BA European Business Administration
BASS	BA Social Science
CAT	College of Advanced Technology
CNAA	Council for National Academic Awards
DipHE	Diploma in Higher Education
ECT	Enfield College of Technology
EITB	Engineering Industries Industrial Training Board
FE	Further Education
GCE	General Certificate of Education
GCSE	General Certificate of Secondary Education
HE	Higher Education
HEAC	Higher Education Advisory Centre
HEFC	Higher Education Funding Council
HNC	Higher National Certificate
HND	Higher National Diploma
ITB	Industrial Training Board
LSE	London School of Economics
M for B	Mathematics for Business Degree
MandM	Methods and Models
NATFHE	National Association of Teachers in Further and Higher Education
NELP	North East London Polytechnic
NPL	National Physical Laboratory
ONC	Ordinary National Certificate
OND	Ordinary National Diploma
OU	Open University
PGCE	Postgraduate Certificate of Education
PIC	Programmed Instruction Centre
RAC	Regional Advisory Council
RSA	Royal Society of Arts
SSRC	Social Sciences Research Council
UCL	University College London
UGC	University Grants Committee

Introduction

TOM BOURNER and TONY CRILLY

> *'Nobody reads introductions, they serve no useful purpose, and they give no pleasure,..'* (H. G. Wells, 1915, p.5)
>
> *'The word introduction spooks me; nobody reads introductions. Most readers want to get to the meat of a book ...'* (Safire, W. 1997, p. xiv)
>
> *'Nobody reads introductions' might be described as a publishing truism, however painful to the feelings of an author who has made considerable efforts to explain key facts about their book.'* (Knowles, 2010, p.71)

Apparently, introductions to books do not always get read. So we'll keep this one short. This introduction seeks to answer a number of questions. We thought we'd list these at the outset to help you decide which, if any, parts of the introduction you want to read. The questions are:

1. What is this book about?
2. What kind of book is it?
3. What is the rationale for this book?
4. How did it come about? What were its origins?
5. What are aims of the book
6. Who wrote it?
7. Aren't lots of accounts of people's experiences of the same college likely to be subjective, repetitive and/or idiosyncratic?

What is this book about?

This is a book about Enfield College of Technology, which existed between 1962 and 1972. Enfield College of Technology is often abbreviated by the contributors to this book by 'ECT' which is also an abbreviation for 'error correction term', 'extended combat training' and 'electro-convulsive therapy'. We thought you'd like to know that.

The book is about what it was like to work and study at ECT. It is also about higher education (HE) in England outside of the universities at a time when HE was starting to change at an unprecedented rate. And it is about an experiment in HE.

What kind of book is this?

The book comprises reports of the experiences of twenty-eight people who taught and/or studied at ECT in the 1960s and early 1970s. These contain a set of first-hand accounts of the college at that time. The book also contains some contextual material about education in England at the time and some historical context on the college before it became ECT. In addition, there is a concluding chapter, which provides an account of the college that is as compatible as possible with the twenty-eight reports that are at the heart of the book.

What is the rationale for this book?

A book about a college of technology that existed for less than a dozen years in the Ponders End part of North London, about half a century ago needs some justification.

Higher education in Britain changed direction in the 1960s. At the start of the 1960s there was considerable dissatisfaction with Britain's university-led higher education. Although it was, for the most part, publicly funded, higher education offered little preparation for most of those who did not pursue an academic career and its research was subject-centred with relatively little concern for its social impact. Also, it was elitist in that those from the working class, the lowest and largest order of society, were massively under-represented, particularly in the most prestigious institutions of higher education. That dissatisfaction was most evident in the Labour Party (Taylor and Steele, 2011) but was also present in the Conservative Party and eventually found expression in the announcement of the Robbins Committee in 1960 by Harold MacMillan's Conservative government.

In the early 1960s less than 5 per cent of school-leavers attended university and when they graduated, most (about two-thirds) of the new graduates remained within the higher education system

(Bourner and Rospigliosi, 2008).[1] Universities were relatively unconcerned about preparing their students for employment outside of academia or the impact of their research outside of the academic disciplines within which it was located. A decade later much had changed. The percentage of school-leavers gaining degrees had more than doubled and groundwork had been laid for the transition from an elite system of higher education to mass higher education. There was increasing concern about the vocational relevance of higher education and more people were recognising the potential of research to impact society, the community and the lives of individuals. Arguably, the colleges of technology in Britain played a significant role in that change and ECT was a leading example. This book explores what it was like to have been part of that college during this key period in British higher education.

Why is this worth recording? There are several reasons. First, the role of technical colleges in the development of British higher education has been neglected; most attention has been focused on universities as the more elevated part of the system. Second, Enfield was a particularly interesting technical college, alive with the ideas that prompted the creation of the binary system of higher education. Third, it is now 50 years later and possible to see ECT in historical perspective. An account written at the time would have contained much speculation of the 'what would happen if' kind. We now know what actually happened and with what consequences.

How did the book come about?

The origin of this book was a conversation between the two editors (Tony and Tom) in the café of the Wellcome Foundation in 2016. We first met at ECT almost 50 years previously and we were reflecting on what a remarkable place ECT had seemed in the late 1960s but we had difficulty identifying what was so special about the place at that time. We thought it would be really interesting to read about other people's thoughts on their experiences at that time.

So the main factor prompting the production of this book was that ECT seemed to have been a remarkable place. Arguably, it was

[1] They became teachers, researchers, scholars, education administrators or went on to further academic training.

the place that pioneered the application of some new ideas about higher education in Britain in the early 1960s and made a significant contribution to the transformation of higher education in Britain in the second half of the twentieth century. Certainly, it was a place that was interesting, exciting and influential on people who taught there.

Our evidence for that last sentence is that we found no difficulty in persuading people who worked there at some time between 1962 and 1972 to write about their experience. Even though that experience was over 50 years ago in most cases, and many of the contributors are therefore 'old' by any reasonable definition of that word. Moreover, in so doing, we discovered that others before us had spoken about recording in book form what had happened at ECT in the decade after 1962. Also, we pretty soon discovered the website *Science, Society and Creativity at Middlesex University* which contained a copy of an article, '*Sparks Flying*', on the history of ECT (Carr and Roberts, 1998). Unfortunately, our attempts to contact the person, Andrew Roberts, who set up that website (Roberts, 2002-) have met with no success, prompting us to question whether he is still alive.

In addition, there was our own experience of teaching at ECT that convinced us that something was happening there that was interesting, exciting and significant. So our personal motivation for assembling this book was to find out if this was also true for others and, if so, why did it seem so special and significant? We were also curious about the different perspectives of those others. Basically, we wanted to learn more about what had gone on at ECT.

What are the aims of this book?

The book has three main aims. First, to explore what had happened in what was a leading college of technology at the birth of the binary system of HE in England. Second, to discover what, if anything, was so special about this particular college at that time. And, third, to help contribute to remedying the lack of study of English HE outside of the universities at an important time for HE in England.

Who wrote it?

The contributors of this book are not a representative sample or even a balanced sample. Most of the contributors are people who the book's editors are still in touch with or people that those people are in touch with. Some are the result of happy accidents, like spotting a letter to the editor of a newspaper from one of the contributors, or pure serendipity, including a chance meeting in a supermarket. So this is a convenience sample with all the caveats thereby implied.

It turned out that some of the participants had worked in the engineering/technology part of the college, some had worked in the business studies part and some had worked in the areas of social sciences and humanities. It also turned out that some had joined the college in the early days (1962-64), some in the middle period (1965-69) and some in the last years (1970-72). So fortuitously, there is some representativeness and balance in this collection of these accounts of working at ECT.

The brief for the participants was simply to write an account of their experiences of ECT. Most chose to start with their account of how they got to ECT and what they did after they left. That provides some information about where they were coming from (literally and metaphorically) and what they subsequently did with the experience they gained at ECT.

Beyond that, there is great variety in the accounts contributed. This is unsurprising because, as noted, some of the contributors were in the engineering/technology part of the college and others were in social sciences and some were there at the start of ECT while others were there in its final years and remained there when it was part of Middlesex Polytechnic. In addition, some of the contributors were in relatively senior positions while others were in relatively junior positions when they were at ECT. Some threw themselves into the politics of the place and others steered clear of that. Some were very active in course development and all that implied at ECT whereas others were more focused on the development of the subjects they taught. All these factors and others would have impacted on their experience of ECT.

The result therefore is not a book of twenty-eight different accounts, or different perspectives, on a common Enfield experience. Rather, it is a book of twenty-eight different experiences depending on where and when contributors were at ECT and on the contributors themselves, including their values, beliefs, gender, age and, not least, their politics.

Aren't lots of accounts of people's experiences of ECT likely to be subjective, repetitive and/or idiosyncratic?

Yes. From our perspective this also makes them more interesting, revealing and authentic. There is much that is hidden from 'objective' accounts or accounts based on official documents. The hidden subtext includes what if felt like to be part of the place, which, of course, impacted greatly on what actually happened in the college.

We hope this book will shed light on a range of issues including what it felt like to be a lecturer and student at ECT, what was unique, or at least distinctive at the college and what contribution ECT made to the development of HE in Britain in the ensuing decades.

1. Education in England when Enfield Tech became Enfield College of Technology

TOM BOURNER

This chapter provides some context for the establishment of Enfield College of Technology (ECT) in 1962. It gives a brief account of the educational system in England at the start of the 1960s, adds some additional detail on higher education (HE) in particular and then looks at how HE was changing at that time.[2] All social phenomena are affected by their contexts and ECT was no exception. The chapters in this book are deliberately subjective, partial and personal. In order to make sense of what happened at Enfield and assess its significance it helps to recognise the broader educational context within which it occurred.

Education; primary, secondary and tertiary

The early 1960s was a pivotal time in the development of the education system in England. By that time the provisions of the Education Act of 1944 had worked themselves out and it had become clear what they meant in practice. Also, there was increasing recognition that participation in HE was lower in the UK than in other countries that were overtaking Britain in terms of economic development, combined with a growing belief that education and, in particular HE, was a key factor in Britain's future material wellbeing. And there was increasing concern about excessive specialisation of subject-centred HE within single-subject Honours degree courses.

Primary school education, at the start of the 1960s, was, for the most part, comprehensive. The large majority of children went to state schools, which were nearly all mixed schools. They had set periods of reading, writing (mostly 'composition') and the acquisi-

[2] To have included the education system of the rest of Britain would have led to a much longer chapter as it would have included many exceptions, qualifications and accounts of variations in practice. And it is not clear that the educational variants in the other parts of Britain had a significant impact on development of Enfield College of Technology even at a contextual level.

tion of some numeracy skills. In addition, they had the contextual studies of history and geography, and some additional studies to broaden pupils' educational experience including art, music, religious knowledge, PE and possibly nature study. A small minority of children, however, were in private education and an even smaller minority attended schools that followed an alternative philosophy of education, such as Montessori Schools, Steiner Schools and 'free' schools such as Summerhill.

At the end of their primary school the pupils could take the eleven-plus examination, which determined what kind of secondary school they would attend. In theory, there were three kinds of schools: 'grammar schools', 'secondary modern schools' and 'technical schools' (officially 'secondary technical schools' and in some areas described as 'technical grammar schools').

Those who passed the eleven-plus went to grammar schools, which provided a more 'academic' education than the secondary modern schools. It was believed that most of the children going to grammar schools would progress to non-manual occupations and most of the children going to secondary modern schools would go on to some form of manual employment, skilled, semi-skilled or unskilled.

The academic education provided by the grammar schools was largely determined by the examinations of the General Certificate of Education (GCE). There were two levels of GCE: ordinary level (O-level) and advanced level (A-level). These examinations were not set by the schools themselves but by examination boards run by groups of universities, each offering slightly different syllabuses in a slightly different range of subjects.

The large majority of grammar school pupils took O-levels at the age of sixteen in between 6 and 10 subjects depending on perceived academic ability of different pupils and the ambitions of different schools. In order to progress to A-level study it was normally necessary to pass at least 5 subjects at O-level.

Of those who stayed on after O-levels, the large majority of students took A-level after two years of further study, i.e. at the age of eighteen. The A-level examinations were also run by groups of universities. A-level studies were much more specialised than O-levels with most students studying three related subjects. Thus, for example, a popular combination of subjects was pure mathematics, applied mathematics and physics. Students choosing that combination could spend the majority of their time studying only mathematics.

There was much criticism of the excessive specialisation at GCE A-level. Subject specialists, however, particularly those in universities, pointed to the high levels of attainment that specialisation allowed and saw A-levels as the 'gold standard' of education at school. Some university academics defended that specialisation as necessary to enable them to maintain academic standards and realise academic excellence on university courses. In response to the narrowness of A-level studies many grammar schools put on courses of general studies and eventually a GCE A-level in General Studies was introduced.

There were two main ways that the universities exercised control over what was taught in grammar schools. First, the syllabuses of A-levels (and O-levels) were set by the consortia of universities. Second, entry to a university course was based, for the most part, on competition in terms of grades attained in those A-level examinations. The result was that majority of grammar school students would receive an education aimed at preparing them for university study even though only a small minority of them would go on to university.

In addition to the pressure to prepare students for university entry, the education provided by grammar schools was influenced by perceptions of the nature of education at elite public schools, a legacy of the idea of liberal, classics-based, education inherited from pre-war educational provision. Thus, for example, in the early 1960s most grammar school students would learn Latin for a number of years.

When the secondary modern schools were established after the 1944 Education Act they embodied no clear philosophy of secondary education. According to the Ministry of Education, they were intended to 'offer a good all-round secondary education, not focused primarily on the traditional subjects of the school curriculum but developing out of the interests of the children' (Ministry of Education, 1947). Most of the new secondary modern schools simply offered more of the same sort of education that had been provided in the pre-war elementary schools. Some, however, offered studies with a more vocational orientation in one or a few specialist subjects such as arts/crafts, furnishing, seamanship, shorthand and typing. And in some secondary modern schools it was possible for the more academic students to take some GCE O-levels examinations.[3] Most secondary school pupils would take no external examinations.

Those who went to secondary modern schools received an education that proceeded at a slower pace as befits a group of students which the eleven-plus examination had deemed less intelligent. And for most, it ended at the age of fifteen when the large majority would proceed to employment or vocational training. The term 'vocational education' was usually used as a euphemism for education aimed preparing students for some sort of manual employment of a skilled, semi-skilled or unskilled kind.

In addition to the 'grammar schools' and 'secondary modern schools' there were also, in theory, 'technical schools'. These completed what was known as the 'tripartite system' of secondary education in the state system of secondary education. The idea was that the technical schools would be for able pupils whose interests and aptitudes were more orientated towards industrial or commercial matters. In practice, many local authorities did not provide technical schools, partly because they were unable to recruit qualified teaching staff with technical skills, partly because some people in the local education system thought they were unnecessary but most often because the technical schools were overshadowed by the status and prestige of grammar schools. So even where a tripartite system existed, the places at the technical school were given to those who failed to get the grades needed for grammar school.

In 1963 there were only 204 technical schools compared with 3,906 secondary modern schools and 1,295 grammar schools (Burgess, 1964). Moreover, that was 16 fewer technical schools than in 1962 and their falling number reflected the fact that they were a failing project by that time.

On leaving school at age fifteen, most pupils from secondary modern and technical schools would go directly into employment, sometimes through an apprenticeship or take a course of further study at a local technical college. Day release from employment was

---

[3] In 1961/62, 5.7 per cent of school leavers from secondary modern schools were entered for one or more GCE O-levels (Burgess, 1964). In a very small minority of secondary modern schools it was possible to study for A-levels.

a common option. In 1961 Enfield College at Ponders End was such a technical college.

At the 'local tech' students could take vocationally orientated courses. These courses can be classified into short courses and long courses (Cowling, 1998). Most of the short courses were administered by the Royal Society of Arts (RSA) or the City and Guilds of the London Institute. These bodies determined the syllabuses, assessment and how units could be combined into awards.

The long courses lasted for two or three years of part-time study or two years of full-time study. They were usually based on combinations of units, similar in size to the short courses. The most common part-time course was the Ordinary National Certificate (ONC) and the most common full-time course was the Ordinary National Diploma (OND). These courses were administered by a number of different bodies, each responsible for a different sector of industry or commerce.[4]

ONC courses were intended for students in employment and usually lasted three years and it was common for school-leavers taken on as apprentices to spend one day a week (or its equivalent) at the local technical college studying for a relevant vocational qualification. The OND was designed for students not in full-time employment and normally took two years.

Thus, the main difference in practice between a long course and an equivalent number of short courses was the former would be designed from the outset to fit together as a coherent whole. For the latter, the packages of short courses that were defined by the examining boards provided some coherence, but these packages were basically built bottom-up rather than top-down, and the courses themselves were designed primarily to be taken individually rather than as components of packages. Where they were taken individually, then any coherence would depend very much on the individual student making a good set of choices as to what courses to take and when, although obviously the colleges (and industrial training managers in the case of those on apprenticeships) would advise students as to what combinations of courses were sensible. (Cowling, 1998, p.3)

---

[4] They were later (1985) amalgamated into one body called the Business and Technician Education Council (BTEC).

If we were to look for a rationale for this whole system of secondary education provided by the state, then it might go along the following lines. Society needed education to prepare students for the rest of their lives including their employment. Some people would have a job doing non-manual work, which as the term implies, meant they mainly used their heads rather than their hands and others would have jobs which mainly used their hands i.e. manual work. The more senior positions in society were associated with the former and it was believed it would be better for society if these more senior positions were occupied by the more intelligent persons. Developments in psychology during the early decades of the twentieth century seemed to show that it is possible to measure intelligence by means of IQ tests. The eleven-plus examination was largely based on IQ tests.[5] It was therefore intended to identify children who were more intelligent and therefore better suited to an education that would prepare them for non-manual positions where they were more likely to progress to the more senior, more influential, positions in society. The students who failed the eleven-plus were perceived as less intelligent and mostly destined for less elevated employment.

Those who supported the introduction of this system saw it as a major advance on what had preceded it in the 1930s and before, when the most important decisions in society had been taken by socially stratified elites, irrespective of intelligence, when there was very limited social mobility and when many 'brighter' pupils ended up in employment where they were engaged in manual work. The new system offered a way of increasing the likelihood that the more important decisions in a society, largely organised hierarchically, would be taken by those who were more intelligent. It was also intended to enhance social mobility within society, reduce the waste of talent of intelligent children from working class homes ending up in manual employment and diminish the probability that children would end up in the kind of employment for which they were least suited.

By the end of the 1950s, the reality of the system had worked itself out and it became clear that the 1944 Education Act had unintended consequences. Here are three of the larger ones. First, the

[5] The eleven-plus examination varied across the country but testing verbal reasoning and non-verbal reasoning were common strands.

great majority of school children who failed to 'win' a grammar school place were labelled 'failures' at the tender age of eleven and that label was publicly displayed throughout their puberty, their teenage years and beyond.[6] Second, it established a hierarchy based on dubious IQ tests that ran from 'smart' at the top to 'dumb' at the bottom rather than any more sophisticated notions of intelligence (Gardner, 1983) or, indeed, any other talents, aptitudes and strengths of different children. Third, the education provided by grammar schools was orientated towards university admission, with excessive specialisation too early. And the more general education provided by the secondary modern schools was often so dull that many school-children ached to leave the earliest opportunity i.e. at the age of fifteen.

Higher education at the start of the 1960s

In 1961 England, it was possible to pursue a course of higher education in a range of institutions: universities, specialist colleges such as teacher training colleges, institutions of advanced technology and technical colleges.

Universities. The universities can be grouped into Oxbridge, London, the civic universities and the new universities. Oxford and Cambridge had histories going back to the high Middle Ages.[7] Both Oxford and Cambridge started as institutions providing education for students, most of whom would go on to serve the Latin Church. In that sense, they started out as seminaries and, hence, vocational institutions. Each of those universities developed as a conglomerate of more or less independent colleges, which gradually became more integrated.

Towards the end of the Middle Ages, the crisis in the Latin Church produced a crisis in the universities with falling numbers of

[6] Being labelled a 'loser' on the basis of 'objective' assessment could undermine a child's self-esteem, aspirations, self-confidence and self-efficacy (Bandura, 1997).

[7] Traditionally, 1167 for Oxford and 1209 for Cambridge, though the precise dates are disputed.

students and financial difficulties for many of the colleges.[8] Consequently, they sought to recruit students who could afford fees high enough for the colleges to survive and thrive. They increasingly offered a higher education that would attract students who were well-heeled and well-connected. This education included the fashionable new learning from the Italian Renaissance. The universities thereby reinvented their mission so that during the early modern period, Oxford and Cambridge sought to produce Godly gentlemen who could tell good from bad morally, intellectually, socially and aesthetically. To this end, they offered a classics-based liberal education. For the most part, they became finishing schools for young gentlemen. And in the nineteenth century this mission, in turn, was challenged by that of the accumulation of new knowledge and provision of an academic higher education that was specialised, research-led and subject-centred.

The best known response to that challenge was provided by John Henry Newman (1873) who produced an account of an idealised version of classics-based liberal HE as one that favoured breadth of knowledge, development of the powers of the mind and, in the words of Matthew Arnold, an introduction to 'the best that has been thought and said in the world' (Arnold, 1869). Despite this, subject-centred, academic HE continued to make inroads into Oxbridge education. Perhaps the most decisive event was in 1917 when Oxford and Cambridge along with other universities in the country agreed to adopt the PhD/DPhil degree as the highest award for which it was possible to register at a university. This implied a system of HE with research degrees as the highest form of HE and research degrees as specialised, research-focused and subject-centred. There were several more decades of struggle between the claims of classics-based liberal HE and subject-centred academic HE but in

---

[8] Associated with corruption in the Church, confusion caused by the existence of two or more Popes during most of the 14th century and the occurrence of various 'natural' disasters such as famines and plagues (including the Black Plague in the middle of 14th century estimated to have killed 30-60 per cent of Europe's population) which were viewed by many as the Acts of a God displeased with the conduct of Christendom and its leaders.

the post-WW2 period it was clear that the latter had triumphed.[9]

London University was established with the formation of University College London (UCL) in 1826 to be a secular institution, partly a response to the religious tests of Oxford and Cambridge at that time. From the start, it offered courses that were more subject-centred than those universities. It soon established 'external degrees' which made its degrees available to those not registered at the university but based in other colleges that were not universities. Importantly, they were available to part-time students outside of London. In 1888 London was the first university in England to admit women to all its degree courses, certainly a challenge to the idea of a university as a finishing school for young gentlemen.

The civic universities were mostly set up to provide a higher education for the region in which they were located and most were established by an individual benefactor or local community. Owens College in Manchester was the first, in 1851, followed by Yorkshire College of Science in Leeds in 1874. After that, there followed colleges in Sheffield, Birmingham, Bristol, Liverpool, Nottingham, Reading, Exeter, Southampton, Leicester and Hull (Tight, 2008). They started by preparing students for external degrees of London University until the title of university was conferred on them, when they were able to award their own degrees.

In 1960 there was a plan to expand higher education by building entirely new universities rather than by rebadging existing colleges. Actually, a precedent for this had been established in 1949 with the establishment of Keele University (originally the University College of North Staffordshire). In 1960 entirely new universities were planned for Sussex (at Brighton), York, Norwich, Colchester, Lancaster, Kent (at Canterbury) and Warwick (at Coventry). There was some disquiet at the outset that HE had become too subject-centred and specialised so that Newman's ideal of a university education as a broadening and liberating experience had been lost. Consequently, at the first of these new universities, Keele, students had to take a joint honours degree, being a degree involving two (or more) subjects. The second, Sussex, tried to resolve the perceived

[9] Arguably the abolition of at least O-level Latin as a general requirement for admission to Cambridge and Oxford in 1959-60 signified the final capitulation of classics-based liberal HE to subject-centred academic HE.

problem of excessive specialisation by allocating students to broad Schools (such as the School of European Studies) rather than narrower departments. After Sussex, however, most of the new universities offered an academic higher education involving three years of specialised study of one subject or a group of closely related subjects.

Apart from the universities described above there were a few anomalies, which didn't quite fit into any of the above categories. Durham and Newcastle were the main exceptions. Durham was founded in 1832 as a 'federation' of Durham colleges (following the Oxbridge model) and Kings College, Newcastle-on-Tyne. Newcastle later split off to become an independent university.

Between government and the universities sat the University Grants Committee (UGC). The UGC was set up in 1918 to distribute public funding to universities, which had been neglected during the first world war (Shattock, 1994). In the 1950s, its main function was still to receive public funding from the government and then distribute it to the universities. At that time, the UGC was mostly made up of senior university men who had been educated at the older universities in the 1920s and 1930s and had been successful in the university education they provided at that time. They were a largely conservative force in allocating public funds within higher education.

Specialist colleges. The specialist colleges were mostly focused on particular vocations, professions or occupations. Teacher training colleges were an alternative to university for school-leavers who wanted to teach. In 1960/61 there were 110 teacher-training colleges run by local authorities, 49 run by voluntary bodies (including religious organisations) and 27 by universities. Of these, 127 were general colleges and the rest specialised in specific subjects such as art (16), housecraft (later known as home economics and then domestic science) (11) and technical subjects (4) (Burgess, 1964). By 1960/61 there were two ways that a person could become a teacher in England: they could take a three-year course at a teacher training college or they could be a graduate.

Teacher training colleges were one particular type of specialist institution for education after school. There were others, including 166 art colleges, 38 agricultural colleges, about two dozen colleges of commerce as well as a number of specialist seminaries for training future members of the clergy.

Colleges of advanced technology. After WW2 there was an increasing belief in the importance of the application of science for the future of society and the fate of the nation. Computer scientists, alongside other scientists and technologists, had played a key role as codebreakers in the war. The development of radar is another example of the important contribution of technology in the fight against fascist dictatorship. The destruction of Hiroshima and Nagasaki emphasised the power of science and the application of technology were increasingly seen as keys to raising the level of material wellbeing of the populace. Governments, however, found it difficult to influence universities to expand university education sufficiently into these fields because of the UGC buffer between the government and the universities.

Unable to influence the universities to provide enough higher education in technology, in 1956 the government designated a number of technical/technological colleges as colleges of advanced technology. Their brief was to provide higher education in technology that was comparable in standard to that of university education. As colleges of advanced technology, they quickly dropped all their lower level work and adopted the same minimum entry qualifications as the universities. They concentrated on degrees, higher professional qualifications and the Diploma in Technology. The Diploma in Technology was intended to have the same standing as a university honours degree. It was a four-year course that integrated academic study with professional experience in employment and it was required to include a course in liberal studies. That was how it sought to reconcile the prevailing perceptions of higher education as both a broad student-centred liberal education and a specialised subject-centred academic education.

The government also established a National Council for Technological Awards (NCTA) to validate and monitor the Diploma in Technology as a means of quality assurance. The NCTA could thus be seen as the forerunner of the Council for National Academic Awards (CNAA), which played a significant role in the development of Enfield College of Technology in the 1960s.

Technical colleges It was also possible to pursue a course of HE at some of the technical colleges. These colleges are hard to classify. For example, many of their courses were not technical at all as they prepared students for a wide range of O-levels and A-levels. And much of what went on in the specialist colleges, such as the agricultural colleges, could reasonably be called technical. Part of the difficulty of classification is that this was an area of rapid and fundamental change so that old categories were becoming outdated. 'Technical' was a term that had been attached to activities that involved hands-on engagement often involving manual dexterity but the rise of technology had added a growing intellectual component – so much of what had been merely 'technical' was becoming an 'ology'. The old distinction between education for the 'head' and education for the 'hand' was becoming difficult to sustain.

It was difficult also to classify the technical colleges by the level of the education they provided. In some colleges it was possible to study O-levels and below. Many technical colleges offered courses above the level of ONC/OND leading to Higher National Certificate (HNC) for part-time students and Higher National Diploma (HND) for full-time students. In others, it was possible to study for external degrees of the University of London. And in a few it was possible to study all of them in the same institution.

Perhaps the most fruitful way of categorising these colleges is by the size of its student catchment area. On this basis, there were local colleges, area/regional colleges and national colleges. Local colleges had various titles, such as municipal college, technical institute, technical college and college of further education. Most of their courses were part-time, many of them by evening attendance. Most of their work led to ONC, City and Guilds, RSA and GCE O-levels and A-level examinations. Many also offered adult education courses of a non-technical kind, sometimes in co-operation with voluntary bodies such as the Workers Education Association.

As one passed along the spectrum from local colleges to area/regional colleges to national colleges the student catchment area tended to increase, the academic level of work tended to rise and the proportion of part-time work tended to decline.

Technical colleges as unlikely engines of change in higher education

The conventional view of higher education at the start of the 1960s would have seen the universities as the leading institutions of HE and Oxford and Cambridge as the leading establishments within the university sector. And that viewpoint would have placed the technical colleges, a ragbag collection of institutions with a majority of sub-degree work and no coherent or cohesive philosophy, at the rear. Arguably, however, the reverse was really the case; the universities, especially Oxford and Cambridge, proud of their traditions, were the most resistant to change and it was the technical colleges that led the changes in HE that occurred during the subsequent decades.

There are a number of strands to this argument. First, we have seen that the government wanted to expand HE in the application of new scientific research i.e. technology, but there was a problem in so doing and that problem was the University Grants Committee (UGC). The UGC acted as a buffer between the government and universities and this was seen as having many positive effects. It ensured that government would be unable to unduly influence what was taught at universities. It ensured that university research would occur in areas determined by academic experts rather than for the short-term or political advantage of particular governments. It enabled universities to 'speak truth to power' without the individual academics involved suffering retribution. In other words, it supported academic freedom.

On the other hand, democratically elected governments in the 1950s wanted to expand HE in technology and the UGC was dominated by senior academics from the older universities and the more established subjects who were resistant to much expansion of technology within the universities. For example, historian Sir Herbert Butterfield, Vice-Chancellor of the University of Cambridge in 1959-61, wrote: 'The university ... can teach the basic sciences in a way that may add depth to the mind itself, while leaving the application of these to be supplied by other institutions. Nowadays we are tending to go further than this: and here we come to a stage at which it is necessary to be rather careful. It is not easy to resist the argument that even those whose actual studies are not quite appropriate for a university will gain much from immersion in university life. At this point it is a rather big camel that is pushing its feet into the tent; and some people may not be aware how easy it would be to change the very nature of universities. We must widen the range of considerations involved; for if we take too much technology into our tail, the tail will soon begin to wag the dog.' (Butterfield, 1962, p.59)

Second, universities in the late 1950s were still locked in the final rounds of their own battle between the provision of a 'traditional' university education that was a liberal (classics-based) education and a 'modern' academic (subject-centred) education. Many of the senior figures in universities still espoused Newman's ideal of a university education. Some argued that such education produced graduates with well-trained minds who could apply those minds to a wide range of responsible positions in society. Many other university academics, however, were persuaded by the more 'modern' belief that the primary role of the university was the advancement of knowledge through the discovery of new knowledge and its dissemination via research-based higher education. They took as their text the words of Humboldt that 'At the highest level, the teacher does not exist for the sake of the student: both teacher and student have their justification in the common pursuit of knowledge.' (Humboldt, [1810] 1970, p. 243)

This was still the dominant issue within universities and the UGC in the 1950s with the latter view becoming increasingly dominant with the passing of the most senior and older members of the university hierarchy. Relatively little attention was paid to an alternative ideal of HE, one that placed more emphasis on the growing importance of the application of knowledge in enhancing material well-being rather than its discovery, preparation for new forms of employment which had enlarged knowledge requirements and the ability to integrate the contributions of different academic subjects to tackle practical, professional and social problems.

Third, we have seen that technical colleges were the most ill-defined sector of education at the start of the 1960s. Technological change itself was making old distinctions unclear, such as the difference between non-manual and manual employment. Even the distinction between 'technical' and 'technological' was becoming uncertain. The technical colleges covered a range of levels, modes of attendance and forms of delivery of education from traditional lectures through to periods of supervised work experience. It was the sector that was most heterogeneous and the most fluid. And it was the sector therefore that offered most opportunities of those with visions of change in further and higher education to have most impact. If one wanted to try to do something different in higher education it could be a good place to be.

Another kind of HE?

In 1961 Enfield was a pretty run-of-the-mill technical college and it was slated to be rebadged as a college of technology, a consequence of government pressure to increase the supply of technicians and technologists. When this happened a new Principal was appointed to lead the institution. That person, George Brosan, brought with him a distinctive outlook on education and, in particular, higher education. It was focused on the application of new knowledge, rather than its discovery. There is not space here to provide a full account of Brosan's educational philosophy but here is a summary of seven elements of it that were particularly relevant to his role in leading ECT:

Technology. It embraced technology as the application of scientific knowledge. It also embraced the application of new knowledge more generally, including the application of new knowledge in fields such as business studies and other social sciences.

Vocational. In the late 1950s new knowledge-based professions were emerging. Old occupations were becoming transformed by the accumulation of new knowledge (e.g. librarianship was becoming infused with information science and journalism was already being impacted by new communications technologies). The result was the emergence of new learned professions.

Problem-based rather than subject-based. Academic disciplines were seen as an effective means of discovering new knowledge, but tackling problems (of professional practice or society more widely) was likely to involve drawing on, and integrating, knowledge from different subject disciplines, so students needed to know how to do this. After graduating, most students from technical colleges or colleges of technology would not encounter subject-centred problems, but rather just problems. This meant that it was important for students to learn how to integrate knowledge from different subjects. This underpinned a case for interdisciplinary studies as part of a course of HE.

Situated problems. It is possible to make a case for locating the discovery of new knowledge within establishments that are disengaged from the rest of society but the application of knowledge usually takes place within the context of society and its institutions. So this kind of HE had to be engaged with the world outside of HE institutions. This line of thinking underpinned the case for work placements and other forms of engagement.

Intellectually demanding. The case for placing subject-centred study within higher education is that, for the most part, it is more intellectually demanding than secondary education as it involves the acquisition of the latest knowledge in a recognised field of study and the appliance of critical thinking to that knowledge. Education focused on the application of the latest knowledge, including vocational HE, could be even more intellectually demanding as it adds in the intellectual problems of integrating knowledge from different subject disciplines, identifying domains of applicability of new knowledge and also dealing with the complications of the contextual issues involved. This meant that the application of scientific knowledge, including its application within vocational contexts, could be at least as intellectually demanding as academic education.

Academic subjects defer to the students' courses of study. Within HE institutions, 'courses' are the means of delivering HE to students and as such they are student-centred. By contrast, the organisation of subjects within HE is centred on the pursuit of knowledge within academic disciplines. Importantly, careers within academic subjects are usually best served by pursuing subject-centred activities. This can be dysfunctional for the education of students if subjects become so strong that they dominate the courses. This is less important for single subject honours courses than it is for courses based on the application of knowledge, which draw on a range of academic disciplines. For this reason, in the interests of the students, it is important that on courses of the latter kind, decisions by academic subjects defer to decisions by the courses of study. This thinking favours institutional arrangements whereby the demands of courses take precedence over the demands of individual academic subjects.

Use of new technologies within HE. HE had been relatively slow to accept developments in the technology of teaching and learning such as (in the early 1960s) machine-aided learning, new media such as TV and team teaching. Scepticism about the admission of too much technology into university education spilled over into scepticism about the application of technology into teaching and learning methods in HE (see the Hale Report, 1964, for an account of university teaching methods in the early 1960s)

George Brosan brought considerable relevant experience to Enfield. He had completed a degree in electrical engineering at Regent Street Polytechnic as an external student of the University of London and had been awarded a first-class degree. He had then completed a PhD by part-time study at Birkbeck College and Regent Street Polytechnic while he worked in manufacturing companies. During this time he had also set up his own company making electrical products. In the 1950s he was a lecturer, then senior lecturer and then Head of Department at Woolwich Polytechnic, Regent Street Polytechnic and Willesden College of Technology respectively. From 1960 to 1962 he was senior assistant education officer responsible for further education at Middlesex County Council. He later sold his business advantageously becoming a relatively wealthy man, at least a millionaire. All this gave him experience of industrial employment, the application of his engineering knowledge to manufacturing, teaching in colleges of technology and his time in the education department of Middlesex County Council meant that he understood local authority rules, regulations and politics. Arguably, the fact that he was a relatively wealthy self-made man added to his confidence and willingness to take risks.

Brosan's personality was also a relevant factor. He was entrepreneurial, iconoclastic and proactive.[10] His entrepreneurial spirit meant that he was inclined to take chances. His iconoclasm meant that he was not intimidated by the reputation of universities or university professors, senior civil servants or government ministers. And his proactive attitude meant that, in modern parlance, he wanted to make a difference.

---

10 By some accounts, he could also be impulsive, autocratic and intimidating.

He could not, of course, run the college on his own so he set about recruiting staff who could help him realise a kind of HE that

was different from that which could be found in other institutions of HE in 1962. He would have been the first to acknowledge that there can be a large gap between theory and the application of that theory in practice. This book provides a range of accounts of how it worked out in practice through the personal accounts of people who were recruited to ECT during its life from 1962 to 1972.

Conclusion

The aim of this chapter is to provide some context for the other chapters in this book. It has looked at the educational system within which Enfield College of Technology was established. It has looked in a little more detail at HE in England at that time. And it has provided some historical context on the development of HE up to that time.

The overall education system was dominated by the division of children at the age of eleven into schools that provided an academic education for those destined for non-manual work and schools that provided sufficient education for work with a greater manual content. There were four main paradigms of higher education at that time: liberal (classics-based) education, academic (subject-centred) education and the overlapping paradigms of technological and vocational education. This was not, however, a static position as classical liberal HE was in retreat, subject-centred academic education had recently acquired a dominant position and technological/vocational education was challenging for a larger role within HE.

Within the hierarchy of HE at that time, the technical colleges had least social standing partly because they were a heterogeneous collection of institutions, with a substantial amount of non-higher education work and no cohesive philosophy. In 1962 ECT was established and a Principal was appointed with ideas of what such a philosophy might comprise.

Part of the philosophy was that technological/vocational education can be as intellectually demanding as academic education and that the application of new knowledge can be as important as discovering the new knowledge in the first place. The story of ECT can be seen as the story of how that philosophy of a new kind of HE fared in practice. It can be viewed as an experiment in higher education. The rest of this book contains insights into that story through personal reminiscences and reflections of those who were there at the different times during the life of ECT.

2. How Enfield College came about

TONY CRILLY

In 1962, the rebranded Enfield College of Technology came into being, situated in Ponders End in Eastern Enfield eleven miles by road to the north of the City of London. A little known place, and if known at all, Ponders End in the 1960s was little regarded. Estate Agents ducked the name and advertised houses as being in West Chingford. It did however sheepishly publicise itself as the destination of the buses on the 279 bus route as they headed home to the capacious Ponders End Bus Garage after a day running up and down the spine of North London. Designating the college as the 'Ponders End College of Technology' would never have done, but later student generations would wear their 'University of Ponders End' T-shirts with pride.

History

Ponders End was a place where work was done. In the van of industrialization of the late eighteenth century, mill owners, manufacturers, and industrialist saw it as well connected with London by canals and roads, and it met their needs for an efficient transportation system for goods and manufactures.

For hundreds of years Ponders End was part of the Lea Navigation system. Early in the Industrial Revolution, the finishing and dyeing trading company Grout and Baylis was quickly on the scene. On a smaller scale, silk was to Ponders End what cotton was to the mill towns of Lancashire. In 1809, recognizing the advantages of this location, Joseph Grout and John Baylis set up their manufacturing plant in the area.

Calling Londoner's attention to this unknown place, the *London Evening Standard* (1 Dec. 1829) asked: 'Where is Ponder's-end?' … 'Can anybody tell us where Ponder's-end is?' Answering its own question, it printed: 'In that place is a vast silk crepe manufactory, …, carried on by Messrs, Grout and Baylis, both, we believe, persons of the utmost respectability.' Having succeeded in Norfolk, the company followed the formality of the British way of death, and were suppliers to the funeral business of heavy black crepe and Norwich Bombazine. For widows' weeds read Grout and Baylis. Parramatta silk was best for deepest mourning but bombazine was both affordable and acceptable for most occasions, and Ponders End benefitted from the elaborate funereal rituals of the Victorian era. The firm lasted out the nineteenth century and only when the wearing of crepe went out of fashion, when the formality of the high Victorian period was abandoned, did they cease trading.

At the beginning of the nineteenth century, goods to and from Ponders End went by canal but the stagecoach was the way people travelled, at least for the well-off. But this was changing, and horse drawn omnibuses arrived during the 1830s, and from Edmonton, just south of Ponders End, there was an omnibus every fifteen minutes to the City travelling along the roads of North London through Tottenham, Finsbury Park and Camden Town. This road system of transport lasted for fifty years before it was replaced by the horse-drawn tram.

Connections with London were further improved when the railways arrived and Ponders End station opened in 1845. With this extra transportation method Ponders End further expanded. The London Jute Company, originally from Dundee, set up in 1866, lasted until 1882 whereupon the buildings were replaced by the Ediswan Factory in which light bulbs and other electrical appliances were manufactured. Joseph W. Swan joined with Thomas A. Edison and the two formed a joint manufacturing company, the United Edison and Swan Electric Light Company in 1883. For a new way of lighting home and industry 'Edison & Swan' advertised their 'Incandescence Lamps' for sale in the 1880s and 1890s.

At the beginning of the twentieth century, there were new inhabitants on the Ponders End High Street, and in 1901 Swan bought a house on it which became the 'Ediswan Institute', a building where his employees could socialize by day while it served as a technical school in the evenings. Ponders End became the centre of the electrical and electronics industry, both in its manufactures and educational culture. When Swan died in 1914 he was celebrated locally as the 'Grand Old Man of Electricity.'

In 1907 the horse drawn tram was replaced by the electric tram and this ran along the High Street on its way to Waltham Cross. In the new technological world the Grout & Baylis factory was replaced by the United Flexible Tubing Company.

Technical Education in Enfield

Technical education in Britain was hardly a new idea. As the industrial revolution advanced in the early nineteenth century, Mechanics Institutes were created in recognition of the need for skilled operatives. In the early Victorian era these institutes became firmly established. In 1882 Quintin Hogg set up the Regent Street Polytechnic Institution and by the end of the nineteenth century there were many old-style polytechnics dotted around London: Battersea, Borough, Chiswick, Kilburn, Tottenham, Willesden, and Woolwich. 'Polytechnic' was the name chosen for the larger technical institutes. A fillip to technical education were the Technical Instruction Acts of 1889 and 1891 which empowered Local Authorities to facilitate technical education and provide the funds to employ teachers.

The 'Ediswan Institute' set up by Swan on the High Street became the 'Ponders End Technical Institute' when Middlesex County Council bought the building in August 1905. At a bargain price of £800, the sale included land for further developments. The building included Workshops for Electric Lighting and Carpentry, a Cookery Room, a small laboratory, and classrooms. The Technological and Trade courses involved Electric Lighting, and a proudly presented guiding principle, no less than an educational objective, was the Institute's philosophy to turn out skilled workers as opposed to producing 'automatons'. In the Institute a full-time teacher of Science and Mathematics was appointed with ancillary staff of part-timers. In an early Electric Lighting course there were thirty students. There were also Art and Commercial Classes and in the Commercial course, where shorthand was taught, there were some 220 students organised into three separate classes.

In addition, the Technical Institute housed an Evening Intermediate School for student progressing from the Elementary Schools in the area. In this school, students who worked in the Enfield Small Arms Factory attended courses financed by an annual Government Grant of £45. However makeshift the building, it was successful for the job at hand, and so successful it was rebuilt in 1911 to serve both as a technical institute and junior technical school.

By then there was also a branch of the electric tram system running from Ponders End along Southbury Road towards Enfield

Town. The centre of Ponders End was firmly placed at the junction of the road heading South/North along the Ponders End High Street, and the road running East/West where Southbury Road meets Nags Head Road. In the 1930s further change was afoot when the electric tram was deemed to be old-fashioned and replaced by a trolley bus system, a system of transport that lasted for another thirty years.

At the beginning of the twentieth century, notable products were being produced in Ponders End. In particular the modern electronics industry got underway. Ambrose Fleming invented the thermionic valve, a project begun earlier by Swan, reckoned to be the start of the electronics revolution. Fleming had been taught mathematics by Augustus De Morgan at University College London, and in a dream class of one, by the extraordinary scientist James Clerk Maxwell. With Fleming as consultant to the Marconi Company during WW2 (he died in 1945) the company supplied the valves necessary for the construction of Colossus computer at Bletchley which enabled the German 'Enigma' code to be cracked.

The Modern College

The Technical Institute on the High Street was so successful that the Middlesex County Council bought a large plot of land on the opposite side of the road alongside Queensway. New premises were definitely required and the decision was taken to build a larger college on this site.

In 1936 building began on the new site but was interrupted by of the war. Existing buildings continued to be used and air raid shelters built – which were still there in the 1960s. The old building housing the Technical Institute took a bomb hit in 1940, but was repaired and continued its work of training local technicians and members of the armed services.

The 'genial and popular' Henry Winterbottom Broadbent, a mechanical engineer was appointed Principal in January 1941. With the war and the need for a back-up defence force there was a 'healthy body healthy mind' approach to the education of the 370 boys and young men on the roll call. In 1943 their physical fitness was ensured by the Physical Training instructor a Mr T. H. Clark. Alongside the young men's training in machines, dynamos and other engineering and electrical equipment, this instructor also dispensed sex education. This consisted of moralistic advice coupled with dire warnings of the dangers which might befall those tempted to stray outside the boundaries he specified. (*Daily Mirror*, 4 Dec. 1943)

After the war, a Committee was appointed by the British Government under the chairmanship of Sir Anderson Montague-Barlow to plan for future scientific manpower. The Barlow Committee Report of 1946 estimated 90,000 trained scientists would be needed nationally, but saw there was only an ability of producing 64,000 in existing educational institutions. Herbert Morrison, the Deputy Prime Minister in Clement Attlee's 1945 Labour Government, acknowledged the shortfall. In the course of the following twenty years there was an avalanche of Government Reports addressed to the question of technical education, which was seen as an urgent national issue (see Appendix). There was also recognition that higher education was in need of expansion and coupled with this, the dominance of classical education was questioned.

Enfield College had always been under local authority control. It was, like technical colleges across the country, a local college. Emblematic of this was the constitution of college governance. In 1949, local industrialist George A. Roberts became chairman of the governing body in which capacity he was to remain until 1968. He was the managing director of the family electronics and cabling manufacturing firm of Ripaults Ltd with headquarters a stone's throw away from the college. During his tenure he was also chairman of the Advisory Committee to the Department of Industrial Engineering. Roberts was instrumental in the building of an extension to the main building of the College in Queensway. In his role on the Governing body he was assisted by Eric Pascal, Education Officer of the London Borough of Enfield during the war years and appointed Clerk to the Governing Body in the same year as Roberts had become chairman, serving the governing body for almost as long as Roberts.

After the war, the college reopened, operating under the banner of 'Enfield Technical College' a college consisting of four departments, all of them connected with engineering. A halt in its fortunes occurred when Broadbent dropped dead in the street in March 1950 aged just fifty-four (*Palmers Green and Southgate Gazette*, 24 Mar. 1950). According to a newspaper advertisement a replacement

Principal was sought in the salary range £1350-£1600 (*The Scotsman*, 30 May 1950).

Broadbent was succeeded by another engineer Roderick McCrae who had been head of department of Engineering at Kingston Technical College since 1939. He appeared to be outward looking, and when it was proposed that lecturers at Kingston should involve themselves with research, he showed support by appointing research assistants in his own department. At Kingston he became 'a well known bowler-hatted figure as he traipsed around all the local industries in search of students.' He believed that that 'local knowledge and personal relationships were the keys to successful recruitment.' Later on he acquired a reputation for liking a free lunch and it was noticed he scheduled meetings with local industrialists towards the end of the morning. Both former Principals were remembered: the main building became the Broadbent building and the extension, completed in 1953, initially housing metallurgy and electro-chemistry, the McCrae building.

A government White Paper of 1956 addressed Technical Education and involved Government spending plans. It focused on the organizational structure and the ranking of institutions into Colleges of Advanced Technology, Regional Colleges, Area Colleges, and Local colleges. The 1956 Act on technical education was a turning point in the fortunes of technical and vocational education in England. Following the Act, there was to be an expansion of technical education through full-time, part-time, day release, and sandwich courses, i.e. courses which included a period of experience in the work-place.

These changes in the structure of higher and further education took place against a booming economy with Prime Minister Harold MacMillan declaring to the nation that it had 'never had it so good.' Unlike the universities, colleges like Enfield were tied to Local Education Authorities (LEAs). The 'local tech', including our Enfield Technical College, was at the centre of the local industrial community, typified by the connection with local industries. The college provided courses in automobile, civil, electrical, mechanical, and production engineering, as well as the metallurgy and electro-chemistry courses and also management and trade courses. But Enfield was ambitious, and by 1959 it put on courses leading to London University External degrees.

In the early 1960s Ponders End changed its profile and the shifting scene of the High Street continued. The trolley bus system with buses powered by overhead electric lines was coming to the end of its life and being replaced by motorized buses. The Routemaster 279, which ran from Smithfield to Waltham Cross and beyond, carried students and staff to Ponders End, to the back door of the college via the short lane past the Swan public house and disused air-raid shelters.

The new College of Technology

Britain in the 1960s saw the growth of education in the expansion of existing universities and the formation of new institutions. Twenty-five Colleges of Advanced Technology had become universities following a recommendation of the Robbins Report, and in the remainder of FE/HE institutions there were twenty-five Regional colleges, about thirty Area Colleges and over a hundred Local Colleges.

In 1962 the government announced the increase of student numbers in the higher education sector from 110,000 to 150,000 and an increase in funding to make this possible. In the spring of that year Enfield College acquired a new title. No longer Enfield Technical College it became *Enfield College of Technology.* Following the death of McCrae in that same year, Mr W. T. Pratt was appointed acting Principal until the autumn when a new Principal was to be appointed.

At forty-one years of age George Brosan became the new Principal of the rebranded college. Technically a Hungarian (his family moved to England when he was one year old) he passed through the English education system. In his early twenties during the war, he joined the Royal Electrical and Mechanical Engineers and rose to the rank of Major, and after the war he continued to serve on a reserve basis. He also continued with his academic studies with a BSc in 1947 and PhD in 1951, both awards gained by part-time study.

Prior to his appointment with Middlesex County Council as further education officer in 1960, Brosan was head of department at Willesden College of Technology. If the appointment as an educational officer suggests a placid servant of officialdom nothing could be further from the truth. In the post-war era he had entrepreneurial business interests in manufacturing electrical goods. Rumour had it that he lost a million in one business but remade it in his next enterprise. He was also active as a mathematically orientated engineer, an interest in mathematics that lasted throughout his life. He later became president of the Tensor Society, a mathematical society that sought to exploit the application of 'tensors' (mathematical constructs relevant to the theory of relativity and to engineering).

By the time of his appointment at Enfield Brosan had acquired a broad background in both teaching and administration but more than this he brought to College administration an ability in getting things done.

With his new appointment as Enfield, Brosan outlined his thoughts on higher education in an article entitled 'A New Sort of University' in the *Spectator* (20 Nov. 1964). He started with a critique of the Robbins Report (1963) and argued that future higher education policy was not to be found in development along the lines of the existing universities. Existing universities concentrated on the provision of an academic education, whereas Brosan had something different in mind.

In his capacity as an education officer he had thought about educational organization, and soon after his appointment at Enfield made a proposal to the Middlesex Education Committee that a new type of institution could be formed from a merger of Enfield College of Technology, Hornsey College of Art, and Trent Park Teacher Training College, the arrangement to be set up on a federal basis. Such an institution would cater for 2,000 students enrolled on degree level studies.

Brosan argued that the theme of such an institution, would be different in character from traditional universities, and would provide an 'integrated professional and academic education, drawing into a unity the sandwich methods of colleges of technology and the current educational methods of teacher training colleges to form a 'university of the people.' He continued: 'In this framework of thinking, art, technology and social studies have a part which transcends the boundaries of existing institutions: the whole [new] institution is visualized as something more than the sum of its parts.'

Brosan drew a distinction between 'academic attainment' and 'intellectual attainment' and he suggested the latter should be the criterion for awarding degrees. He labelled the 'conventional academic attainment' the product of the traditional universities whereas 'intellectual attainment' would be the benchmark in the comprehensive institution he envisaged.

Very soon Brosan was joined by Eric Robinson, who, like Brosan, had been a student of mathematics. Robinson was politically active. One of his roles was as national president of the lecturer's union, the Association of Teachers in Technical Institutions (ATTI), and in the early 1960s he was advisor to the Labour Minister of Education Anthony Crosland.

On his appointment Robinson wrote: 'When I came to Enfield in September 1962, I expected to lead a small-scale but intensive educational experiment. The scale of the subsequent development was not anticipated ... on the day I accepted an appointment to Enfield, I sought and obtained only one assurance – that the Principal [George Brosan] was willing to contemplate appointments of young people to the teaching staff at higher grades than they could normally obtain elsewhere. My belief in the value of employing young teachers was largely based on my experience at Brunel [University], which included some research into the problems of improving curriculum and teaching methods.' (Roberts, 2002-)

With Brosan and Robinson in place, Enfield College of Technology was ready to play a leading role in the revolution in higher education, a revolution that occurred in Britain in the 1960s.

PART ONE

EARLY BIRDS

1962-1965

3. The revolution at Ponders End

JOHN CARR

***John Carr** was appointed Lecturer Grade 2 in Geography in the academic year 1963-64, and retired as Principal Lecturer at Middlesex University in the year 2000. In between he was a regular member of the Social Science Faculty Board, Academic Board, and latterly as a staff representative on the Board of Governors. He was appointed as University Orator in 1992 by the Vice-Chancellor Professor Sir David Melville. In earlier years he served as chair of the Geography Board of the Council for National Academic Awards. In the early 1990's he joined the staff group running the Tunisia field courses for the Third World Studies programme, an activity which led to an abiding interest in the social and economic development of Africa Proconsularis (Tunisia) by the Romans. He is an enthusiastic 'indoor rower'.*

My journey to Enfield College of Technology began in the first year of the sixth form in my boy's grammar school long ago. I had decided to improve my science qualifications at O-level and A-level as my profile was rather weak in that respect. I sought an interview with the headmaster and put to him the idea that I be given leave from the timetable in order to enrol in the local technical college for the University of London Intermediate-BSc course in Geology, a foundation course for later Honours courses in that subject. Somewhat taken aback by my presumption, he did agree that this might be a good idea but that the school could accept no responsibility.

Thus I enrolled and joined a group of highly motivated older students whose opportunities for higher education had been curtailed for various reasons. The fieldwork was hard to organise, but the only drawback to the whole experience was the Thursday evening headache brought on by the fumes from the formaldehyde in which various molluscs and other dead things were pickled for dissection. From such beginnings I progressed to higher education.

After a disastrous first term at the London School for Economics, on the advice of the Borough director of Education, I withdrew and, with my Local Educational Authority grant preserved awaited conscription. Directions and a postal order arrived and within a fortnight I was in khaki and a long way from home. During the next two years I learned a great deal and experienced much, not all of it good but a lasting impression was of the high quality of the instructors. They were some of the best teachers I have ever known. When it ended, I went to Reading University and five years later left with two degrees and a very sound knowledge and experience of 'Fairbairn' rowing (Steve Fairbairn was arguably the most influential and revolutionary coach in English rowing in the last century and rowing at Reading was heavily influenced by his methods).

Finding Enfield

Coming to the end of a short-term contract at University College London, I was thinking quite seriously of seeking a position in education but outside the university system. The advertisement in the education press for posts in social science and humanities at Enfield College of Technology caught my eye. The next day I entrained (it takes a long time to bleed out the military speech) for Derby and an introduction to the Principal of a nearby college with whom my parents were acquainted. From him I gained a basic idea of what was being attempted in Ponders End and the advice that if I was looking for a career behind a library desk then I should not apply. Returning to London I assembled my application and sent it off. A few weeks later I received an invitation to interview.

On a damp warm summers day I detrained at Southbury Station and was confronted by three floor-to-ceiling posters stating 'Alight here for Enfield College of Technology'. Turning right from the station entrance I beheld Brimsdown Power Station to the North-East, a gas and coking plant and gasometers to the East, and with 'the eye of faith', an essential geographers tool, the 'famous' Chingford monocline.

Turning into Kingsway and then into Queensway I found the entrance to the 'campus' and walked along the short poplar-lined avenue up the steps, through the great bronze doors and into the foyer with its glassed-in apse. Met by the Bursar Mr H. Carless I was left in the Principal's secretary's office. Ten paces through the door and I was welcomed and invited to sit by the Principal, Dr George Brosan. Seated beside him was Eric Robinson. There were others at the table also. The interview was lengthy and lively. After waiting outside for a while I was invited back in and offered a post. I took it, and decided to tour the campus, and on the High Street I opened a bank account at the brand new Midland branch. Weeks later I presented a cheque across the counter in the huge baroque branch in Derby. The cashier looked at it, at me, and then she cried in a very loud voice, causing the chief cashier to adopt a admonitory frown, 'It exists! Does the 124 go there?' It appeared that to most people beyond the Watford Gap, Ponders End was a figment of Anthony Aloysius Hancock's imagination. I wonder does No. 2 Railway Cuttings East Cheam also exist?

The Diversity of Change

In the main hall, doubling as the refectory, there were tables at the stage end, some with tablecloths for staff. Everywhere was that smell of unperfumed floor polish and damp mops. In the first floor library there was very little room for books, but shelving had to be found – for in the September before term started George Brosan sent all of us on a bookshop raid equipped with special credit cards enabling us to buy everything we could from our recommended reading lists. Our main work programmes were built on London University External degree courses but we were led to believe that whilst this was the 'bread and butter' for the moment, we would be expected to work for a changed prospectus and a changed environment.

With the benefit of hindsight it wasn't so much the material change and new course development that was so impressive, although they certainly were, it was the speed at which it was all accomplished. The BBC sent a camera crew to film what was going on. It was clear from 1965 that if even a limited range of objectives were to be secured a substantial building programme would be needed. I did not know that the Principal and others had presented the Department of Education and Science with a costed proposal for a new building, a new laboratory and modifications to existing buildings. In 1966 we knew that £245,000 had been approved for a new building ('the tower block'), £75,000 for the new Pascal labs and £50,000 for modifications. All this was approved. In the meantime we had the huts. Two wooden H blocks dropped on what used to be tennis courts. These were to last for five years but lasted over twice that. Strange creations they were, walking up the corridors was like trampolining with all the sounds one might expect. Conversations could be heard throughout even if conducted in hushed tones. No lavatories were provided until later, when they were a 'lean-to' against the police station wall – an inconvenient distance from the huts.

In this short space of time a college shop appeared, to be followed by a plan for a bookshop (1971). Saunas appeared in the gym changing rooms and, sometime later, a collapsible squash court. Possession of 31 Derby Road was given to The Student Union with the wardens of the Student Union at 31A (Andy Thomas and myself). It wasn't long before we petitioned the Vice-Principal, Mr William Pratt, to abolish the office of warden as the President and some other officers of the Student Union were much older and probably wiser than we were. Anyway, 31A had no insulation and poor heating. Had we stayed in those offices we could have died of frostbite. In the main building we had established a college club, with a bar which became the centre of college social life. We were so well-behaved, the staff of the local police station applied to join! Not a hope.

A Failed Innovation and a National Change

My own proposal for a new academic programme was to wrap a sandwich system of education around an Honours degree in Geography and a Diploma of the Royal Town planning Institute. We had the Institute's active participation and support with help from Dr Peter Hall, shortly to be appointed as Professor of Planning and Regeneration at University College London. A detailed and comprehensive submission was prepared and sent to the Regional Advisory Council (RAC).

A few weeks later I was entering the foyer at about 9.10 a.m. when I was called into George Brosan's office. On his table was a bottle of Vat 69 beside a well-filled glass, and I was instructed to sit down and drink the whisky because I would need it. I did as ordered (from one former army member to another), the first and last time I have drunk strong liquor at that time of the morning. It appeared that the Principal of another college of technology to the west of us had appealed to the RAC that Enfield was 'getting all the cherries' and he was getting none. There may have been a 'wailing and a gnashing of teeth' but the upshot was that approval for a degree in Geography went elsewhere and our well thought out scheme fell by the wayside. George Brosan's comment could be summed up as 'stick around kid, you ain't seen nothing yet.' Indeed!

A new course approving body emerged from the National Council for Technological Awards in 1964 – it was the Council for National Academic Awards (CNAA). This body was a royal charter institution which could approve colleges as fit and proper institutions to run academic programmes leading to the award of its degrees. The day of the university external degree was drawing to a close. It was hoped by Tony Crosland, the Secretary of State to Education, that these new institutions would not ape the universities, but be rigorous in maintaining standards. They were to be known as Polytechnics.

One of the first to be proposed would include Enfield and Hendon Colleges of Technology and Hornsey College of Art. The latter did not like this arrangement at all but realised that as Enfield Council had invited us to create a new Fine Arts Faculty, to occupy their recently completed Arts building at Cat Hill, the Hornsey folk had the good sense to allow Haringey Council to negotiate their future as that Fine Arts Faculty. Hendon College of Technology did not relish a future with us either and so sought a relationship with Ealing Technical College. That was stamped on and years of heated discussion passed before Middlesex Polytechnic integrated. Our Vice-Principal, Mr Pratt, said that 'nineteenth century politics were like a Sunday School treat compared to what went on at faculty committee meetings.'

The Revolution Begins

We could not wait for these elevated and quasi-secret discussions to conclude – it took four years! In the meantime we had the development of courses to get on with. One of our first great innovative successes was the submission to CNAA of the Sociology of Education proposal led by Rachel Parry. This was an 'accelerated' two-year course, part-time/full-time, for practicing teachers and we had a good idea it would pass the CNAA inspection. On the day of the inspection visit a large room in the McCrae building had been prepared for lunch with the floor covered by a large Chinese carpet which emitted an evil smell and the buffet was seriously short of food. Nevertheless the degree course was approved, and students came from as far away as South Yorkshire. Camper vans could be seen in the car parks and the gym changing rooms were opened early to allow the 'overnighters' to use the showers. We heard much of the doings of an East Anglian wise woman by the name of Beauty Carver from one of them. We could have done with someone with such skills on the campus.

From 1966 to 1968 our attention and efforts were largely concentrated in the creation of a four-year full-time sandwich honours degree in Social Science. Much effort and energy was required. Occasionally beer was spilt and on one occasion a little blood. But what came out of it was remarkable. Complicated and evidently difficult to assess, the CNAA sent out an advance working party to decide how to assess it. It 'passed' in July 1967 with some recommendations for improvement which we duly incorporated. Eventually, students could specialise in Economics, Sociology, Psychology, Social Policy, Planning Studies, and Social Work with all students spending their third year in a placement. It was a triumph, but I would say that wouldn't I as I became course head in 1982.

Then there was 1968! Occupations of campuses were widespread and Enfield was not exempt. Graffiti appeared – usually the sign of a good community spirit. 'LSE today ECT tomorrow.' It was painted over many times but always managed to shine through. Hornsey was occupied but I suspect their graffiti was more arty than ours!

Joining the BA Social Science programme were 21 other diploma and degree courses, pushing our annual intake well beyond 1,000 and sometime up to 1,400. With high survival rates and the student population exceeding reasonable capacity, the library had to expand massively. We had to find room for a Placement Unit and for an HE Placement Clearing System, a collaboration with the *Observer*.

Jonathan Powers joined in 1969 and spoke of our: 'rampaging paranoia and immense creativity.' 1969 was a strange year. More huts arrived, one each in our courtyards for the caretakers, social work, and a nursery. By 1969 the New Tutorial Block (the Roberts Building) was being built on a quagmire, and in the building of it, exposing sixteen surface springs. 'It's Passchendaele out there' said

Eric Robinson. This was the year in which George Brosan announced to a packed staff meeting that he had had enough of the protracted and largely futile discussions on the future polytechnic and was going off as Director of North-East London Polytechnic. William Pratt said of him: 'He had three years to gain momentum and five to change the college out of all recognition.' In the departure, he was followed by Eric Robinson. The assiduous collector of college lore, Andrew Roberts, said: 'By the time that he and George Brosan left, the college that began with an electric light bulb, had an international reputation in the Social Sciences.'

Life had not ended. The Roberts Building was completed and the Pascal Laboratories were ready for use. Someone decided we should have an opening ceremony – perhaps it was the new Principal John O'Neil. On Saint Patrick's Day 1971 the local great and good descended on the campus to witness the Secretary of State for Education Mrs Margaret Thatcher open the Roberts Building at a ceremony in the study area. Students protesting at the government's educational policy sprayed old milk around and then homemade confetti over the platform party. The police arrived and 'arrests' were made. One student complained that what was usually a quagmire was now grass for Mrs Thatcher's visit. There were shouted complaints about higher education policy and meagre grants.

Eventually some kind of 'opening' occurred and then the visiting party made an exit. It is worth pointing out that the students, who had decided not to accept the invitation to attend, cleared up the debris left behind. Four students were suspended for a limited time and apologies made. As philosopher, Mark Fisher, said at the time, 'survival is a grubby business.'

And so to Polytechnic Status

In 1972 Dr Ray Rickett was appointed Director of the yet to materialise Middlesex Polytechnic, and in the middle of BASS examinations we had our first of many annual bomb hoaxes. It was also the year of BASS first graduation. Funds were not available for BASS graduates to participate in any ceremony. Lackaday! So we held our own on the lawn south of the huts. John Farquhar, dressed in full regalia, 'received' students individually, in one of the two sets of CNAA regalia available and which were passed down the line. A fire safety regulations sheet rolled and tied with a sassy ribbon served as a certificate – also passed down the line. Refreshments were an urn of tea and trays of cream buns. Fun was had by all especially when the bar opened!

Two strange course proposals emerged later that year. One from a Dr Pudge for a module in 'the Social Geography of Flange-welding', and one for a Medical Studies track in BASS from Gail N. Mims pointing out that ' absence of a dissecting room was no disadvantage as a preoccupation with corpses merely shows a materialistic metaphysics.'

In January 1973 the Polytechnic was designated; the first proposed and the last to be accredited! *North Circular* became the house paper. Farewell then to *College Times, Staff News* and sundry other publications. On the Polytechnic front more property was acquired; Trent Park through the College of Education; Saint Katherine's Training College in Tottenham, Bounds Green, Ivy House, and several more. The Polytechnic was thus geographically widespread and consequently expensive to run.

Early in the 1980s one change occurred which, although inevitable, I thought to be to our intellectual disadvantage: the great disciplinary migrations. Humanities moved to All Saints in Tottenham thus beginning their 'völkerwanderung' around the campuses; Science and Engineering moved to Bounds Green and Geography moved from Hendon to Enfield.

Thereafter 'like talked to like' rather than across disciplinary boundaries which had been such a feature of life at Enfield. The following two decades were ones of mixed fortune. Poverty of resources forced on us economies in most areas, but academically we did progress especially at post-graduate level.

In 1989 enhancements to the Library were completed taking over the Hall (the Old Refectory to some) with a new mezzanine floor and a lift in the fashionable 'distressed mode.' There were substantial campus improvements to come and Health and Nursing arrived with substantial funds. Down came the Pascal labs to be replaced by the Pascal Building. We became a University in 1992. Much was expected of the new Vice-Chancellor and his colleague Ken Goulding but that regime only lasted five years. Real change could only be a prospect after it was agreed to concentrate on one campus, but that is another story.

4. Opportunity, vision and change: Enfield College in the 1960's

JOHN M. STODDART

***John Stoddart** worked at Enfield 1964-70. From 1966 he led the economics group and then had responsibility of part-time courses in business studies. He left to become Head of Department at Sheffield Polytechnic. Returning to London he took on a broader institutional role as Assistant Director at North East London Polytechnic. In 1976 he was appointed by the newly established Humberside County Council to lead Hull College of Higher Education – an amalgam of six existing colleges, which eventually became a Polytechnic/University. In 1983 he returned to Sheffield as Principal of the Polytechnic and subsequently Vice-Chancellor of Sheffield Hallam University. He retired in 1998 and took on a variety of non-executive roles to balance family activities, travel and veteran rowing.*

'If you can remember the 60's, you really weren't there' or so the saying goes. Well I was there and I know exactly what I was doing. I graduated, taught at a grammar school and then at a college of further education and from 1964-70 I was a lecturer at Enfield College. Moreover, I remember that decade well. It was a decade of political unrest, change, idealism and expectation. It was a decade of increasing prosperity and technological advance, of increasing liberalism and diversity and emphasis on individual experimentation and fulfilment. In the UK the decade brought the end of conscription, the abolition of the death penalty, the Race Relations Act, the decriminalisation of homosexuality, the contraceptive pill, the Abortion Act, the growth of CND. In the USA the decade covered the election and death of Kennedy, the Vietnam war, the rise of feminism, the Civil Rights movement. In both countries the shift to the individual, together with a growing mistrust of authority, led to the rise of a counter culture and to significant unrest in universities and colleges in the later 1960s as students expressed dissatisfaction about the world in which they found themselves and their experience of higher education.

The decade also saw the beginning of a major transformation in education at all levels. At secondary level there was the beginning of the change to a comprehensive system; at tertiary level the boundaries between further and higher education became increasingly blurred and there was an expectation of significant growth in vocational education and training. The university sector was set for expansion; the Colleges of Advanced Technology were re-designated as universities; additional new universities were created including the Open University which was to have a significant influence on adult and continuing education.

My teaching career spanned the final forty years of the twentieth century and I only spent six years at Enfield but, with hindsight, it is clear that the policy developments of the 1960's were largely responsible for the higher education system we have today. Enfield's response to those developments (along with that of a number of similar institutions) helped to shape the system. For those of us privileged to work in those colleges and with the opportunity to influence change, the 60's were exciting and special years. For me, that time at Enfield was transformative. The experience gained, the growth in my political awareness and in self-confidence was to prove invaluable in my future career as a head of department and then Principal and Vice-Chancellor. These reflections look back at what it was like to be involved in further/higher education in the 1960's and on the interplay between national policy and local aspiration and the impact those years had on higher education in the decades that followed.

Positioned for change

Enfield in 1964 was a strong local technical college offering a range of engineering, science and management courses relevant to companies and the professions in North London. It also offered University of London external degrees in Engineering, Science, Geography and Sociology and it was ready to expand. In 1962 Middlesex County Council had allocated additional accommodation for the college, anticipating a growth in demand for vocational courses. Furthermore, with the agreement of the Department of Education, the County

Council had retitled both Enfield Technical College and Hendon Technical College as Colleges of Technology.

The Further Education Officer for Middlesex at that time was Dr George Brosan, a former lecturer and head of department at Regent Street Polytechnic and Willesden College of Technology. At the end of 1962 he became Principal of Enfield College and it is likely that there was an understanding with Middlesex that he would broaden the academic base of the college and to develop further the range of vocational degree programmes in the Arts and Social Sciences. George Brosan quickly recruited Eric Robinson, a prominent advocate of the expansion of further and higher education outside the universities. Robinson was, in 1962, President of the Association of Teachers in Technical Institutions (ATTI) and one of the key advisers to the Labour Party on education policy.

Enfield was prescient – or fortunate – in timing and leadership. The Robbins Report published in 1963 recommended an expansion of higher education to meet the needs of students qualified to enter. Robbins envisaged a more than doubling of full-time students in the universities. Then in 1964 the CNAA was established by Royal Charter with power to award degrees offered in colleges outside the universities. Also in 1964 the Crick Report recommended the introduction of a graduate level award in business studies and linking study with practical experience.

Perhaps, looking back, the most significant event of 1964 however, was the October General Election which returned a Labour Government. Tony Crosland was appointed Secretary of State for Education and a few months later set out, in the Woolwich speech, a binary policy for the development of higher education. This led, in turn, to the creation of the polytechnics. The timing was perfect for an expansion of higher education outside the traditional universities which could build on the long experience of local colleges serving their communities. Enfield already had in place, in Brosan and Robinson, a leadership committed to that service tradition and a small core of staff had already been appointed to develop a range of undergraduate courses.

But if Enfield had with foresight positioned itself well, I found myself there entirely by luck!

Working at Enfield

In September 1964 I knew very little about Enfield College, its aspirations or its leadership. I had applied for the post in order to teach economics (my degree subject) full-time. I had no idea what was in store for me. In the previous four years I had taught at a grammar school and then at a college of further education where I had taught a range of subjects to mature students preparing for professional exams. I welcomed the opportunity to return to economics, not to mention a significant rise in salary and the attraction of rowing with the newly formed national squad based at Chiswick!

I became the third member of the Economics Section and taught on Higher National Certificate/Diploma courses as well as on the London University External BA General and BA Sociology degrees. My immediate colleagues were Alan Hale who, at that time, was standing as Labour candidate for Enfield West, and Tom Evans, a very bright mathematical economist who had been appointed a few months earlier. Both had been active in student politics – Tom had been President of the Student Union at LSE. The rumour was that Eric Robinson had recruited them at the NUS Conference! Both the Economics Section and the Sociology Section were newly established and seemed to stand outside the departmental structure of the college, although the courses on which we were teaching were located in departments. Roy Bailey, with whom I was to work again at Sheffield in later years, was appointed as a lecturer in Sociology around the same time.

The decision had already been taken by the College to replace the London External degrees with a number of vocational, multi/inter disciplinary courses based on the social sciences. The first of these would be a four-year honours degree in Business Studies (BABS). The third year would be spent in a placement gaining business experience. Each course proposal was developed by a multi-disciplinary group of staff headed by a nominated course leader – Alan Hale for the Business Studies sandwich course; Bill Craze for the Mathematics for Business degree; Rachael Parry for the Sociology of Education in-service degree. I joined the development group for BA Business Studies. Apart from Alan and Tom, others in the team were Frank Little (Economics), Roy Bailey (Sociology), Cyril Walker and

Henry Mosert (Accounting and Finance), Derek Willmott (Law) and Jack Sutcliffe (Marketing).

Overall responsibility for new course development in the arts/ social science area was with Eric Robinson who was the Head of the Department of Mathematics. Robinson had previously taught at Brunel College, had served on various national working parties on aspects of education policy and had firm views on the content and structure of higher education. He attended many of the course meetings and frequently challenged our perceptions of what a degree was and what contribution a particular discipline would make to the overall educational experience of the student. The emphasis was on the student and on the multi disciplinary nature of vocational education in contrast to mastery of an academic discipline.

We were all expected to defend our views and debate was often fierce. Meetings became a major form of staff development for all involved. This was of particular importance as most of us had taken single subject degrees at university and had little or no experience of teaching at undergraduate level. It became even more important in following years as new staff were appointed in the social sciences often while still undertaking postgraduate courses themselves.

The challenge of integration

For many colleagues the constant challenging of discipline and belief was irksome at least and very disturbing for some. For Eric Robinson it was a necessary requirement for the expansion of an alternative sector of higher education, a view that would be clearly set out in his book *The New Polytechnics* (1968). There was also an expectation that the course structure would include some form of integrating study and/or project work. The focus on the development of the individual student was reinforced by adopting a personal tutor system where a nominated member of staff had responsibility for the overall progress of the student.

It is tempting to see the approach taken at Enfield to course development and teaching method – with the emphasis on the individual rather than the subject – as an attempt to develop an alternative philosophy of education to that of the then university sector. This was characterised by Robinson as that of the tyranny of the single subject honours degree. However this conclusion would be simplistic – it was indeed the approach taken at Enfield and championed by Robinson but it was also the inevitable outcome of developing vocationally relevant degree programmes. Indeed the Crick Report (1964) was notable in that, in proposing degree level courses in business studies, it sought to break the hold of the single subject honours degree with its assumed narrowness of study and to provide a wider education. The BABS course development group at Enfield followed the Crick recommendations of a two-year broad based academic foundation followed by a placement year and then a choice of specialism in the final year (the so-called thick sandwich course). The three specialisms chosen were Marketing, Finance and Human Relations. To guard against the dangers of a 'cafeteria' approach, where a student takes a number of discrete subjects and any implied synthesis is left to him or her, there was provision for an interdisciplinary seminar and relevance was sought from the foundation disciplines. In addition to the personal tutor system, staff were encouraged to team teach and to sit in on each other's lectures. The course was validated by the CNAA and was soon followed by the Mathematics for Business and Sociology of Education degrees. A part-time degree in Business Studies started in 1968 and a degree in Social Science in 1969.

My experience of teaching on the London External and the BABS in those first years was of large lecture groups (50 plus), seminars of about six students and personal tutorials. At first I shared the lectures with Tom Evans and all the staff taking the seminars sat in. I remember spending hours preparing for that Tuesday 11a.m. lecture!

The challenge of expansion

After a year or so I took over responsibility for organising the Economics Section. One key task was to attract and appoint new staff. A major expansion was required to cope with the large number of students recruited to the new CNAA degrees as well as the London Externals. The Business Studies degree was very popular and intake numbers were set at 100 plus. However it proved difficult to appoint experienced staff particularly those with relevant business experience. Fortunately the college provided attractive employment prospects for young graduates, often pursuing postgraduate work at

LSE. They were enthusiastic and committed colleagues but were at the start of their academic careers and often moved on quickly. They also had considerable investment in their subject specialism and research and did not find it easy to cut across disciplines. It took a few years after the first CNAA degrees were approved to achieve a balanced staff profile. The growth in staff numbers was impressive – in 1964 there were three economists, when I left in 1970 there were over thirty! The numbers were even greater in sociology. Many of the staff appointed in economics and social science in those years achieved prominence in their chosen fields – as academics, as departmental/faculty/university heads, as politicians. Both the Economics and Sociology Sections held regular staff seminars where research papers were discussed. We had many lively discussions in the economics seminar but perhaps not as lively as in Sociology where there was the occasional punch up!

In 1967 Enfield introduced a Faculty structure and Eric Robinson became Head of the Faculty of Arts and Social Science. Within the Faculty there was a course/subject matrix with courses taking precedence. The course heads acted as the Faculty executive. I was asked to take responsibility for the part-time business courses as well as acting as a subject head and became part of the senior management team.

I proposed that we develop a part-time degree in business studies which would complement both the sandwich BABS and the in-service Sociology of Education course. It would not be conceived as a part-time version of BABS but would be designed to take account of the students' circumstances, experience and maturity. Entry to the course would be more open and not entirely dependent on formal qualifications. The student would be able, to a limited extent, to vary the pace and direction of study to take account of variations in his or her personal circumstances. I got the backing of both Brosan and Robinson and established a small development group to take planning forward. I was particularly keen to involve colleagues with experience of teaching mature students and with a career outside teaching. From memory the group included John Munro (Economics), Keith Jones and Richard Nunn (Accounting), Roger Davies and Tony Crilly (Quantitative Methods). The course was the first of its kind in the country and pioneered the growth of part-time degrees in business studies and the professions related to business in what was to become the polytechnic sector. Although, in retrospect, the submission was not as radical or as student focused as we might have wished, the course avoided the inflexibilities of the London External system and moved a long way towards meeting the needs of mature students in employment. Importantly, the course acted as a template for proposals which would follow from other institutions.

The submission was accepted by CNAA and approved to start in September 1968. Despite the difficulties of access to higher education faced by mature students in employment, the course recruited well. Many students travelled long distances to attend classes in the evening or at weekends. In the late 1960s those in employment seeking to achieve a qualification part-time did so via night school or a correspondence course. The OU had yet to open its doors, there was no internet and there was no financial support for mature students.

The rise of the Polytechnics

My final years at Enfield College were lived in the shadow of Middlesex Polytechnic. The government had announced, in 1966, its intention to designate a number of Polytechnics based on an amalgam of local colleges which would be the vehicle for the expansion of higher education outside the universities. It was anticipated that Enfield and Hendon, perhaps with Hornsey College of Art, might merge to form a Middlesex Polytechnic. Inevitably there was much speculation, talk, posturing, positioning within and between the colleges.

Both George Brosan and Eric Robinson were seen as candidates for the leadership of any merged institution. Both had national reputations, both were well respected and each had much to offer. Robinson was an educational visionary, well connected politically and had set out an agenda in his influential book, *The New Polytechnics* (op. cit). He expressed himself forcefully, disliked compromise and could be abrasive and curt. Brosan was an experienced college principal who understood the political balance between college and local authority and had proved adept at making sure that Enfield was well served by the County Council. He was willing to challenge authority and push assertively when necessary. Both were ambitious and wanted to lead one of the new institutions, possibly Middlesex.

Working closely with both of them had always been lively, now it became tense and somewhat competitive.

For Brosan and Robinson the situation was complicated by timing. Local Authorities had been invited to put forward proposals for polytechnic designation with academic development plans. The Secretary of State would then decide designation. It was likely that institutions formed from one college (e.g. Hatfield) or from a large technical college and a small college of art (e.g. Sheffield, Leicester) would find it easier to develop a proposal than a complicated merger which required considerable discussion and negotiation. The earlier designations were at the start of 1969 (Hatfield and Sheffield); most of the London ones came in late 1970 and Middlesex not until 1973.

In the event, neither Brosan nor Robinson was destined to lead Middlesex Polytechnic. George Brosan became Director of North East London Polytechnic (NELP) in 1970 and John O'Neill succeeded him as Principal of Enfield. Shortly after that Eric Robinson was appointed Deputy Director at NELP with the expectation that it would probably be short term, prior to Eric being appointed to one of the later designations. Middlesex was one of the last polytechnics to be designated in 1973 and Ray Rickett, Deputy Provost at City of London Polytechnic was appointed Director.

I left Enfield College in December 1969 to join the newly designated Sheffield Polytechnic as Head of the Department of Economics and Business Studies. But I was to work with Brosan and Robinson again when I went to NELP as Assistant Director in 1972-76. By then their relationship had become perhaps less productive although both shared a similar vision for vocational higher education and the polytechnics. At Enfield their partnership had been highly creative – George, always a larger than life figure, brought the skills of an experienced leader and Eric the passion of an educational missionary. Both wanted change, both challenged the status quo. Possibly there was less room at NELP, a wider and more diverse institution than Enfield, for two buccaneers!

Towards 'necessary arrogance'

My years at Enfield were characterised by constant change and development, rapid growth in student and staff numbers, increasing levels of responsibility and, above all, an environment and colleagues that allowed me to work through my own views on various aspects of education. I was very fortunate to be given leadership responsibilities at a relatively early age and trusted to get on with the job. As head of a subject group, then as a member of the Faculty Management Team and with responsibility for a group of courses I became involved not only in staff appointments and course development/organisation but also with wider college issues – course and subject matrix, teaching methods, student support services, library development, etc. I saw at first hand some of the interrelationships (often heated) between college management and the local authority. Prior to Enfield, for me teaching was a job, challenging in the range of subjects to be taught, but with a highly prescribed curriculum. After Enfield, education was more of a vocation with a commitment to opening access and to expansion, to part-time education and to serving the local community. I was influenced strongly in my views about higher education by Brosan and Robinson and I was particularly grateful for the freedom they gave me to explore and innovate. The experience and confidence gained and (as Brosan would describe it) the acquiring of the 'necessary arrogance' served me well in my later career.

One among many?

Did Enfield have a wider significance in the development and expansion of non-university higher education in the 1960's and the subsequent emergence of the polytechnics? It is sometimes argued that the 'Enfield Experiment' was a precursor to the polytechnic expansion in the social sciences. Undoubtedly Enfield, in 1970, had one of the largest social science staff groupings in the country and had approaching 1,000 students on degrees in social science and business. The staff were young, bright and politically aware (many were veterans of the student activism at LSE in 1968). However it was only one of a number of local authority colleges preparing for a major expansion in undergraduate vocational education, broadening their academic base from science and technology into business and the social sciences and experimenting with new academic and management structures.

Many of these colleges had significant strengths and also had strong and well-connected leadership. As the opportunities offered by polytechnic designation became apparent, the major colleges became involved in merger discussions with neighbouring colleges which led to larger and more comprehensive institutions with different problems and wider potential. Size, merger and a bold political decision provided the context which was at the heart of the development of the polytechnics.

The key contributing factor was the coming together locally of a number of specialist colleges (of technology, of commerce, of art and design, and later to be joined by education), each with its own strengths and traditions rather than anything a single institution was able to offer alone. This released a vitality and creativity that was able to flourish in the expansionary context of the time. This dynamism could not have been sustained without the support and encouragement of some professional bodies and particularly the opportunities for course development and experimentation afforded and encouraged by the Council for National Academic Awards.

The Enfield influence

Along with other colleges Enfield was quick to recognise and engage with the changes taking place in higher education at that time – the shift in student demand towards the social sciences, the business-led demand for vocational relevance and for higher level business and management education and, importantly, student dissatisfaction with aspects of the higher educational experience.

Enfield, with its background in the responsiveness which was and still is the hallmark of Further Education, was a crucible for new ideas and for educational change. Students were at the centre of the educational process. The college advocated vocational relevance, part-time courses, multi- and inter-disciplinary approaches to teaching and learning, forms of integrative study, large lectures and seminars rather than classes and personal tutorials. Enfield took these values and its experience into its merger discussions with Hendon and Hornsey Colleges.

The emphasis on the development of the student rather than the development of the subject was taken further at NELP with the establishment of the School for Independent Study offering a Diploma in Higher Education (DipHE) and eventually a degree programme. Both Robinson and I were involved with this initiative, led by Tyrrell Burgess which, for a while, sparked national interest. I was also able, as Assistant Director (Academic Affairs) to progress my interest in mature students and part-time education and to persuade the CNAA to accept the principle of accreditation of work experience. This focus on the student was also encapsulated nationally in the development of the number of faculty or polytechnic-wide modular programmes submitted to CNAA in the 1970's, including one developed at Middlesex.

In 1976 I left NELP to become Director of Hull College of Higher Education (later Humberside Polytechnic). This was a merger of six colleges (technology, commerce, nautical studies, art and design and two colleges of education). Eric had moved north as well, as Principal of Bradford College, and we were in frequent contact. My Enfield experience of staff development and of putting the student first proved invaluable in the Hull merger process. We decided to submit a range of new degree programmes to CNAA and fortunately I was able to appoint Mick Harrison to my senior team with a responsibility for new course development (the Eric Robinson role at Enfield). Mick had been a colleague at Enfield where he headed the Sociology Section and again at Sheffield where he was a Principal Lecturer. He was to go on to become Vice-Chancellor of Wolverhampton University. At Hull he led a small course development unit which was very successful and which was firmly rooted in our shared Enfield experience.

George Brosan retired from NELP in 1980 and Eric retired as Director of Lancashire Polytechnic ten years later. That year the polytechnics celebrated twenty-one years of growth – not only growth in student numbers but also in stature and self-confidence. We had, as it were, acquired the 'necessary arrogance'.

The inevitable convergence of sectors

Binary policy had achieved a great deal and the distinctiveness of the two sectors – university and polytechnic – had assisted in marketing a distinctive image. It had enabled what had previously been considered non-traditional higher education – part-time study, access programmes, degrees in newly emerging occupational fields and so on – to gain legitimacy without directly challenging the traditional university model. It had enabled greater student choice of course and institution and had allowed expansion at a lower cost than if it had taken place in the universities.

But the resultant approximate equal balance of student numbers between sectors, as well as the polytechnics coming out of local authority control allowed comparisons to be made between sectors and for questions to be asked as to the differences and for issues such as quality assurance, cost effectiveness, accountability and responsiveness to be raised in a transbinary context. This led to an unsustainable position and made convergence inevitable. The polytechnics could no longer be viewed by Government as a tap that could be turned on or off dependent on the buoyancy of demand for university places. Nor could they be sustained to provide higher education on the cheap. The universities could no longer be ring-fenced while the national agenda of expansion of the qualified workforce was left to the polytechnics. A unitary sector was the inevitable outcome of the success of the polytechnics and of the vision of those, like Brosan and Robinson, who had encouraged and led their development.

Paradoxically, having been a strong supporter of binary policy and of the CNAA throughout my career, I found myself, as Chairman of the Committee of Directors of Polytechnics (CDP) from 1990-93, leading discussions with both government and university vice-chancellors about the end of binary and what the new system should be and what should replace the CNAA. We believed that the polytechnic sector was strong enough for our commitment, mission and ethos to survive and that we could continue to transform the scale and ethos of post secondary education in this country. A unitary framework would not be a uniform system but would allow for diversity and competition and allow institutions to position themselves according to their strengths. Ironically I found myself discussing post-binary possibilities with two ex Enfield colleagues – Tessa Blackstone, who was shadow and later Minister for HE and with Bryan Davies who was shadow spokesperson for Business, Innovation and Skills. The issues at that time were those of access to research funding by the soon to be ex-polytechnics and the arrangements for quality assurance to be put in place for the unitary system. Interestingly title was never a major issue although there were some local difficulties and disagreements. The 1992 Further and Higher Education Act allowed the polytechnics to use the university title if they so wished. There had been limited discussion in CDP about the possibility of sticking with the title 'polytechnic' but it was felt that that would perpetuate a binary divide and that, given a more competitive higher education climate, the title of university would be better understood. We believed that we were strong enough to change, over time the meaning of the term 'university', to incorporate our mission and achievements. We certainly did not see it as promotion!

It is now almost twenty years since I retired as Vice-Chancellor of Sheffield Hallam University. Probably those years have seen more change in higher education than ever before. Universities now appear to have less autonomy and there appears to be more State intervention. The Higher Education Funding Council for England (HEFCE) has migrated from the role of buffer to one of an agent of government and is now set to be abolished and replaced by a new set of agencies. Student numbers have continued to grow despite the introduction and subsequent increases in tuition fees. There are considerably more international students. Vocational courses are well subscribed; higher education is increasingly diverse and better understood; universities are major players in their regional economies and have developed strong links with their local communities. The 'polytechnic vision' is now mainstream. Universities continue to innovate and challenge.

Looking back on my career, the Enfield years were very significant in pointing the way, giving experience and confidence and giving a shared identity with a wider educational movement which was to transform the very restricted and elitist university system of the 1950's and 1960's. I am fortunate and privileged to have been part of that transformation. The foundations of a mass higher education system were laid in the 60's, and Enfield was there!

5. My time at Enfield

SVEN HAMMARLING

Sven Hammarling *came to Enfield in 1964 as a student on the Mathematics for Business course and, on graduating in 1968, joined the lecturing staff on the same degree, teaching numerical analysis. In 1979 he went to the National Physical Laboratory on a three-year research contract. He then joined the Numerical Algorithms Group in Oxford, where he worked in various roles until retirement in 2013, when he was made an Honorary Principal Consultant. Since 2006 he has been a Senior Honorary Research Fellow in the School of Mathematics at the University of Manchester.*

I was a student on the Mathematics for Business, BSc. degree at Enfield College of Technology and became a lecturer on the same degree the term after graduating. I am grateful to Tom Bourner and Tony Crilly for the opportunity to tell you something of my story.

Life Before Enfield

I went to school at Mount Grace in Potters Bar, one of the first comprehensive schools in Middlesex, starting the year after the school opened. Being an early comprehensive and a new school meant that many of the teachers were young and enthusiastic about the new system, something very much in common with Enfield College of Technology when I started there as a student. At school, I greatly enjoyed mathematics and somehow knew that my career would be in mathematics.

During, I think, my fourth year at Mount Grace, Vic Marchesi joined as a mathematics teacher and we became close lifetime friends. Although older than many of the new teachers, Vic certainly shared their enthusiasm for the comprehensive system. One of the teachers persuaded me to stay on at school to do a scholarship year, but it turned out that he was not actually capable of teaching to scholarship level. Nevertheless, I had a good year studying English literature and joining Vic as what we would now call a teaching assistant in his A-Level classes. We also ran an evening class on Modern Mathematics for Parents at a time when topics that many parents were not familiar with, such as matrices and set theory, were being introduced into the syllabus. It was good fun and good experience for the future. Vic will appear again later in this story.

I also first met my wife Pam at Mount Grace and we still see several friends from those days, so it holds plenty of happy memories.

I knew that I wanted to continue with mathematics after school, but guidance on university courses was somewhat limited. For reasons that I cannot now remember I decided upon Bangor in North Wales. Perhaps they were the only college to offer me a place! So off I went on the train, new overcoat given by Mum up on the rack and there it stayed, perhaps still travelling! Nevertheless, I thoroughly enjoyed life there and made good friends, but the course really did not suit me and to make matters worse, my father died just before my examinations. The tutorial system at that time was non-existent, so no one asked how I was coping. Anyway, after two years I failed the exams, perhaps my love of bridge didn't help!

I then spent a year doing various jobs, such as bar tending at my local pub, working in a book warehouse and supply teaching. How times have changed; it would be impossible now to teach without more than A-Level qualifications. I loved my time supply teaching at a primary school and I can imagine that if things had turned out differently I would have become a primary school mathematics teacher.

During the year Vic Marchesi told me about a new mathematics degree course, called Mathematics for Business, that was starting at Enfield College of Technology in Ponders End. The new degree sounded much more my cup of tea and so I made enquiries. I was accepted onto the course and, surprisingly, I was able to get another grant. What a contrast to today; I feel so sorry for the financial burden that students today have to suffer.

A Student at Enfield

Prior to 1964 colleges like Enfield, that did not have university status and hence a Royal Charter, but wanted to run degree courses typically offered external degrees from a university, usually London. In

1964 the Council for National Academic Awards (CNAA) was established by Royal Charter and so was able to grant degrees. The Mathematics for Business degree, which started in 1964, must have been one of the first degrees anywhere to be approved.

The Principal, George Brosan, had been recruited in 1962 and together with his deputy, Eric Robinson, changed expectations as to what educational opportunities colleges, such as Enfield, might offer. See for example (Robinson, 1968). The idea, of course also taken up by other colleges of technology, was to take comprehensive education into the colleges, to give everybody the opportunity to develop, flourish and have a full education irrespective of ability and talent. So, as well as degree courses, one could take various diploma courses and study part-time and in the evenings. The colleges of technology were funded by the local authorities and there was a real sense of community. As far as I am concerned all that was lost when Margaret Thatcher removed local authority control of the polytechnics, paving the way for converting the polytechnics into universities.[11] Middlesex University seems to have been one of the more successful new universities, but the sense of local community has inevitably been lost.

At the time, the Mathematics for Business course was a unique kind of mathematics degree. The applied subjects in the degree included statistics, operational research, finance and econometrics. It also included computing and numerical analysis, which became the main subjects of my future career. The lecturers were all enthusiastic, mainly young, and some just starting their careers. One notable exception was the wonderful Stanley (Stan) Millward who, soon after the war, joined what was then, I believe, Ponders End Technical Institute, shortly to become Enfield Technical College and, in 1962, Enfield College of Technology. Although I was not aware at the time, he had taught an amazingly wide range of subjects such as pure mathematics, physics, statistics, astronomy and engineering, and had even been a Physical Training instructor. At the time of starting the Mathematics for Business course, the college did not have a numerical analysis specialist, so they had turned to Stan to teach the subject,

[11] Somewhat ironically, the new Roberts building, or tower block, was opened by Margaret Thatcher on Wednesday 17 March 1971.

which he agreed to do. I don't believe that any of us students realised that he had never taught the subject before!

Nine of us students started the course, but sadly just three of us finished with a degree, a BSc., so let no one say that CNAA degrees were easy. A Business Studies BA course started at the same time as the BSc Mathematics for Business, but did not receive official approval from the CNAA until 1965. It was typical of Brosan's optimism and enthusiasm that he would allow the course to start without approval. Students who graduated with me on the degree were Mel Williams and Hazel Chapman.[12] As I recall, Mel went to the Milk Marketing Board using his operational research skills and at some point joined British Airways, where he had a stellar career.

I believe that it was in the second year of the course that we were able to take computer programming as an option. Once again, not having any other expert, Stan Millward agreed to take the course! The college did not have its own computer, so we travelled either to Hatfield College of Technology to use their Elliot 803, or to Elliot's themselves.[13] We used a computer language called Algol 60, which was Europe's answer to Fortran and fed our programs into the computer on paper tape. (The Elliott company was close to the Elstree film studios and their magnetic tape bore a close resemblance to film tapes). I thought that Algol 60 was really a very nice language, but ultimately it could not compete with the IBM backed Fortran and it became obsolete. The actual computer that we used at Hatfield is now restored and is in the National Museum of Computing at Bletchley Park. I am not sure if I should be pleased or depressed that the first computer I used is now in a museum! Either way, I am proud of the fact that I wrote and ran my first program in 1965.

In common with many CNAA degrees in those days, it was a four-year course with the third year spent working in industry. I spent my industrial year at Arlington Motors, across the road from the college, working on a model for stock control. I don't believe that the results were ever used by Arlington's, but it was a very en-

[12] If anyone reading this knows of Hazel Chapman, I would love to hear her news.

[13] According to *Wikipedia* Hatfield purchased a digital computer at a cost of £29,201 in 1962 so that a computer science degree could be established. Hatfield became a Polytechnic in 1969.

joyable experience. Hazel Chapman worked at Belling and Lee, and Mel Williams at Idris.

As Pam lived in Potters Bar and Stan Millward, who didn't drive, lived in nearby Brookmans Park, I often gave Stan a lift home in my 1949 Austin A40. I had stuck a number of labels in the car and Stan was convinced that it was the labels that held the car together! Stan was an inspiration to many of us at Enfield, both staff and students, and was another lifelong friend. Ray Barons, for many years a lecturer at Enfield, told me that when he first arrived at Enfield his head of department was nowhere to be seen and had not asked anyone to show him around. Stan took it on himself to do just that and Ray has never forgotten this generosity.

No doubt in large part due to Stan's teaching, I found a real enthusiasm for numerical analysis and, in particular, for numerical linear algebra. In the final year of the course we had to write a mini thesis and mine was entitled Latent Roots and Latent Vectors.[14] In length, mine was very much more than mini. The two external examiners for the course were Ernest Albasiny, Head of Mathematics at the National Physical Laboratory (NPL) and Professor George Smith from Brunel University, who was an expert in PDEs (partial differential equations).[15] They seemed to have approved of the thesis and I was fortunate to obtain a first class honours degree, mainly on the basis of the thesis. Much to my surprise they encouraged me to publish the thesis and, with further work, it was published as a book two years later, in 1970.[16] Much of the book is now out of date, but the experience was wonderful and rewarding and I think that it is testament to the college and the staff that it was possible.[17]

A Lecturer at Enfield

At the end of the course I decided that numerical analysis and computing were what I wanted to continue with, and that I would like to be a lecturer. I was encouraged by Stan and others to apply to Enfield. I was short-listed and called for an interview. After a long wait,

---

[14] Nowadays they are referred to as eigenvalues and eigenvectors.

[15] Yes! We had two.

[16] Hammarling [1970].

[17] Not financially, though!

wondering what was happening, George Brosan emerged from the interview room and said 'Chairman's option, you are appointed.' and disappeared as quickly as he had appeared. Amazing!! It seemed to have upset the local councillor, who phoned me up later to interview me over the phone, but in any case, there wasn't much he could do.[18]

Pam and I married on 7 September 1968, had a week's honeymoon, about six miles away from where we now live, and I started work as a Lecturer on 16 September. I became a Senior Lecturer in 1971.

I loved lecturing and tutoring, principally in numerical analysis and computing. Enfield bought its own computer in the late 1960s, a Honeywell 120 if I recall correctly and not really suited to an academic environment. Input was via punched cards, which we had to leave for computer operators to feed to the computer and collect our output sometime later. In the mid-70s, probably by the time the college became a polytechnic, Enfield bought a DEC PDP-10 computer (from memory), which was a time-sharing machine, much more suited to an academic environment and we could access it via a terminal! I wrote several user callable routines for the DEC and still have the documentation for the linear equation solvers, as well as a guide I wrote for the DEC SOS editor. I also have a number of my numerical analysis lecture notes.

In 1970 Vic Marchesi left Mount Grace and came to Enfield College of Technology as a lecturer. As with Mount Grace, he was drawn by the new approach to higher education. He taught mathematics on a number of courses, particularly engineering courses. Vic never had any pretensions about being a great mathematician, but he was a great teacher because he knew how to instil confidence in his students, especially those for whom mathematics did not come naturally. The students were always free to phone him and to visit him at home for tutorials. Vic and Candy's (Vic's wife of 55 years) home had many mementos from grateful students, a testament to how much they cared about him. To Middlesex's credit, they kept him on as a part-time lecturer until his death, some thirteen years after his formal retirement. I am sure it gave a one-time racecourse bookie

---

18 Of course, nowadays it would not be possible to get such a lecturing job without a PhD so, in retrospect, I feel very privileged.

cause to smile, knowing that he had become a university lecturer! Would a modern university take on such a teacher? I doubt it.

There were many communal activities at Enfield. Vic was a keen football supporter and player, playing well into his sixties and I remember that, until the football pitch was built on, we had a staff football team. Probably our best player was Bryan Davies (see Chapter 7) who left in 1974 when he was elected as a Labour MP for Enfield North. Vic was also instrumental in organising end of term get togethers for the staff, either at a restaurant, or often at someone's home. They were lovely occasions and helped us to get to know people from other departments and courses. He also organised the occasional end of term shows, which were great fun.

The college had a number of somewhat obsolete mechanical hand calculators and Stan, Vic and I, and maybe others, used to demonstrate them at the local schools, as one of the efforts to engage with the local community. The pupils seemed to really enjoy using the calculators and it was not unusual to find a pupil, who apparently had been having difficulty with arithmetic, suddenly understanding the process when seeing it in action on the calculator· It reinforced the knowledge that some students need a different perspective when learning a subject.[19]

Stan Millward formally retired in 1971, but also continued part-time until finally retiring in 1976 and even after that coming in for the occasional guest lecture. He was the epitome of a gentleman. He also had a wonderful sense of humour. In the days of chalk that was supposed not to produce dust, I remember another lecturer called Charlie Dust coming into Stan's class to ask if he had any spare chalk. Stan as quick as a flash said 'Ah, the chalkless Dust!'. One day when Stan had an optician's appointment, Vic and I drew arrows on the floor from Stan's room in the temporary huts towards the opticians in Ponders End. Thankfully, Stan enjoyed the joke[20]. I know that Tony Crilly also saw Stan regularly after his retirement

[19] The mechanical calculators were operated by hand, rather than being held in the hand! The ubiquitous modern electronic calculators and computers are wonderful developments, but we have largely lost the ability to see the arithmetical processes in action.

[20] The temporary huts were not so temporary, they were there for many years!

and they worked together producing, I think two papers, a great help in keeping Stan stimulated.[21]

I have concentrated on two of the people who were particularly important to me, but of course there were many others who contributed to the success of the college, such as Bill Craze who was in charge of the Mathematics for Business course when I started; another person who cared deeply about the students, including making provision for disabled students and late developers.

A notable feature of that time were the discussions, or even arguments. We had plenty of them, but unlike later times after Brosan and Robinson had left, they were about educational issues and student needs. It was a wonderful place for me to start my career.[22]

Life After Enfield College of Technology

Enfield College of Technology became part of Middlesex Polytechnic in 1973, initially combining Enfield, Hendon College of Technology and Hornsey College of Art. Initially, life and the ethos at Enfield did not change too much and even well into Polytechnic days, the staff at Enfield continued to try to engage with the local community and to have the education of students at its heart. For example, in the spring of 1976 Tony Crilly and I launched *Middlesex Mathematical Notes*, aiming at one issue per term, which was usually achieved! It was aimed at students and staff with an interest in mathematics and we also distributed copies to the local secondary schools. Tony kept it going until 1982.

In 1977, in large part due to Bill Craze, we enrolled the Polytechnic's first blind student Paul Holliman onto the Mathematics for Business course. I think that it is fair to say that it was a humbling, but fulfilling experience for those of us involved. There were, of course, challenges, principally in turning written notes and computer output into forms suitable for Paul, as well as thinking about appropriate teaching methods, something that I am sure we as teachers benefited from. To its credit, the Polytechnic agreed to purchase a

---

21 Crilly and Millward, 1988, 1992.

22 They became respectively Director and Deputy Director of North East London Polytechnic in 1970.

Braille printer for the computer, not a cheap option, and many of the staff put notes onto cassette for Paul. Notably, Stan Millward, who had retired by then, and Ivor Grattan-Guinness devoted considerable time to helping Paul. Ivor and Paul subsequently wrote an article about the experience.[23]

But over time, the fact that the college was no longer on one site and was in more than one community did have an effect. The discussions and arguments seemed to move away from education. Andrew Roberts points out, on his web page about the history of Middlesex University, that the first edition of the Polytechnic newsletter, *North Circular*, in 1973 had the headline 'Row brews over faculty boards.'[24] Sadly, that sort of discussion seemed, all too often, to replace discussion on student education.

Life After Middlesex Polytechnic

Thanks to the external examiner of my degree, Ernest Albasiny, I was given the opportunity to have a sabbatical year at the National Physical Laboratory (NPL) with James (Jim) Hardy Wilkinson, which I happily took in 1975. Although I am not sure I realised at the time what an honour it was, the experience changed the course of my career. Working with Jim increased my desire to do more research and in 1979, on Jim's retirement, I left Middlesex Polytechnic to take up a three-year contract as a Principal Research Fellow at NPL, working with Jim's small group. At the same time, Paul Holliman spent his industrial year with us at NPL. If I remember correctly, Paul achieved a 2.1 degree.

Soon after acquiring a VAX computer the college installed the library of the Numerical Algorithms Group (NAG), a collection of numerical and statistical routines for solving numerical problems, which at that time was given free to colleges. We used the Library on the Mathematics for Business course in the teaching of numerical analysis and, of course, people could use the Library for their research problems. NAG started in 1970 as a university project funded by the then Computer Board, releasing its first Library in 1971, but was spun off in 1976 as a not-for-profit company. In about 1974, or

[23] Grattan-Guinness and Holliman [1983].

[24] http://studymore.org.uk/ssctim.htm.

so, whilst at Enfield, I contributed routines for the 'singular value decomposition' mathematical problem to the Library and in 1976 I became a member of NAG, thereby pledging £1 if the company should go bust!

At the end of my contract at NPL in 1982, I joined NAG and remained there for the next thirty-two years, the last seven working part-time, still computing and working on numerical analysis. NAG encouraged collaboration with academia and being non-profit, the emphasis was on the technical work, both of which suited me very well. I was still able to give occasional lectures and indeed was lucky enough to hold a visiting professorship for twenty years at Cranfield University, Shrivenham. From 1994 to 1997 I was even a member of the Science and Engineering Faculty Advisory Group at Middlesex University! In 2006, I became an Honorary Senior Research Fellow at the University of Manchester, a position I still hold (and love) at the time of writing, so I retain a strong contact with academia.

NAG even allowed a colleague and myself to be involved in open source software development for numerical linear algebra, developing a *de facto* standard for a set of Basic Linear Algebra Subroutines (BLAS)[25] followed by a linear algebra package called LAPACK[26] to utilise the BLAS. At the time of writing, the software is widely used worldwide and is included in the libraries of chip manufacturers, such as Intel[27] and AMD[28], as well as in many computer packages such as MATLAB. LAPACK is a project that I am particularly proud to have been involved with, the result of an interest in numerical software that started in 1965 at Enfield. Like Enfield, there was a wonderful camaraderie at NAG and I loved the work. At the time of writing, I still have an honorary position at NAG.

I could not have been successful at NPL and NAG, and involved in academia and projects such as LAPACK without the educational opportunities that Enfield College of Technology provided in those magical years. I am eternally grateful.

---

[25] https://en.wikipedia.org/wiki/Basic_Linear_Algebra_Subprograms.
[26] http://www.netlib.org/lapack/, https://en.wikipedia.org/wiki/LAPACK.
[27] Math Kernel Library (MKL).
[28] AMD Core Math Library (ACML).

6. What do you do here that's so important?

SIMON STANDER

> ***Simon Stander*** *joined the proto-polytechnic in 1965. At various times he was, inter alia, Head and deputy Head of the BA Social Science, senior economist, and during this period raised Erasmus funding to set up joint courses with French and Spanish universities. He took early retirement in 1990, spent a number of years in the USA and as a professor of Peace Studies in Central America, retired again, wrote a couple of books and is in foreign climes again trying to find the time to finish his book on cinema and war by watching as many war films as possible.*

Let me say at the start, notwithstanding any subsequent jaundiced comments I make in this chapter, that Enfield College of Technology provided me with one of the best educations in the social sciences I can imagine. I began as a lecturer in 1965 at close to double the salary I was earning as second in the history department of a large and unruly comprehensive school in King's Cross. This was untold riches for me and was very welcome. Despite a BA in Economics and Economic History, a part-time Master's degree from the London School of Economics, and five years as a qualified schoolteacher, I found myself quite ignorant in those early days at Enfield College of Technology, soon to be more aptly referred to by some of us as Ponders End where it was actually located. It was some distance from the old coaching town of Enfield. The name, Ponders End, comes from the description of where the debris from the last ice age finally came to rest. I suppose it was important not to become metaphorically part of that detritus. We did our best.

Trouble-making to building

The circumstances of my appointment may to some extent indicate the mindset of the prime movers, Tom Evans and Eric Robinson and George Brosan. I was teaching in a dreadful comprehensive school in London, where in each class room there was a speaker fixed to the wall and was impossible to turn off. The headmaster sat in his office at a microphone for most of the day relaying messages during class time, perhaps five or six per forty-minute period. The interruptions, not to say the content and triviality of the messages, made discipline, already horrendously difficult, even more so. On one occasion for a whole month I wrote the content of the messages down in an exercise book, took the result to the headmaster and threatened to give it to the HM Inspectors who were due that term. The headmaster was, naturally, furious. During the Inspectors' visit there wasn't a single broadcast until they had left. I never did show the exercise book to anyone. Shortly afterwards I went for interview at Enfield College of Technology and was offered a post. Tom said I got the job because when he phoned my headmaster for a reference he said: 'Don't employ Stander as he's a troublemaker'. Tom said that was just the sort of person they were looking for! I doubt being labelled a troublemaker is the normal route to employment.

While at one level being at Enfield was like being at one long seminar, violence of opinion was normal and actual violence at time not far removed from debate until by the early 70s such debate more or less disappeared once Enfield had been absorbed into the Polytechnic and the early prime movers had left. Not a few times the expression 'you can't make an omelette without cracking eggs' was heard; it was a bold person who would say aloud 'so where's the omelette?'

I arrived just a year or two into the project. Already in place were George Brosan and Eric Robinson. The latter had made himself Academic Head of Department with an already existing colleague as Administrative Head. Eric was responsible for the appointment of his main henchman, Tom Evans, former Student President at the London School of Economics (LSE). He was only about twenty-three years old. The college had cleared all the lower level work and taught an external London Degree plus Business Studies. The aim now was to introduce an all embracing Social Science programme that would consist of maybe 150 students per year and, lasting for four years, was to include an innovative sandwich element, unique to social science higher education at that time. The future Polytechnic would have on its hands an unprecedented degree programme of up to 800 students. It was planning for this that led to the prolonged seminar from 1965 to after the inauguration of the programme in 1968. A few years later some of us came uncomfortably to read a fictionalised account of the leadership directives for the massive CNAA approval Board that was due to visit, an event satirised by Tom Sharpe in his over the top farce, *Wilt*, in which a College of Technology is desperate to attain Polytechnic status through an innovative degree programme: 'What we have got to stress to the members of the CNAA committee is that this degree is an integrated course with a fundamental substructure grounded thematically on concomitance of cultural and sociological factors in no way unsuperficially disparate and with a solid quota of academic content to give students an intellectual and cerebral [experience] ...Furthermore we have only until tomorrow to structure our tactical approach to the visitation committee.' Our jargon was not quite so nonsensical but jargon it was.

Several objectives had to be achieved quickly. One was the expansion and design of accommodation for staff, students and administration in the existing building was quite inadequate for what was planned and so temporary space had to be found as well as a more permanent and adequately designed premises had to be provided. Central, of course, was the new social science degree. The general 'innovative' lines had already been agreed by Tom and Eric. There was, too, the question of the bar; there wasn't one and some politicking had to be done to get one. The catering was done in what was much like a school hall and was basic though I don't recall much complaining except from a young part-time woman lecturer; she complained that there was only lump sugar, unsuitable for her yoghurt. She turned out to be Tom's wife, now Baroness Blackstone with no doubt limitless supplies of granulated sugar at her fingertips in the House of Lords.

Crucial to the formation of the polytechnic was the integration of several colleges from three different local authorities: Hornsey College of Art and All Saints Teacher Training located in Haringey, Hendon College of Technology and Ivy House in Barnet and Enfield College of Technology and Trent Park Teacher Training College in the Borough of Enfield. The eventual long delay was largely a result of the problems among the three London Boroughs in agreeing on how to control the process of establishing the proper form of authority for setting up the institution, and for financing and for running it. Once the Polytechnic had been formed, *North Circular* was chosen for the title of its official in-house newspaper. This was in reference to the large number of campuses located round the north circular road. At least one colleague suggested at the time that we could do away with the campuses and simply have classes on buses travelling round the heavily congested pre-M25 ring road.

How to work committees and get things done

In addition there was the issue of 'democracy' versus 'management'. I recall the muddied politics providing a lesson to anyone of us academics who was prepared to make sense of the blur of academic board and its composition, faculty boards and their composition, committees, sub-committees, minutes of the last meeting, matters arising, agenda and how to work them, any other business, elections to boards, amendments and amendments to amendments. Tom, who had been a student politician, and Eric a trade union activist saw themselves as top manipulators in this world with techniques to ensure stuff went through or was blocked or was properly prepared and votes counted before meetings took place and corridor talks and words in ears and alliances struck. I am sure the Houses of Parliament and the US Congress and all other allegedly democratic institutions work in much the same way. It was a training of sorts though I only recall one of our ilk ending up in the House of Commons from which he has now been removed to the Upper House. In due course, however, in what was the spirit of the times, the students eschewed the committees and what I suppose was a rigged form of democracy, in favour of sit-ins and direct protest. The students threw milk at Margaret Thatcher when she came to open our brand new six-floor Tower Block. This was 'our' contribution to her downgrading social science to social studies, no doubt.

We had to envisage a university-type institution where tutorials became the most important part of the teaching methods and that involved providing office/study space for teachers and seminar rooms for students of groups supposed to be not more than ten. Hence the design of our temporary huts which were in material terms not unlike the post-war prefabs that my Aunt Stella and Uncle Alan had inhabited on London Fields. As most of us were from the lower reaches of the lower middle-class or the upper reaches of the working class, apart from our very own Old Etonian, there were few complaints at the basic nature of our surroundings. Indeed, our very own

Etonian seemed to enjoy the fact that he was slumming it as if in an East End Settlement, rather like the disgraced John Profumo.

In due course there were two parallel rows of huts set at right angles to each other. The rooms were all of a uniform size and would accommodate either seminar groups of ten or so and others were set aside to house lecturers at two per room, each had a desk, a filing cabinet, a chair or two and no telephone or equipment of any kind in the rooms. The floor was covered with a kind of lino but carpets were not to be found. There was one telephone in the corridor of each of the blocks that was available to everyone; this provided no privacy as every word could be heard through the thin walls. On one occasion I even overheard our Old Etonian trying to volunteer on the phone for the Israeli Army in the Six Days War. Basic as the huts were, they were an improvement on the first year. We had previously shared rooms with somewhere around six or eight per room and maybe had a table and chair each. As for teaching, the classrooms were usually too large for seminar groups or too small for large lectures. I did once have to conduct one-to-one tutorials in a broom cupboard and was to read some years later that Howard Jacobson experienced the same in his fictionalised Polytechnic as portrayed in his first novel *Coming From Behind* (1976) in which his Poly has no redeeming features. After the huts went up plans were set forth for a six-floor building that imitated the huts in design but with one block plonked upon another. Thus it was that Enfield set about erecting a building in much the same way as in *Wilt* (1974), to impress the CNAA. In our case no-one buried a blow-up plastic doll in the foundations. Tom Sharpe's proto-Poly failed to get their joint honours passed whereas we did succeed with our BA Social Science. The main loss with the building expansion was the playing field. No more student-staff football matches on site. There were surprising talents among them: one colleague went on to play for the House of Commons football team, a team full of talents no doubt. And, of course, there was our very own 6' 3" Old Etonian charging down the wing without so much as breaking into a sweat.

To begin with there was a small number of young appointments who tried to make sense of what was supposed to be done and how to do it. There was no bar and the odd tight caucus, in which for a short time I was included, met in either the nearest pub, The Goat, or the nearest cafe. This meant walking across the playing field not yet sacrificed to buildings or car park, past the WW2 bomb shelters (later put to use as storage for past examination scripts and thus inadvertently relatively safe from nuclear attack), along a small gravel path where if you turned right was the pub immediately to hand or if you turned left a ramshackle cafe not untypical of Ponders End High Road. It is the cafe (run by Ossie) that has stayed most clearly in my memory and somehow exemplifies how basic everything was. I recall repairing there on several occasions with Tom Evans, John Stoddart and maybe one or two others. We would always go upstairs where few ventured and we would be guaranteed privacy. John, being an international oarsman requiring massive reserves of energy, would spoon about six sugars into his tea, granulated sugar being available here unlike in the canteen where the future Baroness was deprived of it. The tea would immediately spill into the saucer not simply because of the amount of sugar but because the floor was at about a twenty-degree-angle and everything liquid would overflow. At times one might be in danger of slipping off one's chair. Perhaps someone might order a hamburger which came in a lightly grease-proofed bag with the words either 'whit oinon' or 'whitout oinon' stamped on it. Here I learned how to influence the outcome of meetings, not always, in my case, successfully however.

It wasn't long before the staff increased in number: economists, sociologists, philosophers, historians were all claimed from school teaching or straight from some post-graduate common room or other (but most likely LSE) with the promise of well paid employment, a start to an academic career, possibly advancement, possibly space to write or to finish a PhD or other post-graduate work. Following first the Robbins Report and then Crosland's proposals for rapid expansion of higher education these few years of the 1960s and early 1970s led to what was to be a short-term opportunity for entry into higher education teaching or, in some cases, a management career in the new institutions.

Eric Robinson was determined to steer well clear of such entrenched positions as Liberal Studies. He was after 'integration' whatever that was; it supposedly meant interdisciplinary work, as a defence against the dead-hand of subject specialisations with what he claimed was their non-vocational irrelevance. Any new administration in the new institution was to reflect this and he promoted a so-called matrix structure on academic/administrative lines. In addition, numeracy was promoted though he wanted students to be freed from their usual number blindness in innovative ways and shift them into a bright new field of mathematical awareness.

In order to bring this about Robinson established a weekly meeting to discuss how his educational ends might be achieved. It wasn't long before we had our fair share of 'creative conflict' that went on for several terms until the CNAA submission began to take form. Among the influx of new lecturers were a small number of Leicester-educated sociologists who via their own teachers were inspired by Talcott Parsons, generally regarded as a social conservative and in vogue at the University of Leicester. This group increasingly faced a whole range of Marxists, marxologists, fellow travellers, leftist mavericks and the like, many from the London School of Economics. But there were plenty of the middle-of-the-road Economists, Historians, and Philosophers who held to a form of rationality that involved listening to arguments. But, as was heard from both extremes, anyone who stayed in the middle of the road stood the extreme risk of being run over. As a middle-roader myself I felt run over several times in those early years.

In due time two significant compulsory courses developed for first year students, delaying their entry into specialised disciplinary courses: one to introduce students to innovative forms of numeracy: the course was called 'Methods and Models' but soon became labelled, once in the heat of the classroom, 'methods and muddles'. The great interdisciplinary course was called 'Man and Society' but hastily renamed in more politically correct terminology SHE (society, history and environment). While many cohorts of students were thrust into the deep-end of knowledge on these courses, the ideas they incorporated never saw the public light of day in the form of publication. The same was true of the compulsory course for all second year students that we called the Socio-Economic Foundations of Public Policy. One of the key textbooks on the course was Ralph Miliband's *The State in Capitalist Society*. I wonder now if his politically ill-fated sons Ed and David ever read the book; there seems to be no evidence of it. All three of these courses were taught by teams, sharing lectures and seminars. Whatever we were trying to get over has now been lost in the mists of time as there are no publications to record what was, at least to begin with, a fervent exchange of ideas.

Our treasures

To some extent the youthful lecturers were handicapped by the lack of administrative support and the under-staffing among the secretarial help. On the other hand the secretarial help, bearing in mind that there were no word-processors or photocopying facilities and teachers and students hand wrote everything, did a terrific job. Some of our colleagues wrote in the most horrendous scripts. I think the worst was that of Mick Harrison, who led the Leicester faction and eventually became a Polytechnic principal and later Vice-Chancellor. Perhaps he always received the benefit of the doubt when he was making a written point.

As I remember it, only the most senior colleagues had access to a secretary and the principal's secretary, Gertie Beckett, appeared to rule the roost. A close second was Audrey, Eric Robinson's secretary. They all seemed to be middle-aged though anyone over thirty-five appeared to be middle-aged to us. Most had matriculated and could have gone onto university in this latter age of higher education. They had the indignity of having to serve a generation of lecturers (and later, students) who were reaping benefits denied them, though they varied a great deal in background. One, Daphne, said that her favourite past-time was watching old black and white films. When I asked why, she said she was in many of them as she used to have small parts and double for the British star of historical films of 1940s, Margaret Lockwood especially as she was a dab hand at riding a horse.

The secretary of the BA Social Science programme from its first intake in 1968 had also matriculated but her background differed a great deal from Daphne's. If the term 'old school' means anything then it certainly applied to Iris. She refused promotion because she would not contemplate earning more than Jack, her husband. She insisted on working part-time, thirty hours per week, so she could be home to put Jack's dinner on the table. When the three-day week was introduced during the troubles of the early seventies, she asked me, in a state of exasperation, why educational establishments were kept open five days a week and Jack, a highly valued tool-maker, could only work three days. 'What do you do here that is so important?' she asked. 'I think what Jack does is a lot more important, you know.' She was probably right especially as many of my colleagues turned up only three days a week anyway (some even less!).

Enter the CNAA

With the lack of secretarial or administrative support and few office facilities, some of the lecturers pitched in. One of the most enthusiastic was our Old Etonian winding away at the Gestetner duplicator, collating, punching holes and binding pages as rapid a rate as, when he ran up the wing when playing football, outpacing everyone, without breaking into a sweat. He once described me as lazy but softened the comment by saying lazy people are usually efficient. Lazy true, efficient, I doubt. He physically produced the massive two volumes required for the CNAA submission. There was an extensive introduction written by Eric, Tom and a handful of others. This was followed by syllabus after syllabus written by the designated lecturer(s) each with an introduction, a week by week teaching programme, seminar titles, essay titles and reading lists. All written by hand, then typed on Gestetner skins, checked, duplicated, bound. In addition, there were CVs of the teachers and publications (this latter somewhat thin).

This paperwork turned out to be the heavy artillery with which to bombard the score or more of visiting professors from the CNAA. The teachers provided the small arms fire at the numerous meetings. Sociologists, Economists, Historians, Land use Planners, Geographers, Philosophers, and Mathematicians among them. The proposal was for a four-year degree, which included a placement year; there were arguments justifying integration and delayed specialisation; much was made of the so-called matrix system of management and teaching (using structural-functional arguments). The massive ideological differences were plastered over.

Some of the courses caused a few eyebrows to be raised but no serious dissenter among the CNAA board. I recall one course in particular entitled ‘Strategy and Tactics of Revolutionary Movements’ or some such. This referred to Marxist style revolution and would now no doubt cause some alarm. If we had a patron saint, it would surely be (Saint) Thomas Kuhn and his paradigm shift, which became the keynote of our early introduction to the social sciences. One of the approaches that carried us through was the extensiveness of the teaching programmes and the reading lists, many of which were more up to date than those used by the visiting professors who belonged to an earlier generation. I do not recall how we managed to cover the fact that few of the books were in what had been a dilapidated library, though the librarians had done an excellent job in getting in as many books as possible with George Brosan making available as big a budget as he could muster.

Epilogue

For a time it was clear that Enfield College of Technology was a proto-Polytechnic. Principles such as breaking down subject boundaries, taking on mature students without formal qualifications, interviewing all students for selection, pushing numeracy in the curriculum, pursuing compulsory interdisciplinary courses rather than the multidisciplinary courses of the dreaded modular forms so beloved in the USA, delaying specialisation, putting teaching before research were gradually whittled away. Maybe other Polytechnics followed suit while others were under the thrall of universities to which they aspired. Something of Enfield remains out there I am sure but a lot less than we might have hoped for. I do recall at least one external examiner, an eminent professor at London University (government adviser and subsequently a Baron), being impressed by our syllabuses, reading lists and teaching schemes and he said enthusiastically and regularly how much he was indebted to them for his own teaching. I don't know how far we influenced other university teachers who came to inspect us as members of the CNAA but there was at least this one person of influence who benefitted from our committees, our youth and our Very Own Etonian's Gestetner machine.

Those early days teaching at Ponders End was an education for all of the young men and few women who experienced it. It may or may not have been unique. The sad thing is that the atmosphere did not last and the promise was only partially fulfilled. We were not best served by the top leadership; academics were increasingly replaced at the top by non-academics; 'democracy' within the institution was progressively weakened, and most of the leading lights left for promotion or career change quite soon and before we became a Polytechnic. In due course teachers were kept firmly at the chalk face; research began slowly to replace teaching as the status grab.

But I am glad I was there... In the last few years I have published a couple of books (actually one and three-quarters) which I think both bear the hall-mark of that early education in the second half of the 60s. So, in the days before the UK even joined the Common Market and with the term globalisation not yet coined but with my head becoming full of theoreticism, empiricism, relativism, absolutism, Marxism, capitalism and much else, I, at least, was prepared to face the future, never mind whether the students made head or tail of it all.

7. Enfield College: a unique educational experience

BRYAN DAVIES

> ***Bryan Davies*** *joined Enfield College in 1965 as a lecturer in History and was principally involved with the Social Science degree. He was active in NATFHE (the lecturer's trade union), the Academic Board, and the College Governing Body. He was M.P. for Enfield North in 1974-1979 and was a Government Whip in the 1970s. He served as Secretary of the Parliamentary Labour Party until 1992 and was M.P. for the Oldham Central constituency 1993-1997, and in this period was the Shadow Minister for Higher Education. Created Lord Davies of Oldham in 1997, he has held several ministerial appointments in the House of Lords and is currently a Shadow Treasury Minister.*

My parents were from Tredegar, South Wales. It was there that I was born although we moved within months to my father's new job in Redditch in Worcestershire. Dad was a highly principled socialist, chairman of his constituency Labour Party for 20 years, extraordinarily well read for someone who left school to work in the local coalmine at fourteen. For most of his life he was a painter and decorator craftsman but always frustrated by the intellectual limitations of the job. He had two modest ambitions for his son that he should play rugby for Wales and become Labour Prime Minister. I of course achieved neither. My Worcestershire grammar school played football and my political career fell far short of a Cabinet post let alone PM. Somewhat scant reward for endless late night discussions on how to realise the dream of a socialist Britain.

My grammar school education got me to University College in London where I enjoyed reading for a History degree. I was duly grateful to the school although well aware that it took in the 5 per cent of the local children who passed the eleven-plus and discarded two thirds before higher education could even be considered. I loved UCL, captained the soccer team, made the cricket first eleven, challenged speakers in College debates, served as Secretary of the Athletics Board and got a good degree. A year later I achieved a distinction in the post-graduate teaching course and was persuaded to go for one of the Institute's plum jobs to teach history at the Latymer School in the Borough of Enfield. I loved teaching, taught almost solely examination classes and was delighted when some children from deprived homes obtained university places. I grew however increasingly critical of the culture of the school. I was the National Union of Teachers representative but the majority of the staff were either anti-union or in the Grammar School Associations. Near the end of my third year at the school, Enfield College of Technology advertised for a History lecturer, a post which I delightedly secured.

Exciting prospects

Eric Robinson addressed the first meeting for new staff. He expressed brilliantly, and with great passion, the creative future which lay ahead for the college. It was to promote the comprehensive principle in further and higher education, widening access for students, replacing the London University external degrees in favour of degree courses which would have strong vocational relevance. They were to be sandwich degrees with the third year spent in employment. The emphasis for staff would be on the effective teaching of students rather than on research so characteristic of existing universities. I soon learned that Eric Robinson was a crucial figure in the Further and Higher educational world. He was part of the triumvirate of the Secretary of State, Anthony Crosland, the lead Civil Servant in the Department of Education and Science, Toby Weaver, and Eric himself. If this policy were implemented rapidly the flow of resources to Enfield would be considerable. So it proved. Within three years the College had secured approval of several major degree proposals from the recently created Council for National Academic Awards and obtained in due course a six-storey building for teaching purposes. The seventy plus seminar rooms embodied the teaching principles of limited lectures but intensive teaching in small groups.

Meeting the new challenges

The change to its physical aspects was as nothing compared to the changes in the staff. The old college had been dominated by the technical crafts and higher-level courses particularly in engineering. Engineers were still numerous but the college expansion into Higher Education had been predominantly in the humanities and sciences for London External degrees. The very rapid pace of change which now ensued flowed from the development of the new CNAA degrees in Business Studies and in the Social Sciences. The latter in particular saw the employment of a large number of new staff many of whom had worked or studied at the London School of Economics. That institution was at the centre of the intense student challenge, also in evidence in Paris in the late 60s. The majority of the student body were seeking greater influence on the decisions taken in the institutions in which they studied but the more radical students wanted a total transformation in their Higher Education experience. This involved intense interest in the content and administration of the courses. Enfield's Social Science degree was a key battleground. It was a very large and challenging course. Its intake was two hundred students which meant that within two years it would approach the total student body of the early years of a new university like Sussex established in the early 60s. One significant feature designed to realise the vocational nature of the degree was the third year sandwich element.

The sandwich element involved the massive task of obtaining external placements with employers for 200 students. The energy and commitment this represented amongst staff was testimony to the professionalism of the somewhat disparate staff employed on the degree. Academically also, the Social Science degree sought to emphasise interdisciplinary study with each of the social sciences contributing to the core theme of the analysis of public policy issues. Ideological differences between staff on the theoretical politics and sociology areas of the degree were reinforced by the growing divisions between students many of whom were profoundly ideologically committed. The majority of staff took fairly orthodox positions and were accustomed to compromise to aid educational advance. For the various branches of Marxism however there could only be an agenda of constant challenge. For the extreme left I was a marked man in the college.

Politics

I stood as the Labour candidate in Central Norfolk in the 1966 General Election and joined the Enfield College Governing Body as staff representative a short while later. In addition to my teaching duties which were on the key central part of the degree I was also the examinations officer. Part One was examined at the end of the second year. We consulted intensively across the college and particularly with students on the degree in order that the assessment should employ several examination techniques: an unseen written examination, a seen examination paper for which students could prepare in advance how they intended to respond in three hours, and a submitted thesis on a given subject. On one occasion two students had submitted identical theses despite extensive prior warnings that there should be no collusion. The majority of the examination board considered that the students should be failed, but a counter argument was presented that examination was merely the internal diktat of the demands of the unfair capitalist system and that rules governing examinations were a form of oppression. As examinations officer my orthodox argument had to carry the day. It did, but not without intensive challenges to my reputation.

Mrs Thatcher

More overt external events threatened the course and indeed the college. Margaret Thatcher, Secretary of State for Education came to the college to open the new tutorial building. Just why the Principal, John O'Neill thought this a good idea I will never know. Outrageous heckling by radical students forced her to abandon her speech. She left the platform but not before seizing the microphone again and with a raised voice said she was not going to forget this experience at Enfield College! At the subsequent Academic Board, the Principal, a decent enough man in normal circumstances, revealed that he had deployed cameras at the opening ceremony to secure identification of troublemakers if a demonstration got out of hand. As a member of the Board and a regional representative of the lecturers union I said such an act on his part was alien to an educational institution. Any punishment could prove to be counterproductive and very damaging to staff-student relations. No further action was taken.

A merger ahead

Not long afterwards the governing body of Enfield began the long process of merger with the more conventional Hendon College and the very distinctive Hornsey College of Art. Many such mergers were to take place across the country and new polytechnics were formed but few could have contained such divisive factors as the emerging Middlesex Polytechnic. Nevertheless Government policy was clear so three disparate colleges and three local authorities, one Conservative Finchley, one Labour Haringey and one marginal, Enfield, duly laid the foundations. As the Enfield staff representative I now had a significant role in the embryo governing body of the nascent polytechnic. Progress was hard earned and slow. Locally based politicians had limited perspectives on the role of future polytechnics. I, firmly wedded to national policy and with a clearly identifiable political voice, was sometimes appreciated but equally often disregarded as far too radical which scarcely squared with my reputation with many Enfield staff and students.

The new Director

The most important decision in which I played a prominent role was the appointment of the new Director of the polytechnic. Among the accomplished and interesting university applicants who showed in most cases disappointingly limited vision of the role of the new polytechnics one candidate was very different. Dr Ray Rickett was Assistant Director at the City Polytechnic. He certainly had firm ideas on the future of the Polytechnic, subscribed fully to government aims but had very unorthodox views on the structure of new CNAA degrees. He intended to introduce the modular system characteristic of American higher education which was innovative but scarcely matched the integrated structure of the Social Science degree. Nevertheless he overcame our reservations and my group and students on the governing body backed him. I never saw entirely eye to eye with Ray Rickett in the short time I served in his employ but we respected each other. I was now a Principal Lecturer and being lobbied to take up the position of Dean of Humanities. That would have taken me out of the Social Science degree to which I was so committed but would have guaranteed a major role in the future development of the Middlesex Polytechnic which was the last such institution to be designated in 1973. It was an exciting role which I was bound to enjoy.

Onwards

In January 1974 however I was selected as the Labour candidate for Enfield North partially as a result of my reputation at the College. The seat was clearly marginal but we won in March 1974 by just over 3,000 votes and in October by just over 4,000. I was now to take my educational arguments to a national forum but my Enfield years had been a rich experience and I left with some regret as well as the greatest enthusiasm for becoming a Member of Parliament in which my parents took enormous pride. I rapidly became Parliamentary Private Secretary to the Deputy Prime Minister, Ted Short, but my starry rise dimmed somewhat when Prime Minister, Harold Wilson unexpectedly resigned and was succeeded by Jim Callaghan. I was a regular columnist with the *Times Educational Supplement* and in 1977 was offered an Honorary Doctorate by Middlesex. I was delighted to be so honoured by the Institution to which I had devoted myself for nearly a decade and for which I will always retain the greatest respect.

8. No need to waffle about aesthetics

GRENVILLE WALL

Grenville Wall *began at Enfield by teaching on the external London University degrees before moving to home-grown Enfield courses validated by the CNAA – mainly the part-time BA Sociology of Education and the BA Humanities. He remained when Enfield became part of Middlesex Polytechnic, and then Middlesex University. He was involved with NATFHE union affairs, and became a regular letter-writer to the North Circular eventually being rewarded with a 500 word fortnightly column, 'Off the Wall'. He took early retirement and with his wife decamped to sane Finland from where he views Britain's increasing irrationality with alarm. He still continues with general education and in his spare moments tries to answer the Big Questions.*

The Job Advert

I saw the job advert in the *Times Educational Supplement* (there was no *Times Higher Educational Supplement* in those days). It was for an Assistant Lecturer Grade B in the history of philosophy. I had never heard of Enfield College of Technology (the recently re-christened Ponders End Technical Institute) and wondered why such a place wanted to appoint a philosopher. Fortunately, one or two of my fellow postgraduates at Birkbeck had ears to the ground and had picked up gossip to the effect that Enfield was ambitious and bent on going places. Remember, this was 1965, not long after the publication of the Robbins Report (1963), which had recommended a big expansion of higher education, and David Hamlyn, the professor in the philosophy department, suggested I might ride on the wave of this expansion. The blurb the college sent me said that they were teaching the External London BA General of which History of Philosophy was one of the tracks and hoped that the successful applicant would assist with the teaching of aesthetics. The External London BSc in Engineering and the BA/BSc in Sociology were also on offer.

I put in my application and tried, best as I could, to immerse myself a newly published aesthetics reader (the subject never having been a draw for me) in the hope that I could waffle convincingly about it in an interview.

The Interview

On the day of the interview, I got off the 259 in Ponders End and my heart sank: it was a grubby and unlovely bit of 1930s suburbia. Still, I had higher hopes of the Queensway of the college's official address, imagining a wide road with imposing building on either side. When I found it, I thought that either the road nameplate or my *A-Z* must have been wrong: it was a congested, narrow thoroughfare, lined by cheaply built 1930s small factories. The snob (and newly-discovered aesthete) in me asked whether I was really prepared to walk down such an unprepossessing 'Queensway' every morning. The students must be the compensation! At least the college looked a bit smarter than the factories.

After a long wait, the interview arrived and went like a dream. I had had the presence of mind to spend some time imagining what questions an interviewing panel in a college of technology, with probably only one philosopher on it, might ask. On target every time! Then an unexpected bonus came. No need to waffle about aesthetics because I let slip that I was attending the current re-birth of the philosophy of education under the leadership of R. S. Peters at the Institute of Education next door to Birkbeck. Thanks to Doreen Harris, my future mentor and immediate boss, I discovered that this fitted in with the teacher education plans the college was beginning to think about. I was offered the job and got back just in time for the evening seminar at Birkbeck.

The Stimulation

What I never anticipated was that the daily visit to Enfield would be the source of such stimulation – both academic/intellectual and social/political (with a small 'p'). Conversation with social scientists and even some engineers and scientists (!) were natural and fruitful. Unlike C. P. Snow, I didn't have to move between Bloomsbury and South Kensington to bump into the Two Cultures – it was here in

Enfield in a compact and reasonably amiable and non-flamboyant form. The stimulation of working closely amongst both arts (humanities) staff and social scientists staff continued and I found myself reading Durkheim, Weber and some Marx, alongside Leavis, Christopher Hill and, as cultural background to Greek philosophy, Homer, Hesiod and the tragedies, and much else. Then there was the loss of my innocence and the discovery that academic politics was a game you couldn't opt out of if you wanted to join in the advancement of a significant project. And, of course, part of the fun was sparring with Eric Robinson – see below.

My First Students

Teaching brought many surprises too. An early one, in my second year, was to find myself teaching pre-Socratic philosophy to 18–19 year-olds in a north London suburban and predominantly engineering college – an utterly non-utilitarian activity in the most utilitarian of settings! How Mrs Thatcher would have raged! I thoroughly enjoyed learning about pre-Socratic philosophy for the first time, but I'm not sure what my students made of it. I couldn't imagine how it might engage with their minds unless they already had an interest in really ancient Greece (which I tried to raise) or unless they were truly struck by the strangeness of a lot of it in comparison with modern scientifically-informed common sense.

Then came the time for their first sessional exams. I set the papers, marked them and invigilated. Once having started the students off on the exam, I remember looking proprietorially over them and feeling a strange emotion: a mixture of pride and affection – much as I imagine a father might feel for his children for having stuck at some arduous task. On the whole I was pleased with their performance, though there was plenty of scope for constructive feedback! Widespread routinely badly written English was still some ten or more years in the future.

Eric Robinson's Seminar

There were two educational heavyweights at Enfield: George Brosan (the Principal, later the first Director of North East London Polytechnic) and Eric Robinson (Academic Head of the Faculty of Arts and Social Sciences, later the first Director of Lancashire Polytechnic). Eric Robinson, a fair-haired Lancastrian, of great fluency, full of self-confidence and with an irritatingly egocentric touch of charisma, was a self-proclaimed socialist educationalist and was also former president of the Association of Teachers in Technical Institutions (the name of our union as it was then). He was an advisor to the Labour intellectual Tony Crosland and had the ear of the learned Conservative, Sir Edward Boyle. He was undoubtedly the visionary and the main educational driver of the policy to create new polytechnics, bringing with them vastly expanded opportunities. He liked to think of them as 'the people's universities'.

For my first two years Eric held a Tuesday morning seminar, which was expected that all Arts and Social Science staff would attend. I was never quite sure what it was supposed to be about. There was no printed seminar programme or reading list. Was it a Robinsonian T-Group (therapy group) in which Eric played the therapist? But what did we need therapy *for*? Was it a session for letting off steam about the faults in our own higher education so that we might do better in the future? Was it supposed to be a bonding session, or perhaps one in which like-minded groups might begin to coalesce? Perhaps it was a mix of all of these. But it was also a vehicle Eric used to impress upon us his educational 'philosophy' – that it should be student-centred (rather than subject-centred), based on student needs, etc. I thought such maxims, high-sounding though they might be, were empty because they were not embedded or constrained by any clear educational values. For example, should course programmes meet students' nutritional and sexual needs? Clearly not! So what delimits their specifically educational needs? Colleagues who dared to defend some educational arrangement 'For the sake of the subject' were liable to be slapped town with a rhetorical 'Subjects don't have sakes' – to which the reply is, of course, 'Neither do people' – but that does not mean that there is anything wrong with asking something to be done for someone's sake.

Later I gathered criticisms such as these together and put them into a paper on the 'theoretical' chapter in Eric's book, *The New Polytechnics* presented to a special seminar. I only have a faint memory of the discussion, but my guess is that Eric and I did not properly engage with each other.

One feature of Eric's thinking which had a lot of substance to it and of which I approved was the desire to open up opportunities in the Further Education/Higher Education system by building bridges across the otherwise almost exclusively vertical pathways through it. It is now hard to appreciate just how rigid those pathways once were. For example, there were only limited opportunities for mature students without A-levels to get onto a degree course of any kind and it was still extremely difficult for those who had progressed through the Further Education route to transfer to a degree programme. Another of Eric's substantial positions was that more Higher Education should have a vocational character. I was inclined to agree, but could foresee that as more money was poured into the system, the greater the pressure would be to succumb to a crass economic instrumentalism. I wanted to explore how far a moderate vocationalism might be squared with some of the ideals of liberal education so that an instrumentalist collapse might be resisted. This was the subject of my first published paper. But back in the 60s none of us foresaw the awful tide of marketization that was to come, the conversion of education into a commodity and the re-casting of the student into a consumer.

The CNAA

The Council for National Academic Awards was created in1964 to enable colleges like Enfield to propose and design courses of its own and gain national validation. The external London degree courses we ran gave us a valid claim to have experience of teaching at this level. Soon we were beginning to plan our own degree courses. The big one was the multi-track social science degree. But the first one off the block (I think) was what we called 'the teachers' degree', or to give it its proper title, the BA Sociology of Education.

Eric Robinson pointed out to us that there were large numbers of schoolteachers with teaching qualifications but without degrees and whose opportunities for career advancement were increasingly blocked. A degree course offered part-time which combined a predominantly social science look at education (then very fashionable) with some upgrading and updating of their teaching subjects would attract them. We designed the course and got through the CNAA 'visitation' (as if it involved a scary appearance of a supernatural body – which some thought it did). On the evening of our success Eric had a two-minute spot on the BBC's South-East News, and letters of inquiry poured in over the next few days. To begin with we had intakes of a 100 or more.

Such large groups of part-time students were hard to manage and keep track of and to supply with the appropriate learning materials. Handouts had to be written (in a hurry!), printed (often at the last minute) and sometimes material had to be posted to students (raising new questions about costs). But I think that after the initial shock, it was great fun. And there were some marvellous (if sometimes cantankerous) characters amongst the cohorts. One was an ex-guardsman, about 6' 3'' tall, a jovial but somewhat cynical character (like a tall but smart Onslow from *Keeping Up Appearances*) who, from his great height, took pleasure in discomfiting us (me at least) by calling into question my authority to teach anything (especially philosophy). But, at length, he graduated and to my surprise returned to take the MSc in Criminology. Eventually, he explained, he'd got the 'study bug' but missed the intellectual company. The last I saw of him he was working on his PhD thesis! Gradually the intake was broadened and included social workers, librarians, nurses and others. I was particularly stuck by the philosophical prowess of two police inspectors.

From my second year onwards and for many more years to come I had evening teaching, twice a week on alternate years. I lived a long way south of Enfield and didn't have a car. So one of my most vivid memories of those early years is of waiting for unreliable trains on cold and windy nights on Southbury Station, the station being often enveloped in a strange smell which someone once told me was connected with the manufacture of zinc products in a nearby factory.

Another vivid memory is of The Swan, the pub on the High Street and at the bottom of the playing field-cum-car park. I and a couple of colleagues used to go there after teaching finished at 1.00 pm on Fridays. It was like stepping back to 1948. An elderly lady, always sporting a marcel wave hairdo (if you know what that was) probably in her late seventies, was the licence-holder (her husband having died many years before). She was assisted by her two daughters, the elder of which was the *de facto* manager and principal barmaid. The younger sister (also sporting a marcel wave) rarely made an appearance in the bar but seemed to be the spirit at the top of the dumb waiter. Going to The Swan usually entailed a significant wait for service. If you wanted a sandwich (as I usually did) there were none ready prepared. The elder sister would ring the dumb waiter's bell and then shout up the order to the younger sister. She, in turn, would put on her hat and coat and pick up a shopping basket and could be seen going to a local shop for a bit of cheese or ham and a few tomatoes. About half an hour later, the dumb waiter's bell would ring again, there would be a rumble as it descended and the elder sister would call out (very discreetly) to alert the customer. As you might imagine this system was prone to nervous breakdowns when several people wanted sandwiches! But at least it seemed to be of the same period as the Ponders End Technical Institute.

My most abiding memories are, of course, of my colleagues, how they dressed, their mannerisms, their speech habits and, above all, their voices – I can hear them clearly when I choose to. Then, they feel close to me and the intervening years drop away

9. Humanities at Enfield College

NORAH CARLIN

***Norah Carlin** joined Enfield College of Technology in 1965, teaching English and Economic History on the London BA General. As an Associate Lecturer from 1970 to 1992, she remained at Middlesex Polytechnic, teaching modules the social and political history of early modern Britain and Europe to undergraduate and postgraduate students. Especially after returning to full-time status just as Middlesex became a university, she played an active part on the NATFHE union committee and served as a University Governor (1997-2001). She retired in 2002, and since 2006 has lived in her native Edinburgh, still researching and writing about her favourite subjects.*

I arrived at Enfield College of Technology in 1965, to teach English history and economic history on the London University BA General (External). The college had introduced this course one or two years earlier with a view to expanding its subject range, as the baby boom generation flooded into higher education. Despite the lack of prestige that a general degree carried in those days, it was a very demanding course for the students. At the end of three years' study at Enfield, they had to attend the examinations in central London and take three three-hour papers in each of three different subjects. (This may sound like the invention of an obsessive numerologist, but it was just an extreme version of the normal BA structure at the time.) There was no formal cross-referencing between papers even in the same subject, no intermediate examinations or assessed course work, and a lot of 'question spotting' – by staff as well as students – when finals approached. Teaching at an external institution, we Enfield lecturers had no official existence in the eyes of London University, and found ourselves trawling past examination papers for information on what they expected our students to know and understand.

This meant, however, that we were free to choose which topics to teach, and to set wider-ranging coursework, so long as we adhered to the syllabus sufficiently to get the students there in the end with a reasonable chance of succeeding according to their own ability and application. There were always rumours that some particularly bright student at Enfield had been awarded a degree without ever having attended any of our classes. I am not sure this was ever true, though I find it interesting that many years later the writer and broadcaster Mike Phillips, to whom this feat was credited, seemed to think that I was one of his lecturers at Enfield despite the fact that he never actually enrolled on any of my courses.

The London BA General was not just a humanities degree. In the late 1960s it was also an umbrella for subjects such as geography, economics, politics and sociology, which in the early 1970s would become part of social science or business degrees at Enfield under the Council for National Academic Awards (CNAA). Despite some promising beginnings, notably Len Jackson's BA Communications Studies proposal turned down by the CNAA, there was no independent humanities degree at Enfield until after the merger with Hendon and Trent Park, and the new BA Humanities was eventually launched in 1974. We were always a minority at Enfield, and to many people I suppose we were a marginal one. In some ways, I think, we were left behind because in academic terms we did not easily fit into the innovatory schemes of George Brosan and Eric Robinson, though I believe most of us were fully on board with the project of providing an alternative to the universities and a non-elitist higher education for the masses.

In many ways staff like myself, who had recently graduated from old universities, were thrown in at the deep end. Few of us had postgraduate teaching qualifications, and the general view of the courses available at that time was that they did not provide relevant training for higher education. Our role models were often the academics who had taught us in our own student days; and these were mostly very poor ones to follow, as teaching skills were not high on the list of priorities for academics at the most prestigious universities. The positive side of this was that most of the Enfield staff in humanities were committed to regular one-to-one tuition centred on the student essay, and small group discussion based on the seminar format instead of lectures. In 1968, thanks to intensive lobbying of the Department of Education and Science by Enfield management, work on the new six-storey tower block planned for the college was brought forward, and redesigned to be adaptable for small tutorial/office spaces or larger classrooms. By the time it was up and running, the college had grown so rapidly that the temporary modular 'huts' erected a few years earlier remained in use for a couple of decades longer, stifling hot in summer and freezing cold in winter.

Interdisciplinary

Looking back, I find it hard to separate George Brosan's educational philosophy from his obnoxiously authoritarian management style, but I admit that I was attracted to the two principal ideals for which he is remembered: breaking down the traditional distinction between vocational and academic education, and an interdisciplinary approach to solving problems. There were several specific obstacles to the application of these ideals to humanities in the 1960s. One was the fact that the academic boundaries and examination format of these subjects had been institutionalised for well over a century, not only in the universities but in the Victorian civil service entry examinations – a millstone which did not weigh down the newer disciplines. Another was that humanities subjects are not easily categorised in terms of career orientation, being multi-vocational in the sense that they provide a critical intellectual grounding that can be adapted to many different occupations. But perhaps the main issue was the inability of either Brosan or Eric Robinson (who was Academic Head of the Faculty of Arts 1967-70) to realise that they could not apply the same models that they had successfully introduced in engineering, business or social sciences. I think this was because they never understood – or even asked us about – the specific learning aims of our subjects. We might not have understood the question then, but we could have learned much by being asked it. Robinson especially spent a lot of his time pressurising humanities staff to come up with something that he was unable to define clearly himself. He had appointed a lot of young staff, perhaps because he expected us to be less hidebound by tradition, but it seems to me that he regarded us as bear cubs to be licked into shape by his genius, and was frustrated by our frequent refusal to submit to this process.

Our own humanities version of an interdisciplinary seminar, centred on the study of texts, was introduced quite early in this period. A pair of staff from different subjects were expected to introduce each mixed group of students to a 'core' text of their own choice. Not surprisingly, both input and outcomes were pretty random, and the BA Humanities core course was eventually to be based on a more thoughtfully planned list of texts. Teaching staff on the BA General were also urged to breach the boundaries of academic disciplines themselves by attending seminars on scientific or technical subjects. I had not had a narrow humanities-only education at my Scottish secondary school, and was enthusiastic about the new world of computing in which a family member was employed. The college had already got a head start in the new discipline, and its latest computer (probably the Honeywell) was specially housed in a hut of its own big enough to be converted later to a seminar room. So I joined one of the computing classes recommended. It was not adapted to humanities subjects, however, and I confess I gave up after one session on how to use Fortran – or was it Cobol? – to perform mathematical operations on a matrix, because I had no idea what a matrix was for and no one explained it to me.

Meanwhile, academic development meetings for staff laid the groundwork for the innovatory courses Enfield was to develop under the Council for National Academic Awards. The function of the academic board set up in 1967, with student and staff representation, was to advise the Principal in planning the introduction of new and phasing out of old courses. Brosan did not always accept the board's advice of course, and at first its membership was numerically weighted against the new subject areas. A number of innovatory courses, in subject areas from engineering to trade union studies, were introduced in the next few years, and new degrees in business and social sciences were approved by the CNAA. Nevertheless, I remember one member of management arguing at an academic board meeting against a proposal for a social services qualification in child care on the grounds that 'child care should be left to Dr Spock'.

With the arrival of funding restrictions under the 1970 Conservative government, competition for resources sometimes dominated the meetings; I recall a colleague from a lab-based subject suggesting on one occasion that we didn't need new library books every year. Humanities had a slight advantage in being considered a low-cost area by Dr Brosan, who once argued at a meeting that humanities staff did not require sabbatical leave because 'philosophy research can be done in the bath'. Some humanities subjects did find a place on the BA Sociology of Education, a successful evening course enabling local schoolteachers to keep up with developments in their specialisms as well as the core content. Apart from that, the liberation of humanities from the London BA General straitjacket had to await the coming of the polytechnic.

Extracurricular

I remember all kinds of staff at Enfield College being much more sociable than those of Middlesex University in later years, when collecting our mail from pigeon-holes seemed to become the only regular use made of the staff common room. In the 1960s and 1970s it was sometimes difficult to find a seat in our common room at lunchtime, for it was soon filled (and smoke-filled) by various card schools, cliques and groups of friends from all academic disciplines and other areas of work. Meanwhile the bar, converted from a quiet student common room, was the interdisciplinary learning environment of choice for many staff and students. My own narrow education was significantly broadened as I took (mostly a marginal) part in well-lubricated discussions of philosophy, sociology, linguistics and many other subjects. My grasp of these was revealed to be slender when Mark Fisher and Grenville Wall debated Kant and Hegel, or Len Jackson and others argued about the relationship between thought and language. In time, these evenings typically ended with a rousing chorus of Monty Python's Philosophers' Song.

The bar also had a colour television – a luxury item then manufactured at Thorn's up the road – on which I remember seeing the first landing on the moon and feeling that the reality wasn't as interesting the science fiction I had recently begun to read. The students engaged in more sober extracurricular activities, too, in those days of free tuition and maintenance grants when they did not have to take on part-time jobs to survive. Their amateur productions of Camus's 'The Just' and Dylan Thomas's 'Under Milk Wood' were as high quality as any I saw produced by specialist drama students at the polytechnic in later years. Summer end-of -term parties were held in the picturesque surroundings of Capel Manor, and the annual Guy Fawkes fireworks party in the pavilion at World's End Lane sports ground.

Political

It was at Enfield that I was also introduced to Marxism, when I went along with my colleague's suggestion that the interdisciplinary seminar we shared should study the Communist Manifesto. Other political ideologies were of course on offer in the staffroom; my first colleagues in history were the late Julian Ayer, an incorrigible Tory, and Bryan Davies, now a Labour peer. I got involved locally in campaigns against nuclear weapons, apartheid and racism, and the mass movement against the war in Vietnam (where, incidentally, I first encountered Jeremy Corbyn). I lived throughout these years in the down-to-earth environment of north London's industrial areas, in Tottenham and later in Edmonton, while I think most colleagues resided either in gentrifying inner-city areas or in leafier suburbs to the north and west of Ponders End. It was in Tottenham, where furniture, duplicator and engineering factories and their trade unions still flourished, that I was introduced to the Campaign for Nuclear Disarmament, and soon afterwards to the International Socialists (later renamed the Socialist Workers Party). For years I regularly handed out leaflets or sold socialist newspapers outside factories which were gone by the turn of the millennium.

Politics arrived at the college itself mainly through the staff and student unions. I seem to remember that from 1964 to 1968, all employees of the Labour-controlled London Borough of Enfield had to join a union, and teaching staff at the college belonged to the rather staid ATTI, the Association of Teachers in Technical Institutions. Our first political campaign in the local branch was to get support for the union's affiliation to the Trades Union Congress, which was achieved despite one of our more traditional members objecting, 'We are not a trade union: we do not engage in trade.' Membership of the TUC gave us a place on Enfield Trades Council, where our representatives brought ATTI members into the campaign against Harold Wilson's wage freeze. For us, the outcome under a later Labour government was the Houghton Report (1975), which recommended raising the pay of public sector higher education lecturers closer to the levels prevailing in the universities. In 1975 the ATTI merged with the union for teachers in colleges and departments of education to become the National Association of Teachers in Further and Higher Education (NATFHE).

Meanwhile, the political left began to triumph in students union elections, though controversial political motions were always hotly contested. In May 1968, the student rising and general strike in France raised the hopes of many students and staff that a different and better world could be brought about by a revolution from below. In the same month, Enfield students held the UK's first sit-in to take place in a non-university institution, in the corridor outside the Principal's office. The action lasted all of three hours, protesting against Brosan's proposal for a quota on overseas students that was subsequently ruled illegal by the Department of Education and Science. The official college magazine, *IntellECT* [sic], was challenged by an underground publication with a double-entendre variation on the acronym, whose provocative challenges to the obscenity laws occasioned much hilarity – and some trouble from the college authorities. In 1971, when the new tower block was ceremonially opened by Minister of Education Margaret Thatcher, many students demonstrated outside against the Conservative government's funding and education policies, while others got into the reception room and ate all the sandwiches. In 1972, groups of striking miners picketing the local power station enjoyed a more hospitable reception in the college bar.

Diversified

The opening up of higher education to non-traditional students was of course a major part of the college management's aims, and our student body was fairly diverse for the time – certainly more so than at the older UK universities. Many school leavers came to study humanities or social sciences at Enfield because they had never been thought of as 'university material' by their teachers, or had applied to universities and been turned down because they were too radical, not fluent writers or smooth talkers, or just from the wrong class or ethnic background. We took in many mature students who had not even thought of applying to universities when they left school, often at the minimum age of fifteen, whether or not they had passed the eleven-plus. We also recruited growing numbers of Asian and Caribbean immigrants and their offspring; while among the overseas students in humanities subjects there was a regular contingent from Mauritius, the original home of Pierre Chopin, head of French.

One of the notable changes during these years was the increasing presence of women on the teaching staff. When I arrived, the majority of female staff at Enfield worked in other indispensable though undervalued capacities, such as propping up course leaders who had more intellectual or technical than administrative skills. Some of these very competent women – notably Audrey Hardwick and Gertie Beckett – had already worked at the college for decades: Gertie had started as a seventeen-year-old secretary in the year I was born, and Audrey joined her as a school leaver in the year I started infant school. Both worked there through many transformations, and Audrey kept the Enfield staff reunions going well into the new millennium. I do not remember any female lecturers from the college's traditional areas of engineering and science, or even from mathematics or business until about 1970, but our numbers grew exponentially with the expansion of humanities and social sciences. Several women were appointed subject or course heads in humanities and other areas, but I don't think any held a managerial post during the College of Technology days.

By the early 1970s male domination had not come to an end by any means, but the visible and vocal presence of women teaching staff (especially the many younger ones) had substantially transformed the culture of the college. Not that you would know this from reading over the other chapters in this collection, whose authors are over 80 per cent male: I am astonished and saddened at how rarely these men mention female colleagues even in passing. So for the record let me name first some Enfield colleagues in humanities who, like me, stayed on into the polytechnic and even the university era: in English, Mary Shakeshaft and Susanna Gladwin; in French, Deirdre Welsh and Christine North; in philosophy, Doreen Harris (later, by marriage to one of her ex-students, Doreen Maître). We were perhaps not so colourful as some of the women in the social sciences, such as Jeanne D'eath and Rachel Parry, the surely unforgettable Ilona Phombeah (Halberstadt), or Julie Ford who speaks for herself below! Women mathematicians included Kathryn Braithwaite, Barbara Frost and Margery Reinhart. In the social sciences, women were especially numerous in the field of social policy. Among them I remember especially Barbara Waine, Lesley Jordan and Jean Cooke. Professor Eleonore Kofman, now internationally recognised for her work on gender and migration, left Middlesex in 1992 but returned in 2005 and is currently head of the Social Policy Research Centre. Jean Cooke was also a hard-working and indispensable colleague on the NATHFE committee, and I recall being told that the sight of Jean and myself (as Casework and Negotiations Secretaries respectively) advancing on a head of school at the turn of the millennium could still cause trepidation.

When the feminist ferment of the 1970s arrived at Enfield I was less involved, because I had chosen to take a 0.4 Associate Lecturer's contract when my first child was born. At that time maternity leave was guaranteed only for a maximum of four weeks before and six weeks after the birth. For the next few years I was no longer regularly attending meetings outside my reduced working hours or spending evenings in the bar. A combination of funding cuts and the polytechnic's appointment regime kept me 'fractional' at 0.4 for many more years, and I did not regain a full-time position until 1992. Long before then I was working many additional hours on part-time pay and was fully involved again in academic and union affairs. But fractional appointments, along with fixed-term contracts (which I had fortunately avoided) were the declared preference of Middlesex Polytechnic's director long before zero-hours contracts were invented, and after the change to the status of a university these became middle management's preferred way of filling vacancies economically.

Retrospective

Enfield's history staff moved to the former College of All Saints (Tottenham campus) in 1979, with a short-lived return to Enfield in 1989-92, but the MA course in Industrial and Social History which I later headed stayed on at Enfield for many years. During one of these periods, when I was NATFHE campus rep at Enfield, I remember running off copies of our local bulletin on an ancient duplicator (it may even have been one of the old Gestetner ones manufactured in Tottenham). I called this sheet *Enfield Matters*. And it did matter – especially to me and many others who experienced their formative years as staff or students in the environment of that place in Ponders End. The Enfield College of Technology years were a vital stage in my own education as well as my development as a teacher.

We had at that time been conscious participants – and mostly very willing ones – in an 'Enfield experiment' promoting the idea of polytechnics to provide a new and more progressive kind of higher education for the working class. The college was strategically located between the early twentieth-century industries of the Lea Valley and the 1930s electronics factory strip along the A10. Most of these industries, as well as Middlesex University, have now disappeared from the area, to be replaced by retail and residential developments. With this de-industrialisation of the Lea Valley, education for the working class there came to be orientated towards the expansion of 'white collar' and professional occupations less directly related – or not related at all – to production. I suppose the 'ticket out' on the 1970s wave of social mobility was more in accordance with Robinson's ideal than with Brosan's vision of an enhanced industrial experience.

In the long run, Middlesex Polytechnic was not the outcome of this experiment as it was originally envisaged. The pull of 'upgrading' to a university – which Eric Robinson had once characterised as High Table, mortarboards, and renaming the canteen the Refectory – overrode any remaining pride in the polytechnic tradition, on the excuse of securing the institution's place in the international education market. The same eventually happened in all the former polytechnics, including those that Brosan and Robinson had each headed after they left Enfield, which does suggest that the ideal of an alternative to the traditional university model left no lasting legacy. Middlesex University's marketing priorities from the 1990s onwards also meant that money was spent principally on advertising those courses which could claim to be directly vocational, because in the age of upfront fees students would supposedly expect 'value for money' in this form. Some of our humanities subjects successfully reinvented themselves in a truncated form as vocational courses (e.g. English as creative writing, French and Spanish as translation studies) but others suffered declining student numbers before finally being extinguished in the new millennium. The management that sealed their fate – under the leadership of the first university vice-chancellor to be a polytechnic graduate – was not simply dismissive of the relevance of humanities subjects, but often seemed to see them as part of the old elitist enemy.

Finally, Middlesex University has also abandoned the Lea Valley. When I sat on the governing body from 1997 to 2001 (though elected by the academic staff, I was repeatedly told that it was not a representative role) we had an ambitious plan for a large new campus on a derelict workshop site purchased by the university at Tottenham Hale. This never got further than a university flag planted incongruously on a tarted-up pub building – to the puzzlement of passers-by. Its failure seemed to be due not only to problems with funding but also to what I understood as poor financial management. I now suspect that some of the governors already had a different plan in mind. Within a decade, all the university's campuses in or near the Lea Valley were sold off: Tottenham, Enfield, Bounds Green, Cat Hill and finally Trent Park, to be replaced by a grandiose university complex at Hendon which I have not visited, though I can pick it out on the skyline from certain trains coming into Euston. The idea that higher education could and should be rooted in working-class and ethnically diverse communities as well as the more salubrious and prestigious middle-class areas seems to have become the last casualty of twenty-first century ambition as far as Enfield is concerned, and although I no longer live in the area I find that regrettable.

10. Enfield College: catalyst and stepping stone

JOHN VINCE

John Vince *joined Enfield as a student in 1961 and stayed twenty-five years. Although his studies focussed on electrical engineering, he was diverted by the emerging technology of digital computers, and joined the computer centre at Enfield College. He was appointed to the academic staff in 1967 and taught computing on the Mathematics for Business course. He became absorbed in computer graphics and developed PICASO, one of the first computer animation systems as part of his PhD. He left Middlesex Polytechnic in 1986 to join Rediffusion Simulation as a Research Consultant, and rose to the position of Chief Scientist. He has written and edited over 40 books on mathematics and computer graphics, and retired in 2006 to spend time gardening, DIY and continue writing.*

During the second-world war our family was evacuated to Brancaster in Norfolk where we discovered the local seafood. The war over, and after consuming large amounts of brown shrimps, Stiffkey mussels, samphire, oysters and Cromer crabs, we returned to Tottenham, broken biscuits and food rationing. Being a sensitive boy – that's my excuse – my cognitive development suffered, I failed my eleven-plus and was banished to the newly-built Cheshunt Secondary Modern School in Hertfordshire. Mr Smith was the Headmaster; he was a gentleman, whilst his deputy, 'Basher' Bates, was not. The sleeve of his jacket concealed a long, thin cane that could cut an outstretched hand in the wink of an eye, thus preventing me from becoming an international pianist, the likes of André Previn!

My favourite subject at school was mathematics, taught by Mr Short, who was short, but stood head and shoulders above his peers. His pedagogic skills were responsible for one of my General Certificate of Education successes. The other two were English language and Art.

My best friend was Harry Webb, and towards the end of our days at school we had formed a singing group called the Quintones.

We, and Lonnie Donegan, were the UK's answer to America's Bill Hailey and the Comets! The Quintones met regularly at the Cheshunt Holy Trinity Youth Club, where we practiced our songs and sang for other club members. We also sang at my sister's twenty-first birthday party in Cheshunt. After leaving school, our English teacher, Jay Norris, invited some students back to take part in various plays. One of my parts was Mole in Wind in the Willows, with Harry playing Ratty. We also played together in A Midsummer Night's Dream; I was Tom Snout, one of the 'mechanicals' and Harry played Nick Bottom. Harry eventually changed his name to Cliff Richard, whilst I retained mine and sought my fortune in the Midland Bank. We stayed in touch for many years after.

Banking was our career adviser's suggestion; he knew nothing about careers or banking. Being a sensitive boy – I know! – I took his advice and joined the Midland Bank's Moorgate branch. My job title was Waste Clerk. I took cheques accepted by cashiers and reconciled their total with the associated paying-in slip using an electric adding machine. It was mind-numbing, involved no Calculus, and a complete waste of my time. Waste Clerk was an accurate description! When I resigned my position, the manager told me I was managerial material. Did he mean I would make a manager a good suit? I never found out.

I secured a trainee engineer's job at Cosmocord Ltd. in Waltham Cross, which manufactured piezo-electric, stereo gramophone pickups, microphones and accelerometers. I was now eighteen and starting a career which would eventually take me to Enfield Technical College. I spent time on the shop floor, in the tool shop, stores, sales, marketing and the R&D department. George Bush was responsible for R&D and showed me how he used differential equations to represent dynamic physical systems, and how resonant frequencies were controlled using viscous damping. George was a superb engineer, and I admired his skills.

Studying at Enfield College

Having failed my eleven-plus and left school with only three GCEs, I had a lot of catching up to do. I decided to study for the National Certificate in the evenings at Enfield Technical College. I passed GCE physics in 1961, the ONC in Electrical Engineering in 1962, and A-level mathematics and pure mathematics in 1963. By then, Enfield Technical College had become Enfield College of Technology.

Enfield College was unusually well equipped for a technical academic institute. There were labs for testing the tensile strength of metals and the bending moments of beams, and other labs for configuring electric generators, a.c. and d.c. motors, and three-phase power systems. I recall a clever technician, Jack Deacon, who was very funny, and helped with my experiments.

Once a week, a Land Rover arrived in the evening containing an early computer – an Elliot 803, with 8KB of main memory. I can't remember the programming language, but it was very primitive. In order to use it we prepared our instructions on paper tape in advance of its arrival. One of my programs calculated the area of a triangle from its side lengths, which refused to work. The technician working with the Elliot took my paper tape and read the instructions and data using only the patterns of holes. After a while he proclaimed: 'It's an impossible triangle. One side is longer than the other two together!' He impressed us all with this amazing skill.

Eventually, Enfield College acquired its own computer by collaborating with English Numbering Machines Ltd., which was located along the same road. This was a Honeywell 120 computer with a massive 24KB of ferrite-core memory, 4 magnetic tape drives, 2 disk units, a printer, card reader and paper-tape reader. It required a raised floor to hide the connecting cables and an air-conditioned environment. I learnt to program the Honeywell using FORTRAN D punched onto 80-column cards and became reasonably proficient. I learnt COBOL, WORDCOM, the assembler language EASYCODER, and the computer's binary machine code. Little did I realise that programming was becoming my area of expertise.

By the time I completed my studies as an electrical engineer, I was a competent programmer, and after leaving Cosmocord, I joined the Enfield College of Technology's Computer Centre, paid by English Numbering Machines. To start, I helped with the day-to-day running of the Honeywell and eventually became responsible for the computer operators, who worked three shifts around the clock.

In 1967, the manager of the centre suggested that I applied for a lecturing post in computer science and electronic data processing, for which I would be paid an annual salary of £1,875 plus £70 London Area Addition. At the time, I had been studying numerical analysis on

Wednesday evenings in classes given by Stanley Millward, who agreed to provide a testimonial for my job application. I still have the letter containing the sentence: 'Mr Vince is a man of excellent character and of hard-working disposition. He has a quiet but effective manner and has a sense of humour.' I agreed with him and got the job. With this new wealth I bought a Triumph GT6 sports car.

Early Lecturing Duties

Although I had not received any formal teacher training, I found the role exciting and satisfying. I began teaching programming on the popular Mathematics for Business BSc course. I was also asked to lecture on a 6-week, Systems Analysis course designed by the National Computer Centre (NCC). The objective was to prepare future analysts of computer systems that would arise with the spread of computers. I did not like this work as I was not familiar with the subject, and the course material provided by the NCC contained too many mistakes.

I remember teaching a blind student, Paul Hollingdale, on the Mathematics for Business course, and in order to increase his understanding of mathematics, I traced shapes of graphs on his back with my finger. It seemed to work.

Extra-Curricular Activities

For some unknown reason, the Computer Centre attracted a wide range of outside people with all sorts of problems and projects. For example, in 1968 Cornmarket Press asked if we could computerise their publication *Which University*. Naturally we agreed, without fully appreciating the magnitude of the task. Basically, it required punching onto cards course name, entry requirements, course content for every university in the UK, full-time and part-time! Perhaps one of the reasons for accepting the task was that our Honeywell's memory had been increased by 33 per cent to 32KB.

The project was a collaboration between the Higher Education Advisory Centre (HEAC) based at Enfield College and the Computer Centre. After many months the task was completed and the Honeywell sorted the data into subject sequence. Cornmarket provided a brilliant programmer who designed a program to output the course data to a large-format film plotter, for final printing. The book was published in

1969 and contained around 400 pages. It was a great success. My payment was a free copy of the book, having designed and implemented the system! I was not a businessman.

Afterwards, the HEAC proposed that the data could be used for an advisory service, in collaboration with the *Observer* newspaper. An analyst with a PhD was appointed to undertake the system design. Very soon it became apparent that he was out of his depth, and I was summoned to a meeting with the College Principal, Dr George Brosan. During the meeting I referred to the analyst by his surname without the title 'Dr' George Brosan, sorry, Dr George Brosan, pulled me up sharply and asked me to use his correct title. After this discussion about titles, George – Dr Brosan – asked me if I could undertake the task. I accepted and it was agreed I would be paid extra. I have forgotten how much, but the sum twelve shillings and six pence seems to ring a bell!

I designed a disk-based system that would collect course data, maintain it, and allow it to be randomly accessed from enquiries received via the *Observer*. The project gave me the opportunity to master disk files and random-access file processing. As an example, it identified the institutes in the south of England offering part-time courses in pig husbandry, with the relevant entry requirements.

One day, Mrs Winifred Venton who was consumed by Shakespeare's sonnets brought an unusual project to the Computer Centre. Mrs Venton believed that William Shakespeare was born Edward VI, the son of Henry VIII. Although he died in 1553 aged fifteen, Mrs Venton believed that he lived on under the names William Shakespeare and Francis Bacon. Bacon was known for his use of cipher codes to hide messages. A simple code substituted a number for a letter. For example, A = 0, B = 1, C = 2, … Z = 25. Mrs Venton believed that the strange punctuation of the sonnets was there for a reason. She had analysed most of the sonnets by dividing them into groups of four lines, and added, for example, a fifth line 'Five full stops, six commas, and one colon'. Applying Bacon's cipher code to the five lines gave 3771. If it didn't, Mrs Venton looked at the punctuation again and expressed it in a different way until it did. The same procedure was applied to the rest of the sonnet revealing the repeated number 3771. Unfortunately, a sonnet contains 14 lines, which is not divisible by 4, and I forget how this was overcome. I wrote a Fortran program using Bacon's cipher code and confirmed or otherwise, Mrs Venton's calculations. When the work was done, Mrs Venton paid to have the book published, and I was given a free copy for my work! Still no businessman!

An equally-mad project came from a group representing the Knights Templar. They believed that the Holy Grail was hidden somewhere in France. The precise location was the geometric centre of certain towns where the Knights Templar had bases. I was sworn to secrecy and given a map of France and a list of towns. I found a formula to compute a circle's centre from three points, and applied this to different groups of towns. The result was a mess of circles identifying possible centres from Calais to Cannes! The Holy Grail was never found, and I was never given a free copy!

One researcher, with whom I still work, forty-five years later, is Professor Patrick Riley. Patrick had originally contacted Enfield College to use its analogue computer run by Bob Bowker. For some reason Bob left, the analogue computer closed down, and Patrick was pointed in my direction. Patrick's research was concerned with the uncontrolled growth of cancerous cells, and he wanted to visualise competing groups of normal and cancerous cells. Initially, he was only interested in a petri-dish simulation, which I represented by a matrix of hexagons, like a honeycomb. These hexagons were seeded with cell numbers and type, and the rules of a growth model applied. Over a period of time, cancerous cells overwhelmed the healthy cells and I plotted the results numerically and graphically. The images were graphically stunning.

The next step was to extend the model to three dimensions (3D), which I resolved by simulating a 3D matrix of inter-locking dodecahedrons. I admit that the programming of this structure was extremely challenging, but successful. However, the real problem was how to visualise this solid volume of cell colonies. At the time, colour computer graphics had not been invented, and I had no choice but to draw consecutive slices through the volume.

As Payroll was a process for early computerisation, I wondered how this could be exploited dishonestly. I imagined a scenario where the payroll programmer was collaborating with a computer operator to increase their weekly pay-packet. I wrote a demonstration program that would stop at critical points and permit the computer operator to update specific parts of the computer's memory. The computer then printed out payslips which included enhanced amounts for the programmer and operator. The result of this experimental research resulted in a short course I gave to some large accountancy companies to make them aware of this new form of crime. Today, millions of people are discovering the dangers of cyber crime. I have been a victim, but not a perpetrator!

I was now a reasonable programmer and a good systems analyst, and my thoughts turned to the misuse of computers. I remember writing a noughts-and-crosses program that never lost! The unsuspecting player was asked via an electric typewriter, whether they wanted to play, to which they answered 'Y' or 'N'. Their reply made no difference, as I ignored it and started the next question, which was 'Do you want to be noughts or crosses?' to which they answered 'N' or 'C'. Again, their reply made no difference, as I ignored it. I then displayed the familiar pattern used for noughts and crosses and the nine playing positions, identified by the digits 1 to 9. A game started by asking the player for their starting position, identified by a single digit. Once more, I ignored it and placed them in one of the corners. I then displayed the current state of play. The computer chose the centre as its response, followed by the new state of play. The bemused player was not sure what was going on and continued to play. Eventually, the computer declared 'I won. Another game?' to which the player agreed. They couldn't understand why they had lost, and were even more determined to win. The same procedure was repeated and again they lost. The next time they replied 'No' to the question: 'Another game?' but it made no difference, the computer carried on relentlessly. The only way to stop the game was to physically stop the computer! Today, millions of people play poker online, unaware of what is happening inside a computer.

Introduction to Plotting

Although I was aware that a 12" drum plotter was connected to the Honeywell, I never bothered using it, until I saw Stan Millward looking at a picture of a cube using red-and-green anaglyph glasses. He offered me the glasses and I saw a 3D image of a cube. I asked how he did it. First he declined but then described how to obtain a perspective projection from three-dimensional coordinates by dividing the x- and y-coordinates by their corresponding z-coordinate. It was an epiphany for me. I went away determined to master the Calcomp plotting software.

I thought that I would find a range of programs for drawing perspective views of objects, only to discover a program which would move the plotter's pen from its current position to a new position, either with the pen up or down! I spent eight years developing a library of programs called PICASO, which greatly simplified the creation of computer-generated images. As lines are represented by numbers inside a computer, 3D objects appear as though they are made from wire: there is no automatic process for removing lines hidden by an object's volume. This is known as the hidden-line-removal problem and consumed the attention of the computer-graphics community of the day. There were some very elegant, yet time-consuming solutions. My own partial solution was discovered while I was on a steam train between the Enfield and Waltham Cross stations! A colleague, Paul Hughes, eventually wrote a general hidden-line removal program for PICASO, using a much larger computer.

One interesting problem in computer graphics involves transforming one shape into another, and I designed a program which could transform any 2D shape or 3D object into a corresponding shape or object by a specified percentage. For example, it was possible to transform an elephant into the shape of Africa by a factor of 50 per cent. It created some amazing graphical results, but I did not yet appreciate that this was an inbetweening program for computer animation.

Principia Computica

One of my favourite philosophers is Bertrand Russell who wrote about difficult subjects such as the nature of mind and matter in the simplest of languages. One of his early works, *Principia Mathematica*, written with Alfred North Whitehead, attempted to analyse the foundations of mathematics. I remember borrowing the three large volumes from the Cheshunt Library, but returned them quickly after looking at page one! Russell's *Principia* inspired me to publish *Principia Computica*, an internal publication of the Enfield College Computer Centre. I wrote most of the articles on programming, and Stan Millward contributed others on mathematics. It ran for about a year, before I gave up.

Brunel University

In 1970 I attended a conference on computer graphics at Brunel University. It was organised by Professor Mike Pitteway, who convinced me to enrol on a new, two-year, part-time Masters degree in computer science. It was a challenging, yet extremely useful course. I learnt about compiler design, Alan Turing, further mathematics and more advanced topics in computing. My thesis was about computer-generated music and its annotation. I designed a system called Compusing, which generated melodies using controlled random numbers. One could select a key, time signature, number of bars, key changes and the melodic note ranges. The program then went berserk and printed out hundreds of possible masterpieces on sheets of printer paper. For example, a quaver played on middle C was printed 'QC4', where 4 means the fourth octave. Understandably, it was impossible to sight read this code so I wrote another program to output the melody using the normal stave, treble clef, time signature and key signature. In spite of all this effort, my system never created a single melody that could even compete with 'Happy Birthday to You'! Nevertheless, today, all new music is typeset using computers.

Having passed my Masters degree in 1972, Professor Pitteway suggested I continue with a part-time PhD under his supervision. Naturally, I agreed and the title would be PICASO: A System for Art & Design. After four years of further research, I submitted my thesis and a portfolio of artwork. After the viva I was awarded a PhD, subject to minor modifications, which involved enhancing the references. By 1976 I was a 'Dr'!

Working with Artists

My PICASO system brought me into touch with researchers at the Slade School of Art and students at Hornsey College of Arts and Crafts. In 1973 the latter joined Enfield College and Technical College to become Middlesex Polytechnic. I recall that most students were not enthralled by the prospect of computers encroaching into their sensitive world of art and design. I remember writing on a blackboard at Hornsey College, a PICASO program, to which students added their own numbers, when copying the program onto punched-card coding sheets. One student deliberately copied a blackboard screw-head onto his coding sheet, and I deliberately ensured that this was interpreted as an '*' in their program, making it useless. I became quite good at recognising uninterested students!

I met a variety of people at the Slade, but two who really impressed me were Chris Briscoe and Darrell Viner. Chris had a fine-art background but was equally at home soldering new circuits into his computer or building a robotic arm wielding a paintbrush! He eventually created his company Digital Pictures which was responsible for some incredible computer animation. Chris had asked me to join the company, but I preferred the security of academia. Darrell was also a Fine Artist and saw the potential offered by computers. I wrote many programs for Darrell, but perhaps the most interesting was one cross-hatching random lines. The process began with a collection of computer-generated random lines, which were given to a cross-hatching program, but instead of drawing these new lines, they were stored and crosshatched. This was repeated a few times, until the output was drawn out as a 4" square on an A0 plotter. After drawing out a hundred of these small squares with different random lines, Darrell selected those for drawing on quality paper at A0 size. The only way to control colour was to stop the computer, change the plotter biro for another colour, and restart the computer. Fifteen minutes later, or so, one had an incredibly complex shaded image, that defied description. Darrell framed them and released them into the art world for a lot of money. He was a businessman!

Working with Colour

Back in the early 1970s two American researchers published computer algorithms for shading coloured images. This required a frame store, which was 1MB of memory, capable of holding one image. Somehow, one was bought for the Prime computer. It cost over £50,000, which was a lot of money in those days. I then discovered that I knew virtually nothing about colour. After much research I extended PICASO with a suite of shading programs called PRISM (Picaso's Rendering Image SysteM). It could easily take one hour to render a single image, which meant one day was needed for every second of animation! Nevertheless, we persevered and created some excellent sequences. The next problem was to capture the image on videotape or film, which required more equipment and know-how. Today's PCs are so powerful they can easily render complex images in real time! How things have changed.

Working with Television

Enfield was not very far from Alexandra Palace, which housed part of BBC2's Graphic Design department. Somehow they became aware of my work in computer graphics and asked if I would create some animation. By that time we had acquired a Prime computer which used interactive terminals and a large A0 Calcomp belt-plotter. I admitted that I knew nothing about animation, but was willing to learn. I was asked to plot onto animation cel (transparent plastic) a sequence of drawings showing the paths of planets and the sun, where the Earth is the centre of the solar system, the Ptolemaic system or geocentric model. Next, I had to plot the paths for the heliocentric model where the sun is central. It was an easy project and opened the door into the world of computer animation.

I was then approached by Chris Fynes, a graphic designer at BBC TV, who could already program in BASIC, and was working on the Money Programme. Chris introduced me to an animator's peg bar, which keeps sheets of animator's cel in registration. I wrote a suite of programs to draw registration marks on each cel with its number. After each drawing, the program paused whilst we removed the cel, attached a new sheet, and restarted. Each drawing could easily take a minute, which meant that one second of animation (24 frames) required approximately thirty minutes. It was boring work. One of the problems with this approach is that we couldn't visualise how fast or slow the animation was, until a line test was made. This required photographing each cel, developing the film, and projecting it. I then adjusted the program to reflect the changes. Chris gave me his design for a pound sign, which I digitised into a collection of coordinates. I then wrote a PICASO program to place a 3D observer very close to the image and allow the observer to withdraw, at the same time rotating. Chris then arranged for the cels to be coloured. It was very successful, and I used to watch it every week on TV and say 'I did that!'.

Over the following years I worked on dozens of opening title sequences including The Angels, Swapshop, Parkinson, Newsnight, Panorama, Bergerac, Horizon, Face the Press, South Bank Show, The Two Ronnies and even the special effects for Superman III.

The Following Years

When Middlesex Polytechnic acquired university status it moved to Bounds Green. I also went and continued my work in computer animation. I designed a one-year MSc course in computer graphics and a one-week course introducing computer animation to TV graphic designers, which was attended by BBC TV, ITV, Channel 4 and Yorkshire TV. I even translated the course into French for a group from TF1, Canal Plus, and others. Two days into the course, the attendees told me that they spoke fluent English! At the end of the week I was given a bottle of Champagne Cognac!

Marion Locke ran the university's Consultancy Services Organisation, which managed my PICASO system by hiring it out to other academic institutes throughout the UK.

In 1986 I was approached by a head-hunter who persuaded me to leave academia for industry, with company cars, free medical insurance and company credit cards. How could I resist? I joined Rediffusion Simulation Ltd. as a Research Consultant. The project was top secret, for we were about to develop the world's largest and most powerful, real-time image generator. It took us ten years to make it work, but in the process the company ran out of time and money and Rediffusion was sold to the French Thomson Group. I had risen to the position of Chief Scientist and was made redundant in 1996 and returned to academia at Bournemouth University where we established the National Centre for Computer Animation – a centre of excellence for teaching film special-effects and computer games. I was given a personal chair and later made Head of Department.

Over the years I have written and edited over forty books on computer graphics, virtual reality, computer animation, digital media, the internet and mathematics. Brunel University awarded me a DSc for my contribution to virtual reality and computer graphics. But none of this would have happened if it had not been for Enfield College.

11. Fourteen fun and formative years at Enfield

ALEXANDER ROMISZOWSKI

Alexander Romiszowski *joined Enfield in 1963 from industry, where he was accidentally 'pushed' out of a motor vehicle (engineering) career into the emerging field of educational technology. He was then 'pulled' into Enfield by John Hamer, to offer educational design services both internally and to external client organizations. After ten years full-time plus four years part-time at Enfield, he worked for a decade as consultant in Brazil, then for a decade as professor at Syracuse University, USA. The last two decades since 1997, officially semi-retired, he lives in Brazil but works worldwide and is busier than ever before.*

The Road to Enfield – littered with lucky accidents

I was born in the Polish town of Wilno (now Vilnius, the capital of Lithuania) a few months before the start of WW2. My father, a young army officer, defended the city against the Soviets while this was feasible and then followed the last orders of the Polish army's high command to 'withdraw and regroup, joining the French army on the Western front'. How he crossed Soviet-held territory to the Baltic and swam to a ship which took him to neutral Sweden, where the far-from-neutral Polish Embassy organised his transit to France, is another story for another book. But, had he not made it and, when France capitulated, had he not been evacuated via Dunkirk to Dover with other Allied units, my mother would not have tried to reach Britain and I would not have made it to Enfield.

In Wilno, the Soviets decided to play the role of 'liberators of the proletariat' and, as part of the charade, opened a travel agency – anyone with an entry visa to some neutral country could apply for an exit visa and travel permit. In response, the Polish Embassy in Stockholm – still functioning due to Sweden's neutral status – hatched a scam: fake visas to the island of Curação in the Caribbean. Once you had the visas, you would take the trans-Siberian railway to Vladivostok, cross to Japan and then to the USA – stopping there.

This scam worked until Japan entered WW2 in late 1941 and transit to the USA was no longer possible. My mother applied for one of these fake visas, but the reply from Stockholm contained a visa to Sweden. On the day her letter arrived, the Embassy was 'officially' closed due to pressure on Sweden by Germany. A small stock of Visas-to-Sweden-for VIP's was sent to random applicants before closing. So, by a lucky accident perpetrated unwittingly by the Nazis, we 'won the lottery' and in mid-1940 my mother and I boarded a civilian plane bound for Stockholm.

We lived in Stockholm for over a year, as it was only in late 1941 that it became possible for civilians to fly from Sweden to Britain. By then, the war-game had changed and a new army composed of Polish refugees, many released from Siberian work camps, was being formed by the Allies. Officers for this army were trained in Britain at Black Barony, a castle (now a hotel) not far from Peebles. My father became one of the trainers. So, by 1942, I was living in Scotland – still a long way from Enfield.

From 1944 came education, for me, a process of constant change of schools and locations. My dad's diverse military postings kept him away from home until 1950. My mother was teaching in Polish-language boarding schools for girls that the British Government set up to accommodate the refugee children that arrived in Britain. These schools would merge and move to new locations as refugee numbers dwindled. So, I lived with my mother in a secondary boarding school for girls, first in a mansion in Scotland, then a country house in Buckinghamshire and finally in barracks that had been a WW2 US-army hospital in the Cotswolds. I attended four different primary-level boarding schools for boys and then two different secondary schools – one of these was in the Cotswolds – the other was in Oxford, which became our family's home town once my father was out of the army. Oxford was chosen because it was a renowned university town. So, it was not accidental, but carefully engineered by my parents, that I ended up applying to study at Oxford University. But it may well have been a lucky accident that I got in, as the competition was fierce in those days – in sciences, only one per cent of applicants were successful. In 1957, I took four entrance examinations to four different Oxford colleges before, luckily, I was accepted to study Physics.

My university career was also marked by changes, more accidental than planned. As much of my first year at Oxford University was dedicated to rugby, racing go-carts and rebuilding classic cars, my academic results were not spectacular and my tutors suggested I should consider a 'fresh start' in an area better matching my interests and practical bent – Engineering. I took their advice. But as I reached the end of my studies in Engineering Science I was still undecided as to career paths. I put off the decision and I remained at Oxford to study for a Post-Graduate Certificate in Education, thus qualifying as a teacher.

So, when I had to start looking for a job, I had two quite distinct career paths open to me – automotive engineer or science teacher – and I explored both. Also, my nomadic childhood had instilled a love for travel and adventure, but my links to Oxford through university, school and home were strong. So, it was tough when one day I found myself in the position of having to decide between two offers of employment: as a physics teacher in a secondary school in the town of Kano in Nigeria, or as a 'Graduate Apprentice' in Oxford at the Pressed Steel Company. After some indecision, Oxford won and I took the first step along the career path that took me to Enfield.

The year was now 1961. The Graduate Apprentices at the Pressed Steel Company would spend one to two years in a variety of departments, receiving on-the-job training and gaining experience, until finding their best-fitting 'niche' in the company. In my case, less than one year after starting my apprenticeship the training manager offered me a post in his own department, as 'training designer' responsible for a project to write self-instructional materials in the programmed learning format for the initial training of automobile industry apprentices. I knew nothing about programmed learning, but I accepted the challenge and set about learning how to do it, thus falling (accidentally) into the educational technology and instructional design field, the work I would do at Enfield.

John Hamer – the head-hunter

As luck would have it, I led one of the UK's first ever major projects to apply programmed learning – the 'educational technology of the day' – to industrial training. The potential benefit in this specific context was that the packaging of theory in individualised self-study format allowed the integration of theory with practice in the workshop, or on the factory floor, in a way that a timetable of classes for the whole group just could not do. The project at the Pressed Steel Company was very successful, both in promoting effective learning and in reducing learning time (typically by over 80 per cent) and it became quite famous for a time. Its success was also due to advice and support in the form of mentoring which I received from John Hamer.

John had joined Enfield Technical College in 1947, from the Royal Air Force. Initially, he taught mathematics. Later he also taught courses designed to improve the mathematical knowledge and qualifications of schoolteachers. Thus, he developed an interest in educational psychology and this led to a special interest in programmed learning. In 1960 he arranged a study tour to the USA where he worked with Professor B. F. Skinner at Harvard University and visited many research and development centres working on emerging technologies applied to education. Because of specialist knowledge gained during his USA visit, John was invited by the Pressed Steel Company to orient the project I was directing. In 1963, John asked if I would by chance be interested in joining the staff of a new Division he was setting up at Enfield. After deep thought about moving from Industry to Academe and from a university city to the light-industry environment of Enfield, I decided to give it a try. Maybe doubling my salary clinched it.

The new College of Technology – and my three roles there

In 1962, Enfield Technical College was renamed Enfield College of Technology by the Ministry of Education and George Brosan became the new Principal. Between 1962 and 1970, together with a team headed by Eric Robinson, he set about turning Enfield into a 'New Polytechnic'. The College began to offer a much wider range of courses, adding to its 'traditional' fare of technical skills new degree-level courses in areas such as business studies and sociology.

In 1963, John Hamer set up the Division of Education and Psychology as an integral part of this change process. On the one hand, it allowed him to implement his ideas on use of programmed instruction as a means of facilitating learning, by setting up a Programmed Instruction Centre (PIC). On the other hand, the new Division also included a Learning Systems Unit (LSU) to help implement the revolutionary ideas of the Brosan/Robinson partnership by offering in-house consulting services on the systematic (and systemic) design and development of courses and learning materials. The Division of Education and Psychology undertook three types of activities:

- courses in education, teacher training programs and specialist workshops;
- consulting and support services for other departments and for students in general;
- Research & Development activities in education – especially, the emerging field of educational technology.

To implement this range of services, John needed help. I was the first, and for some years the only, additional staff member of this new Division, starting my duties in the 1963/64 academic year.

Courses and Workshops for teachers and trainers

The new Division of Education and Psychology provided courses for teachers and trainers designed to prepare students for professional qualifications in education. In line with the trend towards the 'polytechnic' model, the Division also provided courses in psychology for students in other departments of the College. I was responsible for the planning and delivery of short courses on Programmed Learning and other emerging educational technologies and running workshops on Programme Writing. These workshops were offered both internally for College staff and externally for all types of education and training institutions. During the decade 1963-73, nearly one hundred such workshops were run. Only around 20 per cent of them were for internal College faculty, and most of these were given during the earlier part of this period. Over time, the internal demand diminished, but the external demand continued to grow – especially from industry and business.

The Industrial Training Act (1964) empowered the Ministry of Labour to establish Industrial Training Boards (ITBs) to 'provide or secure the provision of training and other facilities in their respective industries.' The 'early birds' such as the Engineering Industries Training Board (EITB) were followed by some twenty more ITBs serving diverse areas of industry. Training designers, as well as providers, became very much in demand. There was a parallel increase in use of educational technologies, hence a growing demand from industry for the services of the Learning Systems Unit at Enfield.

There was a similar growth of interest and demand for our courses from educational institutions, especially other technical colleges and some of the newly formed universities. One of the earliest workshops I ran was attended by staff from Huddersfield College of Education (Technical), who then adopted self-instruction in a big way and became a competitor rather than a client when they set up their own programmed learning centre. However, rather than competing, Enfield and Huddersfield chose to collaborate, running several workshops jointly, for participants from other colleges.

We also collaborated on projects implementing educational technology solutions in schools, such as the project using programmed learning to introduce student-directed learning in Leicestershire schools. This project, led by John Leedham, was an integral part of the historic 'Leicestershire Plan'.

The reference to Leicestershire reminds me of our collaboration with the Centre for Advancement of Mathematics Education in Technology (CAMET), at Loughborough University of Technology, on a project to develop programmed learning materials for teaching mathematics as a 'tool subject' for non-mathematicians. The collaboration sprang from mutual interests of the team at CAMET and our project at Enfield to introduce a Remedial Mathematics Service (described later). In the long run, this led to my PhD thesis, defended at Loughborough University in 1976: 'A Study of Individualised Systems of Mathematics Instruction at Post-Secondary Levels'.

During an early workshop in 1964, two lecturers from the Civil Engineering Department of the University of Aston in Birmingham decided to use programmed learning to help overcome problems in their large classes where many students encountered learning difficulties due to inadequate mastery of content they should have learnt earlier in school. Typically, these students would fail unless they received individualised tutorial help to overcome their weaknesses. But how do you offer such individualised help when you have over 300 students in your class? These two lecturers decided that for their workshop project they would cease giving lectures for one discipline in the first year of their civil engineering degree programme – *Struc-*

tures – and would replace the lectures with weekly hand-outs of printed materials in self-study format. Their 'stroke of genius' was to add one additional page at the end – where students would note the numbers of the test items and exercises that they got wrong or could not solve and the serial numbers of the sections (called 'frames') of the study materials which they considered to be difficult or incomprehensible. This feedback was then analysed and used to plan a series of 'difficulty-specific tutorial sessions.' Each student would receive instructions to attend specific tutorial sessions – maybe no session at all, maybe several at different times to cover all identified difficulties. The results were quite spectacular and influenced many other projects, including Enfield's Remedial Mathematics service.

The Programmed Instruction Centre also had a significant international impact. We ran several workshops in Europe and some further afield, for individual organizations or international agencies like the Council of Europe and UNESCO. Not only did we impact education and training in many countries, but we were impacted by contact with many diverse national cultures and customs – and we had a lot of fun in the process. In 1971, a workshop in Egypt, with a week's break to tour the antiquities, was not only *fun* but also *formative* as it taught us how we must take cultural and religious differences into consideration when designing any type of educational intervention – from a single module to a total system.

At a workshop held in Ireland in 1967, one participant's practical project was a programmed text to teach bar employees how to pour a pint of Guinness whilst maintaining the 'head' of foam at the top of the glass within acceptable limits. This project arose due to a court case in the UK; the plaintiff sued the Guinness brewery alleging that he was not getting his rightful measure. The Guinness Company's defence was that the 'head' was a well-known characteristic and indeed a 'trade-mark' of this beer. Guinness won the case, but the judge ruled that the 'head' could not be more than 5 per cent of the full measure. It now became a 'problem' for Guinness to ensure that all barmen performed legally, so an Irish project 'done for fun' transformed into a major contract for the PIC. After many visits to breweries and pubs we 'solved the problem' – but not through training – and in the process, we learnt much about (and even contributed to) the emerging technology of 'Human Performance Improvement' – another project that was both *fun* and *formative*.

Services for the College: the PIC, the LSU and Remedial Mathematics

When I arrived at Enfield in 1963, I encountered the Programmed Instruction Centre already set up and equipped with the latest educational technologies. The Teaching Machine Laboratory had a wide range of equipment ranging from simple *linear machines* which presented printed materials in a step-by-step manner, to more sophisticated *branching machines* which presented alternative paths through the material depending on the responses of the learner. The PIC also had a library of self-instructional programmes on subjects of relevance to courses offered by the College. Notable among these were the teaching programmes stored as a series of slides (or 'frames') on 16mm film reels which, when loaded into the branching machines, would be accessed and presented to learners in a sequence determined by their responses to questions, registered by pressing a combination of buttons. These machines presented learning materials similar in structure to the computer-based courses of today, but in a technically more primitive (and noisy) manner by winding and rewinding the film in search of a given frame – once located, the *whirring* sound of winding reels was replaced by a *clunk* – a room full of the machines in use sounded like some factory production line.

The PIC's teaching machines laboratory, together with the library of programmes in both filmstrip and printed form, were available as a service to College departments and to interested students, as a library of interactive learning materials on topics relevant to specific courses. A particularly impactful use of the *PIC-as-a-service* arose in consequence of the changes in courses and organizational culture as Enfield College of Technology evolved into Middlesex Polytechnic. New degrees in areas such as Management, Economics and Sociology attracted new groups of target students. However, unlike most traditional universities which tended to cater to recent school-leavers, the Polytechnic continued the tradition of the College of Technology, catering to more adult students, often already in employment and some years since completion of basic schooling. This meant that some of the students registering for the new degrees were ill-prepared in terms of pre-requisite knowledge and skills. This was particularly critical in the case of mathematics.

The PIC designed and implemented a self-study programme in Remedial Mathematics, which focused on the competencies that were essential pre-requisites to these new degree courses.

The self-study materials required to implement this service were already available in the Programmed Instruction Centre. All we wrote were the tests to measure each key competency. These were taken by all first-year students, allowing us to identify the 'missing' mathematical competencies of each individual and suggest a sequence of study units. Students would then study the first unit in their suggested sequence, followed by the post-test, which would lead to one of three possible recommendations: the next unit to study (in the event of successful mastery of the competency); an alternative study unit (as a second chance); an individual tutorial session, at a given time and place, with one of the available mathematics teaching staff (a third chance for those very few who failed to learn from the self-study materials).

The design of this Remedial Mathematics service was similar in some respects to the system implemented in the *Structures* course at the University of Aston in Birmingham. However, our course management system was computer-based and automated. The tests were on sheets of paper which the student would complete and then hand to the computer department, where an assistant would transform the data into punched cards, these would be processed by the computer, the tests would be scored automatically and new study recommendations for each student would be generated. The system also generated cumulative data on individual and all-group progress – tracking and improving the performance of our system was a *fun* and *formative* experience.

Another service activity was offered by the Learning Systems Unit as an integral part of the process of new course creation, as the College of Technology evolved towards Polytechnic status. The LSU was instrumental in this process by supplying 'learning designers' (like me) to work on course design teams. We collaborated with the academic staff of most of the departments as they planned new courses. Our role included ensuring that the courses were 'relevant to target-student needs' and 'acquired competencies were assessed appropriately'. Also, we would see it our duty to point out whenever the course planning process seemed to be drifting away from what we saw as the correct path.

On occasions, I pointed out that the course planning process seemed to be driven more by internal departmental convenience or by personal research interests of given staff members than the interests or professional needs of the target students. I recall that this type of intervention tended to make me and the other staff of the Learning Systems Unit somewhat unpopular with some academics. In those pre-email days, internal communications were distributed by notes placed in mailboxes ('pigeon holes') of relevant staff members. Sometimes, the announcement of a planning session for some new course would mysteriously not arrive in my pigeon-hole until it was too late to attend. Although not that much *fun*, these experiences were most certainly *formative*. Despite such reactions, the LSU persisted – with strong support from the Brosan/Robinson team.

This aspect of my work led to an invitation in 1968/69 to join a team of consultants working on the design of the operational methods and systems for the UK's proposed Open University (OU). Enfield's small *Learning Systems Unit* was one of the models for the OU's *Institute for Educational Technology*. The *Course Team Approach* which the OU adopted for design of its courses was also influenced by the Enfield approach. I recall that, just as earlier at Enfield, the approach was not so popular with academics. Brian Lewis, the first Director of the Institute for Educational Technology, told me that the unrest of some faculty members almost caused the OU to abandon the Course Team Approach. But Brian defended it and won – the dissident faculty were told to 'do it our way or find another job' (and some did choose to do so). This systematic (and systemic) approach to the design of all aspects of the OU's operation is an insufficiently-emphasized reason contributing to its success and sustainability. It is a matter of some pride that Enfield's LSU contributed to this.

Evaluative research on the design of learning materials

My first 'research' work at Enfield was to evaluate the programmed learning materials designed and developed by others. This was an essential activity on programme writing workshops – *formative evaluation* of the projects undertaken by participants. However, early in 1965, an opportunity to do this in a real-life context came about through a visit to the PIC by Philip Kogan. Macmillan Publishers had identified a commercial opportunity in the publishing of programmed texts and Philip's job was to locate potential authors and decide whether to publish the programmes these authors wrote. Philip approached the PIC to seek help in evaluating the quality of texts submitted for publication. I evaluated the first-draft versions of many dozens of programmed-instruction texts on various topics, by various would-be authors, and wrote detailed evaluation critiques which Philip would share with the authors. The authors would then contact me to seek further explanations or to share rewritten drafts. It was an enjoyable task, rather like running a correspondence course on programme writing, but I often felt I was learning more from the exercise than the would-be authors – another example of work at Enfield that was both *fun* and *formative*.

My North American study tour

In 1967, the College of Technology granted me a leave of absence to engage in Research and Development. Following John Hamer's 1960 example, I arranged a 3-month study tour of R&D projects in North America. It was a busy schedule: a few days at Harvard University, reviewing the latest research on programmed instruction; a visit to Ontario Institute for Studies in Education in Toronto to see some of the earliest work on computer assisted instruction; a visit to New Mexico to see Zuni Indians studying in their villages by means of a system of learner-directed, on-demand, video (in 1967!) and so on. However, the part of the trip that is most strongly rooted in memory is my visit to the San Francisco Bay Area. Part of the reason was the time and place – San Francisco in the summer of 1967, at the height of the flower-power movement. But that *fun* experience was incidental to the *formative* impact of my visits to several projects that influenced my own research for years to come: Berkeley University, where programmed instruction was being used to teach productive thinking skills; Stanford University, where they were using computer managed instruction in the teaching of arithmetic; the American Institutes for Research (AIR) and its 'Program for Learning According to Needs' – Project PLAN – which was using computer-analysis of learning progress to select suitable materials and activities for each individual student. I returned inspired and enthusiastic and by the following year (1968) had implemented some of the ideas from

Berkeley, Stanford, and the AIR in Enfield's Remedial Mathematics service.

Getting hooked and high on academic authorship

In 1967, Philip Kogan, with Terry Page, founded Kogan Page Limited – a publishing company which initially specialized in practical 'how to' books and then added other categories of specialist publications. Philip suggested I write some books that he would then publish. I was quite unsure, but he convinced me to try. I wrote one of the very first books published by Kogan Page: a short (150 page) 'how to' book for teachers: *The Selection and Use of Teaching Aids*. The book sold well and the experience set me on the path of writing many more books – another 'accident'.

In earlier years (1963-64) John Hamer conducted a survey of the use of programmed learning in British schools and then in 1965-66 I conducted a similar survey of the use of programmed learning by UK industrial and commercial organizations. These reports were published internally by the College of Technology and distributed, at no cost, by the PIC. A third survey we published internally was *Programmes in Print* (1969), a catalogue of instructional programmes available worldwide. However, such survey data should be regularly updated, so the PIC decided to produce a yearbook. Kogan Page offered to publish it and APLET – the Association for Programmed Learning and Educational Technology – sponsored the project. The '*APLET Yearbook of Educational and Instructional Technology*, compiled by the PIC at Enfield College of Technology' was born.

However, the task of annually updating all this survey information proved to be too much for the small staff of the PIC, so right from the start, the 'yearbook' became a bi-annual publication. I compiled and edited the first two editions (1970-71 and 1972-73) and co-edited the 1974-75 edition with Anne Howe, who had then joined the PIC staff. From the 1976-77 edition, we changed the name to *International Yearbook of Educational and Instructional Technology* to reflect the ever-broadening field we covered and the audience we served. Anne and I co-edited the 1976-77 and 1978-79 editions and, from the 1980-81 edition, Anne was the sole editor as I had by then cut my ties to the Polytechnic.

Taking leave of Enfield – in fits and starts

In fact, my ties to the Polytechnic started to loosen much earlier. In late 1973, I received leave of absence to undertake a UNDP (United Nations Development Programme) assignment in Brazil. I did, however, keep in contact with the Polytechnic, particularly the Enfield site, into the 1980's, and I am to this day in contact with Anne Howe, who was the longest-remaining member at the new Polytechnic of the old PIC's staff. I have also on occasions visited the Enfield site, now part housing estate and part industrial zone, quite divorced from the College-turned-Polytechnic-turned-University which it sired and housed in my time. I recall my last visit before the Enfield site shut down. The PIC had closed and the teaching machines had been scrapped, but other stuff was still awaiting disposal, so I picked out a few mementos. So, here in Rio de Janeiro, I have a circular can containing a 16mm film – *Learning and Behaviour: what makes us human* – a CBS newsreel from 1959, showing Professor Skinner and his team at Harvard University demonstrating the application of operant conditioning principles to the training of rats, pigeons and humans. This is the very film that John Hamer brought to Enfield from Harvard in 1960.

The film is now brittle, so I have not screened it since I saved it from the Polytechnic's dumpster. But luckily, others have placed a copy on YouTube: https://www.youtube.com/watch?v=hR675X49GLU Maybe, if I ever retire from active consulting and project management, I will find the time to select some other items from my collection of media saved from the Programmed Instruction Centre and place these on YouTube to illustrate my *fourteen fun and formative years at Enfield.*

PART TWO

MID-TIME ARRIVALS

1966-1968

12. Business Studies at Enfield 1966-71

ARTHUR HINDMARCH

***Arthur Hindmarch** joined Enfield in September 1966 as a lecturer in Accounting. His main task at the time was to join the group led by Alan Hale in developing the BA Business Studies Sandwich degree programme. He was a member of the group, also under Alan Hale who developed the BA European Business Studies Sandwich programme. Afterwards he stayed at the new Middlesex Polytechnic and what eventually became Middlesex University moving from Enfield to the Hendon campus. At Hendon he led the group which developed the BA Accounting and Finance programme. He retired from Middlesex in 2001 and now spends his time in classical middle class activities: gardening, grandchildren, golf and lots of exciting holidays.*

I was born and lived in Sunderland until I left to go to university when I was twenty-three. My father spent all his working life from the age of fourteen at Wearmouth Colliery. The Colliery is now long gone, but it's existence is represented by the sculpture of the miners lamp which stands outside Sunderland's football ground, the 'Stadium of Light', which was built on the site of the mine.

I was one of two pupils to pass the eleven-plus at my primary school, and so in September 1947 I joined the Bede Grammar School, at the time the only grammar school in Sunderland. I graduated with reasonable A-levels, but decided I needed a job to earn some money so I joined Lloyds Bank in September 1954. In February 1955 I was called for two years National Service. I rejoined the bank in 1957 where I worked for another two years. I became dissatisfied with work at the bank and with the help and encouragement of my old Headmaster applied successfully for entry to the London School of Economics. A life changing decision which I never regretted.

I was a student at the LSE from 1959 to 1962 and graduated with a BSc Econ and an accounting specialisation. I decided to study for a professional accounting qualification. In September 1962 I joined Arthur Andersen & Co., an international accounting firm with headquarters in Chicago. At that time the firm had recently become established in London and was rapidly expanding.[29] One of my colleagues at Arthur Andersen was Peter Bird. He was also an LSE graduate but soon left the firm to take an academic post at the LSE. He subsequently became a professor and head of the accounting department at the University of Kent.

I stayed at Arthur Andersen until I qualified as a Chartered Accountant in 1965. At that time I decided to leave the firm. Peter Bird was a useful role model and he encouraged me when I decided to try accounting education as a career. In September 1965 I joined Barking College of Technology as a lecturer in accounting. As a new lecturer I was assigned to teach courses which prepared students for professional examinations. I was of course faced with the difficulty of adapting to my first year of teaching in an environment very different to the one I had left in the city. Towards the end of my year at Barking I was doubting whether I had made the right move in leaving the accounting profession for a teaching career.

It was at this time in summer of 1966 that I received a phone call from someone I had never met, an accountant called Henry Mosert. Henry said he had been given my name by Professor Peter Bird of the LSE and was I interested in joining him at Enfield College of Technology. I was intrigued by the call and I agreed to go to Enfield to meet him.

I had lived in Bloomsbury since my LSE days and was not enthused by the train journey from Liverpool Street to Southbury Road station and the walk to the College in Kingsway which was an unprepossessing road in Ponders End. My visit to Enfield turned out to be an informal interview with Henry Mosert and Eric Robinson.

I was impressed by their enthusiasm and with the plans they had for the development of education at Enfield. They must have been sufficiently impressed by my academic and professional qualifications because the result of this meeting was the offer of a lecture-

---

[29] Arthur Andersen continued to expand in the UK but their whole international edifice was brought down as a result of the Enron scandal in 2001. At the time Arthur Andersen was one of the five largest accounting firms in the world. 85,000 employees lost their jobs as a result of the firm's demise in 2002.

ship in Accounting and I joined the college in September 1966. Reading the contributions of my colleagues Tony Crilly and Tom Bourner who joined Enfield in 1967 and 1969 it is clear that the arrangements for interviews were then more formal than in 1966.

Accounting at Enfield

Henry Mosert was what you might call a 'marmite' character. He was an energetic individual, a chartered accountant of small stature but with big ideas. He did not 'suffer fools gladly' and consequently easily made enemies. He did however have well thought out ideas on the future of accounting education. Luckily he and I respected each other and we worked well together during our time at Enfield.

I did not realise at the time that my other interviewer, Eric Robinson who was the Head of the Arts Faculty at Enfield, was to be one of the significant influences in the development of Enfield in particular and of the Polytechnics in general (Robinson, 1968).

When I arrived at Enfield I discovered that Henry Mosert was the only other member of staff teaching accounting. The college had recruited a bright group of students on to a Higher National Diploma (HND) course in Business Studies which included a significant amount of accounting teaching. The students had been led to believe that there was a possibility of the development of a degree to be built on the foundation of the HND. My first task at Enfield was to quickly develop and teach a syllabus for these students.

Thus my first experience of teaching at Enfield was with these HND students. It is now fifty years on from that experience but I remember how bright they were and how I just (I think) managed to keep one-step ahead of them with a great deal of preparation. An experience I am sure facing many a new teacher.[30]

It was Henry Mosert's view that the traditional technology college teaching of accounting was not suitable for the Enfield HND course, especially if the HND was to be the basis for a Business

---

[30] One of these students Miles Atchison, eventually became an accounting lecturer at the Polytechnic of Central London. He is also one of the joint authors of (Hindmarch et al., 1977) based on the approach to accounting teaching which eventually developed at Enfield.

Studies degree course. In my year at Barking I experienced teaching on programmes which were designed to prepare students for professional accounting examinations. This experience helped to confirm my support for Henry's approach to developing accounting teaching at Enfield in a different way.

Based on my experience of being a student at the LSE, followed by my studies for the examinations of the Institute of Chartered Accountants and my teaching experience at Barking College I had critical views on the way that accounting was traditionally taught. I felt that existing introductory accounting courses concentrated too heavily on methods and techniques. Students progressing to more advanced work would then belatedly be introduced to discussion of the conceptual basis of the subject. My view was that it would be more logical to introduce a conceptual framework of the subject at the beginning of the course before building the superstructure of accounting methods. The implementation of this approach to the accounting syllabuses in Enfield courses took several years and was eventually presented in (Hindmarch et al., 1977).

Business Studies at Enfield

At the time I joined in 1966 Enfield had small nucleus of staff led by Alan Hale, with strong and exciting ideas on the future of tertiary education in general and business education in particular. Alan made it clear that Enfield was keen to develop a degree in Business Studies as recommended in the 1964 Crick Report on *Higher Awards in Business Studies*. Other important influences at the time were the establishment of the Council for National Academic Awards (CNAA) in 1964 and the 1966 White Paper, *A plan for Polytechnics and Other Colleges*.

The immediate dilemma facing Alan Hale and Eric Robinson was whether it would be possible to design a Business Studies degree and have it approved in time to incorporate the HND and its existing students.

This small group of staff was augmented in 1966 an 1967 by the appointment of young lecturers to help develop an exciting range of new courses in Business Mathematics and Social Science, as well as Business Studies.

My recollection of that first year at Enfield, in addition to the volume of teaching preparation, is of endless meetings to discuss the content and submission of the BA Business Studies degree. The structure of the degree was discussed at great length. We agreed that we were seeking to provide a broad based business education and a limited specialisation in the functional areas of business. To this end each syllabus had be agreed by the group. Preparation to meet the CNAA included rehearsals with interrogation by colleagues outside the business studies group. Then the meeting with the CNAA in their offices in Grays Inn Road and finally their visit to Enfield and the wait for their verdict.

I also recollect the energy, excitement and the general atmosphere of optimism and the enthusiasm for the future of business education. I also remember the long 'business lunches' in The Pied Bull and the staff against students football matches on the pitch alongside the 'huts' on the Enfield campus.

BA Business Studies

The course which developed from these meetings was structured with a two-year Part 1 followed by a sandwich placement year and a final one year Part 2. The first two years consisted of:

Accounting
Business Mathematics
Economics
Law and Politics
Sociology and Communication and Technology.

The sandwich year had to be a real job with an appropriate salary. The student was required to complete a project arising out of the work experience. In the final year the students specialised in one of the following areas:

Personnel, Planning and Administration
Quantitative Economics and Accounting
Marketing Analysis and Research
Marketing Overseas.[31]

[31] The options Marketing Analysis and Research

The content of the two-year Part 1 was designed to reflect the multidimensional nature of business problems whose solution requires an understanding of a range of disciplines.

There was a general agreement of the importance of the one-year sandwich placement. The students were visited during the year by a placement tutor. One of the tutors' tasks was to help the students identify and complete a project arising out of the work experience. The project was assessed and contributed to the degree classification.

The importance of the sandwich placement was emphasised by the allocation of resources to set up a special unit to find suitable placements across a range of courses. As well as in Business Studies, sandwich placements were also a feature of BA Social Science and BSc Mathematics for Business. The head of this unit was Julian Ayer, in some ways an unexpected member of staff of a college of technology. Julian was an old Etonian and the son of the philosopher A. J. Ayer. He was an excellent head of the placement unit and worked tirelessly in finding suitable sandwich placements. He was also a fellow member of the staff football team in matches against the students. He was a typical public school footballer, running in straight lines demolishing anything that came in his way. He was a charming colleague and in later years I was sad to read that he had died in the Boxing Day 2004 Asian Tsunami.

The final year specialisations reflected functional areas within business organisations. They were designed to enable students to specialise in areas which interested them and which could provide potential career opportunities.

When the BA Business Studies degree was approved by the CNAA in 1967 it was the first such degree to be approved. The first students to graduate were the original HND students who were given retrospective approval – 14 graduated in 1968 followed by 34 in 1969. They were the first students to graduate with Business Studies degrees of the CNAA.

An important element in CNAA approval and subsequent monitoring was the role of external examiners. We were fortunate to

---

and Marketing Overseas overlapped significantly, but the latter demanded an overseas third year placement. This option eventually provided the foundation for the innovative BA European Business Administration (BAEBA) degree.

have in my area two examiners who were particularly supportive. One was Professor Peter Bird of the University of Kent. As mentioned earlier he had been instrumental in my entry to academic accounting and he continued to be very helpful as an external examiner. The other examiner was Professor Maurice Peston of Queen Mary College of London University (later Lord Peston). He was a strong supporter of the development of the polytechnics and was influential at the CNAA, and over the years he was very helpful in the development of our Business Studies degree. He was also very involved in the development and approval of the Enfield BA Social Science degree.

I have referred earlier to Alan Hale. When I joined Enfield in 1966 he was course leader responsible for the development of the HND Business Studies into a degree course. He led a diverse group of academic staff successfully through the machinations of CNAA approval. He was keen for the group to recognise the interconnection between the subjects taught on the degree, particularly in the first two years. To this end he set up an 'inter-disciplinary seminar' in which staff and students attempted to discuss, with varying degree of success, the relationship between their subjects.

His importance in the development of Business Studies education and his support of a broad based and inter-disciplinary approach was recognised by the publisher Macmillan. Alan persuaded Macmillan to produce the 'Macmillan Business Management and Administration' series edited by Alan Hale. The series comprised:

- *Accounting – An Introduction* by Arthur Hindmarch, Miles Atchison and Richard Marke
- *Sociology of Industrialisation – An Introduction* by David Brown and Michael J Harrison
- *Managing Mathematically* by Terry Green and John Webster
- *Computers in Business* by Peter Haine and Ernest Haidon
- *Psychology and Work – An Introduction* by Peter Ribeaux and Steve Poppleton

Alan was also a strong advocate of our links with the École Superieur in Rheims. His enthusiasm guided us through the difficult initial meetings in Enfield and in Rheims. This liaison eventually resulted in a new degree, the BA European Business Administration (BAEBA).

Conclusion

I joined Enfield in 1966. I remained at the same institution for the next 35 years although the name changed from Enfield College of Technology to Middlesex Polytechnic to Middlesex University. The first five years from 1966 to 1971 were undoubtedly the most exciting and stimulating of my teaching career.

n I have often been asked what made the Enfield experience distinctive. How did it differ from other institutions? My knowledge of other colleges during this period is limited. However, I suggest that the experience of those fortunate enough to be a part of Enfield at this time was based on leadership and self-confidence. George Brosan and Eric Robinson were outstanding in their vision of what was needed to change in Higher Education and Alan Hale provided the leadership in the Business Studies area. During that time there appeared to be endless resources to finance new ideas and enthusiasms. I consider myself fortunate to have been part of the Enfield experience.

13. Mostly happy memories of Enfield days

RICHARD BAILLIE

***Richard Baillie** was at Enfield between 1966 and 1970 and graduated with a BSc in Mathematics for Business. Subsequently he took an MSc in Statistics at the University of Kent and a PhD in econometrics at the London School of Economics. He worked as an economic statistician in the Central Statistics Office and has subsequently worked at several universities in the UK and USA. He is currently the A J Pasant Professor of Economics at the Michigan State University and professor at Kings College, University of London and his research is primarily in the areas of time series econometrics and international finance. He lives in Putney, London and East Lansing, Michigan.*

The Enfield College of Technology (ECT) campus may have had some detractors; but I had nothing to compare it with when I first saw it in 1966. It was neither good nor bad in my eyes, just an anonymous three or four storey building off the Southbury Road, in Enfield. I was a naïve eighteen year old who had spent all of his sheltered life in the confines of Barnet, north London and the small Hertfordshire town of Potters Bar. I had made a visit to Essex University for an interview but my poor A-level results had left me with no clear future in August of 1966. My pure mathematics teacher, Donald Toms at Mount Grace comprehensive School in Potters Bar had sufficient faith in me to suggest I stay on at school for a further year to retake the A-level exams. Donald Toms also spoke to one of his other mathematics-teaching colleagues, Vic Marchesi, who had personal contacts at ECT. Based on their efforts, I was admitted to the Mathematics for Business degree at Enfield in 1966. I remain eternally grateful to Donald Toms and especially to Vic Marchesi for their help in engineering my going to Enfield.

Higher Education in the UK

In the 1960s only about 5 per cent of the eighteen year old cohort went into higher education, and, in my eyes, the UK higher education system was divided into several strata from Oxbridge downwards. The system was hierarchical with a certain amount of snobbery with regard to the rankings of institutions.

When I first went to the US in 1979 I worked at Wayne State University in downtown Detroit and was struck by the very wide open access to higher education with over 40 per cent of the eighteen year age cohort going to higher education of one form or another. Furthermore, most of the degree courses were multidisciplinary in nature, the transferring of credits between colleges and universities and the opportunity to work part-time as a student were all common practice. In short, the system was extremely flexible and there existed a vast range of types of institutions from community colleges, state universities, liberal arts colleges, private universities, etc. I wonder how Tony Crosland and Eric Robinson would have regarded the US system? In many ways it appeared to represent virtually all of their goals.

One other feature of the US higher education system, which has been different to the UK system, is the fee differential between different universities and colleges. For example, liberal arts colleges such as Williams, Swarthmore and Oberlin aim to provide very specialist high quality undergraduate teaching with very small class sizes and faculty members who specialise in teaching rather than research. Fees for undergraduate courses at these select liberal arts colleges are generally considerably more than fees at the major research orientated state universities. So market forces are allowed to play a large role, with a substantial premium on small class sizes and specialist teaching at the undergraduate level. In the US the arguments for high participation rates in higher education were framed in terms of increasing personal opportunities and increasing human capital and was presented as beneficial for the country and society.

Writing in 2018 we see there have been enormous changes in all the UK higher education institutions. Polytechnics have been granted university status and in general it appears that many university degree programs have become more vocational and practical and many ex-polytechnics have sought to become more pure in academic terms. So the objectives of these institutions have gradually merged. Overall, I believe these changes have been positive with now over 33 per cent of the eighteen-year-olds in the UK participating in some form of higher education. Now funding has become an issue. Government funding with only 5 per cent participation rate was trivial in the 1970s compared with trying to finance 33 per cent with accompanying high national debt and record private sector debt.

The Enfield Experiment: 1966-1970

As Enfield students, we were conscious that we were in the vanguard of some new experiment that would challenge the current status quo of higher education and might provide better education in some sense than the traditional universities. Most of the staff on the BSc in Mathematics for Business degree seemed to be genuinely concerned with the welfare of the students and the quality of the degree course. CNAA degrees were relatively new and I remember it being stated that the staff were more focused on teaching as opposed to research compared with a university. To further reinforce the idea of these people's universities being practically orientated there was the concept of a sandwich degree where one year of a four-year degree course was spent in industry. This idea seemed to originate in the CATs and is still used by some ex-CAT universities, such as Bath and Surrey today.

Following my time at Enfield, I became an assistant statistician in the Civil Service and they sponsored me to be a cadet statistician, so that I could take a one-year MSc course in Statistics. I chose to go to the University of Kent at Canterbury, or UKC as it was known. The general environment of Canterbury was another world after Enfield and Ponders End. For one thing, the terms were known as Michaelmas, Lent and Trinity and walking across the campus for a nine o'clock lecture in November I will always remember the spires of the cathedral appearing through the mist below the hill of the campus of UKC; a really wonderful sight. Another student on the Mathematics for Business degree, Graeme Blanchard also began at Kent at the same time as me and took an MA degree course in Economics. We took some joint courses, including econometrics, and at times we were made to feel slightly uncomfortable from the reaction of staff, or other students, when we were asked where our first degrees were from. However, we soon became convinced that our undergraduate training was at least the equal of many of those students whom had been to more established universities. So when we were confronted by questions concerning our previous degree, we started to refer to Enfield Tech as UEPE, i.e. the University of Enfield at Ponders End. Then once we had discovered that the nearby Wye College in Kent was a distant outpost of the University of London; we daringly referred to Enfield Tech as 'Enfield College, Cambridge'. However, we recognized that coming from ECT, or Enfield, was nothing to be ashamed of, quite the contrary in fact.

In appearance the physical environment of Enfield was clearly fairly drab and rather depressing. There was no beauty there. Office space for staff seemed extremely limited with temporary huts being used. However, there was Ossie's café where I and my student friends spent many a happy hour talking over cups of Ossie's strong tea. The Enfield student body was a rather disparate group and included many part-time and full-time engineering students wearing jackets and ties, mixed in with a smaller group of flower power orientated sociology students studying London External degrees. It seemed that most of the students, at least 85 per cent, were male, which was disappointing. There was widespread sympathy for the external London degree students whose chances of getting a good degree were regarded as much lower than those students studying for CNAA degrees.

The late 1960s and especially 1968, were of course eras of radical changes, exciting music and challenges to the political system. While not Essex or LSE, Enfield nevertheless had its moments, with the local NUS calling college-wide meetings to debate the many new political ideas of the time. There were some local issues at Enfield involving, I think, student files, and there were much wider issues of the 'LSE gates', and Danny Cohn-Bendit and the student disturbances in Paris. Some Enfield students inevitably became heavily involved with the local NUS.

***Mathematics for Business degree*.**

However, there was a good creative academic spirit present in many of the staff and students. Also, the late 1960s was an exciting time of change and fresh ideas in many areas and Enfield benefited from these influences. One of the distinguishing features of the Mathematics for Business course was the attempt to be really *inter*disciplinary in nature as opposed to being merely *multi*disciplinary. Hence instead of just offering different and almost unrelated courses, the Enfield experiment focused on course units meshing in with one another and the topics in a course reinforcing those in other course units. This obviously required very careful planning and cooperation, but I believe succeeded in many cases. As such, the degree was probably ahead of its time and broke down many conventional boundaries.

Also, much of the teaching on the BSc Mathematics for Business degree was genuinely first rate. In particular there was Alan Cox, who taught various courses on probability and statistics. I believe he had been very influenced by taking an MSc course at Birkbeck taught by David Cox, who is generally recognized as being one of the truly great statisticians of the twentieth century. Certainly Alan Cox's courses and notes were extremely clear and were very influential for my subsequent interests in the subject. Raj Vasudeva also taught courses on inferential statistics which I thought were good.

The pure mathematicians at Enfield were Tony Crilly, Allan Findlay, Ivor Grattan-Guinness, Margery Reinhart and Sarah Lofthouse. Ivor Grattan–Guinness was primarily interested in the history of analysis, and his courses on mathematical analysis were at quite a high level and relatively abstract. I remember in one of the earliest lectures he used Newton's original terminology of fluxions and fluents when describing differential calculus. The book assigned for the course by Apostol was formidable and rather intimidating for many of us taking the course. At some stage I came across a book by Spiegel (1962), *Advanced Calculus* in the Schaum Outline Series. The front cover of the book, which I still possess, proudly states that it contains '925 solved problems, completely solved in detail.' I found this text to be extremely helpful since it contained detailed examples of calculating Fourier series expansions or Riemann integrals for particular mathematical functions. Suddenly I found myself understanding the theory in Ivor's course. At one tutorial Ivor saw me carrying the Spiegel book and appeared to be horrified that I would read something so 'non-rigorous'. Nevertheless, I think Spiegel's book enabled me to pass the Analysis examinations at Enfield! Years later I independently came across Ivor Grattan-Guinness's writings on synchronicity and related work.

In 1992 I walked into Ivor in a bar at the London Coliseum during an interval of an operatic performance. This started quite a long friendship and in 2005 I invited and arranged for Ivor to come to Michigan State University for a few days to give two seminars on the history of Jevons and some area of statistics. We frequently used to meet for lunch at UCL and on these trips to London, Ivor would often visit the Masonic library for research into the history of mathematics. He was a remarkably independently minded and determined researcher and always provided stimulating conversation at these lunches.

I think Allan Findlay was primarily interested in logic and philosophy. He taught linear algebra and for a while was acting head of department. As head he seemed very kindly towards the students and seemed to genuinely care for them. He was also extremely thoughtful and would ponder and consider any idea carefully before replying. I remember he would sometimes take students and secretaries out for lunch and listen attentively to the students' views. His level of concern and decency towards the students was really quite exceptional and may have been partly due to his thinking that many of us 'university rejects' required special help and time for us to be successful. Allan also seemed to genuinely enjoy talking with us.

Tony Crilly also taught linear algebra in my second year. One of the many good aspects of Tony's course was that it was extremely well integrated with the course on mathematical programming given in the final year by Gautam Appa. Both courses used books by Hadley with vector-based notation and were very clear and even exciting to see linear programming explained so well. This is in contrast to a course I took at Kent which illustrated very clearly that the simplex method (for Linear Programming) is hard to explain. With linear algebra it all becomes very clear.

Another very memorable lecturer at Enfield was Stanley Millward who gave superbly organised courses on numerical analysis. Even in 1966 Stan could be described as *old school*. Everything about him was immaculate; including his appearance in neat suits, sometimes with white coats to avoid the plague of chalk dust, his very precise notes and examples on the board, his delivery and lecturing style. He was a true professional and a delight to take a course from; he was also exceptionally courteous towards all the students. I did not know him really, but sensed that he was a remarkable man. Raj Kapoor also provided good computer-based course. He was also a very kindly and well-disposed lecturer, gave a computer BASIC course which complemented Stan's numerical methods course.

The economics teaching was in the hands of Sami Daniels, Sally Holtermann and Ruth Towse. The micro theory course was quite high level and it was based on the book by Henderson and Quandt and required optimization theory and multivariate calculus. This course was very clearly delivered by Sally Holtermann and it dovetailed well with the advanced calculus courses we were studying simultaneously. These days game theory would be substituted for much of the optimization theory; but the micro theory from Sally was very up to date for the time.

However, somehow I seem to have completely missed out on macroeconomics! I know it was taught at Enfield, but it made no impression on me. The time I really got to understand macroeconomics was when I was lecturing at Wayne State University in 1979 to second year undergraduates and learnt the material myself, including the details of the basic Keynesian IS-LM model which I believe still remains an ideal way for teaching macroeconomics to second year undergraduates. However, I don't really think I developed any economic intuition or learned to think like an economist at Enfield. This skill really requires more introductory courses based around real world economic issues of the day.

Patrick McMahon (1939-1993) was full-time at Enfield in 1967-68 and then part-time in 1970. He taught courses in econometrics and combined enthusiasm with great eccentricity and he also had a big influence on me personally. I well remember his first lecture, which was on the econometric estimation of the consumption function when he took ten minutes in the middle of the lecture to describe how some Irishmen who were regulars at the Springbok pub in Shepherds Bush had a low marginal propensity to save and would break chairs over each other's heads in fights outside the pub. It is strange how odd little jokes and anecdotes in lectures can have such an impact on students and stay in your mind for almost fifty years! I also remember Patrick telling us about the Gauss Markov Theorem and saying that we should know the assumptions 'inside out, backwards, upside down and sideways'. He often repeated this phrase and it stuck in my mind. I subsequently heard another Irish person use the phrase in connection with the *Catechism.* Another feature of Patrick that I remember were some rather amusing examination questions that he set. For example: 'Two econometricians meet, Econometrician A says 'Two stage least squares is a special case of instrumental variables'. Econometrician B says 'No, instrumental variables is a special case of two stage least squares.' Discuss.'

Years later in 1976 when I was a PhD student at LSE and attending my first ever academic conference in Helsinki, I met Patrick again. Then in 1977 I moved to the University of Aston in Birmingham and in 1981 I became one of his colleagues at the University of Birmingham. From 1977 onwards we enjoyed a long friendship and productive relationship; we actually co-authored and published one book, (Baillie and McMahon, 1989) and nine articles in academic journals. We helped each other in different ways and Patrick's sudden and unexpected death in 1993 was a big blow for his family and friends such as me and Anne my wife, as we had shared so many experiences with him. He was a remarkable man in many ways who really loved academic life, research and education in the broadest sense. He came from a Gaelic speaking background on the west coast of Ireland and was the eldest of seven and managed to escape a poor background by becoming a student at Trinity College Dublin and subsequently at Oxford and Birmingham. He appreciated the fact that Enfield was in the vanguard in broadening higher education in the UK and he encouraged his siblings and children in the same way. He also had expert knowledge of wine and classical music.

Operational Research was clearly a difficult subject to recruit staff and in the first year Terry Butfield gave good courses on networks, critical path analysis, practical simulation methods, etc. He and Aviva Weingarten also worked afterwards in British Airways. In my first two years at Enfield I thought OR would eventually be my chosen career. In my final year I actually interviewed for a job at the National Coal Board's OR department. My father who was rather risk averse, was apprehensive about the potential job, since he prophetically believed the coal industry would be in decline and that the NCB would not be secure employment. As it transpired, I was not offered the job.

For much of the time I was at Enfield, Bill Craze was the head of department. He seemed very energetic and always seemed to be concerned about the students and making sure the courses were going well. In fact he was the apparent powerhouse behind the course and was involved with the CNAA and overall administration of the Mathematics for Business course.

Sandwich Year of the Mathematics for Business Degree

I would think that organizing a sandwich degree and finding appropriate placements for students in their third year could be very difficult. I eventually got placed at the British Oxygen Company in Cricklewood and I also occasionally worked in their office in Hammersmith. Much of the work was clerical and quite mundane in nature involving tabulating sales data. We were also required to make forecasts of future sales revenue from selling gas containers and various welding products. There were some elementary calculating machines and I managed to perform some regressions of sales on so-called leading indicators, like lagged GDP. There was also a program on the calculating machines for exponential smoothing forecasts. In a strange way this led to my subsequent research career. It seemed pretty obvious that simple exponential smoothing was a very sub-optimal way of using the past history of sales to produce forecasts. I found this very interesting and started to read a book by R. G. Brown (1962) on higher forms of exponential smoothing. While considerably more general, it still seemed to require guesswork on the part of the user and did not really have any satisfactory statistical method for model selection. Then I came across the works of Box and Jenkins, and during the Christmas vacation, I spent a few days in the Imperial College Library reading their various journal articles that were partly statistical and partly control engineering. Then their book appeared in 1970 and this really changed my life and career as I will explain later. In fact for many months I would always take the book and read parts of it on the underground on my way to work in the civil service. So, in Patrick's words, I got to know it inside out, backwards, upside down and sideways.

Early Academic Career: Mostly in the UK

After leaving Kent, or UKC, in November 1971, I started work in the Central Statistical Office in Whitehall. I spent almost three years working in the division on production data and Input-Output analysis. Then in 1974 I was moved to their research section and I then had the opportunity to pursue some issues on time series analysis again. This turned out to be a great opportunity for me since Jim Durbin, a professor of statistics at the London School of Economics (LSE), was a consultant in the research section of the Central Statistical Office. The topics of seasonal adjustment, trend estimation and forecasting were regarded as important areas for us to work on. I took the opportunity to go to LSE and registered as a part-time MPhil student. I took some econometric courses at LSE and started to do work in my spare time on time series and econometric prediction problems. Eventually LSE transferred my registration to that of PhD.

The Civil Service had a policy of transferring statistician and economist staff every two or three years and in the summer of 1976 I was assigned to be moved from the research section, which by then felt like home for me and I was reluctant to leave. Most of the possible jobs were really administrative in nature and I felt that after five years in the Civil Service that this was the time to leave. At that time my ambitions were very limited. My ideal would be to have remained the rest of my career as a lecturer in some part of the University of London and I had no particular desire to leave London where most of my and my wife Anne's family and friends lived. I had no idea that getting my PhD and being an academic would propel me on to a totally new way of life that involved great joy at times, some conflict and also becoming a world traveller. I also am reminded of Henry Kissinger's remark that 'academic politics are so vicious because the stakes are so small.' But if you spend so much time and energy researching a topic the issues seem extremely important.

I left the Civil Service and after a few months working on my PhD full-time, there followed a few months in Manchester, before I obtained a lectureship in econometrics at the University of Aston in Birmingham in 1977 and I completed my LSE PhD in the summer of 1978. At Aston I was in a small group of statisticians and economists in a management centre which was not particularly academic. The flagship course was a BSc in Managerial and Administrative Studies with an intake of about 160 students a year. However, the mathematical content was very low compared to the Enfield Mathematics for Business course. The Aston degree was also a sandwich course with the third year spent in industry. The one professor of economics at Aston insisted on teaching an extraordinary introductory economics course that contained virtually no concepts and was based around the government National Income Accounts Blue Book. It was the most boring and uninspiring way imaginable to teach economics and not surprisingly very few students continued with economics as an option after the first year. I taught a second year course on econometrics and had between six and twelve students.

By this time I was in regular contact with Patrick McMahon, who was just down the road in Edgbaston at the University of Birmingham. Patrick knew that Wayne State University in Detroit was looking for a time-series econometrician and David Smyth (1936-2015) was the chair of the Wayne State department and had been a colleague of Patrick's at Birmingham some years before. Consequently I went to Detroit for an interview, the first time I had ever been to the US and managed to take unpaid leave of absence from Aston and start at Wayne in September 1979. The year was a great success in virtually every way and Anne and I loved it. I could have stayed on at Wayne and it was with very mixed feelings and rather heavy hearts that Anne and I returned to Birmingham in October 1980.

All seemed to be doom and gloom on the academic front in the UK at that time with the beginnings of the cuts in higher education following the election of the Thatcher government. Fortunately, the University of Birmingham was advertising a lectureship and I managed to get the job, although right until the last moment there was a possibility that it would not be funded! So, I quickly resigned from Aston and started work at Birmingham in early 1981. I was in the Department of Economics at Birmingham and it had a strong research culture and much less teaching than Aston. There had been some very famous people in the department over the years, but the department was in a definite decline before I went there. Overall, I had some good times there and the premier degree was a BSc in Mathematics, Economics and Statistics, which had quite a lot in common with the Enfield Mathematics for Business course but without the sandwich year. Aston was in an industrial and grimy part of the northern side of the city and was surrounded by the motorways that had been constructed around the city. The University of Birmingham in contrast was in the leafy southern suburb of Edgbaston near Selly Oak and the Quaker Bournville estate. So my move in 1981 was reminiscent of transferring from Ponders End to Canterbury in 1970!

Incidentally, David Smyth, the chairperson of the Economics department at Wayne State became a great friend and was also briefly associated with Enfield twenty years later. When he was just short of sixty, David suffered a severe stroke and ended up retiring from Louisiana State University, where he had been working. He made a relatively miraculous recovery and two years later was offered a research chair at Middlesex and was based at the Hendon campus. He bought a house in Hendon and knew many of the people at Enfield such as Ivor Grattan-Guinness. Unfortunately David was not quite the same man as in his pre-stroke days and his wonderful sense of humour and approach to life were slightly different. David was forced to retire when he turned sixty-five and I went to his retirement party at Hendon and fortunately reconnected with many of the Enfield staff again.

Later Academic Career: Mostly in the US

The academic environment continued to be quite poor in the UK in the early 1980s and there were constant rumours of departments being closed and of academic job losses at Birmingham. By 1985 I was getting itchy feet; I was publishing quite a lot and was being sounded out for some interesting possible academic jobs in Canada and the USA. So, without really meaning to, I was getting into the academic rat race. Also, we had been living in Birmingham for about seven years and needed a change. In the Fall of 1985 I became a visiting associate professor at the University of Toronto and then in 1986 was a visiting professor at the University of California San Diego (UCSD), where I met Clive Granger and Rob Engle, who were both recipients of the Nobel Prize in 2003 for their work on time series econometrics. It was a very fortuitous move for me since it changed my area of research and gave my work a big impetus.

Since that time I have mainly been at Michigan State University (MSU) in East Lansing which is attached to Lansing, which is the state capital of Michigan and is relatively close to Detroit. I have generally been in the Department of Economics and for part of the time had a joint appointment with the Department of Finance in the

Business School. I was given an endowed chair in 1999 which has involved slightly reduced teaching and some other perks. MSU have also been generous about giving me unpaid leave of absence so that I could be a part-time professor at Queen Mary University of London and more recently at King's College in University of London. This has satisfied our desire to spend more time in London and Europe. It is strange how life develops; Anne and I have been dual citizens for many years and are pretty much equally at home in either country. East Lansing is a peaceful place with a sizeable intellectual and academic community, while Putney has the advantage of being close to the river and many commons and all the attractions and chaos of life in the congested city of London.

In terms of research my career has been as multidisciplinary as the Enfield Mathematics for Business degree course. I started off as a theoretical econometrician working on time series prediction and model specification issues. It was obvious at the time that after the work of Box and Jenkins (1970) there was a huge need for modern time series methods to be incorporated into the specification and estimation of econometric models. Hence the methods used by Box and Jenkins needed to be extended to a multivariate setting, which at the same time incorporated restrictions from economic theory. So this was a great area to work on in the 1970s and 1980s. Then Patrick McMahon and I together with Bob Lippens, who was a mature PhD student at Wayne State, published a paper on testing rational expectations in financial markets. This arose out of conversations with Bob Lippens about the underpinnings and implications of the popular monetary model of exchange rate determination. Our paper, (Baillie, Lippens and McMahon, 1983) used a general multivariate time series representation and provided a framework for testing these theories with high frequency data. Fortunately for us the paper received a lot of attention and generated a lot of citations. This got me more involved with more macroeconomic issues and also with financial markets and led me to do a lot of applied work in the area.

Another main area I have worked in was the idea of modelling volatility in economic time series and my time at UCSD started my interest in the area. These contributions have generally been quite applied and have been concerned with estimating economic models of risk premium and various quantities used in financial economics. Then in the mid-1990 I did a lot of work on long memory processes which are a flexible type of stationary, or almost, or not quite stationary time series process with a lot of interesting properties – see (Baillie, 1996). In particular these models are now widely used in fields as diverse as climatology, electrical engineering and financial market volatility or spreads in maturity times of bonds. They also represent processes that have been subjected to certain types of structural change. Much of my work in this area has been concerned with applications. However, I have also got involved in theoretical disputes as to the type of methodology, a kind of debate which seems to come with the territory in academia.

When I look back at my career I see that many of research publications have involved technical points improving econometric practice and with many applications. I rather wish I could have done more on influencing policy and been really applied. Perhaps it is not too late for this? I am also trying to finish a book that I have been working on for fifteen years. As I have become more mature, I have become more concerned and critical of the goals of much of the research going on. However, overall I think there is still important work being done.

I have no regrets about being an academic researcher in statistics and economics. It has been very satisfying to do creative work and to be associated with others working in this area. I have made some wonderful academic friends all over the world. I like going to conferences and travelling to far-flung places. With the Internet I find, like most other academics, that I rely less and less on colleagues in the same department or university as me. I currently have co-authors all over the world.

At the same time, I have in all honesty had to pay the price for being in the academic rat race. Grinding out as many papers as possible from each idea has been necessary to stay in the race, while there have been times when I wish I had been more adventurous and tried different areas to work on. The publishing game has generally got harder with longer refereeing time and more competition with more people working in the same field. Publishing a paper in a good journal still gives me a burst of adrenaline and positive endomorphins and rejections from journals can still feel like a kick in the teeth. The nature of research has speeded up it seems in the sense that ideas and new methods do not seem to remain fashionable for as long as in the old days.

The Future and Concluding Remarks

In the thirty-nine years since I was awarded my PhD I can see that universities have fundamentally changed, not always in desirable ways. Funding from the state and federal levels have been greatly reduced in the US leading to more emphasis on grant awards, endowments, and cash-producing courses especially in business schools. This has tended to make the job more pressurized. I have seen similar phenomena in the UK and for some time at Queen Mary University of London where the department of Economics was recruiting 600 students for MSc courses a year, with the incentive to have as many overseas students as possible since they paid three times the fee of domestic students. Not surprisingly, it has been very hard for many universities to recruit reasonable quality students given the intense competition for students from universities fighting for income. Apart from teaching graduate courses in various aspects of econometrics or asset pricing I have also taught a second year undergraduate course at MSU titled, 'Introduction to International Economics.' I have enjoyed making this course more policy and current problem orientated since I noticed that the students have become less tolerant of theoretical models. Sometimes I have classes as large as 280 and it is a challenge to stimulate the students who seem to find concentration increasingly hard. So short films and jokes have to be included with the lectures.

After all the above experiences, I have come to believe that the Mathematics for Business degree at Enfield was pretty much the ideal course for me. I needed something multidisciplinary and it somehow suited my mind which tends to roam across topics. Enfield also provided solid teaching by a group of lecturers who were committed to the students. The Enfield experience has also probably contributed to my own desire to break down boundaries between departments and to promote the modular approach in universities where I have worked.

14. How I learned to teach

RUTH TOWSE

> ***Ruth Towse*** *began work at Enfield as a Lecturer in September 1966, teaching economics on the Mathematics for Business, Business Studies courses, and to engineering students. She left Middlesex Polytechnic in 1983 and after a decade of part-time academic and research appointments, she joined Erasmus University Rotterdam becoming Professor in Economics of Creative Industries in 2006. In 2007 she was appointed to a professorship at Bournemouth University, a position she still holds. She is also CREATe Fellow in Cultural Economics at University of Glasgow and from 2018, she joins a research project at the University of Oslo. She lives in a village on the edge of Dartmoor and is active in the local community.*

Somewhere in late Spring of 1966, I had a phone call from Sami Daniel asking me if I would consider applying for a Lectureship in Economics at Enfield College of Technology. Sami and I had been firm friends since our days together at London School of Economics doing the MSc (Econ), which he completed in 1965 and went to work at Enfield but I took my time and finished in 1966. Our friendship began when Sami asked me (one of only three women on the MSc course of sixty-five students) if I would take part in the LSE Weekend cabaret, which I did, to the great amusement of Mark Blaug, whom I had recently met and with whom I went to Margate for this splendid event.

In this phone call, it transpired that the application date was the next day and that Sami had in fact kindly filled out the application form and signed it for me. I could hardly refuse! I was in fact fairly well qualified as I had already done some teaching at the College of Estate Management, the Brixton School of Building and at LSE as a class tutor (which in fact revealed how little I really knew!). My first degree from the University of Reading in Political Economy had barely prepared me for the rigours of the MSc (Econ) – but I struggled along! Soon after the phone call I was called for interview, about which I remember very little except that I was asked by a local councillor on the board whether I planned to get married (to which I obviously answered no!).

It all seemed so easy – and indeed it was. The LSE MSc (Econ) was the first taught master's degree in economics and it coincided with the expansion of the university sector, the development of the Economics Group in the civil service and the potential for degree teaching in local education colleges which were soon to become polytechnics. Already in 1966, Enfield had developed two degrees which required economics: Mathematics for Business and Business Studies and I taught on both. My first lecture, however, was to about 200 engineers whose interest in macroeconomics seemed relatively slight! Of course, this was all chalk on blackboard stuff – key points were written in chalk and the first thing one had to do on entering the classroom was to wipe off the former teacher's efforts. I hated chalk! (Some of the engineering lecturers, I remember, used to wear a nylon jacket for teaching so as to avoid it getting in their clothing). We social scientists were rather scathing of them – and they spent the lunchtime playing cards! Before photocopying came along, there was an interim type of machine that used purple ink, which got on one's fingers and clothes which was hardly an improvement, though the thing allowed you to give hand-outs to students.

'We social scientists' were initially sociologists and economists between whom there were the inevitable doctrinal disputes. Like us economists, several of whom knew each other from LSE (including my long-time friend from those days, Sally Holtermann, with whom I shared an office for several years), the sociologists were also recently hired. Already in the growing economics group were Tom Evans the Head of the Economics Group and John Stoddart (whom I knew from my days at University of Reading). Looking back, I realise we had some impressive colleagues.[32] We all had to pull together despite our differences of approach on these new

---

[32] Colleagues in other subjects included Ivor Grattan-Guinness, who was recognized as the leading historian of mathematics: see https://www.theguardian.com/education/2014/dec/31/ivor-grattan-guinness and Stanley Cohen whose work in sociology and criminology was highly acclaimed; see https://www.theguardian.com/education/2013/jan/23/stanley-cohen. Tom Evans, who moved to the London Business School early on, died tragically young.

degree courses for two reasons: one was the ever-present Dean of the Faculty, Eric Robinson and the other was the CNAA (Council for National Academic Awards). I later came to fully recognize the debt I and others owe Eric.[33] He refused to allow us to simply teach our subjects as we had learned them; we had to adapt what we taught to the degree course and to the other disciplinary courses. He was loyally backed by the Principal, Dr Brosan. When the BA Social Science degree got going a few years later, we all had to take tutorial classes in each subject taught in the first year – including philosophy, sociology and land use studies. As I have spent most of my academic career in multi-disciplinary departments I fully appreciate those early (if aggravating) lessons in how to teach non-specialists.

The CNAA was another source of irritation! In the pre-polytechnic days it awarded the degrees and monitored the syllabuses and the exams. University professors, whom we knew from recent experience did not always live up to the high standards they now set us, came along to check out that we had read the works on our reading lists etc. These luminaries included Mark Blaug with whom I was by then living! Mark was also an external examiner for quite a while on the Social Science degree and was always very impressed with the teaching quality, especially in statistics. I had served for a year on the academic board of the soon-to-be-Middlesex Polytechnic; it seemed almost unworkable at the time, but one advantage we perceived was that we could regulate our own degrees and loosen the grip of the CNAA.

Another memory I have of those early days was that we were excused four hours' teaching as research time. I was registered for PhD at LSE with Megnad Desai (now the Lord Desai) on the measurement of technical progress. I did a lot of reading for it when a book came out that dealt with everything I'd thought of and more besides, so I gave up. Research days on Friday were very popular. (I had to do my PhD when I moved to the Netherlands in 1999 as it is required by Dutch university law for a permanent appointment; by then I had sufficient articles to put together as a book, which then had to be defended in public).

---

33 https://www.theguardian.com/education/2011/mar/09/eric-robinson-obituary

In 1969, Mark (whose post was in Economics of Education at the Institute of Education, University of London) was hired by the Ford Foundation to go to Thailand for a year to work with Thai civil servants on their educational planning strategy. Thailand was then a closed country and we got married so that I could go with him. During the year, I taught at Thammasat University along with the Rockefeller professors who had started a Masters degree taught in English there. It was an interesting though difficult experience. I had had unpaid leave for the year abroad and resumed my Lectureship in September 1970, when we returned. I was by then expecting my son (born in April, 1971). It transpired that under local authority rules (and Enfield was still a College of Technology at the time), pregnant women were required to withdraw after the fifth month! I was not the only pregnant woman at the time and basically we defied the rule but I was not paid after a certain time (and I cannot now remember when). I know I finished the academic year, teaching while pregnant and then marking examinations after the birth. However, I was by then fed up with the same old teaching and disgusted with treatment I'd had so I resigned and I spent the next year and a half at home.

The next phase of my serendipitous hiring at Middlesex came when Mark bumped into Klaus Heidensohn, then Head of Economics, who asked if I would be interested in going back to work there! I said I would on a 0.4 FTE basis as long as I could teach something new. I was offered a course in Location Theory as part of the Social Science degree and took it on. As there was no crèche (1972/3), I arranged home care for our son and had about four hours a week for preparing lectures in a new subject and doing all the other routine work, such as marking, so it was quite a challenge. I think that turned me into being fully professional. I also taught on a new course that enabled mature students without A-level to join the BA Social Science degree if they passed (I cannot remember the title). That course was located at Trent Park – a notable change of venue from the 'grot' of Enfield! I also started having singing lessons at that time and eventually had hopes of becoming a professional singer – soon to be brought down to earth (though I had a good crack at it and a wonderful time!).

I left finally in 1983, being well 'sent-off' by Bryan Davies, who was then MP for Enfield North (and now Lord Davies of Oldham!), with whom I had worked in the early days. My kind colleagues gave me an excellent recording of the Barber of Seville, which I still have. By then, however, my old friends from the 'early days' had left long ago: Sally Holtermann to the London Business School and then the Civil Service and Sami Daniel to Kingston Polytechnic. It did not seem quite the same! Nevertheless, I had seventeen years at the now Middlesex University.

After some years of doing various research jobs, I got a Leverhulme grant and wrote a book on the economics of the singing profession (*Singers in the Marketplace*). After that, I started to work on cultural economics and am still doing so (at present revising my *Textbook in Cultural Economics* for a 2nd edition). I now specialise in economics of copyright and am very active professionally in that area. I had to retire in 2008 due to my age from Erasmus University Rotterdam, to which I had moved in 1999.[34] We returned to UK and Mark died in 2011 and I continue to live in Peter Tavy on the edge of Dartmoor in Devon, to which we moved in 1988. I have been Professor of Economics in Creative Industries at Bournemouth University in the Centre for Intellectual Property Policy and Management since 2007 and am also CREATe Fellow in Cultural Economics, University of Glasgow. I am busier than ever with publishing, workshops, conferences, summer schools and intend to keep it that way for as long as I am able to.

---

[34] As a university teacher I was Dutch civil servant and at the time, prior to the EU 'Age' Directive, all civil servants had to retire at sixty-five.

15. It was a long time ago

SALLY HOLTERMANN

Sally Holtermann *was a Lecturer in Economics at Enfield from 1966 to 1970, teaching mainly on the Mathematics for Business degree course. Following two years at the London Graduate School of Business Studies, she moved to the Department of the Environment as an Economic Adviser and later Senior Economic Adviser. In 1981 she left London to live on a working farm in mid-Wales, and from there she worked as a freelance economist until her pensions arrived and volunteering took over. She enjoys growing vegetables and wildflowers, making fruit wine, visiting Italy and playing with her two granddaughters, who live nearby.*

I was at Enfield for four years from 1966 until 1970 and I taught economics on the Mathematics for Business degree course. When I started I was twenty-four and it was my first ever 'proper' job, after doing a BSc (Econ) and MSc (Econ) at LSE. In those days of rapid expansion of higher education it was relatively easy for graduates to get good jobs, especially if they had a Masters degree. There was no need for research or teaching experience, no need for a PhD and no need for teacher training.

Working life

I lived in Swiss Cottage and I commuted out to Enfield. There was little traffic compared with today and few traffic calming measures, and I drove much too fast – 60 miles an hour down Bishop's Avenue! The college buildings, I now realise (because, doing a Google search, I find they are listed), were quite distinguished. The car park was scruffy, but I loved the bindweed climbing up the wire netting fence around it and producing massive white flowers in the summer.

Our offices were in the 'huts', lines of temporary buildings put up to house the expanding staff. They were basic and not beautiful, but adequate. I shared with Ruth Towse. One year we organised the planting of daffodil bulbs around the huts, and someone told me many years later that they were still there, though I doubt they are now.

Office technology was primitive, no computers and no typewriters except in the typing pool. Was there a telephone in the office? Was there a photocopying machine in the college? I remember reproducing student handouts on the college Banda machine, which produced copious amounts of mucky blue ink as a by-product, usually on my hands.

The college had adopted a tutorial system, which meant that we saw students in pairs in our office and there were, I think, no classes outside lectures. We gave conventional lectures, though I remember in our first year Ruth, with some imagination, devised an 'experiment' which we carried out with new students. We asked hypothetical questions about how much beer they would drink a week if the price were £x per pint, then variations around that price. Not very scientific but the students loved it and they generated a pretty good downward-sloping demand curve.

In tutorials the students were often shy and lacking in confidence and it was hard to get them to express themselves. How much more effective it would have been to have classes, as we'd had at LSE, where the few students with confidence could dominate, as usually happens, leaving the quieter ones to be how they wanted to be – quiet, while still learning. I often ended up, in effect, giving the recent lecture all over again in order to help them through. But perhaps that reflected my own shortcomings as a teacher. I found it hard work. It is surprising how tiring it is to talk a lot. I used to get mouth ulcers by Christmas, though that was perhaps also the effect of the nasty cigarettes I smoked. I've just had the horrible thought that we actually smoked in those offices. I'm sure that wouldn't be allowed now. Or at least it shouldn't be. Not just for health reasons, but those prefabricated huts must have been a fire hazard. Did we have fire extinguishers?

There was a college dining room but Ruth and I mostly used to go for sandwiches in a nearby pub not frequented by college staff. I'm not sure why. Perhaps the food in the college was awful, but the sandwiches weren't very special either, and by going off like that I think we must have cut ourselves off from a lot of the socialising and intellectual interaction that went on in the college. To be truthful, student contact hours were low – the figure of thirteen hours per week is stuck in my mind – and I wasn't actually in the college for a lot of the time as I did lecture preparation and marking at home. Some staff put much more into college life. There was a staff magazine and a couple of years ago I found an old copy, along with other mouldy papers, in a damp corner of the spare bedroom. It had articles by Bill Craze, Simon Stander, Julian Ayer (along with photographs of them) and others. I put it out for recycling thinking I'd never need it again. I didn't even read it. I'm so sorry. Moral: never throw anything away unless you have to.

We weren't much older than the students, and the distinction between staff and students was blurred in a way that wouldn't be approved of now. This was the swinging 60s. I remember great student/staff parties, and dancing to the Rolling Stones' *I Can't Get No Satisfaction*, wearing a very short dress. I remember one female colleague wearing at work a diaphanous gown that concealed little. How did the eighteen-year-old college boys cope? That makes me wonder: does anyone have any statistics on the gender balance among our students? My recollections tell me that there were very few girls.

We had sit-ins when it was the time of student unrest and demands for student representation on college bodies. We (that is Ruth and I and many of the staff) were sympathetic and took them seriously and I remember visiting Hornsey College of Art, which was more prominent in the protests, and eventually became part of the Middlesex Polytechnic. People from outside Hornsey were allowed to observe but not take part in the debates. In retrospect it seems extraordinary that college authorities opposed student involvement.

I taught mathematical economics on the Mathematics for Business course. My boss was the mathematician Bill Craze. Bill was very supportive and patient with his young staff. In my case he needed to be and I'm grateful. I think that Mathematics for Business was already an up-and-running degree course when I arrived but I'm vague about that. I think the syllabus was already written, but maybe it was still under development, and maybe I had a part in that. I remember some jubilation, especially of course from Bill, when we got CNAA approval. I remember external examiners' meetings, and perhaps some of those had to do with development of the syllabus. Rather than the big issues, small details have stuck in my mind. One in particular, of an external examiner – an ambitious and soon-to-be eminent economist – carefully folding his raincoat inside out and putting it over a chair so that the Harrods label showed.

Economics for undergraduates

In retrospect I wonder what we did to our students. I was young and inexperienced, and in teaching and course development all I could do was pass on what I had only just learnt (and in some areas hadn't learnt too well). The mathematisation of economics was already well under way in academic economics in the 1960s, and as an undergraduate with A-level mathematics I was naturally channelled in that direction, and it suited my inclinations. At the time I finished my Masters I really didn't know much else. When I started teaching at Enfield I had no research experience of my own and little teaching experience. I hadn't had time to absorb and evaluate what I had been taught at LSE. I just reproduced it. I would want to design a very different course now.

I ask myself now whether teaching mathematical economics to undergraduates is sensible. Indeed I wonder whether mathematical economics isn't just an intellectual dead end. And even if mathematical economics can be defended, was it appropriate for these particular students?

In particular, I do remember that our syllabus on microeconomics included general equilibrium theory and Pareto optimality – I've even found some old lecture notes – and that's pretty heavy stuff (and tedious too). When trying to understand why economic systems behave as they do it is the practice of economists to start from some assumptions and build on those. The reasoning quickly becomes complex. Without using mathematics it is laborious and confusing to follow all the logical implications just through words or diagrams, which takes lots of time and intellectual effort by students, leaving little time for a broader look at the economic system and the real world. By expressing the assumptions and their outcomes in mathematical form, the mathematics can be an aid to logical thinking, but in academic economics it sometimes seems as though it is an end in itself, and I rather think that was the case too in our syllabus. We may have focussed on mathematical economics just because the students were studying mathematics.

Is mathematical economics worth the bother? Economic theory has often been criticised for the unrealistic nature of its assumptions. But their lack of realism can be accepted if they provide a useful starting point for working out the consequences of those assumptions, following which the implications of variations in the assumptions can be explored.

Departures in the real world from the usual assumptions of the model – perfect competition, perfect information, no increasing returns to scale, no external effects, etc. – are ubiquitous and readily acknowledged, and much more recent work has been done on relaxing them, for instance by acknowledging and incorporating uncertainty and imperfect information. An implication of the standard assumptions is that with the final equilibrium set of prices, output and consumption is 'Pareto optimal', which means that no one can be made better off without making someone else worse off. This is quite an appealing result; though that is as true of an equal distribution of starting income as it is of a highly unequal one, and that is less appealing. In an important result (Lipsey and Lancaster, 1956) showed that if you move the economic system closer to the assumptions – for instance by curtailing firms' monopoly power – there is not necessarily an improvement in welfare, so you have to look at each policy change on its merits. Yet lots of policy effort goes into trying to get closer to the paradigm. I'm not sure that my example is a good one: monopoly power can be and is used to make consumers pay more than necessary, and surely that is not good. Their work often gets a nod of acknowledgement – indeed my old lecture notes tell me that we covered it in the Mathematics for Business course – but then ignored.[35]

Other critiques of economic theory have been made. An example is the 1994 book by Paul Ormerod, himself an economist, *The Death of Economics*, which contains a swingeing attack on conventional economics, but this didn't derail the train either. I gather that mathematical economics (and econometrics) are still dominating what gets you kudos in academic economics, and that undergraduates are still being put through a similar curriculum to the one we

[35] This is an insightful essay on the subject http://www.economist.com/blogs/freeexchange/2007/08/making_the_second_best_of_it, with quotes from Mark Blaug and Richard Lipsey.

followed in the late 1960s at Enfield. Perhaps entrenched academic interests and career pressures make it very hard to depart from normal practice and retain respectability.

But if you discard this approach what can you replace it with? Recently Joe Earle and colleagues, initially in revolt against the excessive formalism and lack of relevance they were experiencing in their undergraduate economics teaching, went on to examine the content of economics degrees more widely and found a heavy reliance on multiple choice questions and little requirement for critical thinking (Earle, J. et al., 2017). Many of their criticisms applied to the economics part of Enfield's Mathematics for Business course in the 1960s. At least in our examination papers we didn't have multiple-choice questions.[36]

So I would, now, go for being less ambitious in the coverage of economic theory, and devote much more time to applied economics, even on a Mathematics for Business degree course. Even though it would not have involved so much mathematics, our students would have learned about much more interesting and important things, and they would have had to do some hard thinking. Social cost benefit analysis, poverty and inequality, international trade issues, macroeconomic management, financial systems, financial events such as the 2007 financial crisis, the pros and cons of monetary union: these are all topics that are relevant to the world we live in and to understand them needs a certain amount of logical and, at times, mathematical reasoning, as well as factual and statistical evidence. Students would have benefited from thinking and writing about these before discovering them for themselves in the world outside. Industry or organisational case studies could have been incorporated in their fourth year, building perhaps on the experiences these students had in their sandwich year. By then, they would have had more business experience than I have ever had.

I also think our syllabus was too hard for our students. Perhaps that's why their faces were so blank at tutorials. I remember one examiners' meeting where we had to reduce the pass mark on one paper to an appallingly low level in order to avoid failing too many

---

[36] There's an interesting review of Earle et al at https://www.theguardian.com/books/2017/feb/09/the-econocracy-review-joe-earle-cahal-moran-zach-ward-perkins.

students. The borderline students really didn't understand the material.

Studying conventional economics is a miserable experience. I certainly found it so. And I now regret that I inflicted so much of it on other young people. But I've usually added that studying economics opens up the possibility of addressing important and interesting questions in the applied field, and maybe you do that work better if you have endured an undergraduate degree in economics. There is the old cliché, that studying for a degree teaches you to think, and maybe the traditional economics degree does do that, but I think we could have done better things for our students.

Departure

After Enfield I moved far away from mathematical economics in my subsequent career, and out of academia. In my fourth year at Enfield I found myself increasingly thinking that I really didn't want to go on teaching, so I started looking for a job in economic research. I got a post as a researcher at the London Graduate School of Business Studies. After two years there I moved into the Government Economic Service, mainly in the Department of the Environment, working on urban policy and housing, but I also had a two-year spell in the Department of Health and Social Security. I was applying economic reasoning to questions of government policy and public sector investment and I was very happy doing that for ten years. I abandoned my unfinished PhD thesis on the theory of externalities. Then, after I left London in 1981 I worked as a freelance researcher in public sector economics and the application of economics to social issues. I found it rewarding and I felt it was useful. But I wouldn't have been allowed to do that if I hadn't done an economics degree. So rightly or wrongly that degree was an entry ticket to all sorts of things, and I'm sure it still would be.

I made lasting friendships at Enfield and I had some life-changing experiences. One in particular stands out. I was chatting with a group in the staff common room (the coffee was memorably awful) and the conversation turned to holidays. I asked if anyone could suggest a place in Britain that was remote, beautiful, and away from tourists. Alan Cox, one of the statisticians, said 'Mid-Wales?'. A couple of weeks later I came across an advertisement in the personal column of the *New Statesman* for 'Holiday cottage in peaceful beautiful valley in remote Radnorshire hills. £6 a week'. That wording may not be quite right but the rental was exactly that. Thus began the first of many holidays I took in that cottage, and I will always be grateful to Alan. I wrote my first academic article there - it was on externalities and public goods. And since 1981 I have lived permanently in mid-Wales, which is still beautiful, and still relatively remote and not overwhelmed by tourists.

16. Once upon a time in Ponders End

TONY CRILLY

Tony Crilly *was appointed at Enfield as a mathematics lecturer in 1967, and taught mainly on the Mathematics for Business degree and the Business Studies degree (Part-Time). The experience of being at the beginnings of a Polytechnic enabled him to spend two years abroad helping to set up the City Polytechnic of Hong Kong. He completed a PhD in the history of mathematics in 1981, and has found writing books to be a pleasant and hopefully useful thing to do. Having retired in 2007, he lives in St Albans and enjoys a family of children and grandchildren.*

How I got there

We were £10-Poms emigrating to Australia in the early 1950s and where I completed my secondary education at the end of the decade. There was little likelihood of going to university in Sydney where we lived. Few scholarships were available and it would have cost a great deal of money. Anyway, I cannot remember any encouragement to continue into higher education after the Australian Leaving Certificate. On return to England, I was sent back to a grammar school in Bristol for A-levels.

Tiny classes like those in Alan Bennett's 'The History Boys' was my experience in Bristol, but it was 'The Mathematics Boys.' In the Sixth Form there were just half a dozen of us studying for the single specialist papers in Pure Mathematics, Applied Mathematics, and Physics at A-level. The crucial influence at school was a graduate teacher from Bristol University who taught us as part of his teaching practice and afterwards when he was appointed to the permanent staff. He was the inspiration through which mathematics became my academic interest.

I went on to study mathematics at Hull University and I stayed on to complete an MSc by research, this followed by two years in the United States at the University of Michigan in Ann Arbor. When I returned to Britain I needed a job.

Arrival at Enfield

Hoping to live in the London area I wrote a round-robin letter to Education authorities in the north London area enquiring into vacancies in the teaching profession. I had a couple of positive replies including one from Enfield.

In the summer of 1967 I was invited for interview at Enfield College of Technology. I had no idea where Enfield was and not much about the job I had applied for. On interview day the steam train pulled into Southbury Road Station and, after a short walk along Kingsway turning into Queensway, I approached a building looking exactly like a technical college should look – an Art Deco glass plated tower flanked by symmetrical wings in the same style. Job interviews were in full flow. The college secretary Mr Harold Carless was doing his best to keep up with the queue of job applicants knocking on his door. Here was a man not used to the college expansion that was taking place in the 1960s.

Summoned into a large room, the interview itself was conducted by all interested parties: heads of department, student representatives, governors, all arranged around a U shaped table with me neatly positioned between its prongs. At its apex the figure of moon-faced Principal George Brosan squeezed into a three-piece pin-striped suit, the uniform of college principal and businessman merged into one. Questions were fired and answers given before I retired to the staff common room to await the verdict. A flurry of activity amongst panel members took place of which I was unaware, but I found out later that no one in that room was really sure how many mathematical posts were on offer. Was it one, or two?

It is easy to imagine Brosan's exasperation at such incompetence from his administrative support staff, he being a man of action. It was rumoured he had both lost a million at his electronics company but also made a million on the rebound. If nothing else George Brosan was a man who did not dilly-dally over decisions big or small. Somehow the matter of one post or two was decided – there were two posts available and this was very convenient as the two applicants could both be offered jobs as Lecturer Grade II (the other candidate was an American, Margery Reinhart). The annual salary for a Lecturer Grade II was about £1,900/per annum, slightly more than the annual salary of a Member of Parliament. This was a time when there were plenty of jobs for people with degrees; I had also had an offer from ICL (International Computers Limited) for a teaching job at about the same salary even though I knew next to nothing about computers.

The teaching term was to start in October and opening his little diary on the college steps, Allan Findlay, the senior mathematics lecturer on the panel, thought if I came a week before the beginning of term that would be about right. After all, a job should not intrude upon summertime. My teaching appointment at Enfield began on 1 October 1967.

On arrival, I was given my own office in the 'huts', a pair of temporary prefabs of a kind you knew would acquire permanent status. In civil service style, there was one filing cabinet, one desk, a telephone (I think), a little square of carpet, a heater, a postage sized black board and a window looking out into the hut next door. Only the hat stand was missing. My name was soon affixed to the door. It felt like home. During lunch times I met other staff in the dining room – the staff table was the one with the white tablecloth but staff-student barriers were being dismantled and at the hatch we queued for the daily fare.

The first staff meeting for the Mathematics for Business degree included about five new staff members: mathematicians, operational researchers, economists, and statisticians. The head of the course conducted the meeting and introduced the new staff. Later on the big chief Eric Robinson came in, and fiddling with a paper clip as he was wont to do when speaking in his measured Lancastrian accent, outlined the philosophy of the college. This was based on the need to widen access to higher education by the expansion of colleges like Enfield, the philosophy at one with his socialist principles,

There was an underlying cultural clash between College staff already in post at the end of the 1950s and the incoming younger staff of the 1960s. The teaching staff of the 1950s working in a predominantly engineering college had their established network. They frequented the common room at morning coffee and afternoon tea, where many played cards when they were not teaching or supervising in the laboratories. The incomers came into the common room for their post but hardly mixed with the older generation. The engineering staff did not understand longhaired jean wearing social scientists, who in their youthful arrogance classed engineers as mere 'spanner men.'

A social organization in the college which did not survive the 1960s was the Enfield Technical College Entertainments Association. Being on the College staff, teaching and administrative and technical, was not merely to have employment. Coming with the job was an invitation to share in evening communal entertainment, such as dances, socials, and even the organisation of musicals – on one occasion a ballet was performed on the premises. The staff of the 1950s were bound together by shared wartime experiences, and of being 'in it together', not an attitude adopted by the next generation of employees.

Even after the great expansion of education in the 1960s Enfield remained quite small when compared with modern institutions. It was still the 'local Tec' to people on the outside; in 1971 there were 1300 students on full-time and sandwich degrees and 900 part-time students. It was a college under Local Authority control, and with all the changes in personnel, G. A. Roberts a local industrialist was Chair of the Governing Body from 1949 until 1968.

Expansion

By 1967, Eric Robinson was the head of the newly created Arts Faculty, while R. D. Kitchener, a traditional College of Technology figure widely known as 'Kitch', headed the Technology Faculty. Robinson was not a regular presence in the college for he was by this time operating on a national stage, and his natural habitats were the speaking platform, television studios, and rallies at Trafalgar Square. With his educational perspective, he would frequently take the opportunity to lambast the established universities. The 'enfant terrible' (he was barely forty years old) Robinson made such a point of likening them to ivory towers that it was no wonder he was opposed by their Vice-Chancellors. A fierce opponent of the university system in Britain, Robinson had always fought against the hegemony of the traditional universities, and singled out the single subject honours degree as his principal target.

Robinson forcibly argued against elitism and one can only guess what he would have thought of the presently accepted notion of 'good universities', the modern remnant of the 1960s binary model of Higher Education which divided traditional universities from upstart colleges like Enfield.

This was an era of large meetings and there were plenty at Enfield. Regular large and active meetings were those of the ATTI (Association of Teachers in Technical Institutions). These were in the style of political meetings with motions and debate and voting. Some speakers from the floor had highly developed oratorical skills and could have held their own at Speaker's Corner in Hyde Park.

In 1968 staff and students gathered to hear Sir Edward Boyle who was invited to speak at the college. As Minister of Education 1962-64 he accepted the recommendations of the Robbins Report. He was a firm believer in widening access and for a Conservative politician quite radical. He championed comprehensive schools and the notion of 'equal opportunity.' Expansion, as set out in Robbins, was seen as necessary for the country and acted upon, but at the Enfield meeting he admitted the Tory party had made a mistake in founding so many universities. If they had not, he argued, there would not be so many with small departments.

The largest lecture room in the college was '525' in the McCrae Building, an extension to the main College Building (it is now demolished). This was where the huge lectures took place. The quite unique 'Methods and Models' course on the Social Science degree involved such heady mathematical topics as the Greek theory of rational numbers and (Bertrand) Russell's Paradox. It was curious that in my formal mathematical training, to this date seven years of it, I had barely heard of these topics, but here at Enfield, first year Social science students with only a smattering of basic mathematical skills were exposed to them.

Room 525 was also used for overspill staff meetings such as the one conducted by Brosan on the implications for staff as the new polytechnic appeared on the horizon. His intimidating way of dealing with awkward questions – by gazing out the window and scratching the microphone – was well remembered and he made no friends that day. On another occasion Julian Ayer, a member of the Enfield staff, brought his Dad (the philosopher Sir Freddie Ayer) for an evening lecture on philosophy. On such occasions the room was packed. One evening, in a teaching room below Room 525, the College Chess Club gathered and Jonathan Penrose, a psychology lecturer on the staff and renowned international chess champion, easily demolished fifteen opponents in a simultaneous game.

The 1960s witnessed an influx of staff recruited to create and teach on the new degrees being generated notably in Social Science and Business Studies. Social Science at Enfield became one of the largest departments in the country. This kind of activity was a far cry from the normal thrust of a traditional technical college. In the rapid drive to establish itself, the recruitment of staff took on bizarre turns. On one occasion a head of department's job was offered sight unseen to a candidate living in the Far East. In another, an emissary in the college was dispatched to Ruskin College in Oxford to interview for a lectureship in economics and the candidate offered a job on the spot.

While there was work, there was also leisure, and at lunch hour some of the fitter members of staff took themselves off to play football on the scrap of College land near the air-raid shelters or to the Ponders End Park. On Wednesday afternoons an informal 'squash club' played at courts in Southgate (next to the ground where Saracens rugby club used to play). No one could beat Keith Jones, an unusual Australian accountant who practiced for hours hitting the ball an inch from the wall for it to always die in the corner – making a return unplayable. Later on, an engineering member of staff designed an ingenious 'fold-away' squash court in the college gym and Bernie Bellwood, a physical education lecturer, had a Finnish-style Sauna installed.

With the heady expansion at Enfield there was a clear chance of promotion. After just two years as Lecturer Grade II, I was promoted in a batch of appointments to Senior Lecturer, a level previously reckoned to be the career grade acquired after a lifetime spent in teaching at such a college. It was the degree level work which was the clincher in the argument which broke this tradition. In seeing the list of promotion candidates at my time, Robinson half-complained 'but he looks so young.'

With the expansion and the space for staff accommodation limited, many single occupancy offices had to be given up. Being junior staff I shared an office with Dr Sofron Sofroniou. PhD's were still a rarity amongst staff and staff with them usually enjoyed an enhanced academic reputation. Sofron taught on the Mathematics for Business degree. Intellectually he was a man of many parts with a command of languages and philosophy. For a time he was employed by the BBC where he broadcast to Cyprus and Greece on the Overseas Service at Bush House.

Sofron had a Mediterranean approach to life and he was not caught up in the often frenetic activity taking place around him. There was a certain bureaucratic way of administrating Enfield in the early days and in a pre-electronic era, paper memos flooded in. Sofron would glance at them, place them on the corner of his desk, and carry on with his academic work. When the pile was in obvious need of attention, in danger of blocking out the sunlight, he would devote a half-hour to its elimination. Way past their relevance date, he glanced at precious memos summoning him to meetings that had already taken place, and gently slid them into the wastebasket. It was a marvel to watch this efficiency. From Sofron I also learned something of Greek philosophy and the way it applied to mathematics. When dispensing his learning he would say *sotto voce* 'there are some gaps in my ignorance.'

Mathematics for Business

The Mathematics for Business was a flagship degree of the college. This was the brainchild of Robinson who had been a lecturer in mathematics when a young man. Later he had broadened his interests and devoted himself to furthering national education provision and never regarded himself as a mathematician in the traditional mould.

The clever part of the Mathematics for Business degree was the exploration of how mathematics could be combined with business. A more traditional role for mathematics was its support for the sciences like physics and chemistry but now it was combined with everyday needs. Mathematics is a versatile subject of use in many practical situations (evidenced by the importance of mathematics at Bletchley Park). A sub-branch is Statistics and the more recent Operational Research, and both were included in the Mathematics for Business range of subjects. Staff in Operational Research were recruited from the National Coal Board, an organization famous for employing it in their business.

The teaching duties at Enfield were hardly onerous. I taught linear algebra and the classes amounted to about six hours per week.

I was also involved with fourth year specialisms – degree courses at Enfield were invariably four year in duration, the students having spent the third year in business or industry, a feature of Enfield 'sandwich' degrees. The smallness of the degree cohort meant that for some specialisms (Algebra, Logic) there were few students and on occasion there were as many staff as students! This occurred when Allan Findlay and I taught a course on abstract algebra. The teaching on this course was by tutorial, and we did not have to give formal lectures, which involved chalking up mathematics on roller blackboards and preparing notes on the duplicating 'Roneo machines.' We followed the famous algebra text by Garrett Birkhoff and Saunders MacLane. On reflection this was following a feature of the Enfield teaching philosophy of gearing up teaching to the students' individual needs.

As with any group of academics there was variation in the staff's approaches to their subject and to life. A few preferred to plough their own academic furrow by research in their chosen subject area while others contributed to the educational provision offered by the college. There was a strong contingent from the London School of Economics and amongst the mathematics staff, Allan Findlay, Ivor Grattan-Guinness (with whom I later studied the history of mathematics), and Sofron had studied with Sir Karl Popper for Masters degrees in the history and philosophy of science. It was the first time I had come into contact with 'Popperians'. There were other groups of Popper's disciples dotted around the college.

Allan Findlay was my chief guide when I first joined the college. He was the kindliest of men. Quiet in demeanour he was that rare breed who actually listened to what you had to say, took it on board, and gave reasoned responses, even if these were delivered the following day after he had had a chance of thinking about the issues at hand. Although his first degree was in mathematics from UCL (London) he had turned to the philosophy of science after making contact with Popper at the London School of Economics (by writing a letter to him).

When I met Allan he actually had three jobs. Full-time at Enfield, part-time at Hatfield College of Technology, and part-time at LSE where he was Popper's assistant. I would on occasion be in his office when the phone rang with Popper on the other end wanting help with the proof reading of one of his books. Then it was 'Yes,

Sir Karl, No Sir Karl' peppered with advice on the wording on a page, or a mathematical correction. It was clear Popper valued his assistance. When life became more demanding at Enfield Allan gave up the part-time jobs and took a position on the management spine of the college.

Allan was not a modern day thrusting academic. In fact he was decidedly old fashioned, adopting the views of some British academics of earlier generations who saw no particular need to publish their thoughts. He was clearly out of step with the 'publish or perish' mood that was gradually creeping in from America.

Business Studies (Part-Time)

The main duty at Enfield in the early days was attending meetings where future degree courses were planned. I fell in with a group starting a Business Studies degree. I had been hired for the Mathematics for Business degree but there were other opportunities. There was already a *full-time* degree in Business Studies led by Alan Hale but now a variant was to be offered on a part-time basis. The target audience was to cater for those already working in business or industry but lacked formal qualifications. The carrot for students was that a degree qualification would aid advancement in their careers.

The leader of this staff group was John Stoddart a principal lecturer in economics. Initially there were three of us in the team, the other being John Munro, who himself had come late to academia. Having started off his working life as a fourteen-year Post Office messenger, John had taken an interest in Trade Union work and had gone to Ruskin College in Oxford.

Constructed degree programmes were vetted and authenticated by the Council for National Academic Awards (CNAA) an organisation presided over by the Duke of Edinburgh as figurehead. This was quite new as previously the few degrees offered by the college were External degrees of London University. Traditional universities had powers to award their own degrees but Enfield and colleges like it awarded theirs under the auspices of the CNAA. As Robinson used to mischievously point out, 'there are only three bodies able to grant degrees in England, the universities, the CNAA, and the Archbishop of Canterbury.'

The CNAA vetting procedure dominated our lives. The hours of meetings and thought that went into a submission was quite phenomenal. And the big event for any degree team was when the CNAA panel arrived at the college to examine the proposal. The panel was drawn from academics, administrators, business people, educational visionaries and subject specialists from other institutions. There was a set format for the big day: the visiting party arrived and had a private meeting. At this meeting they had probably not met each other before. Then the party would meet those from the higher echelons of the College hierarchy who passed down the main concerns to us foot-soldiers so that we could prepare for the full meeting in the afternoon. The visiting party would then go off to inspect the library facilities, and the prized asset of any college in the 1960s, the mainframe college computer.

The full meeting with the CNAA panel for the afternoon was something we had prepared for – for months. Sometimes the questions from the panel were broad, centring on the 'philosophy' of the proposal. Targeted questions on individual specialized syllabuses were also dealt with though there was little time for much detailed discussion of such questions. Finally the panel met separately and as the day came to an end, there was the judgment. It was either full permission to go ahead, room for further consideration, or outright rejection (rarely given). When the part-time Business Studies degree received the go-ahead, Principal George Brosan marched down the long corridor leading from the Main Building to the college bar, slapped ten pounds of his own money on the counter (pints at 1s/9d) and declared 'drinks all round.'

The part-time Business Studies degree was a highly successful course though it demanded stamina from staff and students. Staff were required for evening teaching and this was not always popular. Ordinarily the degree was five years in length, quite a commitment. The student completing the final part by full-time study could shorten it to four years. In the first year of operation the degree recruited 110 students but such were the demands of the course that barely a dozen of these graduated. It was always smaller than its full-time equivalent, but the students on the part-time degree came with a wealth of business and industrial experience unmatched by the raw eighteen-year-olds on the full-time degree who came direct from school. Lecturers on the part-time degree had the curious experience of teaching students older than themselves, students who had seen much more of the world than they had. For example, Tom Pointon struggled with the study of mathematics but was an entrepreneur and in a former life had been a merchant navy officer operating worldwide (after leaving he went on to complete a PhD at Cranfield).

For the part-time degree we (myself and Roger Davies) devised a different sort of 'mathematical' course, called 'Quantitative Methods.' This concentrated on the applications of numerical thinking which occurred either in their other studies or in their jobs. It was not difficult to find areas in economics and psychology, for example, which demanded numerical understanding. Some students went on to complete numerically based projects in their final year.

In an attempt to get away from the artificiality of the traditional three-hour examination we devised a whole day examination (six hours) in which students were allowed to use previously written notes and make use of the library facilities, as they would in real life. The only rule was that there should be no conferring between candidates. Enfield was an environment in which such experiment in teaching and examining was fostered.

The dozen students who did graduate from the Business Studies (Part-Time) in the first year of its operation were a remarkable lot. Following the degree they formed the British Business Graduate Association, the BBGS. The main instigator was Tom Pointon who inveigled Doddi Rao to do the secretarial work, with Keith Hampson M.P. at the helm

Towards a Polytechnic

In January 1965, Harold Wilson appointed Anthony Crosland Secretary of State for Education and Science. A major educational change was presaged by Crosland's speech at Woolwich Polytechnic establishing a 'binary system' of higher education, in which universities would develop in parallel with a system of new polytechnic institutions which would concentrate on high-level vocational skills. The new polytechnics were, as the name suggests, multi-disciplinary colleges, with an emphasis on teaching rather than pure research and a relevance to the needs of industry and social problems.

In 1966 a White Paper entitled 'A Plan for Polytechnics and Other Colleges – Higher education in the Further Education System' proposed the creation of new polytechnics. In April of the following year Crosland announced that a polytechnic in north London would be formed. Brosan's earlier proposal of a federated institution comprising Enfield College, Hornsey College of Art, and Trent Park Teachers College had come to nothing, but the proposal for a new polytechnic formed by a new amalgamation was an outcome of this earlier thought. Enfield College of Technology was to join with Hendon College of Technology and Hornsey College of Art to form the 'North London Polytechnic.'

Negotiations between the three local authorities involved, Enfield, Haringey, and Barnet, were protracted. Hornsey College of Art, a leading college in the art world in its own right, had no desire to be joined at the hip with colleges of technology – heaven forbid, 'technology.' In 1967 a staff committee at Hornsey listed eleven reasons why it should *not* be part of such a polytechnic. Sir William Coldstream, a leading figure in Art Education in Britain, was clearly of the opinion that the polytechnic plan was not in the best interests in the education of artists. Other amalgamations were explored, and at one point Barnet had ideas of joining Hendon College of Technology with Barnet Technical College and Ealing College of Technology.

The 1960s was a time of radical student action, in the summer of 1968, Hornsey College of Art occupied their college premises. On 28 May of that year, there was a 24-hour sit-in but lasted longer, in which the Principal and Senior Staff were sent into exile to offices in nearby Wood Green. In July the term ended, the students went home, and the Principal and his staff returned.

'North London Polytechnic' proved only a working title for the new polytechnic. It could not be called this since North London Polytechnic was already in the pipeline as the joining of the old Northern Polytechnic to North Western Polytechnic. It was envisaged that there should be five polytechnics in the Inner London area. Unfortunately there were just too many 'Londons' in the offing, and North-East London Polytechnic (NELP) would be an added complication. So the Enfield-Hendon-Hornsey colleges would emerge as Middlesex Polytechnic.

As the polytechnics were being designated, it became clear that the existing college hierarchy of Brosan and Robinson did not see their future careers at the proposed Middlesex Polytechnic. They decamped to neighbouring North-East London Polytechnic and John O'Neil became Principal at Enfield. John Munro took over the running of the Part-Time Business Studies degree.

With the new Principal in place, some of the excitement of the earlier thrust of the swashbuckling Brosan and the Brosan/Robinson axis disappeared. Somehow I found myself on the Academic Board chaired by John O'Neil but for me it was mistake, as I only fully realized when the agenda and inch-thick stack of papers were deposited in my staff tray before each meeting. And those fractious meetings with heads of department arguing for their resources and the ego-driven debates in the smoke-filled boardroom left me drained. The college governance had to take place but that time on the Academic Board was a valuable lesson to me; one year was enough.

As we entered the 1970s it seemed we were almost back to the days of a traditional technical college. A survival of that mentality occurred one evening when I was asked why I was still in the college when clearly I should have been at home sitting down to tea after the day's work. One day I noted the new Principal's disapproval as I came across him in the long corridor, me in casual clothing and he in a dark suit and tie. In the new regime it was now hinted – though not enforced – that lecturers should dress 'properly'.

Moving towards a Polytechnic a new six-storey Tower Block was built on the Ponders End site costing £300,000 and providing staff offices and tutorial rooms. Margaret Thatcher opened the Roberts Building on 17 March 1971. Named after Chairman of governors G. A. Roberts, and not Mrs Thatcher's father, it always known as the Tower Block just as the Broadbent Building was invariably referred to as the Main Building.

Mrs Amy Emsden was 'chairman' of the Enfield Education Committee in the days before chairmen became 'Chairs' or 'Chairpersons'. A Conservative party member who squeaked on to the Enfield Council at the local election, Mrs Emsden served on the London Borough of Enfield Education Committee. In local authority terms she was a power in the land being also the chair of the joint steering committee of the three local authorities which would come together to oversee the new Polytechnic. This steering committee appointed nine of the eighteen governors. Seven others were appointed from those with experience in industry, commerce, and the professions, and two members from Trades Unions. Mrs Emsden was also a member of the Appointments Committee of Senior Officers for the polytechnic, including being in charge of appointing the Director.

The post of Director was advertised at an annual salary of £7,848. In the early stages there were 123 requests for application forms and very quickly 21 of these were completed. In July 1972, Dr Raymond Rickett was appointed as Director, and Robert Hornung Chief Administrative Officer. R. F. Hornby, the chief officer of the CNAA was appointed Chairman of Governors. John O'Neill, who had been Principal of Enfield College of Technology in the period 1970-1972, Dr Ronald Garnett, Principal of Hendon College of Technology, and H. H. Shelton Principal at Hornsey College of Art, all became Assistant Directors of the Polytechnic. Mrs Emsden's work was done and she became Mayor of Enfield in 1977.

The Polytechnic arrives

Middlesex Polytechnic formally came into existence on 1 January 1973. The three colleges that had been in the van of developments came in as the last of the new wave of thirty polytechnics. This event was overshadowed by the national political event of the United Kingdom joining the European Economic Community (EEC) on the same day.

There were 6,500 students in the new institution. High on the agenda for the new polytechnics were the buzz words 'Modularisation', and 'Semesterisation.' In his previous post as Assistant Director at City Polytechnic in London, Rickett made his mark by importing the American system there, and now he would bring it to Middlesex Polytechnic. In his own education he had been in America and had obtained his PhD there and had witnessed this system first hand.

The highly structured British Honours degree would gradually be abandoned – but only after a battle. I had seen the modular system in operation in the American higher educational system during my education 1965-67 at the University of Michigan in Ann Arbor. I had also seen the way the American system valued the PhD. The significance of the PhD was due to the German influence and in America it had become a necessity for all college academics. It was equivalent to a Union card. This too became a prevailing element in the culture of the Polytechnic as it struggled to assert its academic credentials. No longer would staff be promoted for administration and the days of time-tabler being rewarded with a principal lectureship were over.

In an effort to bring about collaboration between staff in different subject areas, we had the 'matrix structure.' Most organisations are built on a hierarchical structure of which the military command structure is the most obvious example. In the 'matrix structure' each member of staff was allied to the courses they taught on *and* also to their subject grouping. In this way the polytechnic was not based on simple command. In my case, for example, I could be a 'mathematician' and also be part of the part-time Business Studies degree and the Mathematics for Business degree. It could be argued (and it was) that the organization was messy but it was a flexible system, and it proved a creative one.

The college building in Queensway which had come into existence before the war and grew and expanded in the 1960s was abandoned by Middlesex University in 2008. The site was sold off to become a mixed housing/school site. It will be the new 'Electric Quarter', a nod in the direction of Sir Joseph Swan the entrepreneur of electric lighting who set up his company in the Ponders End area in the early twentieth century. A memory of the former Enfield College of Technology will be sparked by the preservation of the Grade II listed Broadbent Building, the main building of the old college which has been thoroughly modernised and is now the home of the Heron Hall Academy.

It was both Brosan's and Robinson's belief that the polytechnics did not wish to evolve into universities. Both saw polytechnics as the 'the people's universities' open to all in a comprehensive higher educational system.

Looking back

In retrospect, many of us now realize we were in the middle of something special in the 1960s and that Enfield had been important in reshaping Higher Education in Britain. Staff came from all kinds of backgrounds and from different countries. The informality of the place was a real shock to me having been an undergraduate in a traditional university where ‘professors’ lived in a different zone and you called them ‘Sir’ – if you saw them at all.

There was a kind of missionary zeal which pervaded the place – to provide the opportunity for those who had missed out on post school education in some way or another. Over time the polytechnic arrived and in 1992 a university, but for me the really exciting time was at Enfield College of Technology and it wasn’t even Enfield where it happened. It was Ponders End.

17. Enfield College of Technology: an experience which shaped my academic life

BRIAN EVANS

> ***Brian Evans*** *was appointed at Enfield as a psychology lecturer in 1967, continued as a senior lecturer from 1970 until retiring as a full-time member of the Middlesex University staff in 2007, but continuing to the present as a part-time lecturer in health psychology. He has also taught statistics, mathematical psychology and health psychology as a visiting lecturer at the University of Sussex, Concordia University, Montreal, and City University, London. His first major publication was concerned with eugenics, psychometrics and the IQ psychology and then further in health psychology and consciousness studies. His current enjoyments include family life, jazz music, yoga, and hill walking, including the Alps and the Himalayas.*

I began teaching at Enfield College in 1967, when higher education in Britain was expanding rapidly and with many significant innovations. For example, the Open University, first proposed in 1965 by the Labour government of Harold Wilson, was gradually coming into existence, finally established in 1969 and taking its first students at the beginning of 1971. At the same time the first polytechnics were being established, as described in *The New Polytechnics* by Eric Robinson, a key innovator at Enfield College of Technology. These developments gave rise to the creation of many new academic posts, and I was one of the young graduates who took advantage of this opportunity to embark on an academic career.

What was special about Enfield? At first I did not think that anything was special about it. But within a few years it became clear to me that there was something going on which was unique. What was new for me, and it shaped the rest of my academic life, was the breaking down of the subject boundaries that still dominate in many universities, and the establishment of an interdisciplinary approach. This went far beyond the traditional structure of university courses where students took a single major subject, but were also able to undertake minor studies in one or two other subjects. In those courses the subjects studied were still tightly compartmentalised, with little or no interaction between the staff teaching the separate disciplines. What seemed new at Enfield was the development and teaching of courses jointly by staff from two or more disciplines, staff who, like me, gradually lost their exclusive allegiance to their original discipline.

I do not propose to make a detailed analysis of all the changes that took place in the college during those years. I am focussing primarily on the interdisciplinary developments because they had the greatest impact on me, and because I think that they were done better at Enfield than at any other institution I know. To some extent this chapter is really just a piece of autobiography in which the college plays a central role; but I hope that my own perspective can be combined with those from the rest of this book to obtain a vivid picture. I certainly hope that I can communicate a sense of how much fun it all was.

Recruited by the British chess champion

My life as a lecturer at Enfield College of Technology, and its subsequent incarnations as Middlesex Polytechnic and University, began in March 1967 when I was recruited by psychology lecturer Jonathan Penrose to work as a part-time member of staff teaching statistics and organising laboratory classes for the psychology component of the BA General London External Degree. This was a very traditional course and I was teaching much the same material that I had previously been studying at the equally traditional psychology department of University College London, where Jonathan had also studied some years earlier.

I do not think that either of us in 1967 had any idea of the radical educational developments that were gestating at the institution and which came to fruition in the following years. My reason for taking this workaday academic job had been to help finance me while I finished my PhD, but one reason for feeling excited about it was that, a keen chess player, I would be working alongside Britain's most brilliant exponent of the game. By the time I joined the college Jonathan had already won the British Championship seven times (he went on to win it on a further three successive years from 1967-69).

One of his finest achievements was in 1960 when he beat the world champion Mikhail Tal, the first time since 1899 that a British player had defeated a reigning world champion. In the same tournament he also beat the former world champion Max Euwe and came very close to beating the future world champion Bobby Fischer, finally conceding a draw after failing to convert a won endgame. Fischer's comment: 'That guy Penrose, very strong player, but a weaky in the endgame'. I did not have the temerity to challenge Jonathan to a game but I did benefit from some very useful advice on openings and I enjoyed his many anecdotes about the world of chess, not least his meeting with the chess-loving artist Marcel Duchamp, a meeting arranged by his uncle, the distinguished art historian Roland Penrose.

First experiences of interdisciplinary teaching

Thanks to the support of Eric Robinson, Academic Head of the Faculty of Arts, I was given a full lectureship in September 1967 and encouraged to participate in the development of new degree programmes where the principal aim was to introduce interdisciplinary interactions as a key teaching and learning objective. My first contribution was as a member of a working group set up by the enterprising English lecturer Len Jackson to develop a BA Hons Communication Studies, with the intention to roam broadly over the exciting changes that were taking place at the time in linguistics, philosophy, anthropology, literary theory and cognitive psychology. It was a good idea, but probably overambitious for an institution that was still finding its feet, and it eventually failed to gain accreditation.

Far more successful was the part-time BA Hons Sociology of Education, which we usually referred to as the 'Teachers Degree'. Starting from 1969 this was the first departure for me from teaching on the BA General and I still think that it was both the most innovative and the most enjoyable of all the programmes with which I have been involved. It was aimed at non-graduate teachers seeking to improve their professional status (and income) and it incorporated a strong focus on interdisciplinary interaction, mainly between sociologists, psychologists, philosophers and educationalists. Topics ranged from the causes of educational and social inequality to controversies about the nature of scientific method, and interdisciplinary seminars were held every week attended by members of staff from all disciplines who argued with each other and with the participating students in a very lively fashion.

To illustrate the influence this had on my own academic development and on one of my students I will mention a final year dissertation which I supervised for John Leavold, a bright and enthusiastic Physical Education teacher and high jump specialist, who subsequently became a successful head teacher. The topic was the 'Jensen controversy' concerning claims by Arthur Jensen in the USA and Hans Eysenck in England that race and class differences in IQ and educational achievement were largely the result of inherited differences. Analysing this complex controversy involved some very tricky statistical issues as well as material from a range of disciplines in both the biological and the social sciences. John developed a keen interest in alternative socio-cultural explanations of educational inequality, and I believe that this had a considerable impact on his subsequent career in which he gained a considerable reputation for his ability to 'turn around' failing schools. For my own part this work led me to join the British Society for Social Responsibility in Science where I enjoyed working with Steven Rose of the Open University and others in giving talks at universities throughout the UK opposing the hereditarian viewpoint on scientific grounds.

Later, in the mid 1970s, the controversy erupted again when it was shown that the hereditarian findings on separated twins by the British psychologist Cyril Burt, who had held the Chair of Psychology at UCL, were entirely fraudulent. This in turn led me to work with an old friend, Bernard Waites, social historian at the Open University on our book on eugenics and IQ psychology (*IQ and Mental Testing: An Unnatural Science and its Social History*) which was eventually published by Macmillan in 1980 in a series edited by my Enfield colleague the criminologist Jock Young. The influence of the Enfield philosophy is very evident to me now as I glance through its pages, replete with references to thinkers outside of mainstream psychology including linguistics, philosophy, anthropology and sociology, ideas which I would probably have known very little about if I had remained within a traditional academic psychology department.

Opportunities for my academic development

Enfield proved to be very good for me. My first few years were spent in the company of a rapidly expanding group of young academics, especially social scientists and philosophers, recruited by Eric Robinson and George Brosan to develop new courses. The student to staff ratio was very low, so that we were able to devote many teaching hours to individual tutorials and seminars of six to eight students. We got to know all our students personally within a few weeks of their arrival, something which nowadays in the UK is probably only encountered by undergraduates at Oxford and Cambridge. Most of us were actively conducting research, with considerable support from the college, but we were certainly not put under the pressure to publish fast and frequently as is characteristic of most universities today. It is as a consequence of this lack of extreme pressure that we were able to develop a range of exciting and innovative courses as well as producing published research of a high quality.

The generosity of the institution is illustrated by the help and encouragement I was given to complete my PhD. One day in 1969, while in only my fifth term as a full-time member of staff, Eric Robinson pointed out that the college needed to have more PhDs on the staff, and asked me whether I thought I could finish mine in six months if relieved of all duties at the college. I said I thought I could, whereupon he offered me a sabbatical summer term, which ran on into the long vacation so that I was on full pay from March to September with the sole responsibility to complete my PhD. This proved to be strong motivation and I succeeded in completing my thesis more or less on time and gaining the award in January 1970. This in turn led to my promotion to a Senior Lectureship. My PhD research was in the new field of mathematical psychology and I was also allowed a free day every week so that I could teach this subject to postgraduates on a very high powered Masters programme at Sussex University, an institution whose graduates, along with those from LSE, were concurrently forming a substantial component of the new recruitment of young academic staff at Enfield.

The period from 1966 to 1970 was certainly a period of dramatic change for me, in which Enfield College of Technology played a central role. In 1966 I was a fairly typically confused twenty-three year old with a half finished PhD and a lack of any strong sense of direction, variously working as a colour printer at a film processing laboratory, a swimming pool lifeguard and a junior executive at a market research company. By 1970 I had a secure academic post, quite well paid, a PhD and a lot of interesting work participating in changes in higher education which brought me into contact with many bright young academics and a wonderful range of students, all before I celebrated my twenty-eighth birthday. It is perhaps not surprising that I formed a strong attachment to the Enfield College and eventually Middlesex University, remaining there in a full-time post until I retired 40 years later in December 2007. I should add that I have continued to teach at Middlesex since then, reverting to my former role as a part-time visiting lecturer. The old site at Enfield has gone, but physically it was never a very attractive place, and I have now completed fifty years of teaching at what has always seemed to be the same institution, but now at the much better appointed Hendon campus.

The 1960s and the mood for radical change

In order to appreciate the mood for change which was characteristic of Enfield in its early days it is useful to reflect on the broader changes that were taking place in the UK and in many parts of the world during the 1960s and early 1970s. On the one hand this was the era of the counterculture, the hippies and the various alternative lifestyles that were being explored at the time. On the other it was an era of radical politics including the US civil rights movement, anti-Vietnam protests, CND, the Prague Spring and the rise of many far left groups in the UK.

I was neither a fully-fledged hippy, nor a firebrand of the revolutionary left, but I think that my own history during that period displays the influence of both polarities. It is sometimes said that, if you can remember the 1960s in London, then you were not really part of it. Well, I must admit that I do have rather a lot of memories of the period. For example, I can vividly recall an evening in June 1965 when I had to decide whether to go to the Beat Poetry recital at the Albert Hall, subsequently immortalised in Peter Whitehead's film 'Wholly Communion', or the first British Vietnam War Teach-in. I think that the Teach-In was at LSE but am not certain because I went to the Beat Poetry recital. During the summer of 1965 I was living in a disused windmill on the Balearic island of Formentera, at the time a Mecca for hippies and many expatriate artists and musicians. In 1966 I was at the Grosvenor Square demonstration against the war in Vietnam, and subscribed to the counterculture publication *International Times* as well as the anarchist publications *Black Flag* and *Freedom*.

In 1967, the year I began teaching at Enfield, I became a member of UFO, the now legendary club in Tottenham Court Road which hosted the early performances of Pink Floyd and the Soft Machine; later that year I attended the Dialectics of Liberation conference at the Roundhouse, which included presentations by figures as varied as the anti-psychiatrists R. D. Laing and David Cooper, and the Black Power advocate Stokely Carmichael. At the beginning of 1968 I enrolled at the short-lived Anti-University of London where I can still remember David Cooper beginning one of his classes by proposing that we should discuss the relevance of Che Guevara to modern psychiatry (If you are confused by that, remember '*One Flew over the Cuckoo's Nest*').

During the summer of 1968 I joined many radical young people from all over the world in taking up the invitation of Castro's government to attend summer camps in Cuba. We were of course hopelessly wrong in thinking that this was a progressive government (but note also the popularity with young people to this day of *that* poster of Che Guevara), but it was certainly an enjoyable time travelling all over the island and working part of the week planting coffee alongside Cuban students. My group was known as the Patrice Lumumba Brigade and it included, among other unlikely fellow members, the future Labour MP Kate Hoey and the future journalist and controversialist Christopher Htchens.

The new educational climate at Enfield

At the time that I began my second year as a full-time lecturer at Enfield, shortly after my Cuban summer in September 1968, the changes that were to come were still at the stage of gestation. The engineering staff in the Faculty of Science, older, still more than counterbalanced the expanding numbers of young and radical academics in the Faculty of Arts and more soberly dressed men who we perceived to be looking down on us, regarding us as a bunch of scruffy layabouts. Rather than showing respect for their valuable profession and contribution to education we also tended to look down on them, even sometimes referring to them as the 'spanner men'. But the zeitgeist was certainly on our side and I can think of no better example of this new radical mood than one Monday morning when I arrived at the college and found, painted in huge letters on the side of the engineering block, the slogan 'CONTROL YOUR OWN EXISTENCE'. Was this a manifestation of the counterculture or the Marxist left?

As the college moved towards designation as a polytechnic in 1973 I became increasingly occupied with course development, mainly on the emerging BA Hons Humanities, which evolved from the BA General, and the BA Hons Social Science, the development of which involved many of the staff who had first come together on the Teachers Degree. Both of the new degrees enabled students who chose the right options to obtain psychology degrees accredited by the British Psychological Society, so permitting their progression to further training as a professional psychologist. Inevitably I was required to devote a good part of my time to conventional psychology courses, mainly in cognitive psychology and experimental methods, but I also took advantage of the opportunity presented by the flexible course structures to expand my newly awakened interest in interdisciplinary teaching.

I was able to devise courses for both of the new degree programmes with titles like 'History and Philosophy of Psychology' and 'Controversies in Modern Psychology', and I worked with staff from other disciplines, mainly philosophy, in planning and teaching these courses. Thus we were able to introduce psychology students to the work of a great range of thinkers from various disciplines, including the philosophers Hobbes, Hume, Descartes and Sartre; historians and philosophers of science including Karl Popper, Thomas Kuhn, Imre Lakatos and Paul Feyerabend; and other notable twentieth century figures such as R. D. Laing, Thomas Szasz, Erving Goffman, Noam Chomsky, John Searle, David Chalmers, Colin McGinn, Thomas Nagel, E. O. Wilson, Richard Dawkins, Stephen J. Gould and Richard Lewontin. The topics we covered included biological determinism from eugenics and hereditarian IQ psychology to socio-biology and evolutionary psychology; consciousness, free will and the relation between mind and brain from Hobbes and Descartes to modern materialism, artificial intelligence and advances in neuropsychology; science, pseudoscience and the validity of psychoanalysis; existentialism, existential psychology and psychiatry, and the treatment of the mentally ill.

Preserving the interdisciplinary outlook in later years

After I retired from full-time teaching in 2007 later variations of these courses were developed by two members of staff who had already been involved with me in teaching the earlier versions, Nick LeBoutillier and Richard Barry. In fact both had originally been exposed to my teaching as undergraduates at the college. Although my part-time teaching since 2007 has been solely in the field of health psychology I continue to meet up with Nick and Richard on my teaching days, and I was deeply gratified to learn, from both of them, that my classes had been a significant influence on their decision to embark on a career in academic psychology.

One further way in which the interdisciplinary approach pioneered at Enfield in the pre-polytechnic era has stimulated developments at Middlesex right up to the present day is in the field of health psychology. In the late 1980s under the leadership of David Marks, we were one of the first UK universities to teach this new field and were jointly first with UCL, City and Surrey in starting an MSc Health Psychology. Newly arrived from New Zealand, where health psychology had developed a little earlier than the UK, David rapidly absorbed the interdisciplinary ethos at Middlesex and was keen to promote the understanding of health issues, health behaviour and health promotion as requiring an essentially multi-disciplinary approach. The MSc programme, which I led for ten years, recruited staff from philosophy, sociology, health studies, gender studies, social work and the college counselling service, and included courses with titles such as Health, Morality and Medicine; Ageing and Health; Disability; Gender and Health; Counselling and Psychotherapy. In further promoting our approach we also produced a successful UK textbook of health psychology, now in its fourth edition, and David, with the assistance of various Middlesex people, including myself, developed and continues to edit the prestigious *Journal of Health Psychology*.

Concluding thoughts

Today, in a thoroughly hostile financial climate for education, one can only feel concerned about the difficulties which face students and academic staff. Lacking the benefit of free tuition and maintenance grants, required instead to saddle themselves with huge debts, students find themselves packed into large lecture rooms with only limited opportunities to interact with staff, either on an individual basis or in small tutorial groups. At the same time the academic staff are doing their best to provide a good educational experience while confronted with heavy teaching loads, and required at the same time to publish fast and frequently in order to maintain the research rating of their departments. The consequences are obvious when you browse through current psychology journals and see far too many papers which have been designed to be produced quickly and cheaply, and with a greater concern for their newsworthiness than for any deeper contribution to knowledge. All one can do is to hope for the emergence of a more agreeable political and financial climate for higher education in the UK.

I think that is enough from me. Enfield College of Technology was a great place to start a career back in 1967 and Middlesex University is still a good place to end a career fifty years later in 2017. I learned a lot and had a lot of fun. I hope that my colleagues and students, past and present, feel the same way.

18. Rising to the challenge

BARBARA FROST

Barbara Frost *joined the BA Business Studies team at Enfield in 1967, lecturing on statistics and operational research and, from 1980 – 1984, serving as Senior Course Tutor. In 1993 she took leave of absence and accepted a one-year guest lectureship at the University of Applied Sciences in Reutlingen, Germany. In 1994 she took early retirement from Middlesex University and stayed in Germany, lecturing also at the Verwaltungs- und Wirtschaftsakademie in Stuttgart, until retirement in 2008. Since then she spends a quarter of each year in Germany cycling, hill-walking and singing in the local choir. In England her time is filled by gardening and grandchildren.*

I was invited to join this book project late in its compilation. This had the great advantage that I was able to read the contributions of other colleagues and to see which ground had already been covered. Arthur Hindmarch's chapter covers the birth of the BA Business Studies degree far better than I could have done. Thus I am spared trying to recall details of course development and can limit my contribution largely to personal memories of that period.

Schooldays

I spent my childhood in the small Buckinghamshire town of Stony Stratford, now clinging to its identity on the north-western edge of Milton Keynes. In 1952 I took up my place at Wolverton Grammar School. It was a two-form entry co-educational country grammar with a huge catchment area from Olney in the north-east to Bletchley in the south and all the villages within that nine-mile radius. The school not only offered the usual selection of academic subjects but was also strong on sport and music. I was in my element. Most staff were very good teachers but my two mathematics teachers, one up to O-level and one for A-level, were exemplary role models. Both were women and both were gifted teachers. I was never exposed to the ridiculous attitude that prevails in some quarters that 'girls are not good at maths'. After completing A-levels in pure mathematics, applied mathematics and physics in 1959, I was accepted at the London School of Economics on the BSc (Econ) degree course specialising in statistics. Although it was not my first choice, which had been to do a mathematics degree, I have never regretted it as it prepared me better for my subsequent career.

Culture shock

As I had gone to grammar school a year early, it meant I was very young starting university. That was a mistake, but in those days kids from a humble background like mine had not heard of the luxury/wisdom of taking a gap year. The move from the support structure of family life and school to an independent life in the big city and the need for self-imposed discipline, and the change from doing three closely related numerical subjects to coping with eight widely diverse subjects was a double culture shock. I struggled. Further mitigating circumstances resulted in me taking a year out, repeating a year and I finally graduated in 1964 but with my self-confidence in tatters. I then spent a few months supply teaching in a Catholic boys primary school in Liverpool – the first two weeks were hell, but thereafter it was huge fun and tremendously rewarding – in order to save money for a long-planned year travelling abroad with a college friend. We left in spring 1965. It was to be the most exciting year of my life.

The route to Enfield

On my return in spring 1966, I again did a term of supply teaching, this time in a tiny village primary school, while looking for a career job. That came in the form of a mathematics post in a north London grammar school. Naively, I had expected to find myself in an environment that replicated my own enjoyable schooldays but I was to be disappointed. It lacked the strong school spirit that had been nurtured in my old school. And so, early in 1967, I was glancing through the *Times Educational Supplement* for possible alternatives when my attention was caught by an advertisement for a statistics lecturer at Enfield College of Technology. I had remained in touch with Arthur

Hindmarch, with whom I had been at LSE, and knew that he was working at ECT. I telephoned Arthur to ask if he knew anything about the advertised post. He knew a lot about it – not only about what would be required but also about the difficulties that had already been encountered in that subject area. I expressed doubt that I would be good enough to do the job. Arthur reprimanded me firmly by saying, 'Barbara, get the job and make yourself good enough!' That was the best advice I have ever received and I adopted it as a motto for life – accept the challenge and rise to the occasion.

I applied and was invited for an interview. It was not 'an' interview but three. Before, between and after the three sessions I waited in the staff common room where I felt I had slipped into a time warp, for it seemed that every third person who came through the door had been a contemporary of mine at LSE. One of the interviews was with Alan Hale, who was the 'father' of Enfield's Business Studies degree. I have often wondered if I had a head start with Alan as we had the same *alma mater*. He had been president of the students' union at LSE, albeit before my time. But what I believe really gained me credit in the interview was a little cheekiness on my part. Arthur Hindmarch had told me that one of the problems for those offering the mathematical subjects was that the students came with very different levels of ability and achievement in the subject. Thus I expected to be asked how I would deal with that problem. As I had no idea how to answer such a question, I pre-empted it by saying that I imagined the problem existed and asking how was it was already being dealt with.

I think Alan Hale was so impressed that I had given thought to the existence of a situation where students entered with different levels of ability that he did not turn the question back to me for a solution. My last session of the day was with, amongst others, George Brosan. The post was advertised as starting in September but he asked whether, if offered it, I could start at Easter. I explained that, as I was teaching an O-level class, it would be unfair to abandon them weeks before their examination. George Brosan's reaction was, 'If only all my staff were so conscientious…!' Obviously I had not done myself any harm by not making myself available earlier. Although only one post had been advertised, two of us were appointed. Tim Le Good was given the lectureship and I was appointed assistant lecturer.

The summer of 1967 was spent poring over my statistics textbooks. Also, as that was the birth of the computer era, I thought I ought to know something about it and so attended a course on computer programming. Although I never subsequently directly used the ALGOL learned on that course it gave me a basic understanding of the logic of programming. How distant that era of punched cards now seems!

The early QM years

Tim and I had been given *carte blanche* to do whatever we thought was appropriate in our subject. The brief was, quite literally, 'Do whatever you like. Just make it better.' Our first decision was to change the name of the subject, which hitherto had been called Business Mathematics. We wanted to remove the word mathematics in the hope of reducing the anxiety of those students who had not found maths easy at school. And so the term Quantitative Methods (QM) was coined. It amuses me that, not only did this term quickly become common currency in business studies education throughout Britain but later also in France (*Méthodes Quantitatives*), in Germany (*Quantitative Methoden*) and in Spain (*Cuantitativos Methodos*). It was also appropriate to abandon the word 'mathematics' since the two-year syllabus that we devised was almost exclusively statistics, comprising mostly descriptive statistics in year one and mostly inductive statistics in year two.

I was very content to play second fiddle to Tim Le Good. I felt safer with him leading and me following. What easy days those were! In my first term I had only to hold seminars with four first year groups and two second-year groups per week. Tim took the lectures that first term. That also worked in my favour. I was able to observe his teaching style and to see the level at which he pitched the material. He set a high standard for me to follow as I took over the lectures for the second half of the year. Tim was an excellent teacher and we were in complete agreement about how our subject should be delivered. It was a very harmonious working relationship and we have remained friends, albeit mostly by post, ever since.

We emphasised to the students at the beginning of the year that it would not be at all like school mathematics, that it was mostly statistics that would be taught *ab initio* and that they could therefore discard any negative preconceptions they may have had and see it as a fresh start in matters mathematical. I like to think that we were successful with our efforts, as most students seemed to enjoy the subject and we had good results.

During our first year, Tim and I discovered that the college had eleven calculating machines. These were the size of a heavy, stocky typewriter. They could add, subtract, multiply – by turning a handle clockwise, and divide – by turning the handle anticlockwise. We asked the powers-that-be if the college would buy a further fifty such machines – enough for one per student, so that we could set a 'practical' examination using larger and more realistic data sets. They cost £40 each – a total of £2,000 – a big sum in 1968. But higher education was awash with money in those halcyon days and our request was approved without hesitation. The noise in that 'practical' examination was deafening as sixty students clattered away frantically turning their handles. Of course, within a year or two, the machines were obsolete. I remember too, the college's first electronic calculator. That was twice the size of a typewriter in all dimensions and cost £2,000. It could do the same functions as the mechanical machines and, additionally, could calculate square roots. What progress! I remember it particularly because I asked to borrow it over the summer to help with a consultancy job I had. Allowance was granted but I had to take out insurance for it privately.

Like Tony Crilly, Tim and I were assigned one of the huts – No. 12 – as our shared office. I do not remember the blackboard that Tony mentions. Certainly I never worked on a blackboard. From the beginning I always worked with an overhead projector. Our *modus operandi* was to distribute a handout that had the skeleton of the lecture on it, together with any data sets or diagrams used so that the students did not have to spend valuable lecture time writing down such details. Also distributed was an exercise sheet relating to the new material. Students were expected to complete that prior to the seminar session in which the solutions were discussed and any misunderstandings were clarified. In those pre-computer days we enjoyed the luxury of having course secretaries who would type our teaching material. Later, with the advent of the personal computer, we were expected to become our own secretaries and type everything ourselves. Even then though, my handouts were often handwritten as they included charts, diagrams, mathematical symbols and Greek characters (and sometimes because I only completed their preparation the night before). I would then dash into college in my racy yellow sports car, replicate them on the Banda machine and rush to my lecture with them still hot from the press and smelling of Banda ink.

Unfortunately my teaching partnership with Tim Le Good was rather short-lived. After about four years he was lured away by the more lucrative rewards of industry. But I was lucky. My next partner-in-statistics was Ken Eveson, who was another excellent teacher with whom I enjoyed a close working relationship for the next twenty years.

Seminar groups in those days comprised only ten students and so we were able to hold seminars in our own offices. Only about 10 per cent of business students were female and we deliberately allocated one female to each seminar group as we felt they had a moderating effect on their male counterparts. How the gender balance has changed!

Miscellaneous memories

A weekly feature of those early years was the Wednesday afternoon staff meeting at which Alan Hale bombarded us with his ideas. Apart from the colourful Anglo-Saxon adjectives with which Alan peppered every sentence, he was also a fan of the latest 'management-speak' jargon. We used to while away the afternoon making a tally of the number of times he used the latest 'in-term'. I, who had not yet recovered the self-confidence shattered by my LSE experience, never dared to open my mouth at those meetings, until, after about two years, I could contain myself no longer. I have no recollection of the topic that was under discussion but I was astonished that such heavy weather was being made of it. I rehearsed in my head what I wanted to say, gathered together all my courage, raised my sweaty, shaking hand and made my contribution. There was a stunned silence. Whatever I had said brought the meeting to a hasty conclusion. Alan came to me and said, 'Barbara, you have never spoken before. You must do so more often. You have just crystallised in two sentences what I had been trying in vain to convey all afternoon.' That was a turning point for me – the beginning of the rehabilitation of my confidence.

Another Alan Hale anecdote relates to around 1970. He had been invited to the Marlborough Public School to talk about business studies education. He asked me to accompany him. At that time it was a boys-only school. Shortly before the occasion, Alan was finalising the details by telephone and mentioned the name of the colleague he was bringing with him. There was consternation at the other end of the line. Sorry, he could not bring a female. There were no facilities for females in the school. How old-fashioned that sounds now! Alan wanted to cancel the visit as a protest but I persuaded him otherwise. I thought it more important to spread the word in the public school sector that there was a form of higher education outside the old university sector and outside the traditional academic subjects, than to protest about an insult to me. My consolation prize was a huge bouquet and an apologetic note from the school.

A similar example of the times occurred on one of my early visits to a student on his industrial placement. It was at Courtaulds in Accrington. At the end of my morning's work, the student's in-company supervisor took me to the management's dining room for lunch. He apologised for the fact that there was no 'ladies room'. There was no need for one, as they had no female managers (and, presumably, did not expect any female visitors either).

Arthur Hindmarch mentions the football matches that took place on the patch of ground alongside the huts. I was asked to referee one of those matches. I donned my jeans and hockey boots and raced up and down with my whistle. One member of the staff team, Andy Thomas, became quite tetchy with me as I blew my whistle each time he picked up the ball. He, being a Welshman, was used to a different game and a different shaped ball.

What did we do right?

On a more serious note – what were the positive features of our academic culture? We cannot deny that institutions like ECT, and later, the polytechnics, were regarded as 'second division' and the entry qualifications of our students would probably not have gained them a place in the 'first division' – the universities. However, I believe that, after four years, many achieved results comparable with their university peers thanks to the longer class contact and greater approachability of teaching staff they enjoyed, and of our eagerness to make a success of our new venture. And what did we do right on the BA Business Studies degree? This came into sharper focus for me much later, first when I moved one foot sideways to do half my teaching on our European Business Administration degree and thereby glimpsed how our French, German and Spanish partners did things, but more so in the last phase of my career working full-time in Germany.

In designing the Enfield Business Studies degree I felt we had made a real effort to coordinate the delivery of related subjects and, whenever possible, to emphasise those relationships. That principle was reinforced in a 'subject' called interdisciplinary studies in which all members of staff had to participate a few times a year when it involved a case study to which their subject could contribute. Thirty years later, teaching statistics and mathematics in our German partner university, I was shocked to find that the syllabus for production management in Semester 1 covered quality control methods requiring knowledge of the normal distribution, while the normal distribution did not appear in the Statistics syllabus until Semester 2. Similarly, the economics professor dived straight into complex functions in week 1 while I was only refreshing their understanding of linear and quadratic functions in Week 3.

As far as I could see each professor in Germany was interested only in his (male colleagues only, even in the mid-1990s) own package without any attempt to discuss with others whether we were offering a coherent whole. Another marked contrast was in the style of final year project/thesis. The German equivalent was, in my view, a narrow piece of work, usually examining a very specific problem in the student's placement company. It was often entirely descriptive. That would not have been acceptable to us in the Business Studies degree in England. Amongst other criteria, we expected our students to apply some theory that they had learned on the course, to evaluate the applicability of that theory, to give a critical appraisal of their findings and, although they may have used a specific company example as a case study, we expected them, if possible, to draw some generalisation from it that would be relevant in similar situations.

Conclusion

Those early years were indeed stimulating. We felt we were creating something innovative and useful, and opening up opportunities for the next generation of students. I count myself lucky to have participated in the beginnings of business studies education and to have worked with such a good team of colleagues for twenty-six years. That luck continued into the later stages of my career which were spent in Germany, where I had fifteen more years of challenges, rewards and fun.

I hope my many former students feel that I did, and indeed rise to the challenge. And certainly I believe that we, as a team, rose to the challenge of delivering a new area of education successfully.

19. Exploring new fields in higher education

SOFRON SOFRONIOU

***Sofron Sofroniou** joined Enfield in 1967 as a lecturer in Logic and Mathematics, mainly for the Mathematics for Business degree. He left in 1982 to go to Cyprus where he joined the Cyprus Research Centre. In 1990 he was appointed Adviser to the President of Cyprus. He was thus instrumental in the creation of the University of Cyprus as well as of the University of Nicosia, a private institution where he is currently emeritus president. He also taught at the University of Indianapolis as a distinguished visiting professor for two years. He has published books of extracts with commentaries on Ancient Greek Poetry, Roman life and manners, and a collection of Superior Quotations in English to Educate and Amuse.*

The Road to Ponders End

In trying to write about the past one realises that one's memory is highly discrete and arbitrarily selective. The vast continuity of experience is cut up into little pieces and sieved into just a few moments that exist against a hazy and largely forgotten background. So I find it difficult to make a continuous story out of my life and experiences at the Enfield College of Technology, a life that lasted for about fifteen years from 1967 to 1981. This does not mean that I cannot make a general assessment of that period of my life. I am highly conscious that those were great years ('great' in the sense of the years of one's childhood), that I was happy at the time and that I often recall parts of that life with nostalgia.

I hope to convey what I mean in what follows. Bear in mind though that I will be describing a period of a rather remote past, a period that happened before the momentous revolution of the transistor and its impact on our lives. It was before the transformation that replaced life with virtual reality, a kind of meta-life in front of electronic devices, rather than life with real people and things and real feelings.

From a very young age I saw myself as a teacher either because of family tradition or because I enjoyed learning things and talking about them. Also, I could easily see that teaching was a well-respected and useful profession and that it also afforded generous holidays.

In Cyprus, where I was born, I attended the capital's single gymnasium or grammar school, the Pancyprian, and then the Teachers Training College at Morphou. I taught at both elementary and secondary schools for four years and then went to London for my university education. I made the rounds of London University gathering higher degrees from King's College, University College, and the London School of Economics. I then joined the BBC Greek service at Bush House in the Strand, a part of the 'World Service' of the BBC, from 1960 to 1967. The World Service was at the centre of things geographically, politically and artistically. My job there enabled me to meet some of the representatives of the British and the Greek political and cultural elites and I was quite impressed. I interviewed a number of quite famous people at the time such as actors, writers and politicians. These included the Greek Nobel Laureate George Seferis, the politician Enoch Powell, who in his younger days was a professor of classics, the eminent novelist E. M. Forster who had known the great Greek poet C. P. Cavafy during WW1, the quasi-Elizabethan lady poet Edith Sitwell, Laurie Lee (of *Cider with Rosie*), the Greek Resistance fighter and historian who led a group of fighters to blow up a crucial bridge in German-occupied Greece, Monty Woodhouse (MP for Oxford, and during WW2 commanding some Greek resistance fighters), Laurence Durrell (of the *Alexandria Quartet*), Patrick Leigh Fermor (another resistance fighter in Greece who led a group of Cretan fighters to capture the German General, who was commander of Crete at the time, and sent him to Egypt by submarine), as well as other celebrities.

Yet I was not really happy with a journalistic kind of life and I always longed to go back to education at a higher level than before. The opportunity for this came in a rather unexpected way. One of my higher degrees was on logic and scientific method offered by a formidable philosophical circle around Karl Popper and Imre Lakatos at the London School of Economics. The location of this course was only a couple of hundred metres away from Bush House, the headquarters of the BBC World Service. The other of my colleges was

King's, situated at exactly the same distance, and in the opposite direction, from Bush House, in the Strand. It so happened that the students of both colleges had patronized the Bush House canteen for lunch so that a witty Bush House man had once put a notice at a conspicuous place in the canteen saying 'Would the students of Kings who have finished their lunch, please vacate their places for the students of the LSE to have their own lunch'.

Two other facts conspired to induce me to go back to education. One was that one of the LSE students having regular lunch at Bush House was Iacovos Aristeidou who after graduation from LSE became a lecturer in Economics at Enfield College of Technology. The other fact was that at the famous Popper Tuesday afternoon seminars at LSE there were two postgraduate students, Allan Findlay and Ivor Grattan-Guinness, who were also teaching at Enfield. The confluence of these coincidences led to my own appointment at Enfield mainly, as I found out later, through the recommendation of Imre Lakatos.

So it was that I suddenly found myself far from Bush House in the comparatively remote area of Ponders End, at Enfield College of Technology. This was such a great and sudden social upheaval for me that I could not help but feel like going from Rome to Tomi, a Greco-Roman port on the Western coast of the Black Sea, somewhere in present day Romania. It was for this reason that I often thought of Ovid in exile there during my first year at Enfield. Not that I had any Ovidian pretentions.

The people at Enfield

However, after my first reaction at the change of social landscape I was fully compensated by the fact that I met at Enfield a number of first class people who were actively engaged and working seriously and innovatively in higher education. This was exactly what I was longing for. Besides Allan and Ivor who I knew from LSE I met Tony Crilly with whom I shared a staff room at one of the quasi-military huts surrounding the main building of Enfield College. I liked Tony immediately for himself but also because he reminded me of a good friend of mine from King's, Philip Sherrard, a historian and writer on culture and religion.

I met some other wonderful people at Enfield such as Stan Millward, an older mathematician from King's who epitomized for me the idea of an English gentleman, and who, besides mathematics, had an advanced interest in etymology, one of my own pet subjects. We had some fine walks together around the college and Stan was full of interesting conversation and fine old stories. I remember he once told me of one of his teachers at King's, a considerable mathematician in his time, who, in teaching, applied abstract algebra on operators in a new way, and when one of his better students asked him 'can you do that?' (as one might say, 'can you divide by zero?') he curtly replied 'Who is to stop me?' This unexpected reply gave endless delight to Stan and myself.

Another fine and good man I met at Enfield was Bill Craze the head of the Mathematics for Business course, to which I was mainly assigned. Bill was a most gregarious and friendly man, full of conversation and anecdotes, whose life revolved mainly around the 'M for B' course and its students. His interest in students was deep and abiding to him and he kept it throughout his later life, as I know from his contacts with a number of students from Cyprus.

He was a good organizer and he was also gifted with a kind of natural wisdom and humanity. You could rely on him to always do the decent and kind thing. Some of his linguistic mannerisms were also delightful. He could never say 'now', as he preferred the more highfaluting 'at this point in time.' On one occasion I had a problem at the College and I asked Ivor Grattan-Guinness whether I should to tell Bill about it. After a little thought his answer was 'No, don't tell him, because if you do he will tell you.' He prolonged 'tell' a bit as if to say he will tell you much more than you need to know. We both understood and laughed the problem away.

Another colleague I remember well at Enfield was Sven Hammarling who had graduated from the Mathematics for Business course itself and then joined it as a lecturer. I found Sven admirable in his devotion to his subject and for the continuity of his purpose. His special subject was Numerical Analysis and by the laws of cause and effect he must have done very well in it or in a related field (See Chapter 5).

I also remember well Jonathan Powers, a serious thinker on the Philosophy of Physics whose fine book on the subject was also translated into Greek. We had some talks together on the subject at the lovely Trent Park Annex of the College and I was very pleased when I saw my name mentioned with thanks in his preface, and in both the English and Greek editions (See Chapter 22).

Another colleague I remember well was Joel Gladstone who was involved with a very exciting and very future-oriented course on Society and Technology, an arca that is bccoming progressively more relevant. I met Joel again much later in Cyprus in connection with students intending to study at Middlesex University. I mention this in order to show that my Middlesex connection was continuous but also for a very strange coincidence. Sometime later when I was in London I telephoned Joel in order to arrange a meeting. I asked him where exactly he lived and he asked me back the same question. When I told him at Lincoln Road, East Finchley, he asked me 'Which side of the road?' I could not see the point of the question. I thought Joel was going funny, funny-peculiar, and I retorted a bit impatiently, 'What does that matter?' Then Joel laughed for no apparent reason. When I enquired about the reason for the sudden merriment Joel told me to please open the door of the house and look on my right and when I did so I saw Joel waving at me from his window. That was indeed an extremely rare coincidence bordering on the miraculous.

Mathematics for Business

I also remember well many of the hundreds of students that I taught at Enfield. I am afraid I cannot recall their names except for a handful of students. One of them was called Campbell and I remember him for two good reasons; one, that he was a talented student in mathematics and secondly because he was a supporter of his home football team Cambridge United. I hope Cambridge United is doing as well as Campbell must be doing. I also remember, of course, our student Alan Gully who was a good student of economics and later became a lecturer at Enfield.

When I arrived at Enfield College of Technology I soon felt at home mainly because of Bill Craze's warmth of character but also because of the presence there of both Allan Findlay and Ivor Grattan-Guinness as well as the camaraderie that developed between myself and my room-mate Tony Crilly. I knew Allan and Ivor well especially from our regular attendance and participation in the famous

Tuesday afternoon Popper seminars at the London School of Economics around Popper's philosophy of science and politics, politics as freedom and as criticism with a view to the growth of knowledge.

The Mathematics for Business course was innovative and progressive. It was in this sense emblematic of what most people were trying to do under the academic leadership of Eric Robinson at Enfield. The course tried to combine university mathematics with economics, accounting, operations research, statistics and management. The name of the course was unfamiliar and quite modest but it managed to attract a sufficient number of students some of whom were very capable. A number of them had later reached the higher echelons of small and large businesses while others were well placed to join academic institutions. I know this fact better from what I learned about Greek and Cypriot students who attended the course. One of the latter went on to become a professor at one of the most prestigious universities in Greece, the Athens Metsovion Polytechnic-University. Another of our students had reached a very high position in a well-known company only a few years after graduating from the course. We considered such an achievement as a strong vindication of what we were trying to do.

I still believe however that the name of the course was too unassuming and unfamiliar and that it would attract more attention and students had it been called, and rightly called, something like Mathematics and Management or even Mathematics and Business. It is worth mentioning here an incident in connection with the eminent Cambridge mathematician and philosopher Alfred North Whitehead, the Whitehead of *Principia Mathematica*, when he was teaching at Harvard. At an apparently noisy party there, a colleague mentioned to him that he was teaching Business Ethics. Whitehead couldn't believe his ears. The name of the subject sounded so strange, unfamiliar and incredible to Whitehead that he told his colleague in total incredulity 'You know, I could swear I heard you say you teach business ethics.' Such a subject was unheard of to Whitehead who could understand the teaching of Ethics and Philosophy and Mathematics and other traditional combinations, but not, in God's name, business ethics. This little anecdote shows the importance of the names of academic disciplines and how educational ideas have changed in time mainly through the American influence.

The course was well run by Bill Craze in a most friendly and democratic way. Everything we did was done collectively after a thorough examination and discussion of all relevant aspects. We felt that we formed a special front line group and in that group Allan, Ivor and myself were a special Popperian contingent that was duty bound to spread Popperian enlightenment about science and society as a Darwinian process of conjectures and refutations and survival of the fittest species and ideas. This Popperian gospel that was extended also to mathematics by the rather heretical Popper disciple and successor, Imre Lakatos.

Ivor applied and extended these and many other ideas in an impressive way in his substantial work on the history and philosophy of mathematics and logic. Allan Findlay was also a fine thinker but a very reluctant writer while Tony Crilly has left his mark both in introductory mathematics and in his magisterial work on the life and work of the eminent British algebraist Arthur Cayley.

We, at Mathematics for Business, rather kept ourselves to ourselves, as a kind of chosen people, who could afford to frown on more subjective and dubious subjects, such as new-fangled sociological theories or the obfuscations of modernism and deconstructionism. Another course that I thought was especially worth its salt was the one associated with Joel Gladstone and entitled 'Society and Technology'. This course had, I thought, the right ingredients for making a valuable contribution both to the economy and to humankind as thinking and social beings.

Eric Robinson's enlightened leadership

This brings me to an interesting educational problem. The period of Thatcherism in education can be described as a period of redirecting education, especially higher education, mainly to the service of the economic and industrial needs of the country. This was a laudable aim but it would have been more laudable if education in skills needed for the economy were not divorced from education for human beings who have intellectual and moral concerns. Unfortunately Thatcherism in education became a mostly instrumental and utilitarian exercise and so it was cut from its foundational and historical roots. This policy ignores something important that may sound contradictory to the utilitarian but it is, I think, something that great scientists always appreciated and stressed. I have here in mind mainly Einstein and Poincaré who believed that we become more practical when we are at our most theoretical. Poincaré highlighted this principle in connection with mathematics and the practical and life-saving use of complex numbers that many people considered as fictional complications. In fact, the whole history of modern science bears witness to the validity of this principle of theory being a most practical pursuit. I am reminded here of the great German mathematician Bernard Riemann who in the 1860's was delighted that he had the grand number of eight students in his course. Thatcherism would have closed such a course of studies as uneconomical but the world would have been much poorer after such a step.

In a sense Thatcherism began even before Thatcher. It can even be traced back to the Roman poet Horace who advised that one should pursue 'virtue after riches', that money must be sought in the first instance. The guiding and enlightening force at Enfield at the time, Eric Robinson, was against such attitudes. Eric, the head of academic affairs, was a thoughtful and energetic educationist with a great interest in higher education. He believed and fought for the expansion of education at all levels and classes of the population and in a number of new and relevant fields, fields related to the social and economic needs of the country. He was a Labour Party activist and it is said that he promoted the idea of the New Polytechnics through the highest echelons of the Party.

Eric thought the expansion of higher education should include the proliferation of polytechnic-universities which would serve as 'people's universities.' And when we consider that university education at that time covered only 5 per cent of the population we can appreciate better how necessary and revolutionary were Eric's ideas. Eric's social philosophy was similar to that of John Rawls, as encapsulated in the latter's idea that 'social and economic inequalities ought to be arranged so that they are both (a) to the greatest expected benefit of the least advantaged and (b) attached to positions and offices open to all under conditions of fair equality of opportunity.' (Rawls, [1971], 1999)

Eric was a social democrat whose higher values were freedom, democracy and a fair opportunity for all, especially in the field of education. When he suddenly left Enfield, under politically motivated and rather nefarious circumstances, the sense of loss at the college was widespread and deep. We immediately realized that we lost the leadership of a man of vision, progress, and educational innovation.

The regular meetings of academic staff that Eric chaired at the college were memorable. They enhanced the awareness, the solidarity and the unity of purpose of all who took part in them and they were hugely attended. His informed positions and commitment were truly instructive and even inspirational. For me, personally, they were a high level educational experience. Eric Robinson was one of the prime movers in the educational revolution that occurred in Britain in the 1960s.

Reminiscing again

Another positive aspect of the college that made life there more interesting was its international environment. Enfield College and later Middlesex Polytechnic was a truly international institution. Personally I found it very interesting and enriching to teach students from countries like Iran, Chile (during the dictatorship there), Indonesia, Hong-Kong, Nigeria and various European countries.

As I mentioned in the beginning I particularly remember certain moments of my life at Enfield that may or may not be significant. Let me mention some of them. My journey from North London to Ponders End took invariably thirty-five minutes whatever route I tried to follow in order to shorten my journey. I can boast that I was never late for any class or meeting. In those days we spent most of our time at the college but I remember well the local pub, which I rarely visited being allergic to drinking, the well-stocked library that I often visited and the large machine learning room which was quite progressive at the time (see Chapter 11).

Our secretary Barbara, was always obliging at the Mathematics for Business office. I remember a lady student who had joined the course after teaching classics for some years and doing so well that she later joined the National Physical Laboratory. I also remember my visits to students in firms during their sandwich year from which visits I learned more than the students. I remember the CNAA visits that usually went very smoothly. I remember too some of the external examiners who were always useful to us such as the economist Sir Roy Allen from the London School of Economics and the mathematicians Hyman Kestelman and David Larman from University

College London. And I remember a visit of Mrs Thatcher herself, then Minister of Education and student protests against her for her hard-line-policies. I also remember a completely blind student who managed to graduate from the course and who was a great example to all of us.

After Enfield

I left Middlesex Polytechnic in 1981 because I wanted to work in Cyprus, my country of origin, and because I felt that my experiences from Middlesex Polytechnic could be fruitfully transplanted to Cyprus. I joined a private college as its director and I was instrumental in helping steer it toward a university status under the name of University of Nicosia. I became an advisor to the president of Cyprus especially in educational matters and I was also instrumental in the establishment of the University of Cyprus which is doing very well in international university charts. I believe my own education at Enfield and Middlesex helped me considerably in my later educational endeavours. My son Christopher became an educational consultant and universities' representative and of course Middlesex University is on top of his list of overseas universities. My time at Enfield has accompanied me throughout my life and I feel eternally grateful to all my friends and colleagues there for their cooperation and support.

Good higher education and social and economic order

But I would like to end this rambling note on a more general level. A main objective of higher education is to cultivate and impart to young people the skills and productive capabilities associated with modern life and especially modern technology. But as the Roman thinker Seneca realized a long time ago, and as Aristotle would have told him and us, education should not be cultivated only as a means. It should equally be concerned with cultivating humanity itself, the humanity of human beings. I believe that cultivating humanity also includes cultivating the love of knowledge for its own sake and also cultivating and respecting our own values and the lives and values of other people and also being constantly aware of our common humanity in a mostly hostile universe. Good education has also to vigorously oppose the enemies of knowledge and those who cultivate and impose distorted versions of knowledge or simply falsehoods as knowledge and as ideological means for power, domination and exploitation.

One of the serious problems in the world today is the extreme and absurd levels of economic inequality that applies both within and between countries. Such levels can be described as immoral and offensive. Looking at the past we often discover astonishing and offensive situations and practices. I sometimes think of present situations and practices that our descendants in the remote future may find equally astonishing and offensive. I believe that our present huge inequalities in salaries and rewards in the workplace and beyond will be one such case. How could people tolerate such glaring injustice?

Huge inequalities, besides being so unfair, are also counterproductive. In fact, inequality is one main reason for economic underperformance and even of the all too familiar periodic economic depressions. And yet such inequalities are increasing instead of decreasing throughout the world. Eminent economists, such as Joseph Stiglitz, have argued convincingly about the multiple ill effects of extreme and unjustified inequalities. I believe that one very good way of reducing unacceptable economic inequalities is the widest possible extension of higher education, the highest possible raising of young persons' capabilities. I am sure that this kind of thinking lay behind the thought and movement that led to the creation of the new polytechnics in Britain. Enfield College of Technology played a meritorious role in this connection.

20. Reminiscences of a serendipitous start to an academic career

THANOS SKOURAS

Thanos Skouras *joined Enfield as an economist in September 1967 and moved to Thames Polytechnic as head of Economics in January 1974. He subsequently served as head of the department at North East London Polytechnic for eight years, before returning to Greece in 1986 as professor at the Athens University of Economics and Business, where he has acted as vice-rector, president of the research centre, head of department and is, since 2010, emeritus professor. He has taught at Cambridge University and universities in Belgium and China, was a consultant to the European Commission and other widespread consultancy. He enjoys reading and writing, mostly about current issues in Greece and the European economy.*

Enfield was my first job. I started as an assistant lecturer in September 1967, a little short of twenty-four years of age. I had just graduated from the London School of Economics MSc (Econ) course the same summer and had practically no experience of the real world outside education.

One of the first people I met was Sami Daniel, who became my best friend in the college and one of the few colleagues that I also met socially outside of work. I first went to Enfield a couple of months earlier for the interview and Sami was among the economists I saw before the formal interview. It turned out that he was also from the LSE and we established a good rapport immediately. Sami participated in the formal interview representing the economists though he did not ask any questions. Sometime later, he confided to me that Dr Brosan had been rather reluctant to hire me because of a previous experience with the appointment of a compatriot economist, Rigas Doganis. Rigas (who became a friend a couple of years later and had a distinguished career as a world-renowned expert in aviation and airport economics) had been offered a job at Enfield in a previous round of hiring. Though he accepted the appointment, he changed his mind after receiving a better offer from a university. George Brosan took this as a betrayal typical of Greek economists trained at the LSE. Sami didn't counter this prejudice head-on but argued that Doganis had grown-up and gone to school in London (which was true) and was not Greek but London Cypriot (which was not true). Fortunately, George Brosan was persuaded by this to give me a chance.

My appointment at Enfield had a determining influence in my life, as it set me on a career path that I followed for the next half a century. But, at the time, an academic career was not my main aim and, in fact, had never seriously considered until the spring of 1967. What seemed a great chance for me was that it enabled me to stay out of the Greek army without becoming a draft dodger.

The army coup on 21 April 1967 and the establishment of a military dictatorship had made the performance of my military service, which was my original plan, not only distasteful but even dangerous. A change of plan became particularly advisable following the reaction of the closest person to me at that time. My then wife (we were married the previous summer) had taken part in the first resistance act against the dictatorship, which was the occupation of the Greek Embassy in London a week after the coup. In these circumstances, staying out of Greece seemed essential and an academic job was the only acceptable basis for deferment of the draft. I, therefore, felt great gratitude to Enfield and George Brosan (as well as Sami's deception of him). They had offered me a job that not only allowed me to legally stay out of the Greek army but also made it possible for me to live in London and to further my economics education, both by registering for a part-time PhD at the LSE and, more importantly, by on-the-job training as an economics teacher.

Although Enfield was a dream job in the circumstances, it was a radical change of direction for me. Before that fateful April, my expectation was that, upon getting the mandatory military service out of the way, I would work in the cinema business, in which I had close relatives both in Greece and in the United States. I had never until then seriously contemplated an academic career and hardly felt adequate to the task.

Learning from colleagues

On starting this career, it was clear that I needed to work hard to fulfil my duties. Fortunately, Enfield was a great learning place and my colleagues, who were mostly only a few years older than me, were an important source of knowledge. I was struck from the start by their willingness to explore new ideas and follow novel directions in economic theory. I was particularly impressed by their familiarity with literature that I had never encountered before in my five years of economics studies at Durham and the LSE. They were using in their teaching a recent book by Richard M. Cyert and James G. March *A Behavioral Theory of the Firm*, which was the first ever textbook in behavioural economics. And that was more than a decade before Herbert Simon was awarded the Nobel Prize and the term 'behavioural' was first heard by most academic economists and at least three decades before such an approach started gradually to become a subfield of economics!

I still remember my surprise when Klaus Heidensohn, a good economist and faultless colleague, casually corrected my misapprehension regarding the general applicability of the demand and supply model. Klaus pointed out that it cannot be used for a monopoly and referred me to Lipsey's well-known textbook. Richard Lipsey's *Introduction to Positive Economics* was a book for which I had the highest regard and had read from cover to cover. So it was quite a shock to discover that Klaus was right and that a supply curve can be validly specified only under perfect competition. I suspect that even today most academic economists (let alone their students) are hardly aware of the limitations of the most widely used economics tool. But a further lesson for me was the realization that I had not been attentive enough in my reading and that I still had a lot to learn from a book I believed I knew well.

Another colleague who contributed significantly to my better understanding of economics was Noel Lee, with whom I shared an office in the prefabricated 'huts'. Noel had a very good analytical mind and his mathematical skills were better than mine. We had many interesting discussions from which I learned a lot, we co-authored a paper and also gained a lesson in professional academic politics. I felt there was something wrong with a widely-quoted result in the literature regarding regulated utilities and, through diagrammatic analysis, came to the conclusion that the correct result was exactly the opposite of the generally accepted one. Noel agreed with me but we could not pinpoint the mistake in the mathematical proof of the result, which was published in the prestigious *American Economic Review,* as the mathematics used were quite advanced and certainly beyond our understanding. Finally, Noel worked out an algebraic proof, in addition to my diagrammatic one, and the correction was eventually sent to the *American Economic Review*. We were disappointed to receive a reply indicating that another correction had already been accepted for publication and would appear in due course. The accepted paper didn't look like a correction at all; it was less than two pages of incomprehensible advanced mathematics, totally cryptic and hardly mentioned the result that it meant to correct but, somehow, the message was communicated and from then on the usual references to the mistaken result disappeared from the relevant literature.

There were many other colleagues with whom we talked about economics but Sami Daniel was by far the most important one. Sami had a very inquisitive and imaginative mind and had an interest not only in economics but also in politics and was particularly active and effective in the organizational politics within Enfield. The never-ending discussions about desirable improvements in order to secure the approval of the Council for National Academic Awards (CNAA) for various courses, gave him ample scope for the exercise of his political talents. But this was of little interest to me then and our conversations were almost exclusively about concepts and new ideas in economic theory. The pub in the back of the Enfield precinct was our customary meeting place and, and as I never developed a taste for the English pub, this was the only time in my life that I frequented one and regularly had a pint over an hour of conversation with Sami. I would normally leave to have Greek-hours late dinner with my wife while Sami would stay on to talk workplace politics with other usually non-economist colleagues. Months into this routine, I couldn't believe my ears when one evening Sami said that he had to leave early to see his son's mother. The routine came to an end some time later, when Sami married Susan, his son's mother and the younger sister of Janet Holland, a good friend of ours we knew from the LSE.

Sami was instrumental in bringing about a momentous event in my intellectual development. We were both interested in finding out how the Cambridge school of economics differed from the neoclassical school, which was all-dominant at the LSE, so Sami arranged for Joan Robinson to give a talk at Enfield. In a fully packed hall, Joan Robinson stood up for nearly three hours without a break, giving a spirited talk and answering questions without any notes. Apart from her stamina, we were impressed by her passionate conviction in her criticism of neoclassical theory and felt we should learn more. The following year, it was arranged that Mario Nuti, fellow of King's College, would give a series of lectures on Cambridge economics to our students and this was continued for three more years by John Eatwell, then fellow of Trinity College and now Lord and President of Queens College. I sat in with my students for all these lectures but unfortunately Sami missed them, as he had left Enfield to become Head of the Economics Department at Kingston Polytechnic.

The influence of the CNAA

I stayed on for a few more years until the last day of 1973. By then, Enfield had become part of Middlesex Polytechnic and I had made considerable progress in my understanding of economics (both its strengths and limitations). My teaching had improved a lot and I had internalized the CNAA requirement for continual development of all courses and teaching materials. My first publication was done in preparation of the macroeconomics course I developed and taught, being an extensive review of the differences in the main approaches that could be found in more than forty macro textbooks (probably the totality of such texts in English at the time).

The importance of the CNAA to life at Enfield cannot be exaggerated and its positive effects on academic development were quite remarkable. Maurice Peston (Professor at QMC London and later a 'Lord') was reported in the front page of *The Times* asserting that the teaching of economics at Enfield was better than in Oxford. Professor Peston and Professor Bernard Corry, who was chairman of the Economics Board of the CNAA in its formative period, effectively determined (being outside advisers to the appointments committee) my hiring as Head of the Applied Economics Department at

North East London Polytechnic. The committee that formally made the decision was chaired by the Polytechnic director, Dr Brosan, whom I had not seen since my Enfield appointment ten years earlier. It is for this reason that I have always had a soft spot for George Brosan even though a year later he tried to close down my department – but that is another story.

The CNAA was also inadvertently a major reason that Enfield, as well as the other similar institutions financed by local authorities, did not develop as originally planned. I remember Eric Robinson giving a talk to new staff and asking them to do research and provide solutions for problems of relevance to the local community. This made me feel very uneasy, as I could not see how I could go from book knowledge, about which I was still insecure in my teaching, to giving advice on real world problems of a community that I hardly knew at all. Moreover, even if feasible, this seemed a diversion from the research work needed for career advancement in the academic profession. But in reality, apart from this talk, there was neither institutional pressure nor incentives to do work in this direction and I find it difficult to avoid the conclusion that only lip service was paid to the aim of serving the local community.

If the original aim had been to serve the local community, the institutional setting that was put in place should have ensured that the interests and primary objectives of the local authorities were not misaligned with those of the other actors involved. But this was not the case and there was an evident misalignment of objectives between the local authorities, on the one side, and the CNAA and management on the other. Moreover, it was the latter side and predominantly the CNAA that ultimately controlled the direction of the institutions' development.

It was probably thought that control of the purse by the local authorities sufficed to achieve the aim of serving the local community, since financial control could be used to steer the educational institutions' management to the pursuit of this overarching objective. But this purpose was undermined by the establishment of the CNAA. The CNAA had a national aim, which was to ensure a high level of tertiary education that would be equivalent and by no means inferior to that provided by the university sector. It was, therefore, most likely if not inevitable that it would aspire to academic excellence. In retrospect, it was the CNAA that controlled the direction of the institutions' development, in conjunction with the managerial inclination for growth. As might be expected, the management was mainly interested in the growth of the institution and, in seeking to increase the number of students and staff, it needed the support of the CNAA and so had to satisfy its requirements. This gave the CNAA the strategic advantage in shaping the direction of development pursued by management. There was little that the local authorities could do when faced with a management, like that of Enfield, which was intent on the growth of the institution. They could either approve and share in the success of a rapidly growing and academically respectable local institution or, without any apparent gain to the cause of serving the local community, stifle its development.

The uniqueness of Enfield

Enfield's growth was quite remarkable and its pace was faster than at any of the four institutions I have served in my career. This was a time of rapid expansion of tertiary education but George Brosan's personality and ambition must have played a significant part. Rapid growth undoubtedly contributed, if not actually caused, the palpable dynamism that characterized the Enfield scene and which was noticeable even by outside academics. I remember Max Steuer, an LSE economist with a curiosity and sensitivity for new trends, wondering about Enfield and asking Sami and myself what exactly was going on there. The fact that there was a steady stream of new posts advertised and staff hired also contributed to the buzz about Enfield.

The increase in staff numbers followed the increase in the number of students drawn by degree courses that were on the whole novel to the British academic scene. Business courses, which were long snubbed by universities as unworthy of academic study, were among the first to be offered and proved to be very popular. Enfield was a pioneer in the creation of such courses, which are now ubiquitous in British and European universities. These courses were essentially multidisciplinary and their various components were taught by specialists from a number of academic disciplines. This, in conjunction with the pronounced student preference for social studies rather than engineering, resulted in the staff recruitment of large numbers of social science graduates. It also probably accounts for the remarkable record of Enfield being for a time the biggest academic employer in the country of sociologists, as well as, possibly, of philosophers of science.

A number of these social scientists made an impression on me but it is not possible to explain here the way in which many colleagues, economists and others, were significant to my own development. All I can say is that I am thankful to have known them in those formative years in my life and to have been at Enfield in such exciting times. Enfield thrived in a period in which access to tertiary education in Britain was radically transformed expanding at an unprecedented rate. It was a great fortune to have lived in these times and a great privilege to have participated even a little in this transformation.

21. Giving up was never an option: Enfield and I found each other

RONALD GILES

> ***Ronald Giles*** *was an undergraduate student in the Enfield Mathematics for Business degree 1967-1971 with an industrial year at National Institute of Economic and Social Research. He went on to obtain a PhD in Quantitative Social Science in 1984. His career started at the United Nations Economic Commission for Europe followed by a short time as a UK Government Statistician. He has been a senior lecturer at South Bank and Queen Mary University of London, a visiting lecturer at University of Kent and University of Birmingham and visiting professor at City University of New York and Saratov State University. He also spent a short time as a financial analyst. He is now semi-retired but is an active member of the Society of Technical Analysts.*

Before Enfield

My parents were both brought up in a world of extreme economic deprivation in the east end of London. School time for both of them was limited, and on their fifteenth birthday the labour exchange directed them into manual work. I was born in the post-war baby-boom in late-1948. Knowledge of how the education system in England worked or did not work was not available to my parents. It is summed up in the poem by G. K. Chesterton 'The Secret People'. I went to the local secondary school, as one of the 'Hidden Children'. Most of my friends aspired to become assistant butchers. My view at that time was 'there must be something better than this?'

After school I went to the Sixth Form College as directed by the youth employment office resulting in a short period on an OND course. I hated it so I transferred to an A-level course. I was offered History, Economics and Politics as a 'normal plan' but then a big argument ensued, as I wanted to swap History for Pure Mathematics. This subject was linked with Applied Mathematics, Physics, and Chemistry. The staff at the college thought I was from the planet Zog but my preferences were available on the timetable. The teaching was dreadful and/or non-existent – the Pure Mathematics teacher read the horse-racing column in class and disappeared at lunchtime. So we were mainly self-taught and I was the only one to pass this subject. Professor Richard Lipsey (then at Essex University) published a textbook half way through the A-level course that revolutionised the thinking in Economics at that time. It linked Economics with Pure Mathematics and I felt vindicated (Lipsey and Archibald, 1967).

I was not sure what to do next. In 1967 I found it very difficult to get into University, partly because of the baby-boom, partly due to restricted numbers on courses but mainly because Sixth-form colleges were then considered of the lowest rank. New Universities had been added to the existing Red Brick Universities but demand exceeded supply. There were however these 'other colleges' that were offering degrees regulated by a body called CNAA. I must admit I did not understand the difference between university awarded degrees and those CNAA degrees. There were implicit rankings but not explicit ones at that time. I spoke to a friend who had a second interview at Enfield on the BA Business Studies degree and had subsequently been rejected. He said that as I had achieved Pure Mathematics among my A-levels perhaps I should try for a course described in a leaflet he had picked up in the Enfield college literature. It was called Mathematics for Business. I found later in my career that 'word of mouth' has a high rating in such things as finding employment and selecting a course.

Enfield - getting in.

I phoned Enfield College the week preceding the start of the course and was invited along the next day for interview. Terry Butfield a lecturer involved with Operational Research conducted the interview. He spoke of such strange terms: Analysis, Matrices, Operational Research, Networks, Programming, Calculus, Statistics and Economics. The last three I understood. Naively I said 'will you take me?' After some deliberation, 'Yes' was the reply 'but we start next Monday.'

I went back to my A-level college and showed them details of the course at Enfield. They were quite angry that a degree course existed relating to my A-levels after their previous advice. I then approached my father about starting the course. He was concerned about me supporting myself. When I told him that I could get a grant it was clear that father and son were going in different directions. It took three bus journeys to travel to Ponders End and to his credit my father contributed to me buying a car, a Ford 100E. This was possible as I had been working in a brewery during that summer and had saved some money. The local authority paid for my travel expenses and the car park at Enfield was free.

First Experience

My fellow colleagues on the course were entirely different from those I had met before. They were more confident and many came from local grammar schools. There were also a few from private schools. The head of the course was Bill Craze. He came in from time to time saying that he had resigned from being the course leader, but then suddenly he was back in charge. He would occasionally pop in with new ideas. One I remembered was his advice to the effect that 'You need to write an essay on a social science subject so that you don't inadvertently end up to sacking half the staff in your future job'. For this a politics essays from my A-levels came in handy.

Enfield College was a mishmash of temporary huts and old buildings, and nothing structurally changed during my time there. The temporary buildings were similar to my Sixth form College. My knowledge of higher academia was limited and I assumed that all colleges were similar in layout. Algebra was taught mainly by Allan Findlay and Analysis by Dr Sofroniou. Allan Findlay also taught us some Boolean Algebra but it was mainly matrix algebra. Order was his theme. 'You do not put your shoes on before your socks' I remember him saying. Dr Sofroniou, whom we called Saffron after a popular record at that time, spoke with a cigarette at the corner of his mouth, almost chewing it. I realised that Analysis and I would soon be parting company.

The Statistics taught by Raj Vasudeva was good, and I enjoyed the course. However, he could not pronounce residuals, calling it resdiduals. This endeared us to him. Sally Holtermann, who summed up the 'mod' girl image of the time from the Hampstead set, taught the microeconomics course. She was also a good teacher. Macroeconomics, taught by Ruth Towse, was more difficult for many students, as I found many did not have A-level Economics. Stan Millward taught Numerical Analysis. He always came in to lectures wearing a white overall coat and his notes and presentation were first class. Computing was taught by various staff. I have never found computer people able to convey much information. In the end I taught myself Fortran. Operational research I avoided as much as possible, and I scraped through the first year examinations.

My car broke down with regularity and the Enfield technical support staff were very helpful getting the car started on many occasions. On the way home via Chingford there was a hill called Kings Head Hill that required me to stop half way up as my Ford 100E had no synchromesh between third and second gear. There was no fourth gear.

Christmas vacation was spent delivering the Christmas post, and I remember such employment was against the instructions of Dr Brosan, the principal. During my first year I regularly bumped into second year student Richard Baillie – who appears again later in my story. The student football team at Enfield was poor so I continued to play for my Sixth-Form college Old Boys on Saturdays, while on Wednesdays I took up Judo at Enfield. This was very good but there was a drawback. Some years later I found that I had damaged my atlas bone from the rolling break-falls. My shins are still sore to this day from throws at the leg. On the social scene there were various pop groups and other events. We linked with the teacher training college at Trent Park for joint events. On these occasions we all asked the question: 'Why hadn't Enfield College been moved to such a magnificent place as Trent Park?'

Second Year

In 1968 there was much student disruption in Universities. Essex University was closed down and the London School of Economics was used as a focal point for the press as the location was only a short walk from Fleet Street, then home of the newspaper industry. Student disruption did not greatly extend to Enfield College except for a few students blockading Dr Brosan's office, much to his annoyance as he faced the prospect of climbing over the student protestors.

In the second year of the Mathematics for Business course we were introduced to Patrick McMahon. His Econometrics course was a revelation. He had stories to tell and he regularly brought in other colleagues to give his lectures. He seemed to be having a good time. As I found this course easy relative to other students, my destiny was to follow this route. Ivor Grattan-Guinness gave the last of the Analysis lectures on the course. Ivor's Lecture on Fourier Analysis and Spectral Analysis was like being caned at School. It was painful but by accepting the punishment, it would do you good in the long run. In later years I found this subject very useful in my research and could see the relevance of it. (I bought a tent from Ivor that he advertised on the notice board. It stood me in good stead for many years. His name remained on it when I sold it).

As the second year examinations loomed I was apprehensive about passing, as were many others. Twelve of the thirty-five students who started never returned for the final year. I remember the letter coming in the post. I had passed. I had a clear examination strategy. In the 'applied' paper I had avoided any Operational Research questions, answering only the Statistics questions, and in the Economics examination I answered only the econometric type questions. In the latter I came second in the class. The computing paper had been a six-hour examination, but little things are remembered; I chose to answer the regression question but I forgot to allow for deviations from the mean, as I realised as soon as I left the exam room.

Towards the end of the second year we were allocated an industrial year placement. Most were Operational Research or computing based. The placement and I were becoming a problem. Then as sometime happens, when all seemed hopeless, Ruth Towse managed to secure two placements at the National Institute of Economic and Social Research (NIESR). I was lucky enough to be offered one of these. Thank you Ruth.

Industrial year

NIESR was a different world. I was assigned to work with a Hungarian statistician Laszlo Campbell Boross who had escaped the 1956 Russian occupation. He had added the Campbell part to sound upper-class British. Most of the staff came from Cambridge University and 'High tea' was served on Friday afternoon. The operation was based in Smith Square Westminster, where I saw Ted Heath embraced by Conservative staff after his 1970 election success. All this was a new world to me.

The task of developing a disaggregated model of UK Imports seemed manageable. Economic model building was then in its infancy. The fact that I could cope with the Economics, Econometrics, Statistics and Computing put me at the forefront of their model team. Strangely enough, they had a series of support staff still inverting large matrices by hand, according to the theory the right thing to do, but hopelessly inefficient. Amazing! Electronic calculators did not exist at the time, so logarithmic tables were employed. Changes were afoot and I was sent on a course to understand the programming rudiments of the computer company used by NIESR. I remember the first question asked was ‘can anyone invert a four by four matrix’? Up went my hand – good old Stan Millard. I bet the question was never asked again. During the industrial year I met some of my Enfield colleagues, and it was reassuring to learn that we all had similar experiences of apprehension in approaching the work placement of the third year.

Fourth year

In some sense I did not look forward to returning to Enfield. I found the ‘Industrial year’ had caused me to move on. I would have preferred the degree course to have carried straight on from year 2. On reflection, at least one of my choice of subjects in year 4 was wrong for me. Based on their industrial experience in year 3, students were excelling in different directions. That was the great thing about the Mathematics for Business course.

During the last stage of the degree I faced the same problem that I had experienced after A-levels. What to do next? I went to the Enfield Library – the one and only time I went there! My hand fell upon Kent University post-graduate course booklet. As if by magic it opened up at the Quantitative Social Studies (QSS) course being offered. There it was, the QSS course comprised Mathematical Statistics, Econometrics, Economic and Social Statistics and Finance. This was exactly what I was interested in. I applied and was interviewed by a large team, and during the interview I was unusually quite assertive. They liked the Enfield course and my industrial year so much so that I was offered a SSRC award. Kent University was on a hill overlooking Canterbury Cathedral. Wow! What a view. So this was how students' university life could be. New buildings everywhere, magnificent views, a far cry from Enfield. (I recently returned to Kent University. There were many new buildings and the campus now resembled a town). Having to explain to my father that I would be taking another degree would be difficult. It was beyond his understanding. At twenty-two years of age when would I enter the world of work?

After Enfield

At Kent the Masters degree lecturers were ruthless in their expectations. In structure the QSS course was integrated with the MSc Statistics and MA Economics courses. There were twelve students on my course and probably fifteen on the Statistics and Economics courses. When I arrived, the previous year's students were starting their Masters dissertations. Richard Baillie was one of those students! One of the Students on the Economics course was Allan Ward who had been with me on the Mathematics for Business course at Enfield. The good news is that Richard, Allan and myself all passed the examinations at Kent. Enfield must take some credit for that.

On a rigorous course of this kind where there were few passes I managed to attain the top mark. Similar pass numbers were the norm on the other masters degrees. As the top student I was offered an MPhil/PhD post. In the seven years from the age of sixteen from the days of the Sixth form College I felt I had travelled far.

Career

I decided to defer the option of staying at Kent. My industrial year had afforded me contact with a previous director at NIESR who was then at the UN Economic Commission for Europe in Geneva, and I joined him in Switzerland. On reflection, at the age of twenty-three I was too young for such an expatriate posting. After a while I returned to England and secured a job as a senior assistant statistician with the Government Statistical Service (GSS). Once again I met Richard Baillie at a GSS training seminar. My job was a contract post and a change of government in 1974 resulted in my redundancy.

I wanted to stay in London. Fortunately a lecturing post came up in Quantitative Analysis at South Bank Polytechnic. They even offered me a reduced timetable to start a PhD, with the Greater London Council paying the costs. Unlike now, there was no production line of PhDs and at the time it was a rare thing to undertake. Though appealing I deferred taking up this offer for a couple of years but I subsequently changed my mind and was the first staff member at South Bank Polytechnic business school to complete a PhD. In the 1980s, promotion was non-existent, and I became disillusioned with the time allowed for research. Added to this were the upheavals in the organisational structure of the polytechnic when a new director was appointed. I started to look elsewhere though there was a need to stay in London for family reasons. I kept an umbilical chord with the Polytechnic. In 1992 it became a University, as did Middlesex Polytechnic.

I was an examiner for the professional accountants examination and as part of my duties I had to attend a meeting at Middlesex University at Hendon. Something was missing. It wasn't Enfield! On reflection, those pioneering days at Enfield, where something special was being created aligned to Business mathematics, are now just a happy memory. My career took off with a professorship in the United States, as chief economist for a financial institution, and lecturing posts at several UK universities, ending up as a senior lecturer at Queen Mary University of London. I travelled extensively around the world representing that university. I had made contact via my research with the Society of Technical Analysts and jointly ran their courses, first at South Bank then at Queen Mary. I have enjoyed working in different capacities and different roles including, for example, as a member of the Sizewell B enquiry proposed nuclear power plant in Suffolk.

I am now retired but am active in the education in the Society of Technical Analysts. As I recall at least four other colleagues from my Enfield class ending up as polytechnic lecturers. I am still friends with Richard Baillie as we have similar interests. My two daughters have had their own careers, one as a medical doctor, and the other as a hospital social worker. Altogether we have nine degrees between us. On reflection I have been lucky in how things have evolved and the part played by my early education at Enfield.

Reflections

Located at Ponders End – not the most attractive of locations – Enfield College of Technology had a buzz about it. It was true that the environment comprised old buildings surrounded by temporary huts, but that did not seem to matter. The college was gaining a reputation as an innovative teaching establishment. The car park was huge and free and the college was connected to two train lines by way of Ponders End and Southbury. If the college had moved to Trent Park as part of an amalgamated Middlesex University (as envisaged by Principal George Brosan) it would have scored over its rivals for location and environment. The end of the Piccadilly Tube Line on the London Underground was only a stones throw away.

The CNAA degrees offered by colleges like Enfield were considered more 'applied' than traditional university degrees. Some critics referred to these degrees as 'dummying down'. However, the Mathematics for Business Course was certainly not in this category. It was rigorous; many of its courses were clearly of postgraduate level, for example the Operational Research course, and they were blended into a coherent undergraduate degree. Whoever thought of the structure and content of the course was far-sighted, an innovator. In many ways they were indirectly responsible for reshaping degrees in traditional universities. To conclude my educational journey, it is not where you start but where you end up that matters. In that respect the Mathematics for Business course at Enfield has never been given the full credit it deserves.

22. A more exciting place than Sussex?

JONATHAN POWERS

> ***Jonathan Powers** joined Enfield in 1968 as a Philosopher, subsequently heading the BA Sociology of Education. At Middlesex he worked on Regulations and Planning, teaching philosophy, history, physics, and mathematics, heading the BSc Society and Technology and the BA Humanities, latterly becoming Dean of Humanities. He was appointed Academic Director and one of the first Professors of Derbyshire College of HE, which achieved University status in 1992, becoming Pro Vice-Chancellor, Deputy Lieutenant of Derbyshire, and Honorary Doctor of the University. After retiring he chaired Derby's Multi-Faith Centre, Chamber Music Society, and Playhouse, and now lectures and publishes on the Enlightenment.*

After a very erratic performance as a Physics student who seemed bent on asking the 'wrong' sort of questions, I had become a Philosophy postgraduate at the glamorous new University of Sussex. At the time Sussex had the second largest collection of Philosopher lecturers in England after Oxford University, and buzzed with frenetic interdisciplinarity. With its parkland campus designed by Basil Spence, it seemed the perfect place to be. One of the suites of extra seminars I joined was on Logical Positivism and run by a certain Mark Fisher. To everyone's astonishment he then resigned from Sussex to take up a philosophy post at the hitherto unheard of Enfield College of Technology. And what was even more *incredible* he was reported saying that it was 'a more exciting place than Sussex'.

The image conjured up by his comment was reinforced later when I started hearing about Enfield while applying for other lecturing jobs around the country. At Kingston, for example, the Head of the Faculty told the candidates that he expected that they would become one of the top eight among the New Polytechnics, possibly even one of the top six. 'Well', he said, 'basically there's Enfield and then you can argue about the rest!' Enfield was clearly the place to get to even if one was holding the offer of another job!

I then heard that Roger Harris had just obtained a Philosophy lecturing post at Enfield. We'd been at Sussex together but had first met at the 'Square Circle' (Philosophy Society) in Birmingham when we were first year science students (Roger did Biochemistry, see Chapter 24). I learned that Enfield was looking for more philosophers with interdisciplinary backgrounds, so I fired in an application and rapidly read Eric Robinson's visionary book, *The New Polytechnics: the People's Universities*.

From glamour of 'The Lanes' to the grime of Ponders End

I came up from Brighton for the interview, getting to Liverpool Street and catching the 149 bus to Ponders End. Getting off at the Swan pub, I found myself walking through a narrow pathway, which was lined by derelict WW2 air-raid shelters topped with rusting barbed wire. Emerging into the landlocked site, surrounded by the backs of houses and factories, I found I was viewing a brown-tiled, two-storey, 1930s technical school building across a moth-eaten football pitch. On the left were some nondescript 'terrapin' huts and one more modern two-storey building. Looming in the distance was a huge industrial chimneystack, which (as I discovered) occasionally deposited flakes of soot across the site. I was dumbfounded: I nearly swivelled on my heel and returned to my flat on the edge of *The Lanes* in Brighton with its bracing air and view of the sea. But I kept walking: there must be something really extraordinary about what was going on in this place, given what people were saying – despite (or in the face of) its actual appearance.

Staff induction – the impact of the first morning

The first morning of that September's induction for around two-dozen new staff sprang a surprise or two. The Principal, Dr George Brosan, welcomed us. As an electrical engineer who had become a self-made millionaire, he was an evident force of nature with thinly disguised contempt for anyone pussyfooting around with bureaucratic niceties. It would be disconcerting to be pulled into his First Class carriage at Southbury Station to discuss some urgent matter, when one only had a standard ticket. Thanks to him, a few years earlier Enfield had brazenly jumped the gun by recruiting students to its

Business Studies degree before it had been validated by the CNAA – but he had got away with it, 'in the interests of the students', and because the course and the staff he recruited were so good and so vigorously promoted. At one point, having read an article about the coming 'microelectronics revolution', in *The Guardian* on the train from Liverpool Street, he stood on the Enfield steps to accost Dr John Butcher as he came into college. 'What would it cost for us to get into this?' asked George. Plucking what he thought was an impossible figure out of the air, John replied 'About £30,000.' He regretted he hadn't asked double, because George immediately said, 'Right, you've got it. Get started!' Thus began what for decades was Enfield's (and later Middlesex's) leading high technology research group.

Eric Robinson, as Academic Head of the Faculty of Arts, supplied the institution's intellectual nervous energy. When he'd applied for the job himself, he had sought just one reassurance from George, viz. that youth would be no bar to promotion. If one was going to break the mould one could not have the place dominated by people already stuck in their ways. The prime objective of the traditional universities appeared to be to enable such institutions to reproduce themselves, hence they focussed progressively on narrower and narrower specialisms. But in the outside world problems were always multi-faceted, and if our society in the 'White Heat of the coming Technological Revolution' was to produce people capable of addressing such problems, then they needed to have the skills and principles of more than one traditional academic discipline under their belts. *Proper* Vocational Education would not be less disciplined or less demanding than traditional 'Academic Education'. The supposed contrast was false – 'Academic Education' actually meant 'narrow *vocational* preparation for an academic post in a traditional university department'.

The first morning of the induction ended with the Administrative Head of the Faculty of Arts, Norman Sida. The change of tone took us aback. This seemingly lugubrious figure, rolling his hands together began, 'I think anything I say will probably be waste of valuable drinking time,' apparently expecting us to be impatient to repair to the College Bar, instead of having an interest in visionary educational policy, 'but if you'd like to discuss your promotion prospects, please make an appointment with my secretary.' Promotion prospects?! Ye, gods, we'd only just arrived and were already being paid on a higher lecturing scale than many places were offering! Anyway he had nothing else to say, so we duly trooped off to the recommended watering hole. As we stepped in the first thing we heard was, 'Sida's been sacked!' – this had happened before he spoke to us! However before the afternoon session started we heard he had had to be reinstated, because his barrister had insisted that since he had been appointed by the Borough Education Committee, the Principal had no power to sack him. So instead George moved him 'sideways' and put him in charge of the Car Park. It is never a good idea to injure an opponent only slightly – especially one you have under-estimated – and then to leave him with time on his hands. But it was another year before these chickens came home to roost.

Vocational education needs philosophers!

It was axiomatic at Enfield that everyone needed to study more than one 'subject'. But integration – and handling the problems caused by conflicting assumptions – could not just be left to happen in the minds of the students. What if the assumptions of the Sociologists and the Psychologists, or the Economists and the Accountants, were at loggerheads? There needed to be Interdisciplinary Seminars where such issues were tackled head-on. And this meant one needed a cohort of 'conceptual policemen', who were particularly adept in clarifying and addressing such issues. Hence the fact that Enfield began to recruit a large number of professional Philosophers, most of whom had studied other disciplines as well. When Middlesex Polytechnic was first designated the fact that it had the second largest collection of Philosophers in England after Oxford led to a critical question by Lord Annan in the House of Lords. We had 25 Philosophy Lecturers and 1 Research Fellow at Middlesex, compared with 20 at interdisciplinary Sussex. Only Oxford University with 40 outnumbered us. What their Lordships did not appreciate, however, is that this situation did not arise from abandoning the idea of Vocational Education, but instead from taking it *really seriously!*

The other critical policy affecting the design of Enfield courses was that every full-time degree had to be a Sandwich Programme. The point of this was 'to bring the outside world back inside the course'. Courses could not just pay lip-service to 'vocationalism':

they had to prepare students for their third year placements and then, when the students returned for their fourth year, the students themselves would put pressure on the staff to ensure that 'relevant' issues were tackled, not least in their choices of final year project.

The Enfield matrix versus the Middlesex matrix

From the moment that the CNAA was established in 1964, the College had been taking the opportunity provided to wean itself off London External Degree programmes and HNDs. The Electrical, Mechanical and Civil Engineering Departments had been offering the corresponding London BSc Engineering Degrees, while the Arts and Social Sciences were represented by London's BA General and BA/BSc in Sociology. At the end of that year the College was reorganised into two Faculties, each with its own Academic Head and Administrative Head. To resist the insidious temptations offered by traditional Subject Departments, the prime organisational focus and authority was vested in the interdisciplinary Course Group. 'Subject Groups' existed but had no authority to run courses, or recruit students, though they could engage in cross-institutional development. At a very early stage, the Philosophy Group began operating across the Colleges of the future Polytechnic – advising on the recruitment of staff, participating in course development, and running staff seminars. Indeed during my first year at Enfield, Eric himself came to our Philosophy Staff Seminar to read a paper on 'Absolute Truth' – a notion which was anathema to Eric himself as an ardent Pragmatist.

One of the consequences of any Matrix Organisation is that if there are unresolved conflicts between the different parties involved then the decision goes *up*. However not all Matrix Organisations are the same. When Middlesex was created there was some relief that Dr Ray Rickett, the first Director, rejected the idea of re-imposing traditional Subject Departments, but his 'matrix' was subtly and significantly different from that developed by George and Eric. Ray's matrix was designed to facilitate the *modularisation* of course provision, encouraging the standardisation of interchangeable course components. This actually worked against *interdisciplinarity* and encouraged the development of specialist subject elements, albeit in a multidisciplinary mix. The locus of programme design then became the individual students and their interests and preferences. Restrictions on combinations, or indeed the designation of particular elements or strands as compulsory, were always in danger of appearing 'artificial' or even 'counterproductive' unless supported by student interest, or evident necessity, such as might arise from the requirements of professional accreditation. The 'Enfield Matrix' embodied a different concept of how to make higher education relevant to the world the graduates would face and it worked to different effect in the way courses were constructed.

In addition to the full-time Business Studies provision, and a separate more specialised Mathematics for Business degree, when I first arrived a new full-time Social Science degree was getting under way – incorporating routes in Sociology and Economics. Further new routes in Geography – transmogrified into the practically oriented field of 'Land Use Studies' – and Social Work were in the pipeline, but Psychology had been showing some signs of resistance to the model. Meanwhile a major part-time degree (with an optional full-time final year) in Sociology of Education, for practising schoolteachers, was in its second full-year of operation and it was to this Course Group that I was initially aligned. The course was designed to address the needs of the experienced one-, two-, or more recently three-, year certificate trained teachers, who tended to predominate in the former Secondary Modern Schools. They were particularly likely to lose out to the University graduates in the Grammar Schools during the move to Comprehensive Secondary Education. While the 'top 15 per cent' at the eleven-plus had gone to Grammar Schools only between 2½ per cent to 4 per cent of their age-cohort had made it to University: half the population left school without any qualifications whatsoever.

Experiments in teaching and assessment

The 'Soc of Ed' degree was launched before the Open University came into being, indeed the latter did not recruit its first students until 1971. So we had students travelling to Enfield from all over South East England – some were prepared to travel for up to three hours to get to us! This meant we had to be very assiduous in making the best use of their time. Traditional lectures were displaced by specially prepared 'Handouts', which were then discussed in small seminars with up to ten students. The fact that the seminar-tutorial mode of tuition was dominant was reflected in the design of the new Tower Block whose construction got underway on the site of the old football pitch during 1969. It contained 180 individual staff tutorial rooms, each capable of taking a seminar group of ten students. If this were not controversial enough at the time, the building also contained a large *Student Study Area* on the ground floor. The DES had required strong persuasion to allow such a strange thing to be built!

My own involvement with the 'Soc of Ed' degree began with the teaching of Social and Political Philosophy, Philosophy of Education, and Ethics. But judging that a separate strand in Philosophy of Science was needed – though there was no time available for separate classes – I began experimenting with issuing weekly Handouts accompanied with Multi-Choice Tests. This was very controversial. I was told, 'But there are no *right* answers in Philosophy!' to which I responded, 'There are lots of ways of making mistakes!' I arranged for the hundred or so completed tests to be analysed by a computer programme devised (I think) by Derek Bush, which enabled me to write general follow-up Handouts. I also added the innovation of having individualised printouts for each student, commenting on each of the responses they had chosen. The most interesting cases were those questions which the students who did well overall got wrong, but which those who performed poorly got right. If one had been using this for assessment such items would have been eliminated as 'invalid', but in the context of teaching they were very illuminating. My colleagues quickly discovered that an unexpected side effect of this enterprise was that the quality of students' essays improved – they were much more careful about what they said and how. And the students clearly appreciated it, to judge from the number of Christmas Cards sent to 'Jonathan's Computer'! However there were limits. One day I arrived at the Computer Centre to pick up the result of an exercise on the Philosophy of Measurement, to be told that the machine had spewed out nonsense overnight because my pile of punched cards had 'overloaded the core'! Enfield's Honeywell 120 machine was tended by operators wearing quasi-surgical gear in a room held at positive pressure, which was accessed through an air lock. It had been so expensive (£450,000 in the mid 1960s) that the College had bought the machine jointly with the English Numbering Machines company based in a building opposite the college entrance. It was explained that our hard-wired computational device only had a core of 32K, written in 3-bit words! And it had cost the equivalent of something like £10m in today's money!

One of my other examination innovations was fondly described by some students as the 'Powers Chinese Torture Method' (presumably intending to allude to Empress Wu's introduction of the Examination System for entry to the Chinese Civil Service in the eighth century). Concluding that the traditional form of essay-based examination was defective if it simply became a memory exercise written under time-pressure, I introduced a different regime. I wanted students to be given all day (with a supervised rest room for refreshments) to answer just one (tricky) question. In the end I had to compromise by offering students the option of answering between 2 and 4 questions over a six hour period. This created huge anxiety in the student body, so much so that one of the two cohorts which were being taught in parallel opted out, and insisted on the form of assessment they had originally been promised, viz. three hours to answer three questions which they were allowed to see three weeks in advance. They were not convinced by my argument that this was a pointless way of trying to assess someone's ability to think philosophically.

We had therefore unintentionally arrived at an 'experimental design'. The performances of the students with the Seen Paper were tightly bunched: no-one actually failed since at least some of what everyone wrote had merit, but equally no-one performed outstandingly – everyone had referred to the same sources and there didn't seem to be sufficient time for the better students to demonstrate their superiority. However on the No-Time Limit Examination the results could not have been more different. A student, who had previously suffered from serious exam nerves found he was completely relaxed and having answered two questions in two hours, left early. He obtained a 'starred' First Class Honours. On the other hand another student who wrote intensively for the full six hours and whose four essays filled more than four complete answer books, dug himself deeper and deeper into a hole. His unfortunate failure to understand the questions was inescapable. My colleagues however would not allow me to award the zero mark which it merited and instead gave him a consolation mark of 5 per cent for 'effort'.

On one occasion I recall reading an answer in an unseen examination which had me remarking, 'This is very nicely put. I couldn't have put it better myself...wait a minute!' I found I was reading a memorised verbatim transcript of a paper I had written myself. Fortunately I had a policy of never asking questions in an examination which I had already answered in the course, so I was able to comment that this was indeed an excellent answer (of course!) but to a *different* question. Since the student clearly did not understand this, he had to fail. This experience later prompted me to experiment on other courses with 'Critical Appraisal' unseen examinations, where students would be asked to write a critical response to an article I had specially written. (I used this in a variety of contexts not only in Philosophy, but also in teaching History, Mathematics, Physics, and Research Methods.) What emerged rather strikingly from these experiments was that the normal distribution of marks or grades did not apply. The distributions were *bifurcated* – either the students understood what to do – in which case they did well – or they did not – in which case they failed. Borderlines were virtually non-existent.

'A bit junior to be a senior'

I suppose I had become so involved with trying to reform systems of assessment because they effectively 'operationalise' your course objectives. If you have the method of assessment wrong then you can kiss 'goodbye' to any high-flown educational objectives to which you might aspire. And it wasn't just the Methods one had to get a grip of, it was vital to get a grip of the Regulations and Procedures as well. For the first few weeks at Enfield, I had been happily teaching and getting along with my research on the development of Relativity Theory, when I attended my first Soc of Ed Course Group meeting. I was so shocked by what I saw about the Examinations system that I got up and spoke. Shortly afterwards I was appointed Examinations Officer, and within a month of arriving had been earmarked for promotion to Senior Lecturer the following year. My old friend Roger Harris was promoted with similar rapidity, and commented, 'twenty-five is a bit junior to be a Senior!' Indeed at some aspiring Polytechnics you couldn't be considered for promotion even from Lecturer I to Lecturer II until you were twenty-six. The following year as Deputy Head (and sometime Acting Head) of the course I was shortlisted for promotion to Principal Lecturer, but this was delayed by a year as a result of unexpected turbulence in the institution.

At Enfield this was not that exceptional. Mick Harrison, heading Sociology, had become a Principal Lecturer at twenty-five. Later he became the Director of Wolverhampton Polytechnic/Vice-Chancellor of Wolverhampton University). John Stoddart (running part-time Business Studies, and much else) had been promoted each year like clockwork, only pausing for two years at Head of Department Grade VI before becoming Assistant Director at North East London Polytechnic, and then taking over Humberside en route to becoming Director of Sheffield Polytechnic/Vice-Chancellor of Sheffield Hallam University (see Chapter 4). There were many similar cases: the Enfield policy of rapid promotion, for those who successfully took on major responsibilities, led to the seeding of the whole sector (and institutions overseas as well) with senior people who had been touched by the Enfield ethos.

Meanwhile the development of Examination Regulations and procedures to ensure they enshrined our educational objectives instead of undermining them, became a continuing side-line for me. So I found myself drafting not only the Regulations for the Soc of Ed degree, but the general Regulations for the Faculty of Arts, those for the institution-wide modular BA Humanities degree, and indeed for the new Polytechnic as a whole. The last actually influenced the reformulation of the CNAA's own regulations, and later in my career as an External Examiner (while actually on the CNAA Regulations Committee itself) I often noticed how the little 'memes' and phraseology I had sown into the terminology at Middlesex kept appearing in the Regulations of other institutions around the country!

The peak of interdisciplinarity

During my first year at Enfield, the Swann Report on the Flow into Employment of Highly Qualified Manpower in Science and Technology was published. Along with the Dainton and McCarthy Reports of that period it laid down a challenge to reform scientific education in Higher Education. Roger Harris and I, with Grenville Wall, who had studied Chemistry alongside Philosophy at Keele, started developing an 'academic subject option' for science teachers within the Soc of Ed degree. Many of the Secondary School science teachers had primarily studied biology but were obliged to teach physics and chemistry as well. (Later the supposed 'integration' of science education in school had the unintended consequence of encouraging physics graduates to become mathematics teachers, rather than have to embrace the very different world of traditional biology.) There was an opportunity to explore the physical sciences in some conceptual and methodological depth, which would complement their methodological studies in the social sciences.

While this development was cooking we proposed a full-scale response to the Swann Report in the form of a 'Science Greats' course. Roger, Grenville, and I had weekly meetings with Eric Robinson to explore how best to take the idea forward. Meanwhile a parallel group was emerging within the Faculty of Technology, seeking to integrate technological studies with social science and business studies. A Principal's Study group was formed under the chairmanship of Ron Kitchener, the Academic Head of the Faculty of Technology, and I became its Secretary. But the application to the Regional Staff Inspector (RSI) for permission to develop the course for submission to the CNAA ran into an unexpected obstacle. Hendon College of Technology, which was due to merge with Enfield and Hornsey to create a new Polytechnic, had proposed a Joint Honours Degree in Chemistry and Economics. This rather conventional-sounding and un-integrated proposal reflected the organisational structure and ethos of Hendon, but the RSI insisted that there should be a single proposal going forward.

To address the inter-institutional sensitivities, Andy Thomas, Principal Lecturer in Systems at Enfield was put in charge of the development. The Philosopher who was invited to be involved was Len Doyal, who had developed the 'Methods and Models' first year course on the BA Social Science degree. (Much later Len did pioneering work in the development of Medical Ethics courses in Medical Schools, at the Whittington, then Barts and the Royal London Medical College, latterly becoming Professor at Queen Mary's College and St Thomas' Hospital.) Len introduced a brilliant tool to assist in curriculum planning on a course which threatened to embrace all of human knowledge. He dubbed this 'the criterion of acceptable ignorance'. The course which developed was a four year degree with ten academic terms and a nine-months placement named the BSc Society and Technology. I got to work on it once it was running and, thanks to teaching on the physical sciences strand, even burnished my credentials as a 'Chartered Physicist'. There were huge difficulties both with recruitment and with the contents of the programme however. After a period running the Soc of Ed degree and the Humanities degree, I served as Course Head for about five years controversially negotiating the programme to safer waters by linking it to the Modular Degree scheme, which was headed by Joel Gladstone (a comrade in arms on the course since the earliest days of 'Soc and Tech' when he had constructed its week-by-week integrative maps). However for the students who undertook the programme, their projects and placements were life-transforming experiences. Several dozen from the original cohorts remain in touch with one another and in June 2017 I attended a Fortieth Anniversary Party in Suffolk (supplemented with some international *Skyping*).

If 'Soc and Tech' suffered from problems of coherence and progression, the most tightly integrated and intellectually challenging of Enfield's interdisciplinary, vocationally-oriented courses was the ill-fated BA in Communications Studies. The core of this was rooted in the Chomskyan Revolution in Linguistics, integrating that subject with Philosophy and Psychology, and applying it (with Literary Critical and Language Studies) to the whole field of human communication – it intended to offer placements in everything from publication to journalism. But despite the leadership of Dr Leonard Jackson and a strong and committed supporting team, the CNAA turned down the proposal – on the contradictory grounds that it simultaneously omitted too much material from each of the constituent disciplines to provide an Honours experience, and yet was far too advanced for undergraduate study. Had this course succeeded in 'making it to market' it would have constituted the high water mark of Enfield's interdisciplinarity.

The Enfield diaspora

But there was other 'trouble at mill'. During one vacation both Eric and George went on leave at the same time. At that moment Norman Sida struck, filing complaints of financial misconduct against both of them. Their holidays were cut short as they appeared before the Education Committee flanked by Barristers. All the charges against Eric were dismissed, but it appeared there had been two minor irregularities in George's expense claims for which he was 'reprimanded'. Eric's comment afterwards was, 'Enfield is finished.' The chance of

George leading the new Middlesex Polytechnic had been fatally undermined – he became Director of North East London Polytechnic instead. Eric joined him before taking over Bradford College, en route to the Polytechnic of Central Lancashire. But what they had created at Enfield was not dead – far from it. The group of people who had been nurtured in the institution they had created formed a diaspora, which I believe changed the face of UK Higher Education.

23. Memories of Enfield College of Technology and beyond

DENNIS BARKER

***Dennis Barker** joined Enfield College in 1968 where he taught engineering geology to Civil Engineering students. With the threatened closure of the Engineering Faculty in the early 1980s he decided to have a complete change and transfer to the Business School at Hendon. He completed an MBA and taught Management Strategy and Small Business Development. By the millennium he decided to retire and now, in the words of a song: 'I'm busy doin' nothin', Workin' the whole day through, Tryin' to find lots of things not to do. I'm busy goin' nowhere, Isn't it just a crime? I'd like to be unhappy, but.... I never do have the time'.*

My wife and I were shopping in Morrison's during March 2017 when we happened to meet Tony Crilly, a lecturer I used to know at Middlesex University, who told us about the idea of writing down memories of our time at Enfield College of Technology. I worked there in the Faculty of Engineering from 1968 until 1988, when I moved to the Business School. Although I am over eighty I am still reasonably fit but my detailed memory is quite poor, which may be reflected in the following account.

Between 1962 and 1970 the Principal, George Brosan and his deputy Eric Robinson, worked to turn Enfield into a 'New Polytechnic' that would unite Technology with the Social Sciences and in 1973 the College became incorporated into Middlesex Polytechnic. There was very little cross-fertilisation between the Arts Faculty and the Technology Faculty as far as I was aware, although I did some research later in the 1980s, guided by Peter Sneddon in the Psychology Department, and I published three papers.

Having completed my PhD in Geology in 1964 I had been working for a while as a consultant at Paleoservices Ltd, concentrating on the development of the oil industry in the North Sea. However, in 1967 our business slowed down so I decided to move back into education. I had a few months as a Supply Teacher and then a few months teaching geology to Higher National Certificate students at Enfield College of Technology.

This position became permanent in the autumn of 1968 when the College replaced the London University Degree in Civil Engineering with a CNAA, (Council for National Academic Awards) BSc Degree in Civil Engineering. This was a four-year Sandwich Degree in which the students spent their third year in industry (which they had to complete satisfactorily). Each lecturer was given responsibility for a few students and we had to visit them twice during their employment. At the end of my first year the Lecturer in Soil Mechanics returned to Australia and I took over his responsibility as Year-Tutor for the second year of the degree. I retained this post till I left the Faculty in 1988.

For our degree programme we set up a committee of staff and students to monitor the course and identify problems before they surfaced. Each year-group of students was invited to elect two students and the staff were represented by the three Year-Tutors and the Head of the Course so that the students always outnumbered the staff and did not feel alienated in any way. The committee met about four weeks into each term to iron out any problems with the running of the course.

We started with only thirty-six students in the first year of the new course; I worked with Terry Hawkins, an ex-Geological Survey geologist who had mapped out some of the geology in North Wales. He had been teaching Engineering Geology for the London University BSc Degree in Civil Engineering at Enfield for about two years. The Head of Civil Engineering was Tony Dockerty.

Students in Civil Engineering had over 20 hours of class contact time per week including lectures, lab classes and group tutorials plus a week long field class in both geology and surveying during the vacation. In the 1980s. teaching time for all Middlesex Polytechnic courses was reduced to nine hours per week. This was incompatible with the demands of the Engineering Institutions, a fact that contributed to the eventual demise of the Engineering Faculty.

In the final year of the degree course all our students had to complete a project which involved laboratory and/or fieldwork, write a report and attend an interview with two academic members of staff. During one of the final year Engineering Geology field classes in North Wales the students had to do geophysical work and discovered that one farmer had a large deposit of good sand under one of his fields. We informed the farmer and the next year we found there was no evidence that there was any sand at all. He had extracted the sand and sold it!

I cannot remember the details about the examinable subjects but I do know that until about 1980 our mark for a First Class Honours Degree was 75 per cent. Our external examiners from Southampton and Cardiff Universities, put their boundaries at 70 per cent and since they were satisfied with our work they said they would be happy if we were to lower our grade in a later submission to the CNAA.

Civil Engineering accommodation was spread about the Enfield site. The McCrae building contained the main lecture theatre (Room 525) and the Geology and Soil Mechanics laboratories. The Pascal Laboratories housed the Hydraulics and Structures laboratories plus the Electrical and Mechanical Engineering laboratories. Surveying and the Highways and Traffic Departments were in the old Ponders End Technical Institute on the other side of Ponders End High Street. The department office and most staff were in the huts, and the other staff had offices next to their laboratories. Each laboratory had a technician to prepare materials and equipment for classes, student projects and research.

The College had an Examinations Office, a Typing Pool and a Treasurer, Harry Carless. The mainframe computer occupied an air-conditioned room and operated using punched cards. We supplied numbers on paper which were converted into holes on cards by typists.

When I joined the College it was run on the usual departmental lines. Each branch of Engineering (Civil, Electrical and Mechanical Engineering) had a head of department responsible to the Principal, George Brosan. In large staff meetings in Room 525 Brosan had a habit of playing with his microphone while staff were speaking: the noises were allegedly to put the staff off their stride!

There were two developments of particular note in the late 1960s. The first was the change to a matrix system of college management brought about by the development of new courses in the Social Sciences and a need for extra accommodation. This caused a lot of argument and eventually resulted in a reorganisation which focused on a matrix system based on Courses and Resources. Each department then had a secretary and lecturers allocated to it and was responsible for all its courses, but the Head of Resources controlled the money for the laboratories, staff, materials and equipment. Heads of Courses were not responsible for any money, and this resulted in stress to the system because development of the courses needed funding. For instance Heads of Courses might want to change their courses but had to negotiate for the money needed for staff, accommodation, materials and equipment. In the Engineering Faculty Mr Osborne-Moss was the Head of Resources and Mr Kitchener was the Head of Courses. I have no idea how Osborne-Moss divided up the money between departments.

The second development was the setting up of staff study groups to generate new ideas to further develop the College. This seemed to have lasted about one year!

From Enfield College to the Poly

In 1973, Enfield College of Technology joined with Hendon College of Technology and the Hornsey College of Art to form Middlesex Polytechnic. This increased the number of sites, administrators, and ancillary workers, and new departments were introduced for such tasks as computing and printing. The Engineering Departments from Hendon College of Technology moved to Enfield and a few staff were absorbed into the Civil Engineering Department at Enfield.

In the early days we were able to interview our students for entry to the course and were surprised when we lost them to lower offers from universities such as Salford. Until about the 1980s there was a ladder for those students who failed the eleven-plus examination to enter an engineering degree programme via the HNC/HND (Higher National Certificate/Diploma). Apprentices in industry going to local technical colleges on day-release schemes and evening classes obtained these qualifications. Students with a good HND were able to enter the Second Year of an engineering sandwich degree. This approach relied on the teachers at the technical colleges preparing their students for a more academic approach to their studies. The HNC/HND progression allowed many young people to reach the higher echelons of the engineering professions in spite of being labelled failures at eleven years-of-age. We were very proud of them especially as they were undervalued by the country as a whole.

Since then the approach to apprenticeships does not, as far as I am aware, enable the progression to a degree in the same way. This conclusion is based on my experience in the Business School with undergraduates and in the 1990s with my involvement in the early development of the Management Charter Initiative and National Vocational Qualifications.

From the beginning of our engineering course we found that many students had a problem with mathematics. This was because most of the best students with a facility in mathematics at A-level were able to gain entry to universities. Thus the faculty employed several mathematics lecturers to bring the students up to standard. Since we found it difficult to recruit UK students who were good at the subject we began to recruit students from overseas, and they were very capable in mathematics. As a result our intake rose to over a hundred students in each year over the 1970s with a very high proportion from Malaysia and the Middle East. Some of these students had problems with the English language so the Polytechnic employed two lecturers to improve their language skills.

I ran a geology field class at Tenby during the Iran/Iraq conflict and the local paper must have heard about us because a journalist called at the hotel to ask if he could interview the students. The students agreed to this provided the newspaper did not publish anything by which their governments could trace them.

Problem-solving

During my first year at Enfield I volunteered to be involved in a new course in problem-solving. When I began my PhD at Leicester University in 1960 I thought it would be useful if I read something about Creative Thinking but the library was unable to find anything useful for me at that time. At Enfield George Brosan started me thinking about it again and I found there was an increase in publications of this kind.

The first Problem-Solving syllabus was created in the middle 1960s by George Brosan with the help of an electrical and a mechanical engineer. This was a straightforward statement of the stages an engineer would go through in solving a problem. The second syllabus was part of an engineering degree accepted by CNAA for the use of the three subject areas, Civil, Electrical and Mechanical Engineering. This was much more detailed and covered the relevant psychology. A study group used this as the basis for a scheme of work and a structure for teaching Engineering Problem Solving. I was involved in the first year of teaching to the civil engineers. We arranged lectures and various exercises to stimulate creative thinking.

In the summer of 1970 I felt that we needed more cross fertilisation with the needs of the civil engineering industry so that some of their problems could be adapted for our use. I also found that students often became fixed on a particular solution or were satisfied with the obvious one. The conditioning of students at school and college had made them satisfied with *one* correct answer. There was often no sign left of the creative ability children have in their early years.

We had to change these attitudes, since graduates in industry have to face open-ended problems and problems with more than one solution. There were the civil engineering aspects but also engineers have to deal with people, a factor which introduces an extra element of unpredictability. Moreover they need to be able to consider all kinds of things that might affect the situation such as social or historical problems. As a result, in the early years they were allowed to choose their own problems to solve as personal interest and ownership can often stimulate ideas.

In 1970 I was given responsibility for teaching the problem-solving programme to civil engineers so I began to develop a Engineering Problem Solving (EPS) Course for second year students and I wrote a course handbook *Solving Problems*. By the 1970s a number of systematic techniques had been developed to solve problems so I simplified the EPS programme by concentrating on four stages of the problem solving process:

Understanding the problem
Producing and developing ideas
Evaluating and developing solutions
Adopting solutions

Such a process may have to be repeated a number of times or even stopped part-way through and recycled. The techniques encouraged students to examine all facets of the problem at hand and provide a systematic method of recording thoughts about it. The students wrote reports on their solutions to open problems and these were assessed through a *viva-voce* with staff and the external examiner. The external examiners were impressed by this work and thought we were ten years ahead of other courses.

In 1972 I arranged a full day open Seminar on 'The Role of Problem Solving in Degree Courses' at Capel House which housed our Management School. George Brosan, by this time Director of North East London Polytechnic, was one of my speakers and I thought, since the armed forces were always facing problems, someone from the army would make a good chairman – after all, waging war is problem solving on the run! After a few phone calls I was put into contact with Major General R. L. Clutterbuck CB OBE FICE PhD, Chief Army Instructor at the Royal College of Defence Studies, who was pleased to accept the position of chairman. (He had been commissioned into the Royal Engineers in 1937 and had long list of publications. On retirement he became a lecturer at Exeter University).

By 1975 I had become more and more interested in creative thinking and techniques which could improve it. It became obvious that thinking depends on our use of language. Systematic techniques help but they can make thinking too rigid. Students who used my first booklet *Solving Problems* kept to the routine too rigidly.

Creativity depends on thinking and two quotations pointed to some of the difficulties we faced at the time. In 1967, the astronomer Fred Hoyle suggested that undergraduates were not getting the best from university life: 'There is far too much work, far too little thinking ... it is the quality of thought that should be taught, knowledge they can get for themselves.' Keith Duckworth designer of the successful Cosworth Ford racing engine said: 'probably only about 10 per cent of engineering problems have a purely mathematical solution. The 90 per cent of engineering that involves judgement and decisions is not taught at all. In fact I don't like to be known as an engineer ... I am someone who sits around and thinks. Sometimes I think about motor car engines.'

So my second booklet *Thinking about Problems* dealt with thinking skills as well as the Problem Solving Process.

By 1976 I had developed the above ideas and produced a set of 'Barker Charts' which provided a systematic method of recording the thought process. This booklet was called *Creative Problem Solving*. Jane Moran, one of the English for Foreign Student lecturers, also taught Creative Writing at our Tottenham Campus and she used my booklet to teach Creative Writing as she thought the charts were so useful in helping her students to think creatively.

About this time I recall one of the students looked at the problem of speeding on motorways. He talked his way into joining the police in one of their patrol cars. His solution involved placing coloured poles down the central reservations spaced so that when you reached a certain speed the colour of the poles turned into a solid line of colour.

In the 1970s students chose their own problems to solve but I gradually began to realise that British trained engineers were missing out in marketing their skills and needed to learn how to work in groups. Therefore by 1980 I had the students working in groups of five to solve real problems and eventually arranging for them to work with external organisations. The groups had to make fifteen-minute presentations to Civil Engineering Staff of the organisation concerned, followed by questions. About 1980 my course was recognised by the *Education for Capability* Scheme of the Royal Society of Arts, Manufactures and Commerce. The Royal Society believed that 'a well-balanced education should embrace analysis and acquisition of knowledge. But it must also include the exercise of creative skills, the competence to undertake and complete tasks and the ability to cope with everyday life and also doing all these things in co-operation with others.'

Further developments

Approximately every four years we had to submit our course for re-assessment by the CNAA. This enabled us to bring our courses up to date in terms of standards, methods, equipment, and research. The inspectors consisted of several Heads of Department from polytechnics and universities around the country, the Secretary of CNAA responsible for the subject area and one or more representatives from industry. This enabled both us and the visitors to learn from one another and spread best practice around the country. As an external examiner in later years I always tried to find three ideas I could make use of when I visited other universities.

For our Civil Engineering Course submission to CNAA in the early 1970s we changed our course from three 10-week terms per year to two 15-week semesters, arranged the subjects as modules and included "Open Book" examinations. I think we were the first at Enfield to make such changes but later we found that the original timetable and work patterns were preferable, so in our later submission to CNAA, we abandoned 'Open Book' examinations and reverted to a year long programme and annual examinations.

In Civil Engineering we always marked students' laboratory work, (coursework,) but these marks were not included in the examination marks except in borderline cases, when they would be taken into account by the Examination Board. As an external examiner, years later, I found that coursework marks included in the assessments at other universities were about 10 per cent higher than their examination marks. The coursework marks therefore boosted the total marks, leading to higher grades! About 1980, to our chagrin, the Polytechnic brought in the semester assessments and the inclusion of coursework marks into the assessment process for all subjects.

During my last five or so years in the department I organised two or three lectures each semester from engineers in the industry to give inspiration to the students. I also organised field trips to engineering sites such as the Thames Barrier and the Dartford Crossing as they were being constructed. In addition we built relationships with Schools and Technical Colleges to encourage their students to make their careers in engineering. This approach was similar to the very successful Polytechnic Universities in Germany.

Afterwards

The CNAA and its link with the Polytechnics worked well and encouraged the supply of skilled engineers with a practical outlook. This was dropped when polytechnics became universities and the country is now suffering from a lack of skilled engineers. Engineering Departments in the Polytechnics were industry-based rather than research-based. Although some research was carried out, our approach was to build our contacts with industry, do consulting work and bring up-to-date ideas from industry into our teaching. For instance, in 1968 John Osborne-Moss, Tony Dockerty and Philip Monks went to St Lucia in the West Indies to do some pre planning (locations, materials, roads) for the development of the Tourist industry there.

About 1970 Terry Hawkins put together a team with the Hydraulics Rcscarch Station to study the sediments of the Maplin Sands of the Essex coast. At the time the government was thinking of building a new airport there. Later in the 1970s he went to the Yemen with the Hydraulics lecturer looking for water supplies. Terry also ran an MSc Foundation Engineering course until the civil engineering department was eventually closed down.

The Mechanical Engineering Department at Hendon had a rig for testing baby car seats and other equipment in cars. This was nationally recognised as several manufacturers used the facility and it was a good money-maker for the institution. This was closed down in the 1990s as Hendon required the space to accommodate an expansion in student numbers.

About 1980 the Polytechnic developed the Bounds Green site for engineering. Originally it was a very large warehouse with structural problems which cost the university a lot of money to rectify and adapt for our needs. The architects designed a mall down the centre of the building which connected all the rooms. However, the laboratories were open plan so we were distracted by the noises going on in the other laboratories! The Bounds Green campus was eventually sold off and demolished to make way for housing.

In the 1980s the Polytechnic lost its way and was going through the process of closing its engineering courses because of their costs and pressures from the Engineering Institutions. The enthusiasm and creativity of the earlier years had been lost. Since I was around fifty years old and expected to work for another fifteen years I felt I needed a change and explored the possibility of moving over to the Business School. I was allowed to do this provided I enrolled for an MBA which I duly completed. After transferring to the Business School at Hendon I taught Management Strategy and Small Business Development until my retirement from the institution.

24. Intellectual generosity in a prototype for a new kind of institution

ROGER HARRIS

Roger Harris *taught philosophy at Enfield from 1968, on the Full-Time and Part-Time* BA *Social Science degrees and subsequently also on the* BA *Humanities and* MA *Philosophy courses. He took early retirement from Middlesex University in 2002 He next undertook several property renovation projects, with his son-in-law. In 2007 he began working for a charity providing independent advocacy for people with complaints about their NHS treatment – an alternative to litigation – finally fully retiring in 2017. He and his wife have nine grandchildren and two great grandchildren.*

My abiding memory of Enfield College from 1968 until it merged into the new Middlesex Polytechnic, was the exhilarating collective intellectual generosity of my colleagues. Indeed, this was a characteristic feature of the ethos at Middlesex Poly for a good many years thereafter. As I strove to remedy the narrowness of my university education, I owed something, intellectually, to nearly every one of my colleagues – it would be invidious to make a list for fear of leaving someone out. We had all been tasked with devising interdisciplinary degree programmes which, it had been argued, would be more vocationally relevant than the narrowly circumscribed single subject honours degrees most of us had followed. This route to vocational relevance was championed in the book *The New Polytechnics*, then recently written by Eric Robinson – the head of the Arts and Social Science division of the college. We duly set about educating one another, because we needed to understand what we each were bringing to the table if our courses were to be more than a mere academic smorgasbord devoid of any educational rationale.

I don't think I was unrepresentative in thinking at that time that we might have the opportunity to make a completely new kind of institution, from the ground up, which would remedy many of the defects of the education system from which most of us had so recently graduated. In doing so, many of us felt we would be able to provide, *for each other*, the seed bed in which to nurture our own broadly critical understanding of the intellectual and educational landscape of the time in contrast with the narrow, blinkered approach to the academic disciplines characteristic of most degree-level education in the 60s (and, sadly, since). For me, and many others I am sure, that meant that my initial years at Enfield contributed far more to my real education than most of the schooling and degree courses open to me before I began to teach at Enfield.

We felt, with some justification, that Enfield College was a prototype for a new type of institution which was to spearhead the coming expansion of higher education. For Eric Robinson was rumoured to have the ear of Anthony Crosland, a leading Labour intellectual and education minister at the time. Crosland had already set about dismantling the selective state secondary education system, based since 1944 on use of the IQ test based eleven-plus examination to 'cream off' the pupils into grammar schools to prepare a select few of them for university entrance. He and his successors would eventually achieve a general consensus in favour of comprehensive secondary education – Tory press notwithstanding. They would also succeed in expanding higher education in line with the Robbins Report (but not, eventually, on the models that we, or Eric Robinson had envisaged).

Raised Under the Butler Education Act – Context for My Good Fortune to Teach at Enfield.

While the 1944 Act and the grant funding of undergraduate study at university had represented a massive step forward for equality of educational opportunity, when compared to the situation that had obtained before WW2, there remained massive flaws in the resulting state education system. The education of the broad mass of the population was wholly subordinated to the fundamental task of winnowing a very small amount of wheat from an overwhelming volume of supposed 'chaff'. School syllabuses were dominated by the universities, and the universities dominated by concern for success in pursuing research interests that would advance the careers and prestige of their professors. So, degree courses were devised to teach tightly circumscribed single academic subjects and assessed in order to prepare and select the few who would join their professors' research teams. It was a secondary consideration what benefit might be derived from this education by those who failed to make the grade at this, and at each preceding stage. The selection of pupils which began with the eleven-plus initiated a relentless narrowing and specialisation of curricula once secondary education had begun, culminating in a single subject degree accessed by a tiny proportion of those whose education had been shaped by these imperatives.

Sixth form A-level syllabuses were dictated by the requirements of degree courses which most sixth formers would never enter. O-level syllabuses (precursors of today's GCSE exams) were dictated by the requirements of A-level courses which most pupils would not undertake, and the eleven-plus was used to reject the large majority of pupils who were denied access even to the first rung of the educational ladder leading to university. Less than 5 per cent of the population attended university, of whom a tiny proportion received first class honours degrees and went on to do postgraduate research. The tail well and truly wagged the dog! Even now this pattern still persists to a disheartening extent.

In those days, even overtly vocational university courses adopted this damaging and wasteful ethos: Civil Engineering at my undergraduate university recruited 100 students in the first year, of whom only 80 were permitted to proceed to the second year, and 60 to the third. This meant 40 per cent of their initial intake was discarded *on principle*, irrespective of whether these students knew what they had been taught, and regardless of the waste and harm inflicted on them and on the taxpayer. So, what I felt about the opportunities presented to us at Enfield could not help but be influenced by the way I had experienced the education I had been given within this system.

Tom Bourner has summarised its objective features in his contribution. So, self-indulgently perhaps, I shall outline my subjective reactions, because, by a stroke of sublime serendipity, I could hardly have been more fortunate, ready and willing to teach at Enfield.

Grammar School

I passed my eleven-plus and attended a boys' grammar school. While I had some good teachers, the overall ethos of the school aped the sort of threadbare boarding 'Public' school satirised in Evelyn Waugh's *Decline and Fall*, or Michael Palin's *Ripping Yarns*. Pupils were divided into 'houses', despite there being no boarders; 'prefects' were appointed as licensed bullies (and, at all times, wore half-length academic gowns!); entirely bogus 'traditions' were invented to be solemnly honoured; sport and conformity was valued above everything. All in all, you could almost believe that the 'school rules' had been made to be broken so you would be sensible by mistake.

I was lucky enough to make it into the top form (of four) – the only stream to be taught Latin, needed at the time for Oxbridge entry. However, far and away the cleverest boy in that class – effortlessly top in every subject each year – had a cockney accent. Teachers never ceased to mock how he spoke, and he left at fifteen. So much for 'upward social mobility'! A secondary modern school just up the road took all the boys who had failed the eleven-plus. We grammar school boys were sitting ducks to be roughed up in the ridiculous uniforms we were obliged to wear – a crash course in class antagonism!

In any case, so-called 'upward social mobility' in the UK depended far more on the changing occupational structure of British society than on any facilitation it received from this selective education system, which, if anything, placed obstacles in the path of clever boys with cockney accents. The decline in industry meant that demand for traditional manual occupations was shrinking, along with a growth in the public and service sectors which required 'white collar' workers. Moreover, the vast preponderance of this massive 'deindustrialisation' took place *after* the abolition of the eleven-plus and grammar schools throughout most of the UK, so the fabled merits of grammar schools in promoting the careers of talented poor pupils had no bearing on the social changes which largely took place some time after grammar schools had been abolished almost everywhere.

The expansion of university education urged by the Robbins Report was equally a response to, rather than a driver of, the changing occupational profile of the nation, since the vocational relevance of the degree courses offered then (and still) could hardly be said to have been tailored to the rising occupations.

University

I did not stay on the extra year at school required to attempt to enter Oxford or Cambridge, but left school as soon as I could, to a red-brick university to study biochemistry. This institution made no serious attempt whatsoever, in its curricula, to aspire to Newman's ideals of university education and intellectual literacy. What concession there was amounted to an eccentric frill, rather as *University Challenge* still appears today. Worse, the efforts devoted on my course to teaching its students were derisory. I attended six 'tutorials' in three years, but their 'tutorials' were classes of about twenty-five students in which you were not expected to speak unless you were asked a direct question. Teaching otherwise was accomplished by lectures, usually to audiences in the hundreds. Some were good, many were indifferent, while a good number were quite appalling. One man flatly refused to speak sufficiently loudly to be heard. Another, without a glance or a word to his audience, taught thermodynamics by frantically writing equations on the blackboards until they were filled, whereupon he rubbed them out and wrote some more equations without turning to look at us, much less speak.

More revealingly, another lecturer listed the organic compounds he had succeeded in synthesising, comprising a catalogue of substances which it could be known in advance would have no interesting or useful properties, so that all that could be acknowledged was that samples of these useless compounds now existed and he had made them, employing already well-known procedures of chemical synthesis. Although it seemed to me obvious from the research that we had to study, no lecturer differentiated such mere stamp-collecting from the construction of scientific hypotheses to be tested. You did not ask the question 'What made us scientists?' And, in any case, the answer seemed to be that we wore white coats!

This intellectual passivity expected of science students was among the features of the bifurcation between the 'Two Cultures' –

science vs. humanities – dominant in British universities at the time. Outside Oxbridge, scorn was poured on the idea that science students, outside their studies, should have interests beyond drinking and sport. Meanwhile the arts departments did their best to sequester within their self-appointed cliques the culture they were entrusted to transmit to the coming generation. Reading literature in translation or acquaintance with fine art as reproductions was the focus of the scorn of the cognoscenti. It is hard now to appreciate how revolutionary were the TV programmes of Jacob Bronowski and Kenneth Clark (*The Ascent of Man* and *Civilisation*, respectively) shown while we were teaching at Enfield College, which aimed to spread some general intellectual literacy and even-handedness in the regard for the arts and sciences.

For a number of reasons (my intolerance of the culture of research labs, and, to be frank, a 2.2) I did not pursue biochemistry as a postgraduate, but I was accepted to study for an MSc in the philosophy and history of science at Sussex, along with Jonathan Powers, who had been a friend when we were undergraduates. We were in the first cohort of master's students at Sussex, where, amongst others, one of our teachers was Mark Fisher, who eventually enticed us both to Enfield. I had been lucky, as a scientist, to get in to do postgraduate study at Sussex with a 2.2 and no background in philosophy, but Sussex was in the process of establishing an ethos much closer to Newman's ideal of a university than the benighted institution I'd just left, and was a leader in interdisciplinarity and in teaching styles, which we later sought to emulate at Enfield. We were allowed to gate-crash undergraduate philosophy courses, so, hoping to catch up on wider philosophy, both Jonathan and I pursued a double-weight curriculum for that year (1965/6) in an institution that could hardly have been a more vibrant contrast to the one I had just left.

My Route to Enfield

Before coming to Enfield in 1968 I had enrolled as a part-time PhD student at Sussex (I never finished), which continued to allow me to gate-crash seminars that interested me, and I supported myself teaching General Studies part-time at Portsmouth Art College. This was an eye-opener: I could teach anything I liked provided it could plausibly be entitled 'general education'. Only the fine art students followed a degree level course, the remainder followed Further Education courses in design-related areas. The most illuminating group I taught were those studying for a technical illustration certificate. They were learning to produce exploded 3-dimensional drawings of seriously complex engines, pumps, machine-tools and the like. 'Not a task for the intellectually challenged' would be a gross understatement. These working-class lads (no girls in those days, of course) were very hard work to teach and it was not long before I stumbled on the reason: THEY COULDN'T READ, not properly, if at all. This, despite their lapping up the general science I taught verbally and with diagrams at breakneck speed. They were very happy to learn about electrical circuits, the electromagnetic spectrum, direct and alternating current, levers, pulleys and hydraulic mechanisms etc. (I still knew all that stuff, then!) but I knew I couldn't go anywhere near issues of literacy as I would just get some effing and blinding and lads walking out. Nonetheless, I had found nothing I would rather do than teach, or more rewarding that seeing eyes light up when I succeeded in explaining something new.

Brighton was a very seductive place; after two years of part-time teaching and study I looked around and it was clear, from the streets, pubs and parties I frequented that, if I did not make an effort to leave its shabby gilded idleness, I would find myself in Brighton at forty still doing the same as I had at twenty-four! It did not seem a likely prospect, but I began looking for teaching work in a college in London. I was surprised to see that lectureships in *philosophy* (not general studies) were being advertised at Enfield College and at Kingston Poly. I don't recall the details but I made contact with Mark Fisher, who had taught me at Sussex but had since taken up a principal lectureship in philosophy at Enfield, and he filled me in about what was happening at Enfield. I took the job when it was offered and cried off my Kingston interview. Jonathan Powers has recounted, in his contribution, how he followed much the same route to a job at Enfield.

My Teaching was a Joy (to me, at least)!

Mark wanted 'proper philosophers of science' to help bring rigour to what he feared was the teaching of cultural relativism in the opening year of the new Social Science degree. Perhaps I went 'native', but joining this teaching team was a joy. The course syllabus combined the Weberian thesis regarding the 'disenchantment of nature' and the rise of the physical sciences at the beginning of the capitalist era (where Mark had smelled relativism) with an account of the Popper/Kuhn debate regarding theory/paradigm change, in which the philosophical issue of relativism and the objectivity of physical science was directly addressed. The students were a delight to teach, it was 1968, radical change was in the air and there was a vital case to be made for Reason in the face of nihilistic agitation and irrational reaction. Mark was not wrong about that, even though his suspicion of the 'Methods and Models' first year Social Science degree course was ill founded.

Even better for me was teaching on the part-time degree course in the Sociology of Education which had been developed as I was appointed. Non-graduate teachers, trained on an emergency basis following WW2 or in Teacher Training Colleges which could not then award degrees, were finding themselves leapfrogged in their careers by younger graduate teachers lucky enough to have been to university. Here was a ready market for a part-time course which allowed graduate status to be achieved but also an opportunity for working teachers to study, and us to teach, a course which took a long hard look at the school system that the 1944 Butler Education Act had ushered in. I was able to teach an introductory philosophy course – a sprint through ethics, political philosophy, the philosophy of education and of social science – and subsequently to convene my colleagues to contribute to an 'Interdisciplinary Seminar'.

The reality, week by week, was to address a student body almost all of whom were older than me but almost all of whom were serious enough to attend for six hours a week after exhausting days working in schools. Many of them were already profoundly critical of the system within which they worked, while many others were entirely happy with it, so that seminars (we did not lecture, but issued handouts we had written, week by week, to ground seminar discussions) were uncommonly lively, rehearsing the disputes that already existed between our students. Indeed, some students needed to be separated, or segregated into seminar groups allocated to more robust teaching colleagues, so fierce did discussions become! Students – many old enough to be my dad – would begin their seminar contributions, saying 'Are you seriously suggesting…', 'Do you expect us to believe…' etc. when faced with statistics regarding social class and education which no one now disputes, but which then looked like heresy to teachers brought up on the Butler Education Act. These were statistics that were acted upon by Kenneth Baker no less than by Labour education ministers. The demand for this course soon declined as we worked through the cohort of teachers who had been left behind in the move to a graduate profession, but while it lasted nothing could have chimed better with what I felt about education.

Constraints and Downsides

I may have made my working at Enfield College appear to have consisted in me and others of like mind riding our hobbyhorses to our hearts' delight. There were serious constraints – the college could not award its own degrees, but needed the imprimatur of the Council for National Academic Awards (CNAA) for the new courses we were developing. So, although we were able to innovate quite radically in curricula and teaching and assessment methods, it was necessary, in those days, to provide a rigorous written specification and rationale of any degree course to the CNAA, which then had to be defended during a searching and lengthy inspection by members of one of the CNAA's boards. This was a taxing discipline, especially if the inspecting CNAA members were intellectually hostile (or direct rivals and competitors!).

And there were downsides of our own making. Whatever his major positive contributions might be judged to have been, I feel, in retrospect, that Eric Robinson foisted on us at the time (and bequeathed when he left) a serious lack of civility towards colleagues. I often leapt into some fray that Eric had engendered in ways I now regret, and his cantankerous self-serving style persisted on Polytechnic boards and committees long after he had left. There was much to be said in favour of a 'Matrix' form of organisation where there was, notionally, parity of power and authority between the management structures of interdisciplinary courses and those of the academic subject affiliations of the teaching staff. However, this was never properly institutionalised in a stable form with checks and balances on either side. Eric wanted there to be a continual foment – almost a

Maoist form of 'perpetual revolution' which persisted long after he had left, and its fluidity made arm-wrestling, power struggles, and score-settling even more egregious features of our academic politics than is the lamentable norm for HE institutions. This lack of embedded legitimacy to the 'Matrix' in its many incarnations sadly led, many years later, to the gradual reversion of Middlesex University (with perhaps the exception of the Business School) to the single specialised subject hegemony that Eric and the rest of us had fought against in those days when 'interdisciplinarity' had been our watchword.

PART THREE

LATER COMERS

1969-72

25. My Enfield: the beat of a different drum

TOM BOURNER

> ***Tom Bourner*** *joined Enfield in 1969 as an economist and worked mainly on the part-time degree in Business Studies. He stayed until 1979 when he moved to Brighton Polytechnic where he shifted his focus to HE outcomes and the learning processes producing those outcomes. He retired in 2005 as Professor of Personal and Professional Development and head of research at Brighton Business School. He now spends most of his time enjoying the delights of Brighton, his grown-up family, free-form dance and studying issues ranging from the development of HE to subjective well-being and related areas within the growing field of positive psychology.*

This chapter starts with a bald account of what happened to me at Enfield, followed by a reflection on the highs and lows and then an attempt to recall what sense I made of it at the time. The rest seeks to distil some lessons from that experience and draw some conclusions.

I was not a blank slate when I arrived at Enfield in 1969 and my experience there was influenced by my own personal history, so I start by summarising that history.

Background

I was brought up with my older brother on Canvey Island, near Southend in a working class home; my father was a bus conductor and my mother worked as a shop assistant or in a local factory for most of the time I was at school. At the end of primary school I passed the eleven-plus examination and, as a result, attended the local grammar school, off the Island, in Westcliff. At eighteen I went to university to study economics, clear that I wanted to become a teacher. I was the first in my extended family to attend a university. This is not a large claim for the early 1960s when the university age-participation rate was less than 5 per cent. I studied at University College London and it was an experience that I did not much enjoy.

On graduating, I worked briefly as a secondary school teacher and then got a job as a research assistant at Surrey University. After about six months I got involved in the emerging 'hippie' counter-culture, became restless to expand my horizons and obtained a scholarship to do a Masters degree at a university in Canada. I combined this course with running a psychedelic light show. The stimulation I got from the light show experience was more than from my Master's course which I failed and returned to England where I enrolled on an MSc degree in business administration, specialising in industrial relations. By that time I had a vague idea about working in the research unit of a trade union. I took this course much more seriously and funded it by loans and part-time teaching in a further education college during the evenings. The course, at City University, was titled an 'MSc in Administrative Sciences'. This was part of the development of Master's degrees in Business and Management that took place in Britain in the late 1960s and 1970s. Eventually the preferred title of such courses became 'MBA', following the lead of universities in the USA.

By the time I applied for the job at Enfield I had completed the examinations of the Master's course and still had the dissertation component to complete.

What happened at Enfield?

The first time I saw Enfield College was the day I was interviewed for the post of lecturer in economics. It was housed in an unprepossessing building deep in the heart of the then unprepossessing Ponders End in North London.

The interview was a full-day event. In the morning I was interviewed by a group of economics staff and there was another interview in the afternoon. This was with the principal of the College, George Brosan, several senior members of the college and several members of the local authority, possibly as many as eight people in total.

The interview went well and I started work in late summer 1969 as a 'lecturer grade 2' i.e. a junior lecturer. I was given a place in an office that I would share with an old hand at the college, John

Munro, who I liked immediately. He had entered higher education through the trade union movement, with a scholarship to Ruskin College, Oxford, before completing a degree in politics, philosophy and economics.

He was also the newly appointed course leader of a part-time degree in Business Studies, validated by the Council for National Academic Awards (CNAA). I learned that many technical colleges had prepared students for 'external' degrees of the University of London. Under this system, the University of London set examinations and colleges around the country (and overseas) could prepare candidates by part-time or full-time study. For the University of London this was a form of university extension into the community. For the colleges, it enabled them to develop work at the higher education level. In 1964 the government established a Council for National Academic Awards (CNAA) through which these colleges were able to develop their own degree courses. Enfield had immediately started to replace its University of London (External) degrees by CNAA degrees and then develop new courses in other subjects, including Business Studies.

I was given a timetable with a 'half-load' of teaching for the first term, seven hours of seminars only. John Munro informed me that this was common practice in the college for staff who were new to lecturing. This light load was particularly helpful to me in my early months during which I was able to complete the dissertation element of my MSc course.

Most of my teaching was on the part-time Business Studies degree course. I learned that the college had a policy of assigning the majority of each lecturer's teaching to a single course and the remaining minority might be spread over several courses. This meant that staff felt their primary commitment to the course that provided the majority of their teaching.

I learned also that the part-time degree course in Business Studies at Enfield was the first part-time course of its kind in the country and was in its second year of operation. There was a pioneering feel about the course and those who taught on it seemed proud to be associated with it.

Enfield also offered a sandwich degree in Business Studies. It was based on the 'Crick' model. This involved the students studying a broad range of so-called business-related disciplines such as economics, law and statistics for two years, followed by a 'sandwich' year of supervised work experience and ending with a year of specialised study of a major of a major business function such as marketing, personnel or accounting.

By contrast, the part-time degree in Business Studies was a five-year course for students in full-time employment taught on the basis of evening classes or by a mixture of afternoon and evening attendance. Alternatively, it was possible to commute the final two years of part-time study by one year of full-time study, in which case the students on the part-time degree joined the students on the sandwich degree for their final year.

It was believed that there was a need to provide some integrating studies to help the students find connections between their studies. This was achieved in the latter part of the course by the use of case studies. Case study teaching had been pioneered by the prestigious Harvard Business School and was sometimes called the 'Harvard case study method'. In the early years, however, when the students had little knowledge to integrate, the 'integration' took the form of a course in the philosophy of knowledge. The rationale given for this was that, whatever the differences between the individual subjects in the first two years, they were all branches of a common tree of knowledge and shared similar epistemological concerns. This may not have been the whole explanation, however, as there seemed to be a particular interest at Enfield in Karl Popper's approach to the accumulation of empirical knowledge.

When I received my timetable, I found that, in addition to teaching economics I was expected to lead a one-hour seminar per week in integrating studies, *aka* philosophy of knowledge. As I had no background in this subject I was very grateful for a light timetable during my first year as an opportunity to read furiously about epistemology, philosophy of science and, in particular, the works of Popper.

I later discovered that philosophy of knowledge was taught across a range of courses at the college. And I remember that, a few years later, the *Times Higher Education Supplement* revealed that the Enfield college of Technology employed more philosophers than any other academic institution in the country with the exception of the University of Oxford.

Another feature of the college which I suspected was distinctive was the opportunity to attend the classes of other members of staff. An example of this was the lunchtime classes given by a senior member of the mathematics staff, Bill Craze, on introductory mathematics taught with reference to the historical development of mathematics. It was a weekly class suitable for staff without any mathematical qualifications. Bill would enter the room with a pint of beer from the college bar, his lunch, and try to share his delight in mathematics and his knowledge of the history and development of the subject. There were usually about half a dozen of us present including admin staff as well as lecturers who, like me, were feeling vulnerable about their lack of mathematical knowledge.

Another example of the encouragement to learn from other members of staff was an openness to sitting in on each other's classes. I suspected this had started with staff that were timetabled to lead seminars attending the lectures on which the seminars would be based. I, of course, attended the lectures in integrating studies (philosophy of knowledge) which would be the basis of the seminar with students that I would subsequently lead each week.

By the time I arrived at Enfield a culture had developed in which it seemed that a lecturer did not even feel the need to seek the permission of another lecturer to sit in on their classes. The effects of this were generally very positive, supporting collegiality, learning and openness. But on one occasion, it backfired on me. In what seems like one of the first seminars I led on philosophy of knowledge I found a senior member of staff in the classroom as part of my seminar group. For a young inexperienced lecturer teaching a subject where I felt my learning was only just ahead of the students this was too much. After stumbling and bumbling through the first ten minutes of the class I asked him to step outside for a moment and then explained that I was new to leading seminar groups and this was a new subject for me so his presence was making me too nervous to teach effectively. He apologised profusely and did not return.

There seemed no pressure to do research but there was pressure to keep up to date in the areas I was teaching. During the late 1960s and early 1970s economics as an academic subject became much more mathematical. My own economics studies had been almost entirely non-mathematical. By 1970, however, I was finding that an increasing proportion of the articles in the leading journals in economics were being expressed in mathematical terms and I concluded this was a trend rather than a fad. So I decided to repair the deficiency in my mathematical knowledge and skills by signing up to study A-level mathematics at the local FE college, Tottenham Technical College. To my surprise and delight, I found that I enjoyed studying mathematics at this level and that I was quite good at it.

This was a good experience for me for several reasons. It increased my empathy for the part-time students I was teaching at Enfield, I enjoyed being a part-time student and it made me realise how important motivation is in education. At school I couldn't see the point of mathematics and dropped it as soon as I could but now I had a good reason to study it and that was the difference that made the difference. It gave me the knowledge to start making sense of the journal articles which had hitherto been inaccessible to me.

In fact, it was such a good experience that each year over the next five years I took one, two or three units on the Mathematics for Business degree that was offered at Enfield. I also sat in on courses on econometrics on other degree courses at the college. I went on to teach economic statistics and econometrics on courses at the college but the crowning glory of this episode, for me, was when I later taught mathematical economics on the Mathematics for Business degree itself. More generally, this experience had a significant influence on my attitude to self-managed learning which, in turn, was to have a significant influence on my views on self-development and learning in higher education in later years.

At no time during my time at Enfield College did I feel pressure to undertake research. I was aware that there were people at the college who did pursue research and some, especially amongst the sociologists, had international reputations for their work. Jock Young, for example, apparently had an international reputation for his work on drug-taking and criminology. When I met an old school-friend, who was a young university lecturer in social administration, and mentioned that I was working at a technical college, Enfield, he seemed genuinely impressed saying that in his field Enfield was no ordinary college of technology.

At Enfield, attitudes towards universities seemed mixed. Without doubt, there were lecturers at the college who would have preferred to have been employed in a university. On the other hand, there was a significant belief that the college was doing something different and valuable. This sentiment seemed to be emanating from senior members of staff, particularly George Brosan and Eric Robinson. The sense that I got, as a new lecturer, was that universities had become ivory towers, disengaged from the community and society more generally with insufficient emphasis on the dissemination of knowledge and too much emphasis on research, much of which was of a kind which had little impact on the world outside of academia itself. By contrast, it was the role of the colleges of technology to offer higher education that was relevant to needs of society, disseminating up-to-date knowledge by teachers who drew on the best knowledge currently available across their field. If the primary goals of the university had become the preservation and accumulation of new knowledge then I thought Enfield saw its primary roles as the interpretation and dissemination and application of new knowledge. I later read Eric Robinson's book, *The New Polytechnics'* (sub-titled, *The People's Universities*) which developed those themes into a philosophy for binary education in the UK.

After I had been at Enfield for a year I became the co-ordinator of Year 3 for the Part-time Business Studies degree. In this capacity, one of my tasks was to advise students who were considering whether to commute their final two years of part-time study by one year of full-time study. I 'researched' this issue and reached the intuitively improbable conclusion that for students with a 'typical' profile for the part-time students (i.e. early thirties, married, with young children and a mortgage) to be financially worse off by completing the degree by full-time study they would have to have been earning above the average (median) wage. There were three main reasons for this: (1) the academic 'year', from October to June, was, in fact, only eight months long (which reduced the foregone earnings to only two-thirds of their annual income), (2) the student grant was surprisingly generous for mature students with family commitments, and (3) the academic 'year' spanned two tax years, October to March and April to June, enabling the student to reclaim income tax on the preceding and succeeding year. Later, when I realised how general the option of completing part-time degree courses by a year of full-time study had become during the 1970s I decided to share my conclusions more widely. Accordingly, in the late 1970s, I published my first journal article which I framed as an application of the principle of opportunity cost, 'The Cost of Completing a Part-time Degree by Full-Time Study' in the *Higher Education Review*. For me, this seemed the kind of practical and applied 'research' which resonated with the spirit of ECT.

During this period also, I became a member of the Standing Committee for Part-time Degrees in Business Studies. After the apparent success of Enfield's Part-Time Degree in Business Studies these courses proliferated across the country and the Standing Committee was established to hold regular meetings of people running such courses or planning to do so. This was a valuable vehicle for information exchange in the early years. The people running courses would exchange information on issues such as levels of student enrolment and accounts of validation visits by the CNAA. Moreover, people planning to set up courses could attend the meetings and seek advice from those who had already done so, find suitable people to serve on mock validation panels etc. Again, I experienced a sense of being part of something new and valuable. It fed my interest and enthusiasm for part-time provision of Higher Education.

In 1970 the Head of the College, George Brosan left to become the Director of the new, North-East London Polytechnic, taking Eric Robinson with him as his Deputy. In 1973 Enfield became part of Middlesex Polytechnic, the last of the original set of polytechnics to be established.

So how did that feel?

The last section tried to provide an 'objective' overview of my experience at Enfield between 1969 and 1972. It is objective in the sense that the facts it contains could be confirmed or falsified, at least in principle, by independent witnesses. This section is different; it addresses how the experience felt. In order to make the task manageable I restrict myself to the three main things I felt good about and the three main things I felt bad about during my time at Enfield.

The first high was getting the post at all. As a kid from a working class home I encountered some good and kind teachers in my secondary school, and, as a result, I aspired to become a teacher like them. By getting a job in a college of technology I had already realised my aspirations and exceeded my expectations. Moreover, this was a college that taught degree-level work but without the apparent pretentions of a university. And when I arrived at Enfield I liked the people I was working with; I liked their values and I was exposed to ideas I found new and exciting.

During my first year at Enfield I became aware of what sort of institution I had joined. As I did so I became increasingly proud of being part of it. I discovered that it was an institution with a point of view, even a philosophy. That philosophy included opposition to elitism in higher education and a responsiveness to the community and society more widely. It was a philosophy with which I felt aligned. I also felt excited by the pioneering feel of the college.

At Enfield, the vision coming from senior members of the college was around access, relevance and service. ECT sought to provide access to a wider range of students, in particular working class students who were under-represented in universities. It offered courses that were intended to be relevant to the employments that the students might pursue. And it aimed to serve the needs of the students, the community and society more widely.

The commitment of Enfield to access, vocational relevance and service can all be illustrated by reference to the part-time degree in Business Studies that accounted for most of my work at the college. This course was intended to be accessed by people in full-time employment so it provided for evening only attendance and it drew its students from the local community who had no other access to higher education.

A second thing that I felt good about was the emphasis placed on providing higher education rather than research. When I left school I was clear that I wanted to be a teacher so I felt very comfortable working in an institution that prioritised providing students with a vocationally relevant education. Much of the research published in journals in my subject, economics, seemed of little use or consequence outside of the subject itself. I aspired to be a good teacher who stayed up to date in all aspects of the economics courses on which I taught. For me, that implied that I engage in scholarship rather than research. I later encountered a definition of scholarship as 'critical interpretations of existing knowledge' (Elton, 1992). In other words, I saw my role as a teacher in HE as scrutinising new research in areas that impacted on the subject matter of the courses I taught and incorporating and critically interpreting what I judged to be the most relevant and significant findings into my lectures and seminars.

I also felt a sense of growing, professionally and personally, at Enfield. I believe I became a more effective teacher, I exorcised the ghost of my mathematical inadequacy, I became a better economist, I developed an interest in philosophy and, in particular, thc philosophy of knowledge, I learned much about the world of part-time higher education and I learned a lot about myself, including my strengths, weaknesses and values. In other words, I flourished in the environment that Enfield provided.

What were the three low points or worst aspects of my time at Enfield? First, I felt underprepared for the job. I got no real induction to the college, its work or its philosophy. It is true I was given a very light time-table in my first term and given a room with an 'old hand', familiar with the college and its ways, but I sometimes felt a bit overwhelmed by what I encountered.

Second, I sometimes felt rather fraudulent. In the first couple of years, in particular, I felt I did not know enough economics and that I might be found out. The courses on which I taught were scrutinised and, hopefully, validated by the CNAA and a validation event could be a anxiety-provoking experience. At a validation event we were interrogated by peers drawn mostly from universities, about any aspect of the courses we were submitting for approval including the syllabuses we had written. It could be uncomfortable to say the least.

Finally, I felt that I had arrived towards the end of an era at Enfield. I felt that I'd missed out on something important that had happened at the college in the previous few years.

What was I thinking?

My first acquaintance with Enfield was my interview for a lecturing post there and I was surprised that there were so many senior people involved in the interviewing process. When I started work, I asked my room-mate about that and he said it was because the senior staff were concerned to appoint the 'right' people, particularly those whose values were aligned with those of the college. This would help the college realise those values through its actions and it would also save the time of senior staff in the long run compared with the consequences of appointing the 'wrong' people. That explanation made sense to me and also made me feel good as being amongst the 'chosen ones'.

When I started teaching part-time students and full-time students I soon became aware that I preferred working with the part-time students even though it meant teaching evening classes. I was struck by how much the part-timers were motivated to learn and the sacrifices they made to acquire a higher education. I became an enthusiast for part-time higher education. It seemed to me to be a way of increasing access to higher education and reducing the social imbalance in higher education, a cost-effective way that government could increase the number of people in the country with graduate-level skills and a way of improving the lives of a substantial number of people. Later in my life I was to write several books on the subject of part-time higher education and part-time students (see, for example, Bourner, et al. 1991).

Many of the students on the part-time degree course did not have conventional qualifications in the form of A-levels and some did not have any qualifications at all. I initially feared that such students would have difficulty coping with the academic demands of degree-level work and would drop out. In practice, I found that the main reason for non-completion was not the academic demands of degree-level work but the demands, often erratic, of professional and domestic commitments. I became increasingly convinced that strength of motivation was the key to success in learning. This was confirmed by my own part-time study of mathematics. I concluded that most people can learn most things but there are some things that some people will take longer to learn than others. This provided additional support for my enthusiasm for greater access to higher education.

When I first started work at Enfield I didn't think the college was much different from any other technical college. Over my first year I gradually became aware that Enfield was not just another college of technology. I read Robinson's book *The New Polytechnics* and found an articulation of a philosophy that seemed to lie behind the institution. It was a philosophy that resonated with my own thinking about higher education at the time. I was a already convinced by the need for greater access to higher education and a higher education that was more engaged with society including more vocational relevance, and this book provided a clearer rationale for that case. My relatively incoherent beliefs and inclinations became more coherent and more explicit. I had been unimpressed by my own experience of higher education on my undergraduate degree at University College London and many of the criticisms of traditional university education that I heard at Enfield resonated with my experience as an undergraduate student and this gave credibility to those beliefs. I wanted to be part of providing a better higher education than I'd received.

Being required to teach philosophy of knowledge gave me an interest in epistemology and particularly the work of Popper, Kuhn and the American pragmatists. I wondered why there was not more attention paid to the philosophy of knowledge in higher education as it seemed fundamental to the acquisition of knowledge about individual subjects. Epistemology has remained of continuing interest to me in the ensuing years.

What did I think about the focus on teaching rather than research? It pleased me for several reasons. First, I saw myself as a teacher rather than a researcher so I felt I was in the right place. Second, I was unimpressed by much of the research that was being published in economic journals at the time. It seemed that academic advancement was becoming increasingly dependent on research publication and that much of what was being published was subject-centred and of little interest or consequence outside of the economics profession. I remember a colleague in another of the social sciences criticising much of the research at that time as the pursuit of 'truth without significance' so it seemed that it wasn't just economics.

Thirdly, I believed that over-emphasis on research could actually damage the higher education provided by universities. I had encountered university lecturers for whom teaching was a distraction from maximising the list of their publications on which their advancement would depend. There seemed to be, at least in my subject, a growing flow of publications of low significance making it more difficult to find the new additions to knowledge that were relevant to the world outside the world of academic economics. There was at least the possibility that the crowding out of high-value research by low-value publications could actually be hampering the advancement of knowledge, which would be a counter-productive and ironic outcome.

I saw my role as a teacher and a scholar (but not a researcher) at Enfield as sifting through the newly published material to identify the significant findings that I could use to up-date the knowledge I conveyed in my classes. Over time I became clearer about the distinction between 'scholarship' and 'research'. I saw scholarship as the 'critical interpretation of existing and emergent knowledge' and I saw research as 'the intentional creation of shared new knowledge'. From this perspective, I believed an individual's scholarship as essential to good teaching in Higher Education and an individual's research as a potential impediment.

I believed that the new polytechnics had been developed to make up the deficiencies of universities at a time when such deficiencies were many. Here are ten criticisms of universities in the 1960s that I heard voiced at Enfield that struck me, at the time, as valid:

1. *Universities were, for the most part, elitist institutions in terms of their admissions.* Students from working class homes were under-represented, women were under-represented and students from independent schools were over-represented in the universities. This was particularly the case with the older universities with more prestige, to which most of the other universities aspired. In general, there seemed to be a positive association between elitism and the age of a university. There was also, in general, a positive association between the age of the university and its esteem. And this meant there was a positive association between university elitism and university esteem.
2. *They were elitist also in the kind of higher education they offered.* Courses in the arts and humanities had their roots in the classical tradition and with its aspiration to introduce students to 'the best that has been thought and said in the world' (Arnold, 1869), at least in the Western world. And courses in the sciences had their origins in Humboldt's conception of a university in the early nineteenth century. For Humboldt the dominant goal of the university was not to provide higher education that meets the needs of its students but to serve knowledge: 'the teacher no longer serves the purpose of the student. Instead both serve knowledge itself.' (Hutchins and Adler, 1969, p.350).

3. *The vocational needs of students were ignored.* The courses that universities taught were seen as low on relevance to the work that most of the graduates would go on to pursue after graduating. Compared to, say, the USA where professional Master's level courses, such as the MBA, and professional doctorates had existed for most of the twentieth century, British universities, for the most part, disparaged vocational education in the 1960s. Their courses provided a good preparation for those graduates who would go to become researchers, and academics more generally, in their chosen fields of studies but not those students who would go on to employment beyond the academy, particularly in industry or commerce or public service outside of academia. In the 1960s about two-thirds of university graduates remained in the education system after graduation (Bourner and Rospigliosi, 2008). They went on to research, further academic study, teacher training, other training, education administration or directly into teaching.
4. *Higher education of students was accorded lower priority than the accumulation of new knowledge.* The higher education of their students at universities seemed to be subservient to research. It was symptomatic that research degrees were accorded higher status than taught courses based on scholarship. And, in general, research was prioritised over teaching.
5. *Research was too driven by the pursuit of knowledge for its own sake.* This was exemplified for me when a colleague from the Mathematics for Business degree at Enfield mentioned that the toast of the University of Cambridge Pure mathematics society was 'To pure mathematics, may it never be of any use to anybody.' (attributed to many people, including G. H. Hardy in (Clarke, 2001, p.460).
6. *Research was too focused on the advancement of academic subjects rather than the advancement of society.* The *application* of knowledge was undervalued compared to the *accumulation* of knowledge. Many university lecturers seemed overly focused on their personal research, much of which was of little significance to the world outside of their academic subjects. Consequently, there was a need for more in-

stitutions in higher education that placed relatively more emphasis on the *application* of knowledge.

7. *The development of higher education in Britain could be characterised as a process of academic drift.* Historically, a process could be discerned where institutions of higher education had been established to serve the needs of a locality or region and the needs of their students and success in so doing had led to them to acquire the coveted 'university' title which then resulted in their abandoning their commitment to society and students in favour of subject-centred aspirations. This has been termed 'academic drift' and could be seen in the histories of most of the civic universities of Britain and those new universities of 1960s that had their origins in the colleges of technology. For this reason, it seemed to me important that the new polytechnics should not be rebadged as universities and that they should remain accountable to their local authorities or some other democratically elected institution(s).
8. *Universities had become disengaged from their communities and society more widely.* They had become increasingly disengaged from the practical concerns of the majority of the population, particularly those in the lower part of the social hierarchy.
9. *University autonomy had resulted in 'ivory tower' institutions.* The universities of the 1960s were seen by many as autonomous bodies accountable to no one but themselves. This had allowed them to become 'academic' in the pejorative sense of that term i.e. of little practical value or consequence to anyone outside of the academy, and earning themselves the critical epithet 'ivory towers'. It was their autonomy, i.e. lack of accountability, which had allowed this 'academic drift'. Many people in universities seemed to interpret 'academic freedom' as freedom from accountability to any part of the democratic system or indeed any part of the world outside of academia.
10. *Slow to adapt to the changing needs of society* There seemed plenty of evidence for this from, for example, the continuing requirement into the 1960s of prior study of Latin or Greek for admission to a course in the Arts and Humanities in Brit-

ain's oldest universities through the resistance of the majority of Oxbridge colleges to the admission of female students and on to the resistance of many of the universities to providing a higher education in the technologies. Even some senior Oxbridge academics, such as Eric Ashby of Clare College, Cambridge, saw this as a looming crisis in British higher education (Ashby, 1958, 1974). It seemed that universities were becoming increasingly irrelevant to a technology-based society. During my time at Enfield I believed that the higher education that these universities provided was too slow to adapt to the needs of an increasingly knowledge-based and technological society.

By way of contrast, I saw Enfield as an institution that was:

1. *At least as concerned with scholarship as research.* The work of the college was focused on the higher education of its students and the scholarship needed to support that higher education.
2. *Committed to access and widening participation.* Enfield expressed its commitment to access by developing part-time courses accessible to people in full-time employment. The social origins of part-time students were much more representative of the whole population than full-time students in HE.
3. *Valued vocational relevance.* It was concerned to offer vocationally relevant higher education to provide the knowledge, developing the skills and cultivating the attitudes to support the students in their lives after university. Enfield expressed its commitment to vocational relevance by developing courses like the sandwich course degree in Business Studies that prepared students for employment for organisational settings outside of academia.
4. *Engaged with the local community.* Enfield's part-time courses (usually available by evening attendance) drew their students mostly from the local community. The college library was open to local residents. And senior figures in the college, especially Robinson, exhorted us to engage with the

local community with our research and our teaching including, for example, visits to local schools.

Discussion and reflections

This section looks at a number of issues that have emerged in the foregoing account, including (1) whether Enfield was really unique? (2) the problem of rose-tinted spectacles (3) contexts, including the 2 cultures, (4) the relative valuation of research and teaching, (5) the issue of academic drift (6) what happened next and (7) new times and new agendas.

Was Enfield really unique?

I was 24 years old when I arrived at ECT and 28 years old when it became part of Middlesex Polytechnic. I found the Enfield experience stimulating and motivating. I enjoyed its iconoclastic ethos, its willingness to try new things and its refusal to be cowed by the reputation of elite universities. The contrast with my experience when I moved from Middlesex Polytechnic to Brighton Polytechnic in 1979 was stark. At Brighton, I found an institution that behaved as if it was 'second best' to Brighton's other Higher Education institution, the University of Sussex. Brighton Polytechnic felt more timid with the question 'What would they do at Sussex?' always in the air. Actually, sometimes that question was actually articulated and it annoyed me. At Enfield I heard the term 'a necessary arrogance' to mean the arrogance to which one is entitled when one believes one is doing the right thing.

In the late 1960s I had the impression that Enfield was unique with its own ideas and its own practices. With hindsight, I wonder if that was a form of cultural myopia associated with the limited communication at the time which made it difficult to know what was going on at other colleges. The coverage of higher education in the national media seemed focused on the views and the practices of the universities, so news and views from the colleges received relatively little coverage.

It was then a paper-based world where posted letters, 'snail-mail', played a major role in communication so we had little idea about what was going on in other institutions around the country. In this respect, the *Standing Committee for Part-time Degrees in Business Studies* was a valuable in revealing that there were like-minded individuals in other colleges around the country. Nowadays, with on-line communications the relative cultural isolation of Enfield or any other college would not be possible. Since those days I have spoken with other people who were aware of something happening in HE in Britain of which Enfield was only an example, albeit I suspect a good example. It was, after all, at Enfield that the Eric Robinson wrote '*The New Polytechnics: the People's Universities*'.

Many people, including myself, saw Enfield as challenging the hegemony of the autonomous university sector. Lest that conjures up an image of David and Goliath I think the image of an ant and a giraffe might be more apt. In reality, however, I suspect that Enfield was just a part of a larger movement in higher education that was occurring world-wide in so-called economically developed countries, which became known as the 'massification' of higher education (Trow, 1974). The institutional arrangements of higher education in Britain, with its autonomous universities, had served to keep higher education small with less than 5 per cent of school-leavers going to university in the 1960s. But the demand for higher education was rising in Britain and it was the colleges that were meeting much of the excess demand. Consequently, the percentage of higher education provided outside of universities was rising.

The first crack in the dam occurred in the early 1960s with the creation of ten new universities between in the five years up to 1965 (Tight, 2009). The creation of a binary line probably served to preserve elite university education. The dam finally broke in the early 1990s with the ending of the binary line. The shift from an elite system to mass higher education brings with it many changes in the nature of higher education itself. For example, a few years ago I (with co-author, Asher Rospigliosi) looked at the destinations of university graduates in the 1960s, when such data was first published, compared with the situation in the early 2000s. We found that in the 1960s about two-thirds of university graduates remained in the education system after graduation. By the 2000s less than a third remained in the education system. It seems that increasing the higher education age-participation rate changes the destinations of the majority of graduates and, since a significant part of the purpose of higher education is to prepare graduates for their lives after graduating, this changes the nature of higher education itself. More generally Clerk Kerr has explored, in *The Great Transformation in Higher Education, 1960-80*, other changes that can accompany the shift from an elite system to mass higher education (Kerr, 1991).

Rose-tinted spectacles?

My Enfield experience was an important time of my life during which I believe I developed and grew. However, I recognise that I do not have full recall of events of so long ago but rather memories that comprise snapshots of particular moments and short episodes. And I recognise that I have constructed a narrative linking those memory fragments (Gilbert, 2006). It took place when I was in my early twenties and research on personal narratives has found that people often place particular significance on what happened to them in their early twenties (McAdams, 1993). This is the time when people are transitioning into full adulthood and it is therefore particularly important in identity formation. I also recognise that many other colleges were experiencing the transition from being providers of further education to that of higher education with all the problems, challenges and opportunities thereby involved.

With hindsight, I am inclined to conclude that Enfield was part of a larger movement whereby the UK shifted from an elite system to mass higher education. It was unique mainly in that it was a leading light of that movement. Despite these reservations I remain convinced that Enfield was a remarkable place in the late 1960s with a worked-out alternative counter-philosophy of higher education and a group of staff who were prepared to take actions to which that philosophy pointed.

Enfield and the 'two cultures'

In 1959 C. P. Snow had given the Rede Lecture for that year and argued that British public life was dominated by two cultures. One culture had its origins in the classics/humanities and the education provided by independent/private schools and this had dominated University education until at least the first half of the twentieth century. The other culture was associated with the growing importance of science and technology.

The first culture was based on the classical education with its aspiration to introduce students to, in the words of Matthew Arnold (1869), 'the best that has been thought and said in the world' at least since the birth of civilisation ... at that time believed by many to have been in ancient Greece (Tarnas, 1993). Within university education, the second culture, originating in science and technology, was becoming relatively more important.

In his lecture, Snow claimed that the British political elite was dominated by people steeped in the first culture who were ignorant of science and Luddite in terms of technology, which made them unfit to govern a nation in which technological advance was increasingly important. Snow claimed authority in both scientific and literary fields as he was a trained scientist who was also a successful novelist. The debate was intensified in 1962 when F. R. Leavis, leading academic and literary critic, attacked Snow as a mere 'public relations man for science', whose public standing was out of all proportion to his intellectual gifts. A book by Snow based on his Rede lecture was subsequently published in 1963 and became a best-seller (Snow, 1963).

Britain's political elite, however, seem to have been sympathetic to Snow's criticisms and this supported the belief that higher education in science and technology should be expanded. At the 1963 Labour Party Annual Conference, Harold Wilson made his 'white heat' speech on the consequences of scientific and technological change with 'no place for restrictive practices or for outdated measures on either side of industry.' (Edgerton, 1996). Universities, however, as autonomous institutions were slow to respond. Government had relatively little control over the established universities as autonomous institutions but they could create new universities and they could ensure that a substantial proportion of those new universities were rebadged colleges of advanced technology.

In addition to these moves at the national level, government encouraged local authorities to support the development of science and technology at the local level. This was the climate in which Enfield College of Technology was created in 1962. Colleges such as Enfield were encouraged to develop high-level courses to support the emergent technologbased society.

Relative valuation of research and teaching

There is a view often found in universities today that an academic can't be a good teacher unless they are also engaged in research. 'Research-led teachers' are represented as academics that are in touch with the leading edge of their subject discipline in contrast with their more pedestrian colleagues who are content to convey second-hand knowledge in their classes. Accordingly, research-led teachers are able to convey to students the excitement of discovery as well, of course, as the newest of new knowledge.

There is, of course, another view. Research in most academic subjects takes place through specialisation as researchers focus on a small, sometimes minute, part of their subject discipline in order to advance knowledge. Allocating such a large proportion of their working hours to one small element of their subject means allocating a correspondingly smaller proportion to monitoring the latest knowledge in the other parts of their subject. The dedicated teacher, by contrast, is able to devote a larger proportion of their working hours to scholarship i.e. the critical interpretation of new knowledge across a much wider range of their subject discipline.

These are caricatures but they are not unimportant caricatures. Most undergraduates do encounter in their studies the 'lecturer' whose primary focus is their research on which their advancement depends and for whom their students are a distraction in terms of their interests or career aspirations. And most students also encounter the lecturer who seems to have lost interest in their subject let alone the latest additions to knowledge in it.

At Enfield in the late 1960s there was little pressure to do research though there was much pressure to continue learning. It seemed to me that scholarship, the critical interpretation of emergent knowledge, was more highly valued that research. Most subject groups at the college ran staff seminars, CNAA inspections could expose staff who lost touch with the latest knowledge in their field and staff were encouraged to register for higher degrees. Enfield was an intellectually stimulating place. When Enfield College of Technology became part of Middlesex Polytechnic in 1973 there was still no great pressure to do research. The polytechnics emphasised teaching rather than research. Within the domain of the advancement of knowledge, the universities saw themselves as most concerned with the pursuit of new knowledge and the polytechnics were most concerned with the interpretation, dissemination and application of knowledge.

Since that time, much has changed in higher education, including the elevation of research within HE institutions more generally, the higher esteem accorded research outside of HE institutions and the filtering down of research from the PhD as the pinnacle of HE into other levels of higher education. Research is now the primary criterion for an institution's position in university league tables and it is the primary criterion for academic advancement within most HE institutions.

In the late 1960s it was possible to perceive much academic research as an ivory-tower activity of limited interest to the rest of the world. Since that time the contribution of new knowledge to human well-being, particularly material well-being has become much clearer. The vision of Francis Bacon that the accumulation of knowledge could significantly enhance human well-being probably seemed hopelessly idealistic at the start of the seventeenth century but it is now widely accepted. That acceptance is captured in the popularity of the terms 'knowledge economy' and 'knowledge society' in the last decades of the twentieth century. More recently, and more specifically, the contribution of the accumulation of knowledge to the improvement of the human condition was powerfully captured by the World Bank Study of 2015 showing that in 1800 about 85 per cent of the world's population lived in extreme poverty. Since that time, this figure has fallen year by year until by 1970 it was down to about 50 per cent and by 2016 it was approaching 10 per cent (Binswanger, et al, 2016). My, admittedly limited, studies of the possible explanations of this phenomenon have convinced me that the primary cause is the accumulation of knowledge, particularly in the fields of science and technology (see, example, Fogel, 2004, Clark, 2008, Mokyr, 2011 and Deaton, 2013). It is not difficult of find other equally powerful examples of the contribution of the accumulation of knowledge to the improvement of the human condition, including, for example, the doubling of global life expectancy over the last hundred years from under 35 years to over 70 years (Roser, 2017). Moreover, I see the primary source of the accumulation of knowledge as the institutionalisation of research in universities and other organisations. Bacon's dictum that 'knowledge is power' now seems so obviously true as to be a platitude.

As the importance of new knowledge has increased, its role in higher education has risen. In the late 1960s there was a very clear distinction between a research degree and so-called taught courses. Since that time research 'training' has filtered down from the PhD into Masters degree courses. Nowadays, it is very difficult to find a Master's course without a dissertation component where students are expected to research an issue agreed with their supervisor(s) and present the result in the form of a dissertation. Nowadays too, many, possibly most, undergraduate courses have a 'capstone' course which involves the requirement for students to plan and manage a small-scale research project (Healey et al, 2014). Undergraduate research is now commonplace in USA universities. In 2005 the US *Council of Undergraduate Research* and the *National Conference of Undergraduate Research* issued a joint statement referring to undergraduate research as the 'pedagogy of the twenty-first century' (Walkington, 2015). This is supported by the growing number of undergraduate journals based in prestigious US universities aimed at publishing the results of undergraduate research. These included, for example, the *Berkeley Undergraduate Journal*, the *Caltech Undergraduate Research Journal* and the *Columbia Undergraduate Science Journal*. In the UK, student-led research as part of the undergraduate curriculum has been championed by the *Higher Education Academy* (Healey et al, 2009 and 2014, Walkington, 2015).

During my last years at Middlesex at the end of the 1970s I gradually became more engaged in research. After looking at the cost of completing a part-time degree (see above) I became interested in what happened to my students after they graduated and how well the higher education we were offering prepared students for that. At that time graduate unemployment had not become the issue it became in the early 1980s and my discovery of the first destination statistics prepared and used by careers advisory services in universities and polytechnics opened up the opportunity for more work on graduate employment (see, for example, Bourner and Crilly, 1981). This led me to research on graduate outcomes more generally (e.g. Bourner and Hindmarch, 1981). I believe that my early forays into research were still guided by the spirit of Enfield i.e. problem-centred research aimed at applicable outcomes.

When the polytechnics were rebadged as universities in 1992 there was much more emphasis on research. By that time I had become more convinced of the value of research beyond its (small) contribution to my own teaching. I recognised the value of research in tackling practical problems and led the development of professional doctorates in my own university (Brighton) in support of that end. Whereas I could see little value in much of the research being undertaken in my subject, economics, in universities in the late 1960s I am now an enthusiast for research more generally and, especially, the contribution it can make to the current and future wellbeing of humankind.

Academic drift?

Most of the universities that existed in Britain in the 1960s were of relatively recent origin; most had achieved their university status in the twentieth century. Most had started as institutions of technology founded as local or regional establishments to serve the needs of the locality or region. Most, also, had been institutions with goals that were primarily vocational. A common progression was from local technical college, responsible to a local authority, to college of advanced technology and then on to university and autonomy, i.e. freedom from local accountability.

During this process the institution invariably lost its vocational orientation, its local/regional focus and its accountability to part of the democratic system i.e. its local authority. And it gained control over its own destiny and freedom to pursue knowledge for its own sake.

Typically, in this process it would give up its lower level teaching, particularly sub-degree work, and take on an increasing proportion of post-graduate work, it would reduce the proportion of students studying part-time courses and it would expand the amount of non-vocational higher education that it provided.

In this process also, its staff would become more subject-centred and less centred on the needs of the students for preparation for their lives, including their work, after graduating or on the needs of the community or society more widely. The drift into subject-centeredness manifested itself as prioritising the development of the academic subject and seeking the esteem of subject colleagues beyond the institution. It involved a change in professional identity as allegiance to academic subject became relatively more important and allegiance to the institution, or a course within that institution, became relatively less important.

Some people saw in this progression what has been termed 'academic drift' as institutions moved from being practical, useful and relevant to their communities to institutions that were elite, unaccountable and self-referencing. The consequence was that some first-rate local and regional institutions meeting needs that would not otherwise have been met became third-rate universities meeting 'needs' that were being met by thousands of other universities around the world.

It was this process that the establishment of the binary system of higher education in Britain was intended to restrain. The polytechnics and other colleges remained accountable to their local authorities. As a result, a relatively high proportion of their work remained vocationally orientated, part-time and they continued to offer courses of tertiary education below degree level. (Pratt, 1997)

In 1992, higher education in Britain changed from a binary system with one part (the universities) focused on research and another part (the polytechnics and other colleges) focused on teaching, to a unitary system made up almost entirely of universities. Enthusiasts for the binary system feared, and predicted, 'academic drift' in erstwhile polytechnics and colleges as they placed much more emphasis on research. Although this did, to a considerable extent, occur, the ending of the binary line also encouraged 'vocational drift' in the old universities as they placed more emphasis on graduate employment with disproportionate growth in subjects with more vocational relevance, development of transferable skills and competencies (Barnett, 1994), and, in some subjects, particularly at Masters level, reflective learning for professional development.

Rebadging the polytechnics as universities in the early 1990s has revealed that the story was more complex than the 'academic drift' narrative suggests. Other factors were also at work including the massification of higher education and growing recognition of the value of new knowledge as the basis of economic development and material well-being.

What happened next?

By the time that Enfield became part of Middlesex Poly in January 1973 most of the excitement had gone. When the college principal, George Brosan, left to become the first director of North East London Polytechnic in 1970 (with Eric Robinson following him soon after) he was replaced by a person with less vision for the college and more of a civil servant disposition with both the benefits and limitations of that. By the time I left the polytechnic in 1979 the spirit of ECT seemed to have been lost completely. As far as I was concerned, Middlesex had become just another polytechnic in a way that Enfield had not seemed to be just another college of technology.

When I moved on to Brighton Polytechnic in 1980 much of what I did there was influenced by my experience at ECT. I used what I had learned at Enfield to pursue course development, including a part-time degree in Business Studies, a post-graduate course that enabled part-time students use research methods to tackle problems within organisations and, later, several professional doctorates. I set up a local economy study group where I tried to put my economics to practical use. My work at ECT on graduate employment had brought me to the attention to the CNAA for which I undertook a series of projects ranging from an enquiry into the experience of part-time students and their HE outcomes to the establishment of a transbinary database which, amongst other things, allowed the comparison of HE outcomes across the two sectors of HE. That last project caused me to wonder what was generating the numbers in the database and that developed in me an interest in learning and teaching processes in HE. In this field I discovered in the work of Reg Revans, something called ‘action learning’, which gave me a route into personal and professional development which was the field in which I remained for the rest of my academic career. It is not difficult to see the influence of values and beliefs acquired at ECT on all those activities.

New times and new agendas

The fire has long gone out of many of the debates that seemed critical in the 1960s. Some of the issues have been wholly or partly resolved, such as female under-representation in HE, resistance to vocationalism in HE and a low age-participation rate compared to other countries at similar levels of economic development. And some have been replaced by new critical issues such as university funding and student debt, league tables and levels of student satisfaction with their HE experience. In the 1960s and 1970s we had little idea that within a couple of decades we would be discussing issues like knowledge transfer partnerships (KTPs), professional doctorates and third leg funding to support university engagement with parts of society outside of the ivory towers.

Conclusions

It is almost fifty years since ECT ceased to exist. What do I conclude about it now? I still regard as Enfield as a special place. What was most special about it? There was a great deal of vision at Enfield. There was a willingness to go where the vision led. And in so doing there was a readiness to challenge the established order in Britain's higher education.

I think that the emphasis on the education of the students in colleges like Enfield rather than the accumulation of new knowledge was appropriate for that time for the reasons given above. However, I now see the wider purpose in the accumulation of new knowledge in terms of its capacity to make the world a better place. But, I am still impatient with the justification of research as the pursuit of knowledge 'for its own sake' and subject-centred research that is self-referential and disengaged from the rest of society. That seems to me to be perfectly sound as a hobby or personal pursuit but not something that should be supported from public funds i.e. paid for by the rest of society.

I'm no longer so quite convinced by some of the views I encountered at Enfield, such as those represented by Robinson's *New Polytechnics*. I now see the role of universities in terms of the so-called tripartite mission (contribution to the higher education of students, the advancement of knowledge and service to those outside of the university) and I have tried to work out the implications of this for what it means to be a 'fully-functioning university' (Bourner, 2008). However, I still believe that in the 1960s and 1970s universities were too dominated by the pursuit of knowledge to which the other parts of the tripartite mission played a subservient part. I now suspect that if the ECT of 1962-72 had not existed then HE today in Britain today would not be very much different from the way it is. However, I believe that I would have been very different.

The Enfield experience affected me in many ways. At the simplest level, it provided an environment where I could challenge my ignorance and fear of mathematics and the result of that had a significant impact on my subsequent work as an economics lecturer and my future work-life more generally. At another level, the concerns and ideas I encountered at Enfield contained the seeds of most of the issues on which I have spent the ensuing years of my life working. These include graduate employment starting with the question, 'what happens to my students after they graduate?' and leading eventually to the ideas of a 'new vocationalism' (Bourner et al, 2011) It includes the experience of part-time students and widening participation in HE. It includes work on university-community engagement, especially student-community engagement (see, for example, Millican et al, 2014). And it includes continuing concern with the questions, 'what is higher education for?' and 'what are universities for?'

Finally, my Enfield experience increased my confidence in dealing with universities and university academics when I was a polytechnic lecturer and later when I became a university academic myself. It also helped give me the confidence to move within the domain of higher education from economist to education researcher in the early 1980s and then again in the late 1980s to the more uncharted field of personal and professional development. I'm not sure what I contributed to ECT but it contributed a lot to me.

26. Early days at Enfield: interdisciplinarity, fraternity, and a fair amount of freedom

JEFF EVANS

Jeff Evans *joined Enfield in 1969 and taught Statistics and Research Methods on various courses, beginning with the BA Social Science. He was seconded to the Open University in the mid-1970s, and contributed materials for several course teams. He completed a 'mid-career' PhD on an interdisciplinary topic in mathematics education, Adults' Mathematical Thinking and Emotions. Having retired in 2011, he enjoys having more time to read the papers, to continue academic writing, and in campaigning organisations, particularly Radical Statistics. He also enjoys learning Modern Greek, and participating in a walking group, which eats out regularly, and often goes for walks.*

How I got to Europe

I grew up in a pleasant city in Southwest Ontario – somewhat bigger than the small towns in that area that are described by Alice Munro in her short stories. Leaving school in the early 1960s, I applied to study Mathematics at the new university in nearby Waterloo, which was beginning to have an excellent reputation. Though I had a scholarship to cover my tuition fees and some expenses, there were no maintenance grants – so I knew that I needed to find summer jobs.

One such job involved initial actuarial training at the Mutual Life of Canada, based in Waterloo. The workload was variable, so we had some spare time for reading. In Somerset Maugham's *The Razor's Edge*, I was attracted by the sentiments of the main character who left North America to 'wander and search' in Europe.

One day during second year, I was wandering around the University, and saw a poster inviting applications for an international student Seminar in Chile, in July–August 1965. The Seminar was a marvellous introduction to developments in Chile; Eduardo Frei and the Christian Democrats had won the recent elections in 1964-65, and were implementing what appeared to be progressive changes (Salvador Allende and the Socialists would not be elected until 1970). Besides affording us the opportunity to get to know Chile well, we became familiar with the wider preoccupations and perceptions of Latin America more generally, through reading and travel.

The following year, 1966, I finally took off to Europe in September.

How I got to London

After a year studying 'French Language and Civilisation' in Paris at the Sorbonne and hitch-hiking around western Europe in 1968-69, I completed a Masters degree in Statistics at the London School of Economics. This was a time of political turbulence, as well as political education, at the LSE; many of the most effective speakers in the (direct-democracy) Students' Union were members of the Socialist Society, and many of those were research students teaching at one of the Colleges of Technology around London: Woolwich, Kilburn, Regent Street, Ealing and Enfield.

The following summer, I was offered a post at the Enfield College of Technology, teaching Statistics on the BA Social Science (BASS). I accepted immediately.

How I got to Enfield

On the first Monday of October 1969, I took the new Victoria Line to Seven Sisters and then the overground train from Liverpool Street for the ten-minute trip to Southbury British Rail station. I got in to a compartment with a young person, who turned out to be a student at Enfield (Tom Cashman). When I introduced myself, he said 'Oh yes, you are my personal tutor.' Once at the College, I met Mr Carless, the Bursar and Mr Blockley, the Registrar, and was awarded a salary 'at the bottom of the Lecture Grade 2 scale'. The main building of the College was presentable enough, but the 'huts' where we had our offices appeared somewhat spartan. Fortunately, I knew a number of the other lecturers, from my two years at LSE: Bill Barnes in Statistics, Bernard Burgoyne in Mathematics, Richard Kuper and Mike McKenna in Sociology.

Sami Daniel gave me a work programme: five Statistics practicals with Year 2 BASS Economics; two Mathematics seminars in Year 1 (plus 'one or two' lectures); some help with the Year 2 Sociology Research Methods seminars, and some tutorial work on the (external London) BSc Sociology degree. Thus, most of my teaching was in 'seminars', normally of 10 to 12 students, and all teaching assignments involved being available a certain amount of time each week for on-demand 'tutorials' for students.

The ideas that guided our work

George Brosan, the College Principal (until 1970, when he left to become Director at North East London Polytechnic), and Eric Robinson, the Academic Head of the Faculty of Arts (in which BASS and the other social science degrees were administered) had well-developed, progressive ideas concerning the fast-moving developments in higher education at the time. I did not know the man well, but I began reading Eric Robinson's ideas on *The New Polytechnics* (1968) soon after arriving at Enfield. Robinson was a strong egalitarian, who was committed to a 'steady movement towards the modernization and democratization of post-school education' (pp. 240-41). He was critical of assumed hierarchies of persons, and of those among educational institutions, and of the privileging of full-time over part-time education for adults.

Robinson embraced the ideal that everyone should find 'self-expression through his economic activity in this society' (p.16). In appreciating the different forms and purposes of higher education, therefore, he saw as outdated the supposed appropriateness of *liberal education* – cultivation of the well-rounded citizen – for the élite, and of *vocational education* – imparting of technical skills – for the masses. In contemporary society, he argued 'everybody needs both – the manager needs technical expertise as well as clear thinking, the worker needs understanding as well as manual skill.' (p.92). He was therefore critical of the Robbins Report's (1963) position that higher education should normally be provided in the universities to those who were academically inclined and destined to become professionals – whereas further education, often a narrowly-conceived 'vocational' training, was to be provided in colleges for the rest.

He accepted that the universities would continue to dominate in the provision of 'academic' education – the intensive study of one subject in depth. The polytechnics, he thought, should instead aim to combine liberal and vocational approaches in the courses they offered. He wanted the polytechnics to be 'comprehensive people's universities', and his book provided the basis of a plan for such institutions.

From his discussion of aims for the content of the education there flowed several important principles of curriculum, pedagogy and assessment. In curriculum terms, there was strong emphasis on an 'interdisciplinary' approach to areas of study, and a 'sandwich' period of work experience in Arts courses, for example business studies and social sciences, just as there were in Technology studies. This led in pedagogy to team-teaching in the 'interdisciplinary' parts of courses, and to the use of 'projects' for learning and assessment; the latter were extended pieces of writing on topics where students ideally had scope for choosing and/or for formulating a problem themselves. In terms of 'selection' of entrants to courses, there was a welcoming, not merely an acceptance, of older 'mature' students, even in some cases of those without traditional academic GCE A-level entry qualifications for HE, as long as they had useful vocational or other experience.

In what follows, I will discuss mainly the BA Social Science. I also taught on other courses, which colleagues discuss in other chapters; for example, the BA part-time Business Studies, the BA part-time Sociology of Education (the 'Teachers' degree') and the (non-degree) Diploma/Certificate courses in Industrial Relations and Trade Union Studies. Since most students on these courses were already in work, they had no sandwich element, but each had its own 'interdisciplinary seminar' or similar focus. The Trade Union courses also served as a path into degree studies for some – an early form of 'access studies'.

Interdisciplinary studies at Enfield

When I arrived at Enfield, there were two tracks on the BASS degree, Economics and Sociology, which took in 150 students in total each autumn. This was a four-year 'sandwich' course, with a placement in the third year, usually grant-supported, with only a few paid placements. A limited number of those on the Sociology track could do a Social Work qualification in the last two years, in addition to gaining a Sociology degree. In addition, there were plans for a Planning Studies track and a Psychology track – which would have to be approved by the CNAA during the five-yearly 'Resubmission' of the degree in 1973.

My mentors impressed upon me that BASS was an 'interdisciplinary' degree. This meant several things. As a statistician, I would be contributing to interdisciplinary course components, such as Methods and Models for first year students. And like any member of staff, I would have dual organisational loyalties, within the 'matrix' structure: (i) to the course where I did my main teaching – through membership of the BASS degree course team, led by John Farquhar and Bryan Davies; and (ii) to my subject – through membership of the Statistics section, headed by Alan Cox. Nonetheless, at that time the degree course link was seen as more important, since that is where my 'timetable' and workload were organized.

In 1969-70, only the first two years of the BASS degree were operating as yet. My main role was as part of the staff of the 'Maths' (mathematics and statistics) strand of the Methods and Models (MandM) course in Year 1. This aimed to 'teach mathematics as a cultural thing' as set out by Bernard Burgoyne around 1972. We began with several lectures on the history of mathematics, considered as a series of crises: for example, the students had a lecture on the 'Pythagorean crisis', followed by a seminar examining the proof (by contradiction) that the hypotenuse of an isosceles right-angled triangle could not be a 'rational number' (a ratio of two whole numbers). Another lecture examined the 'crisis of set theory', and the seminar examined Bertrand Russell's paradox. The book we used for this part of the course was Morris Kline's *Mathematics in Western Culture* (1953), which both lecturers and students found fascinating, and which inspired at least one of our colleagues' children to choose to study mathematics at university. As well as the mathematical technicalities, this part of the course considered the social fall-out from the acceptance of these proofs. This led naturally into a discussion of syllogistic reasoning, and the First Term rose to a crescendo, culminating in a discussion of functions and the differential calculus. The Second and Third Terms studied statistics, moving from descriptive statistics to statistical inference, illustrated by the chi-squared test of association, much-used by social scientists.

A number of colleagues in other subjects have used the term 'numeracy' to describe the pedagogic aims of the Mathematics strand of MandM. I don't remember people using this term very much at the time. However, I now realise it had been brought into discussions of British educational policy-making by the *Crowther Report* (1959), as the mirror-image of literacy, a broad introduction to mathematical and scientific reasoning, avoiding statistical fallacies, and so on. It was certainly the sort of broad skills that we hoped our students would develop, as well as the confidence to deploy them – and many students did. This conception of numeracy is much richer than the narrow notions underlying some later policy initiatives such as the National Numeracy Strategy in English schools.

The other strand of MandM was Philosophy of Science, which included a discussion of the history of the natural sciences, focusing on the Scientific Revolution (Copernicus/Galileo/Newton). The text used here was Arthur Koestler's *The Sleepwalkers* (1959). The course went on to discuss the theories of knowledge of Karl Popper and Imre Lakatos (with whom a number of our colleagues had studied at the LSE), and the critique of their work from Thomas Kuhn's idea of paradigms as bastions of 'normal science' in *The Structure of Scientific Revolutions* (1962).

The two strands worked well together. There was a similarity in the historical basis of the material. And the two strands supported each other's content; for example, the Philosophy drew on the discussions of logic from the Mathematics strand, for example for an elucidation of the hypothetic-deductive method, while the Mathematics strand could draw on understandings of falsificationism from the Philosophy strand to help explain the rationale of significance tests.

In the Third Term of MandM, the two strands cooperated more closely, with the aim of showing students how to marshal insights from both for the purpose of evaluating published social science research. A number of examples were used as illustrations in lectures, and students chose one of a range of articles as a focus of their final project, such as Milgram's research on obedience to authority or Rosenhan's study of the diagnosis of apparent mental health symptoms. Assessment in the first two terms of MandM included: essays in Philosophy on the history of science and on social science epistemology, and problem worksheets and an open-book untimed test in Mathematics.

In the early days, lecturers teaching on one of the strands of the course would aim to attend the weekly lecture in the other, and those particularly interested in ID (interdisciplinary) ideas would often attend each other's seminars and contribute ideas, or indeed questions!

At that time, those of us interested in ID work distinguished 'truly interdisciplinary' modules from 'multidisciplinary' ones. These can be exemplified, respectively, by Methods and Models and the Core Theme.

The latter was a module in Year 2 of the degree (full name 'Social and Economic Foundations of Public Policy'), which aimed to show students how to bring to bear their developing disciplinary perspectives to analyse contemporary 'policy problems'. This was staffed by economists and sociologists, and also geographers and psychologists.

The distinction between the approaches was reflected and amplified in an article by Len Doyal (1974): this distinguished between 'pragmatic' ID courses, where subject specialisms are combined to 'shed light' on problems of practical or policy interest, and ID courses based on a challenging 'conceptual and methodological analysis', often historically grounded, of the apparently distinct bases of subject specialisms, Doyal argued several important ideas: that the distinctions between subject specialisms were conventional; but that, nevertheless, it was crucial to acknowledge the centrality of subject specialisms in 'integrated' ID degrees; and also to acknowledge the professional interests of subject specialist 'sections' or departments.

To some extent, the rest of the 1970s at Enfield (and later in the Polytechnic) can be characterised by the struggle between interdisciplinary interests, and those of the subject sections – and the resulting ebb and flow of ID courses. In the Resubmission of BASS, a new module, initially called 'Man and Society' was introduced to complement MandM in Year One (and to displace first year courses in Economics, Sociology, etc.) – but only for the first two of the three terms. It contained a 'concepts and methods' approach to the development of social theory (with historical reference to Britain, France and Germany) in the period from the Enlightenment to the early twentieth century. For further detail on this (and much else), see the website of Andrew Roberts, a student in the early years, and later a lecturer. The module also included short 'taster' modules on topics studied in each of the subject specialisms on the degree.

Another approach adopted by those supportive of ID work was to design entire ID tracks on the BASS, for example, Planning Studies and later Social Policy. A development aimed at promoting interdisciplinary degrees in a different, but overlapping field, the BSc Science and Technology, gained CNAA approval around 1972.[37]

Other Issues of Academic Organisation

We were all expected to do administrative jobs in the College. In my first year I was asked to be take overall responsibility for the 'selection' of students for BASS. This issue is of great importance for the academic success of any programme of studies, along with the formulation of curriculum content, pedagogic methods and assessment requirements.

Because we believed that students had certainly learned a great deal outside of, and after, formal schooling, we interviewed almost all applicants to the BASS, including many 'mature students' (initially those who were over twenty-five, and later to those over twenty-one), including some who lacked formal qualifications for entry (two A-level passes). This allowed us to see potential that was not evident from the student's formal qualifications. It was also a lot of work. We had meetings to collate the results from the many interviewers, so as to select the most promising students overall who had signalled their interest in a particular Track. Occasionally, we would re-interview a student if the interviewer felt that s/he had been too nervous on the day. We were repaid by having students to teach who were capable of marvellous intellectual development, and pleasant in personal interaction – and of course the mature students were often our contemporaries in age terms.

By the early 1970s, it was clear to some of us that modularisation of degrees was on the cards in British higher education. This

---

37 (Doyal, 1974) can be read both as a reflection on our experiences in the early years of BASS –and as an expression of optimism for the future of the BSc Science and Technology,

was originally resisted by many staff, but a modular, semesterised two-year Diploma in Higher Education (DipHE) was started in 1976 at the Trent Park campus of the then Polytechnic. Again this diploma recruited marvellously stimulating students. The working ideology related to ID work on such courses was that the student, who knows best, should him or herself *choose* the modules that would provide the most personally satisfying education. The crucial question then became how students are going to have access to the information needed for such an *informed choice*.

The upshot was that in the DipHE, and in the modular degree that succeeded it throughout the polytechnic, ID studies had great difficulty to survive in the ways created and debated at Enfield. They survived only when there existed a staff group strong enough, and with sufficient internal and/or external support (particularly from External Examiners) to recruit to and to teach a major Set in the DipHE/Modular Scheme. The Society and Technology degree was able to survive in that way. So was the Social Policy track. The Planning Studies staff from Enfield worked together with the Geographers from Hendon in the Polytechnic to create a series of degrees that survived in the increasingly competitive recruitment context of the late 1970s and 1980s.

Looking Back and Looking Forward

In personal terms, I consider that we were exceedingly fortunate to have been 'there', at a place like Enfield, when the opportunities for change were ripe. Key factors included: national and local policy developments, notably the expansion of UK higher education; the concentration of a large group of academic-reform minded staff, who were energised by the critical cultural and political spirit of the time; and of course the availability of a large pool of applicants who turned out to be eminently well 'qualified' for higher education – even larger than the Robbins Report had anticipated in 1963.

What was distinctive about the situation at Enfield? Certainly it helped to have educational visionaries, like Brosan and Robinson, as leaders in the College, but success depended on many others in the college. The diffusion of power through the operation of the 'matrix' structure undoubtedly helped. The general lack of hierarchy in the structure at Enfield was also crucial. So some of our lack of hierarchy may have been cultural, built upon shared beliefs from our previous academic bases, such as the LSE, Sussex, UCL, Oxford and other universities and workplaces.

There was also a less pronounced distance between staff and students. Not only were many students our age contemporaries, but in the interdisciplinary courses, we were often learning together. Besides their evident intellectual development, many of our students knew more about the nitty-gritty of the contemporary London world than myself, as a relatively recent arrival. We often lived in the same neighbourhoods, too: in the 1970s, you might as easily bump into a student from Enfield on the street, as a colleague – especially if you lived, in say Hackney, Hornsey or Holloway. All this resulted in productive and satisfying academic relationships, and often in easy-going social relationships too. A number of students became long-term friends.

Of course there were trade-offs. While colleagues in other departments, or other institutions were writing research articles, many of us thought it important to respond to a demand to back up our teaching – given the interdisciplinary material, and our many mature students – with handouts that required time to draft and to produce, sometimes with only rather elementary technology available.

Yet we also tried to keep up as academics, attending conferences and producing papers. I was also able to produce a 'mid-life' PhD (in 1993) on Adults' Mathematical Thinking and Emotions', which drew on research with students in Year 1 of BASS and the DipHE, and which benefitted from help from colleagues like Peter Sneddon in Psychology, Chris Abbess in Statistics, and staff in the Computing Centre at Enfield and Bounds Green. In due course, the increasing pressure in the Polytechnics for all academics to publish coincided with the apparent decline of interdisciplinary studies. However, it seems unlikely that the apparent decline is terminal, when there seem so many calls at the present time for research, as well as teaching, to be 'interdisciplinary'. Nevertheless, the discussion above indicates how 'slippery' this particular concept can be!

All in all, the experience of Enfield in those heady early days showed us – unforgettably – some valuable ways to present the opportunities of higher education to a motivated group of young and middle-aged adults, in a setting characterised by cooperation and intellectual excitement.

27. Choosing a career path

TONY CRASNER

***Tony Crasner** joined Enfield in 1969 to teach development economics on the BA Social Science degree. At the end of 1976 he resigned to take up a post with the Ministry of Education in Guyana. From there he moved to educational posts in Swaziland and Zimbabwe eventually joining the staff of the European Commission. He was subsequently posted to Brussels, Indonesia and Papua New Guinea. Tony retired in 2010 and divides his time between struggling with Parkinson's Disease and working as a volunteer for an NGO that seeks self-determination for the people of Kashmir.*

Lecturing at Enfield was my first full-time job. I was twenty-four and had just completed a Masters degree in Development Economics at London University's School of Oriental and African Studies. At the time, the logical next step seemed to be to register for a PhD and that is exactly what a lot of my classmates did. Two things, however, made me reluctant to commit myself to a further three years of study and research. The first of these was the impact of the student political movement of 1968.

Except for one torchlight march my involvement in the events of '68 was nil. But being surrounded by classmates of varying degrees of militancy all of whom needed little encouragement to expound vigorously their particular political philosophies served to highlight the incoherence of my own political position. Furthermore, it seemed clear that this was not an issue that could be resolved in the abstract atmosphere of a university library but rather one that needed contact with the physical world of work if a better articulated and sounder point of view was to emerge.

The second factor that made me reluctant to commit to a PhD was simply that I needed a regular salary! At the same time as I started my MSc programme I was able to fulfil, through the generosity of my parents, my lifetime ambition of taking singing lessons with a first rate teacher. After two years of regular lessons it seemed that I did indeed have a voice and one which improved dramatically with training and that a career as a professional opera singer might not be just a dream. This meant finding a job that would give me the time and flexibility to go to singing lessons, rehearsals and coaching sessions. Out of all the available possibilities, teaching in Higher Education looked the most promising. Not only would it give me the flexibility I needed but with a starting annual salary of some £2,300 I could pay for my singing lessons as well as paying my rent and so avoid a continuing dependence on parental handouts.

Job hunting

I started by applying to traditional universities with vacant Assistant Lecturers posts. This was not a great success and I quickly accumulated a file of virtually identical replies thanking me for my interest in the work of this or that Department and commiserating with me that unfortunately the vacancy had already been filled. In contrast, both my initial applications to HE Colleges produced an immediate invitation to an interview.

The first invitation was from Hendon College of Technology which was housed in a sombre neoVictorian building. The post I applied for was in the Business Studies Department. I remember almost nothing about the interview itself, just the formal rather depressed atmosphere and the dark suits on the other side of the table that looked out of place amid the piles of dusty notes headed 'Memorandum To All Staff' in the fading blue ink used by a spirit duplicator. However, the interview must have gone reasonably well as they offered me the job on the spot! I thanked them effusively for the offer and said I needed a couple of days to decide. I did not tell them that I had an interview at Enfield the next day!

The atmosphere at Enfield was very different, much less formal and more alive. For a start the vacancy was in the Social Science Department which meant that economists, sociologists and academics from other disciplines were required to coordinate their different approaches to social science. Then the campus was full of prefabricated 'huts' which served as offices and as teaching rooms giving the institution an air of being in a state of transition. Most of the Social Science staff seemed to camp out in these temporary spaces. The Head of Department did wear a suit but had the relaxed air of a country gentleman rather than the stressed look more appropriate to the

CEO of a large International enterprise. Nobody else wore a suit although I did see one or two pass the window of the hut in which the interview took place. Then too the staff seemed to be genuinely friendly and there was a feeling of adventure in the air that recalled the atmosphere and the spirit of '68. Yes there was also dust and spirit duplicators were clearly used at Enfield too. But whereas Hendon seemed to exist to process students, Enfield gave the impression, on a very brief acquaintance, of existing to enable students to learn! Anyway after half an hour and without apparent hesitation the Interview Panel offered me a job and there I was with two job offers on my plate!

Family conflict

To my Father, who had made the transition with much effort from being the manager of a real factory to teaching management at another London Polytechnic, the offer from Hendon seemed the safest alternative. The Principal of Enfield had a reputation of being an innovator and a liberal and although my Dad was in theory totally supportive of liberal humanism, in practice he was deeply suspicious of things that took him out of his comfort zone or which were just different. So over a family dinner that evening we argued fiercely for and against the two institutions and, for just about the first time in my life I stuck to my guns on an issue of principle and defied him! Next morning I politely declined the Hendon offer and equally politely accepted that of Enfield.

First impressions

My first day in my new job was 15 September 1969. A couple of things about the College struck me immediately. First was how widely read my colleagues were. Not just within their own disciplines where you would expect them to have a good knowledge of the current literature but in all sorts of interesting and what appeared to me to be esoteric fields which they were able to make effortlessly relevant to the core material of the courses that they were teaching.

Students too were expected to read voraciously. Course reading lists were huge while lengthy handouts were routinely distributed during lectures. This emphasis on erudition was exciting but also intimidating! I was confronted with positions that made me uncomfortably aware of the gaps in my own thinking and my background, which I had thought more than adequate for a college environment, now seemed to be narrow and deficient. Would I ever be able to catch up?

The staff, almost without exception, seemed to look on teaching as something stimulating and creative! Delivering a lecture or taking a seminar was treated as a significant activity and not just as something to fill the time between committee meetings or that got in the way of drafting the next research paper. It came as no surprise, therefore, that on the Social Science degree attendance at lectures was considered non-compulsory for students while participation in the seminars which accompanied the lecture programme was mandatory.

But the most surprising feature of College life at Enfield was the explicit recognition by both staff and management that the efficiency of students' learning was directly related to the quality of the teaching they received. Traditionally staff in tertiary education are supposed to be able to teach by virtue of their academic achievements. But once you accept that high academic achievement by itself is no guarantee that the academic concerned is able to impart his/her knowledge and insights to a group of young men and women then what goes on in the classroom in a Higher Education institution becomes a legitimate field of enquiry for anyone interested in improving the learning environment.

Quality of teaching

The 1960's and early 1970's was a time when improving the quality of teaching in tertiary education became a fashionable concern. London University created the University Teaching Methods Unit. Donald Bligh published his book '*What's the use of Lectures?*' The Society for Research into Higher Education published a series of monographs on the measurement of quality in HE teaching including several on students' assessment of the quality and relevance of the teaching they were experiencing!

That Enfield was in the forefront of the movement to transform the conventional wisdom of British Higher Education was something that I only slowly started to appreciate and understand in the months following my taking up the post. At that time the award of qualifications by colleges such as Enfield was overseen by the Council for National Academic Awards (CNAA). In order to maintain the accreditation of courses such as the BA Social Science, the teaching institution was obliged to re-submit the course to the CNAA every five years. The Council's inspection procedures were detailed and rigorous. Curricula were checked against academic objectives, proposed teaching methods and assessment systems. The teaching institution was obliged to justify why certain things were being taught while other things were not and to address head on the issue of what skills the student needed to acquire if s/he was to be considered as a viable professional in any particular field.

Re-submitting to the CNAA

The Social Science degree went through the ordeal of resubmission to the CNAA in 1973. For a good twelve months prior to the deadline of the re-submission there were weekly meetings of a Re-submission Committee together with other *ad hoc* meetings of subject groups and groups that examined issues such as the organisation of the sandwich year, assessment methods, administrative and management issues and so on. In these meetings the debate became increasingly polarised between staff who wished to see more time devoted to specialist subjects and supporters of an integrated approach to the disciplines.

In essence the subject specialists maintained that there was so much material for the student to master in the way of theories, techniques, analytical methods and so on, that every spare minute of class time had to be devoted to deepening and extending the student's knowledge of his/her discipline and requiring students to study what amounted to the development of European philosophical thought was an unnecessary distraction from the task of equipping them with a solid background in their chosen subject.

On the other hand, supporters of the integrated study model argued that mastering a set of methods and techniques however sophisticated without gaining an understanding of the underlying problematic and its dynamics was a recipe for producing narrow specialists. The position of the interdisciplinary group was that tertiary education should focus on encouraging students to acquire those analytical and critical skills which enable individual disciplines to be located in the context of an overall understanding of the processes of social development.

The debate on whether the re-submitted degree should take the form of a loose collection of disciplinary strands or whether it should attempt to offer an integrated approach to the development of the social sciences became increasingly heated as the deadline of the inspection drew ever nearer. Week after week scholarly papers or impassioned tracts were drafted and tabled by one side or the other only to be viciously dismembered by the opposition leaving fragments of an argument to be resurrected as part of the material for the next round of the argument which crept forward at what seemed like a snails pace while the new structure started ever so slowly to coalesce into a viable degree programme.

The eventual outcome was of course a compromise. But an interesting and challenging one. All students would follow a two-term programme to be called 'Man and Society' to be taught in parallel with a programme on Statistics and research methods called 'Methods and Models'. From the start of the third term students would be allowed to specialise in the discipline of their choice.

To support this structure we set up 'Learning to Learn' groups to work with students on the vexed question of study skills and ' Learning to Teach' groups to help relatively inexperienced teachers to rise to the challenge of a packed lecture theatre. For the first year at least staff enthusiastically took advantage of the Learning to Teach groups to try out their lecture material on their colleagues before presenting it to the students. The subsequent discussions were stimulating and thought provoking.

Teacher training and the quality of teaching

Most of the Higher Education institutions I have encountered have tended to take it for granted that all academics automatically know how to teach. It is assumed that every academic is able to select an appropriate teaching method to convey the messages contained in the curriculum and to integrate this method with the learning needs of the students. When the main teaching vehicle is the mass lecture where there is very little interaction between the lecturer and his/her audience any deficiencies in the tutor's repertoire of teaching skills are relatively unimportant. When the main teaching vehicle, however, is the seminar as was the case with the Enfield BA Social Science degree it is essential that the tutor is able to manage interactions within the seminar group and understands the ways in which his/her authority as a tutor can encourage or discourage the development of independent authority by the student members of the group. The skills involved in facilitating a small group discussion are quite different from the tutor's skills as an economist, sociologist or whatever academic discipline provides the material for the group to discuss.

The sense of intellectual adventure that I had felt during my interview at Enfield turned out to be on the one hand the result of the specific challenge of empowering students through the application of small group discussion methods. and, on the other the freedom given to staff to develop curricula which directly confronted the conventional wisdom of the discipline.

The choice of the seminar as the main teaching vehicle for the course brought with it a couple of; important implications! The early 70's were a time of rapid expansion of UK Higher Education. Students rushed to seize the opportunity of getting a degree. Now one Lecturer can cover a particular topic for 150 students in one 90-minute lecture. Total staff-time needed (2 hours preparation time plus the time ended to deliver the lecture) is three-and-a-half person hours. Using a seminar-based approach 150 students will need 10 groups each of 15 students for an hour and a half, plus again 2 hours for preparation. Total person-hours is 10x1.5 + 10x2 = 35 hours! The difference in the staffing requirements of the two approaches is dramatic!

The staffing implications of the more progressive teaching methodology were not the only difficulty. Many of the new staff who were recruited to teach this influx of students were in a similar position to mine in 1969. We were mostly recent graduates, with limited teaching experience. Few of us had any teacher training and we were obliged to teach in ways that were new and relatively untested. In consequence, when we were obliged to prepare two or three classes per week during the first six weeks of term it was inevitable that we would turn to material that we knew well from our own recent studies. The result was that undergraduate economics students at Enfield were often taught topics that other institutions regarded as being post-graduate material suitable for Masters level courses. This was challenging both for the students who were being asked to grapple with very advanced material and for the academic staff who were required to create a high quality learning environment, a task for which for which they were in the main poorly equipped.

Enfield College Management was certainly aware of these problems. We were encouraged to sign up for the in-service training programmes offered by the University Teaching Methods Unit and a group of us participated in Jane Abercrombie's research programme on techniques of small group teaching which was hosted by the School of Architecture of London University. The training we received enabled us to give maximum support to the activities of the Leaning to Learn and the Learning to Teach groups.

The end of an era

I joined the staff at Enfield thinking that I would be there at most for a couple of years and ended up by staying for nearly eight! It was an enriching experience and a privilege to be able to work with such dedicated and committed colleagues to learn from their collective expertise and to make a contribution, however small, to the development of real quality in UK Higher Education. My stay at Enfield equipped me with the skills I needed to tackle the world outside the sheltered niche of Higher Education. It enabled me to break free from one ambition that had become an obsession and to take up alternative goals with the confidence that the challenges they posed could be overcome.

The end came in a quite unexpected manner. In September 1976 I met a group of sixteen final year undergraduates who had elected to take my specialist course in development economics. As usual I used this first meeting to get to know the students and to give them an overview of the main topics we would explore during the course. One of my particular interests at that time was the issue that many developing countries focused on the production of primary commodities which were then exported for processing (which is where the main value-added accrued) in the developed world. The particular example I used was the production of cocoa in Ghana.

At that point I stopped and turned to a student who looked particularly interested and asked him where he was from. He replied that he was from Ghana! I asked what his family did. He replied hat they grew cocoa on the family farm. At that moment I knew that my time at Enfield was over. How could I teach development to someone who had lived with the problems of a traditional society for over half a lifetime? How could I teach the economics of cocoa production when I wouldn't recognise a cocoa bush If you put me in front of one?

Six months later I left both Enfield and the UK for a post in the Education Ministry of Guyana.

Conclusion

The late 1960's and early 1970's were something of a golden age for institutions like Enfield College. Never again would they have the autonomy to challenge the conventional wisdom that stifles creativity in Higher Education nor the resources to take advantage of whatever autonomy might be salvaged from the decline of the sector. Forty years on and my memories of Enfield remain vivid but patchy. One image, however, recurs repeatedly: I am standing in my hut, having got up at 07:30 to catch the early train to Enfield. I have arranged the chairs in a neat but crowded circle and am waiting impatiently for the first members of today's seminar group to arrive. And I am thrilled and excited at the thought of what we will achieve today!

28. At Ponders End

JULIE FORD

Julie Ford *taught Research Methods on the BA Social Science degree and Sociology on the Council for Qualification in Social Work course. When Enfield College became part of Middlesex Polytechnic, she taught on the MA in Deviance and Social Policy degree. At Middlesex University she helped formulate the first nursing degree, instigated the Research Ethics committee and supervised PhD's. Unable to persuade the hierarchy to grant her early retirement – when the internal market replaced academic cooperation with destructive competition – she threatened legal action. She then escaped to the wilderness of a Welsh mountain, but reappeared in this century, and with former Enfield colleagues set up and ran the independent publishing company Superscript.*

The first thing to be said about Enfield College of Technology is that it was located at Ponders End. Yes, really. This was a great source of amusement to colleagues in 'proper' academic institutions, the connotation probably being 'wits' end' as in 'last desperate bid for sanity'. But there is another way of reading this soubriquet: the end of pondering could be the 'Aha!' moment at the beginning of understanding, the gratifying 'Eureka' of discovery. Nowadays this notion of fruitful serendipity is represented as a light-bulb moment with a graphic representation of a lit bulb above the head of the genius. That image couldn't be more appropriate for our ramshackle collection of ill-matched buildings because just across Ponders End High Street was our Swan Annex. It was there that Joseph Swan invented the incandescent light bulb which most people associate with Thomas Edison since it was his company that developed and appropriated it.

I was at Ponders End because, in many ways, I was too appallingly deviant to fit in anywhere else. I was an outrageously dressed barefoot twenty-two year old hippy with a PhD and a very well reviewed book in a respected academic series (Ford, 1970). In 1968 –

the year of the student 'revolution' – I was employed by the London School of Economics on a Temporary Assistant Lectureship. I didn't need to do much as there were strikes most of the time, but what I did do was not exactly welcomed by the LSE establishment. On one occasion I gave a lecture about the role of the police in upholding the iniquities of capitalism. Unfortunately nobody had thought to tell me that the particular class was made up of police recruits.

Before the end of my year's contract Percy Cohen warned me that unless I started wearing shoes my appointment would not be renewed. I was too feral to even care.

Then one day the late Jock Young, author of *The Drug Takers*, a close friend of my ex-husband the late Steven Box (founder of the sub-discipline the Sociology of Deviancy) turned up in my office with an urgent request. He was one of a small group developing a BA in Social Science at Enfield. He reckoned that they had a great gang of staff already but nobody to take control of developing and teaching Research Methods.

My immediate question concerned the necessity of wearing shoes at Ponders End. Reassured on what seemed like the most important issue at the time, I went on to ask what the Hell was to be covered by 'Research Methods'. Jock said, 'Oh you know, statistics, computing, that sort of thing'. I couldn't really imagine anything more unappealing, but there I was, about to be jobless, and the offer was of a Senior Lectureship on a considerably higher salary than I could have hoped for in a university. Not that money meant anything to me, but I think (embarrassingly now) the status probably did.

I remember that just before I left LSE Paul Rock warned me that Enfield would be a big mistake. He told me that nobody ever escapes Ponders End, once there you will be there until you retire, you will be both literally and metaphorically stuck in the mud. It certainly was muddy at first (there seemed always more portacabins going up) but I had no shoes to be ruined, and anyway grass gradually grew between the thirties-style Broadbent building and the burgeoning extensions.

Appropriately perhaps, my memories of my early days at Enfield College of Technology were of just that – technology. The computers were massive and housed in a room with a controlled atmosphere. I took to the counter-sorter machines instead. These belonged to a company called English Numbering Machines located across the road. I loved them because it was easy to explain to students how to analyse data when the stuff was punched on Hollerith cards and fed into these noisy old things which sorted them into sections so you got an immediate visual image of the relative quantities in the different sections and how this related to the tables you needed to produce in order to test hypotheses. The students would gather around the counter-sorters and watch them sorting. Then I would draw pictures of the piles on the blackboard. Yes, we had actual blackboards with chalk and board-rubbers, much nicer than the toxic markers and white-boards that eventually replaced them.

Another essential technology was the mimeograph printer. These involved special sheets that fitted an ordinary typewriter with no ribbon. The keys cut through the sheets which were then fed into a machine which printed as many copies as required with a slightly blackish text that faded to purple in the sun. I must have produced many thousands of pages of handouts for the students on these machines. These were gradually revised, improved and expanded into what we called the Grimoire: a handbook of 'spells' or algorithms for designing, conducting and analysing research. As Enfield turned from tech to Polytechnic these went from fading purple on yellowing paper to a proper published two volume textbook.

Getting to and from Enfield also emphasised that we were at the centre of a technological ghetto. Belling, and then Thorn, electrical and electronic goods were our next door neighbours. There was a huge scrap metal yard between us and the railway station and I remember that, while waiting for the train, we would sometimes lark about in a heap of aluminium discs discarded from the holes cut into electrical goods.

My mind runs straight from the physical machinery to the institutional machinery. The Council for National Academic Awards (CNAA) had been set up in 1964. It was this body, overseeing the standard of educational qualifications awarded, that set the scene for the serious development of Higher Education outside the universities. Enfield's work was already highly regarded on the cosmopolitan academic grape vine, but the ability to grant qualifications assessed on the same scales as those from the more established institutions really opened up the opportunities available to both staff and students. As I see it in retrospect there were probably three main threads of education: technical, professional and academic.

The technical courses consisted of six-month diplomas and degrees. The degrees were known as sandwich courses. The filling in the sandwich was work placement. Some students were sponsored by their employers, others came to the college without industrial contacts. These latter were initially expected to find their own placements and then a member of staff with an interest in that area would take responsibility for visiting them on placement and coordinating it with their college work. Later a proper placement unit was set up with thirty industrial tutors who would visit the 400 odd students who were in placement at any one time. Emphasis was laid on the fact that placement was for training, not for exploitation by the employer and not a situation where the student should play one firm off another to get the highest wage. When the students eventually left Enfield the Placement Unit helped them secure a job.

Professional studies such as Social Work were overseen and examined by the relevant national bodies such as the Council for Qualification in Social Work (CQSW). Mostly these were run and taught by specialists but some academics, such as myself, were required to service the courses with wider disciplines, in my case sociology. I found this quite demanding on a personal level because the students tended to be more conservative than the company I was used to keeping and there was a lot of antagonism towards my bizarre appearance and rather vernacular language. On one occasion a huge row developed over the fact that I was wearing one lime green and one shocking pink sock under ballet pumps held on with rubber bands. Another time I left a class in one of the thin-walled portacabins to catch sight of three of the Social Work staff with wine glasses pressed to the wall. They had heard ribald laughter from the class, considered this out of order and were piously tut-tutting while listening to what was going on.

The academic degrees were really quite innovative. On the one hand, some involved placements which were organised a bit like the technical courses. At the same time the BA in Social Science (BASS) was much more progressive and challenging than the external London University degrees which it replaced. Part of this was due to the central role played by a subject called Methods and Models. This really grabbed the student's imagination as it opened up areas of mathematics and philosophy to which they did not have access at school. I was in awe of the tutors who worked on this course and who never invited me to take any part in it. I think they were probably wise because my own external London degree had left me pitifully ignorant of how to think outside a narrow scientistic paradigm. In fact it took me a few years working on issues raised by compiling the Grimoire before I managed to catch up with the Methods and Models pioneers and come up with my own innovations in epistemology.

Perhaps it was the buzz around Methods and Models that really set the intellectual atmosphere at Ponders End. We thought outside the crudely empiricist box of what some historians of ideas refer to as 'the English way of thinking'. It may be that many of the people who devised and ran that ground-breaking course never achieved wider recognition; but their students will not forget them, or the way they changed their lives. It was, of course, the collective culture that was really important, not any particular individual. Yet out of that wild ferment of ideas came some very notable contributions to wider society.

There is Rick Kuper who founded Pluto press, the invaluable outlet for progressive ideas that went above and beyond the scope of the old Left Book Club. Now in his seventies he still contributes book reviews and is involved with the truly inspiring International Institute for the Propagation of Political Economy.

Then there is Simon Stander who turned his back in disgust at the destruction of Higher Education caused by the introduction of the so-called internal market and went off to help set up the brilliant anti-Thatcher periodical *Scallywag*. Later he worked at the University for Peace in Costa Rica (see Chapter 6).

There is Bernard Burgoyne, the brilliant mathematician from Cambridge University, who worked with Duhem, Popper, Lakatos and then Lacan. After Enfield morphed into a Polytechnic and then a University he became Professor of Psychoanalysis in the department he set up on the old Enfield campus and he is now regarded as Britain's leading Lacanian analyst.

Then there is the utterly lovable Roy Bailey, legendary folk singer, who toured the country with the late Tony Benn in their wonderful joint show *The Writing on the Wall*.

These are just a few with whom I have personally maintained contact. But I am pretty well a recluse so it is certain that there are many other notable Enfield alumni of whom I am entirely unaware.

This must be especially so for the students, one of whom became dean of Social Science at the Open University. Students and staff alike, we were bright and idealistic – sometimes even meticulous – curating noumena and propagating fecund lines of inquiry. Now, in these darkening anti-technical, anti-professional and anti-intellectual times, who knows how permanent our little revolution will turn out to be?

29. Enfield College of Technology: diving in at the deep end

PETER C. GRAVES

Peter Graves *joined Enfield College in 1969 as College Chaplain, and stayed until 1979, whereupon he returned to the mainstream Methodist ministry in churches in Epsom until 1989, and then in North Shields until 1996. He was then appointed Superintendent at the Methodist Central Hall, Westminster until 2000 and afterwards the Chaplain to Methodist Students at Cambridge University until 2008. On invitation he served the Centenary United Methodist Church, Winston Salem, North Carolina, USA during the period 2009-12. He and his wife now live in a village near Cambridge, where with no pastoral charge, he often preaches and leads worship in local churches.*

In January 1969 I stood in the corner of the Refectory of Enfield College of Technology. The hall was crowded, but I knew hardly anybody. Not surprisingly, I was overwhelmed, apprehensive and out of my depth. I had never seen the inside of a College of Technology, and had little knowledge of the subjects being taught there. I had though been appointed as College Chaplain, and now was the time to begin this ministry. I had to dive in at the deep end, and get to know the lecturers, staff and students, and then gradually discover just what shape my ministry there would take.

My background

The eldest of five children, I was brought up in a working-class home in Blackheath, South East London. My father was a carpenter and joiner. My mother had worked in a factory, and later served as a shop assistant. I was something of a late developer, so following the eleven-plus examination was sent to a Central School. After two years the whole school was merged with a Secondary Modern school to become a new Comprehensive. I was badly advised in my choice of GCE subjects at O-level. Although I gained good marks in all seven subjects, including four at A-level, most universities would not consider me without O-Level Mathematics. However I had a strong sense of vocation to the Christian Ministry, and knew that it would be possible to study for an External London BD degree when at Theological College. Wanting to broaden my life experience, I worked in a public library for five months and then was appointed as an Executive Officer in the Civil Service, to work in the Ministry of Pensions and National Insurance.

In 1963, I was accepted as a candidate for the Methodist Ministry, and sent to Handsworth Theological College, Birmingham, for a four year full-time residential course in Theology and Ministry. In 1967 the World Council of Churches awarded me an Ecumenical Scholarship to study abroad in a seminary of a different denomination. I was sent to Union Theological Seminary in Richmond Virginia, USA, which is now known as Union Presbyterian Seminary. I studied for a Master of Theology degree (Th.M) in Pastoral Theology. This included the study of human development, psychology and Counselling, and I wrote a dissertation on ministry with young adults. I graduated in May 1968, but before returning to England, underwent three months of Clinical Training for Chaplaincy in a Psychiatric Hospital in California.

In September 1968, I was sent by the Methodist Church to serve in the Cambridge Circuit as minister in pastoral charge of Goff's Oak and St John Bullsmore Methodist churches. The following month Rev. Douglas Brown, Head of Student work in our denomination wanted to come and see me. He explained that Higher Education in Britain was going through a time of major change. In addition to the universities several other colleges would be united and developed into larger multi-disciplinary institutions. These would eventually become Polytechnics.

In universities the churches had had many years of involvement in student work. Now they were keen to develop work in these new institutions, but realized that as separate denominations it would be inappropriate to do so. Instead they should work together, and that meant appointing Ecumenical Chaplains, recognized by all denominations.

Douglas Brown explained that having already established such a chaplaincy, Enfield College was a pioneer in this development. The present chaplain, Rev. Christopher Lamb, an Anglican, had laid a firm foundation, but was now resigning to become a missionary in Pakistan. The College was keen that the Chaplaincy would continue, and the Anglican, Roman Catholic and Free Churches had agreed that Douglas Brown should see if I would be willing to succeed Chris Lamb as the new Chaplain. Having long been interested in student work, and being committed to the Ecumenical Movement, I was naturally keen to be considered. I was convinced that in a college setting, the key question for students, was not 'Am I Catholic or Protestant?' but 'Do I take the Christian Faith seriously?' and 'How do I relate this to my life-style and my studies?'

Denominational and college authorities, together with the Enfield College Chaplaincy support group were consulted. I visited the college with Chris Lamb, met with Gerald Blockley who would be my line manager, and was introduced to the Students Union and some supportive lecturers. It was agreed that I would serve in a part-time capacity, become an associate Lecturer Grade 2, and start work in January 1969.

For three and a half years from January 1969 my work at Enfield was part-time since I also had pastoral charge of local Methodist churches. Then in September 1972 this changed. I became full-time and was asked to extend the chaplaincy to the other colleges that would be joining the new Middlesex Polytechnic in January 1973.

The work developed and grew, and then for two years from 1977 I also served as Head of Student Welfare. To help develop the Chaplaincy I recruited a small group of local clergy to become honorary chaplains of the various sites of the Polytechnic, and these I coordinated. I was Chaplain for over ten years in both the college era and the early days of the Polytechnic.

When invited to write this chapter I was offered the chance to read the chapters by Tony Crilly and Tom Bourner. These brought back many memories. The days of George Brosan and Eric Robinson were exciting and pioneering. Enfield was certainly an intellectually stimulating place.

We were concerned to provide degree level studies without the apparent pretensions of a university. We wanted to give opportunity to those who had missed out in some way but were really motivated to study. Vocational relevance was valued, and we wanted courses to support the emergent technology-based society.

Understanding the context

I was keen to be Chaplain to the whole college, not just Christians. My first task therefore was to get to know as many of the college community as possible. I met with the student Counsellor and also got to know the college nurse, and visiting doctors. I made a point of meeting academic staff who were known to be supportive of, or in sympathy with chaplaincy. It was important to build up a sense of trust and colleagueship with each other, since there could well be times when we needed to work together. I had a lot of listening to do, and knew I could learn much from these contacts as well as the many other staff that I had not yet met.

Since most part-time students were only on Campus in the evenings, I worked mainly with those who were full-time. To help me meet as many students as possible, I spent a lot of time in the Refectory and other places, where I knew students gathered. I often described this aspect of ministry as 'loitering with intent'. Sometimes a conversation would begin in a very light-hearted way, but would then move on to a discussion of some deeply personal concerns. In such cases we would often go upstairs to a cubicle with frosted glass windows to ensure privacy. Situated by the staircase this had been set aside for my use as an office and interview room.

We had a very good and experienced student counsellor, and many students found it very helpful to see her privately. Some though would open up to me as we chatted in the refectory. Not thinking that their concerns were serious enough to warrant the need for a formal appointment, many found it less threatening to chat with me.

Some of the most meaningful conversations I had took place in the Refectory where often students would raise deeply religious questions. When social or political issues were in the news I would sometimes be approached by students wanting a Christian comment or point of view. Where an increasingly wide variety of subjects was being taught, people were confronted with religious issues and moral questions. Naturally, I was happy to be seen as a religious resource person, who was keen to discuss such matters with them.

One lunch time when I was chatting in the Refectory, a couple of students came and asked me if there was another Christian Creed besides the two well known ones – The Apostles and Nicene Creeds. I said 'Yes, the Athanasian Creed, but why on earth do you want to know?' They both laughed and said: 'Because we're doing a cross-word puzzle!' (At last I thought, my five years of Theological study had come into its own!) I went back to their table and was introduced to a group of their friends. Each one was keen to tell me that they had once been involved with a church, but had now given up. For one, his football team now played on Sundays. An ex-choirboy, he did not like the new vicar, so he left. Another said his family moved to a new town where the local church was not very friendly, so they never went back.

As the conversation carried on, the questions deepened, and I was able to share my own conviction that a living faith, was not only based on truth, but it gave life a new sense of purpose and meaning. Reflecting on that encounter, I saw more clearly what my role as Chaplain might be. All these young men had given up on the Christian faith, but not one of them had a good reason for doing so. None of them asked the really important questions like 'Is it true?' 'Can God be really known?' or 'Will faith make a difference to my life?' Maybe my task was to help students see that the faith they had rejected was too shallow. It bore little or no resemblance to the real thing. Only then would they be able to hear and understand the truth, power and relevance of the gospel.

Students Union meetings usually took place in the Main Hall, also known as The Refectory. I usually attended them because I wanted to really understand what kind of institution Enfield was. It was certainly very left wing, and there was no lack of opinions being vehemently expressed. There was a great deal of Marxist influence, not only in the Students Union, but throughout the college. Other colleges were similar in that respect. It was jokingly said, that if the London School of Economics had boiled eggs for breakfast, we would have them scrambled by lunchtime.

One of the earliest Students Union meetings I attended, hosted a visiting speaker who was very much in the news at the time. Bernadette Devlin a young, recently elected M.P. for a Northern Ireland constituency spoke about the Irish situation. She was obviously anti-unionist, and a keen supporter of the IRA. The meeting closed with a collection for the struggle of the North Vietnamese against the 'horror of American Imperialism'.

After a while we felt it would be a good idea to hold a Marxist-Christian Dialogue. These were quite popular in the late 60s. The Socialist society agreed to work with us, and offered to do the publicity. I should have known better! As we entered the crowded Main Hall, we could see that all the walls were completely smothered with large posters. The message was clear. That afternoon Christian mythology would be smashed by Marxist truth. Some of the posters were very funny. The one I shall never forget featured Jesus hanging on the cross. Underneath were the words 'What a Rotten Way to Spend Good Friday!' Little did they realize how true that was! But out of the horror of the Cross came the miracle of the Resurrection. Christians feared that we would be beaten, but thanks to the excellence of our speakers, and a large number of engineering students, determined not to give in to extreme Socialist propaganda, that was not the case. When the vote was taken, the Christians won with a respectable majority.

Notably 1968 was a year of Revolutions in many European cities and Universities. On 28 May students occupied the premises of Hornsey College of Art, which a few years later would be joining the Middlesex Polytechnic. Student protests were also experienced in Enfield. On 17 March 1971 Margaret Thatcher, as Minister of Education opened a new six storey Tower Block on the Ponders End Site. In the ground floor dining room refreshments had been prepared for invited guests. But by the time the formal proceedings were over, students had occupied the area and eaten the food. Mrs Thatcher made a hasty retreat.

Teaching

In the first few weeks of employment at Enfield, I found it especially helpful to have a definite fixed point in my week. As a lecturer I was asked to lead a weekly seminar for students working for the Higher National Diploma in Engineering. Known as 'Professional Studies', the aim was to improve their written and spoken communication skills, broaden their breadth of knowledge, and discuss contemporary issues. Many of the subjects discussed were chosen by the students themselves. One student asked if, the following week, we could look at the concept of 'Utopia' and ask, 'What is the ideal society?' Out of that came a very lively discussion of the kind of society we should be working for, and on the values and guidelines by which we should live. That was good, but the atmosphere changed and the seminar really took off when one student asked if there was any purpose or meaning to life itself.

Sadly, none of the students felt there was a meaning. Indeed one student even implied that life was 'no more than a meaningless accident.' I challenged some of the opinions that had been expressed in the seminar, and shared my own experience that as a Christian, I found life to have a tremendous sense of purpose and meaning. This could not be summed up in a few pat answers or simplistic statements. Instead we each had to discover meaning for ourselves. All the clues though, and the values and guidelines by which we should live, could be found in the life and teaching of Jesus. I suggested that to discover a living faith in Him, was to find a life full of significance and a great deal of fulfilment.

As we drew nearer to the establishment of Middlesex Polytechnic, I was asked to teach a course in Comparative Religion for Students at the Hornsey College of Art. I soon realized there was a world of difference between the two colleges, and the kind of students they attracted. I learned much from the different interests and attitudes of these two groups and looked forward to working with students studying a much wider variety of subjects, once the Polytechnic became a reality.

In keeping with the policy of the College that lecturers should feel free to attend classes led by colleagues, I joined a seminar in the Sociology of Religion. Although we had studied some sociology at Handsworth, I knew that Enfield had one of the largest departments of Social Science in the country, so I thought it wise to enlarge my understanding of the subject.

Counselling

Being a Chaplain is a very pastoral role. Although I was available to both staff and students, the main focus of my work was the students. I made a point of letting it be known I was always available to lend a listening ear to any student who wished to discuss personal problems with me. Sometimes I was asked to deal with religious issues but students were free to raise almost anything. In times of stress many students came seeking encouragement and reassurance, but also at times, they came when they needed a challenge or some practical advice. I emphasized the importance of confidentiality and promised never to share private information with lecturers or college authorities unless they gave me distinct and specific permission to do so.

Student years can be a very difficult time. Many were away from home for the first time. Now they had to look after themselves. The simplest issue can become stressful if you don't know how to deal with it. One common problem for example revolved around the difference between school and college. Sixth form students are often given clear guidelines as to what is expected in assignments, and when they should be handed in, but in the more adult world of Higher Education, they are usually expected to work out their own timetable and be sure to get their assignments finished on time.

For many, the experience of higher education at Enfield was a whole new world. Early days were often exciting, but for some, they could be unsettling. Some were still exploring their own identity, and discovering the kind of person they wanted to be. Others were exploring deeper friendships or coping with broken relationships. There was no Hall of Residence, and many students had to find their own home. Some lived in a flat with fellow students, others were in 'digs' with a landlady, but some preferred to be alone in a bed-sit. Not surprisingly therefore many felt a sense of isolation and loneliness.

Developing the Christian Community

In my early days at Enfield I was often asked why we had a chaplaincy. As this was a very secular institution, why did we need religion? Indeed some made a point of saying that there was no place for religious indoctrination in the college. With that I agreed, but then I was strongly opposed to any form of indoctrination and saw it as dangerous. I stressed that secularism was one distinct philosophy among many, and that it would be inappropriate for any single approach to claim a monopoly of truth especially in an institution of Higher Education. We must be a pluralistic institution committed to exploring all of life. I agreed with the writer who said that University Level Education was about helping students 'live with big questions and make connections'. We have inherited the richness of Western Civilization, and much of our culture and learning benefits from that.

You cannot understand any culture without taking account of its religious foundations. In Britain, and virtually all Western Culture, that means taking Christianity seriously.

Many students were troubled by the left wing ethos of the college, and sometimes felt threatened when their attitudes, opinions, and indeed their faith, was challenged by their studies, or by the cynicism and even mockery of some fellow students. Some were tempted to ignore the challenge of a questioning approach to faith, and retreat into a simplistic and often superficial approach to the Bible and the Christian message. Others were challenged by atheistic or agnostic attitudes, but could not answer the questions they posed, and so were tempted to give up their Christian beliefs. Understanding these concerns, I felt that we must find a way of helping students discover a faith that had intellectual integrity. They needed to see that Christian discipleship involved a creative dialogue with doubt, and that dealing with questions gave us the opportunity to find a deeper understanding and a more mature faith. This concern led to the foundation of the Christian Community in the college.

When I arrived at Enfield there was a small Evangelical Christian Union led by students. There had been a Catholic Society which no longer had formal meetings. Some students regularly attended Mass at the church in Enfield Town, and one of the priests was recognized as the Catholic Chaplain. There were some other main stream Christians who hoped we could do something meaningful in the college. After speaking with many students and several staff, we eventually decided to form a 'Christian Community' in the college. This would fit in with the approach of an Ecumenical chaplaincy, and would be open to serve the needs of Christians who wanted to grow, seekers who wanted to find and others who were just interested in knowing more.

We believed that the Christian Community should have a strong teaching function. Christians needed to know what they believed and why they believed it. Only then would they be able to give a reason for the faith that was in them.

We began a weekly Christian Forum to discuss matters of Christian Faith and concern. It met in college from 1-2 p.m. on Tuesdays. Tea and coffee would be served, and students were welcome to bring their own sandwiches. It would be run by a student committee in partnership with the Chaplain. Guest speakers, including some Enfield Lecturers, would introduce their chosen subject and then the meeting would be open to questions and discussion. Many local clergy were willing to come and speak, and my contacts with Anglican, Methodist and Catholic Chaplains in London enabled us to cast our net wider and have some really outstanding speakers who were willing to travel some distance to be with us.

We had a large number of Overseas Students at Enfield, and several of them got involved with us. At the beginning of the academic year we drew up posters saying 'Welcome! There's a place for you in the Christian Community. We meet each Tuesday 1-2 p.m. in Room XX.' We asked as many overseas students as possible to write this in their own language. I asked one from Cyprus to do this in Greek. He began immediately, but then stopped in the middle, and said 'It's this word 'Community'. I can't find a word in my language to translate it. The nearest I can find is 'Koinonia.' I replied, 'That's exactly the word I need. In the Ancient Greek of the New Testament, it's the word for "Fellowship", and implies a community that shares in depth.'

Attendances at the Forum were encouraging, but after a while some students expressed their desire for an additional, more intimate meeting for Bible Study and discussion. This really did fit in with our desire to form a community that shared in depth, so I did some research. On the High Street, and only a short walk from the Enfield Campus, was Ponders End Methodist Church. It had a comfortable lounge, next to the kitchen, and the congregation was willing that we should meet there free of charge on Thursday evenings. The students liked the idea and were keen to support it. Each week we would gather in the kitchen for tea or coffee and biscuits, and then move into the lounge to start the meeting with a prayer. We would usually follow that with a passage from the Bible. I would give a brief introduction to the passage, putting it in context so that we could understand to whom it was written, and why. Then having read a few verses at a time we asked what it actually says, and what it means, how we should see its relevance for today, and then apply it. Often students would lead the discussion, but I would be available as a resource person.

Research shows that Christian growth takes place best in the context of relationships, and that small groups provide the best opportunity for relationships to be built. Christian young people often experience peer pressure to adopt secular and atheistic attitudes and life style. They need to be part of a group characterized by relationships of trust and openness, where they can reveal deep questions and find satisfying answers. The group process helps to get people involved.

In his book *Growing Christians in Small Groups*, John Mallison reminds us (on p. 96) of the danger of a purely intellectual approach to Bible study. He says 'Bible study is more than a mental exercise.' A Bible passage is not just a set of doctrines or propositions. We need to see it as mediating God's word in a way that addresses our feelings and our behaviour as well as our minds. It is not just a truth to be understood but also a reality by which to live.

Students away from home for the first time can feel somewhat isolated from friends and family. They need to find a caring support group. I remember meeting one student, Chris, in the refectory. He looked very isolated. After a while I invited him to our Bible study group that evening. He came and seemed to enjoy the experience. When we met the following day I asked him if he had enjoyed the experience. He replied, 'It was great. It was my first meeting, and everybody made me welcome and wanted to know my name. Then when tea and coffee was served, a girl came and asked me to give out the biscuits. Not only was I able to receive, but I was able to give.' He became a regular member of the group.

Bill was an engineer. Just before he graduated he came to say goodbye. 'I've only been to four of your Bible studies, but each time the passage you chose, spoke to my situation. That's uncanny! You didn't know I was coming, nor what was concerning me, but you certainly gave me a lot to think about.'

Ravi was a Hindu student from India. He wanted to learn something about Christianity, so I invited him to the Thursday group. Over the next few weeks, several new members joined us, and each time he was quick to welcome them with a warm smile: 'Hello, my name is Ravi. Welcome to the Christian Community.' He was obviously feeling very much a part of things.'

In addition to the regular meetings of the Christian Community we organized annual residential weekends for fun, fellowship and Christian teaching. Many former students still keep in touch with each other, and speak very warmly of their time at Enfield and their involvement in the Christian Community.

What did my time at Enfield mean to me?

I cannot think of a better way to have begun my active ministry. Not only did I enjoy the privilege the ministry of small but lively local churches, but also my life experience was being enriched by my involvement with the staff and students of Enfield College. I never expected that being Chaplain at Enfield would be easy, but I learned so much about Christian witness from working there. Predominantly secular, sometimes apathetic, and on occasion downright hostile to all that Christians stood for, Enfield was a wonderful learning experience. I had been forced out of my comfort zone, and enabled to catch a glimpse of the real world. Apathy and hostility had to be faced, but there were also many wonderful people facing big issues, and wrestling with real questions, who were prepared to share their searching and their finding with me. I learned so much from working in my churches and in the college. All this proved to be a good foundation for a lifetime of ministry. I also appreciated the support of colleagues, both locally and nationally, at conferences and other meetings organized for chaplains in Higher Education.

Being at Enfield showed me the importance of keeping in touch with the real world, and understanding secular attitudes. It also deepened my understanding of society, and furthered the breadth of my education. All this enriched my preaching as I have always sought to share good Christian Teaching that is both applied and relevant. At Enfield I sought to share the faith with students in a non-threatening way. Helping others find faith deepened my own trust in God, and strengthened my belief in the relevance and power of a living faith in Christ.

Although my work at Enfield was only part-time, it led on to a further seven years of full-time service at the Middlesex Polytechnic. This was followed by many years of pastoral ministry. From 1979 until 2008 I served as minister of some of the largest churches in Methodism, and many of these included work with students and young adults.

I may have had to dive in at the deep end, but Enfield taught me to swim, and for that I will be eternally grateful.

30. Just in time for last orders

DAVID DEWEY

> ***David Dewey*** *was appointed in 1972 as a lecturer in Sociology to teach mainly on the Business Studies degree both full-time and part-time. Later he moved into the Social Science area and, briefly to the Law degree at Hendon. The rest of his time was spent in the Diploma in Higher Education scheme at Trent Park and Tottenham, the forerunner of the Polytechnic's Modular Degree scheme. He retired 2001 and became a parish priest in Hertfordshire. He retired from the Church of England in 2008 but still helps out as needed in the Hertford area. A great deal of time is spent reading, gardening, and family life with nine grandchildren.*

I was a relatively late arrival to the teaching staff of Enfield College when I was appointed as a Lecturer in Sociology in 1972 at the age of twenty-nine. Even so, it was for me a *Damascus Road* experience in that it changed my life. I met some fine and helpful colleagues, an interesting and diverse range of students, and was led into a totally new kind of working environment. A short autobiographical summary might clarify my route to Enfield College of Technology which was shortly to become one of the newly created Polytechnics.

On the face of it, I had no place in such an enterprise spearheaded by people of academic distinction. I had left school, which was quite a respectable Technical School, in 1959 at the age of sixteen. I took half a dozen O-levels and managed to fail them all. Until I reached twenty-one I drifted through various routine jobs that I did not like and where those in authority did not like me. I was a trainee in a laboratory, a clerk in various contexts, all going nowhere. At twenty-one someone suggested that I might give the Civil Service a try: security, pension, discretionary leave, generous sick provision etc. In 1965 I became a Temporary Clerical Assistant in what was then called the National Assistance Board. Here, at last, was a humble start of something worthwhile. The Board performed an important social function for the less fortunate of our 1960s society.

I encountered people in more senior positions whose appointment was sometimes the result of promotion, or sometimes by direct entry to a senior grade by virtue of having specified academic credentials. This seemed unfair to me because these colleagues appeared no brighter or more able than we minions. This experience inspired me to correct my past failures and develop such capabilities as I thought I had.

I began a course with the London University Extra-Mural Department leading to a Diploma in Sociology and there was a range of subjects on offer. Over a three-year period of evening classes I gained the Diploma and discovered that it counted as two A-levels for undergraduate entrance. Armed with this first indication of having done something right, I realised that I would need three O-levels to get the minimum entry requirements. This I did through private study and the result was doubly productive. First, I gained entry to Goldsmiths College to pursue the London Internal BA Hons in Sociology; a four-year course part-time or three years full-time. We could attend classes on both routes as was convenient.

The second boost was to learn that my equivalent to A-levels allowed me to apply to the Civil Service Commission to be a direct entrant Executive Officer. This was successful and off I went to the Ministry of Defence (Navy) to be a Whitehall bureaucrat. My undergraduate studies continued until in 1972 I graduated with First Class Honours to the utter amazement of my family, friends, elders and, not least, of myself. During the years 1968-72 I had a shot at the Administrative Class of the Civil Service. I managed to get to the Final Selection Board where I gained a ‘near miss’, but near enough to be offered the consolation prize of becoming one of HM Inspectors of Taxes. I started the training but did not take to it at all. Compared with the leisurely and civilised atmosphere of the Ministry of Defence it was Dickensian. I returned at my own request to the Ministry of Defence (Army) for a short while until my degree result was published. My professor encouraged and supported me towards an academic career which led to Enfield College in 1972 and my first steps on the *Damascus Road.*

Enlightenment begins

I was interviewed by a panel chaired by Dr John Farquhar and accompanied by Alf Holt, Peter Morea, John Munro, Len Jackson and a representative of the Local Education Authority. I was living with my wife and first child in Beckenham, a long way from Enfield, so would have to endure long journeys to begin with. However, joy of joys, when Alf Holt (Dean of Social Science) explained that I would not need to attend very day, probably three days a week in term-time. Compare that with life in the Inland Revenue, and the *Damascus Road* began to look rather attractive!

My main commitment when I began to teach social science was on the BA Business Studies full-time and part-time. The part-time course involved some evening work so that on one day each week it meant 9.30am to 9.30pm and a long drive home. The Course Head for the full-time BABS was Gus Demesquita, a very fatherly and experienced mathematician. The part-time degree was under the leadership of John Munro, an economist and a magistrate. All my colleagues were more experienced than me and many were part of a large cohort of young lecturers who had joined in the late 1960s. Some are sadly no longer with us but I recall several names with affection: Vic Marchesi, Mike Miletto, Gerry Mars, Bruce May, Barbara Frost, Val Mort, Noel Lee, Tom Bourner, Tony Crilly, Arthur Hindmarch, Lester Clother, Bal Chansarkhar, Gerry Earls, Mike Denton, Steve Culliford, John Ives, and Peter Ribeaux.

The College offered what was known as the Enfield 'thick sandwich'. In both Business Studies and Social Science students spent the third year of the four-year programme out on a placement. This unit was run by Julian Ayer, Mike Denton and Howard Ward. Lecturers would normally tutor at least one student per year on placement which involved visits to workplaces anywhere in the country or, from time to time, in the world. This manifestly vocational aspect of an undergraduate programme served graduates well in their subsequent searches for employment.

If I cast my mind back to 1972 I can still recall the faces and names of students on the BABS full-time and part-time programmes. All the students on the part-time course were male and in employment, most seeking career advancement. The full-time students were very mixed in age and nationality but again they were predominantly male. In later years more women did join the course. Just before Enfield closed there was a reunion for staff, students and administrative staff and it was delightful to meet students I had taught in 1972. The group of about half a dozen had remained in mutual contact for some forty years.

Teaching staff in 1972 were a very mixed bag. In several areas, there were colleagues of national and international renown. Many others were routine graduates in their subjects who had been appointed when recruitment criteria were less rigorous. Following the expansion of higher education in the 1960s these elder statesmen and women had benefited from rapid promotion and held important roles in the College structure. In later years it became significantly more difficult to secure a teaching post. This was partly due to the desire by most of the new Polytechnics to emulate universities as centres of research. Very soon the possession of higher degrees and publications became the *sine qua non* for an academic post. In addition, the ability of staff to bring external research funding into the College was a sure route to appreciation by management.

In spite of positive and negative factors Enfield College was a great place to work. I suppose the factor which made it stand apart from the Civil Service and other jobs I had done was the professional freedom that all teaching staff had. At the beginning of each year everyone tried to secure a timetable that suited themselves. Not surprisingly many colleagues endeavoured to compress their formal duties into Tuesday, Wednesday and Thursday. Some were even more enterprising. I recall one colleague who lived at Porlock Weir on the Somerset/Devon boarder who organised his work into two days attendance per week. Another once told me in the strictest confidence that he actually lived in Germany! It is perhaps fair to say that most academic institutions have had their share of staff that were famous for their scarcity. In general, however, most colleagues worked out a fair timetable and attended faithfully to their duties. Everyone's way and style of teaching was at their own professional discretion and the College, to my mind, was the richer for it.

Day-to-Day Work

My task as a Lecturer in Sociology was to make social science a relevant constituent of a Business Studies programme. An underlying issue was the contrast between the rather right-wing tenor of commerce and more left-wing flavour of the social sciences. I spent a hectic first year having to prepare a new lecture each week and keep myself just ahead of the students. As many newcomers to academic posts will realise my main resource was my own collection of undergraduate notes and essays. My principal message to students was that the social sciences help us to understand the society in which business is conducted and also assist our understanding of commercial organisations.

First year students were introduced to matters of social stratification, educational provision and relative opportunities, gender issues, patterns of family building, career opportunities and expectations together with some introduction to the ideas of the Founding Fathers of social science. Second year students looked more at organisational factors, for example, management systems and practice, human relations in the work environment, studies of working practice, unionisation and the conflict of ideologies between management and workers.

In general, I believe that the 'thick sandwich' worked well. Graduates usually secured employment with little difficulty. The key to this success was thought to be the placement year. Other institutions were producing large number of Lower Second Class students who had not had a placement year so that they were all much the same. Our 'thick sandwich' graduates stood out as different to good effect. This all meant that Enfield became a strong constituent of the newly formed Middlesex Polytechnic (later Middlesex University) and its reputation for Business Studies within Middlesex University continues to this day.

During the late 1960s and early 1970s Enfield College had other strings to its bow. As a sociologist I must confess that I really wanted to move away from Business Studies and work on what was then the BA Social Science which also had a successful placement system, although by the 1970s fewer of the BASS placements were paid than the BABS ones. In the 1970s, the Enfield site of the new Polytechnic also housed the BA Geography, BA Humanities, BA Accounting and Finance, Trade Union Studies and a range of Engineering courses. I was not connected with these but they form part of the whole scenario that defined our place of work.

Over time the transition to Social Science happened and it put me in daily touch with a very difference group of colleagues. In addition, I, like many others, became involved in split-site teaching over the many campuses comprising Middlesex Polytechnic. The whole operation was getting bigger and more spread out across North London. Teaching staff each had a base-site where they did most of their work, had an office and collected their payslips, but there was a great deal of inter-site travel, for which reason it put in place a free domestic transport service.

The Changing Face of Higher Education

As time moved on, the College, like other constituents of the emerging Polytechnic, lost some of its old identity. Courses changed sites, management structures were renewed and many new administrative posts were created. The old Personnel Office had been run effectively for years by one man with some secretarial help. Suddenly it became 'Human Resources', not so much an office as an empire, with a large hierarchical staff and an ability to complicate matters which had been routinely managed in the past. In a changing world Enfield College had to endure its share.

The Polytechnic duly became Middlesex University and at that time similar changes of identity, status, and vision affected other old Technical Colleges across the country. Perhaps the most radical rethink concerned the introduction of modular degrees. This was an American inspired system based upon student choice, mixed forms of assessment, and with semesters replacing years as the teaching unit. It began on the Diploma of Higher Education (DipHE) with top-up facilities to graduate level and was based initially at the Trent Park site. After some years the DipHE became the Modular Degree and this system became the university's way of working.

From a personal point of view the *Damascus Road* upon which I was launched in 1972 brought many changes and maintained a certain dynamism. I cannot speak of Enfield in the 1960s in the way that others colleagues can. To me, names of the old management like George Brosan and Eric Robinson meant nothing except as the subject of anecdotes. In 1972, however, many colleagues both academic and administrative had cut their teeth in that old regime and looked to the future with some trepidation. There were the unsurprising grumbles among longer-serving colleagues about the Brosan/Robinson years. Nevertheless, I always got the impression that they were both regarded with affection. By the time of my arrival the Principal was John O'Neill and his Vice- Principal was John Osborn-Moss, both were engineers.

For my own part I took steps to guard against real or imagined uncertainties in higher education. Very soon after my appointment I undertook a CertEd course of London University to obtain qualified teacher status. This was in case there were to be redundancies, so I could apply for a post in the school system. It never happened. The second step may seem more surprising. I had long been involved in the Church of England as a result of upbringing and personal persuasion. I decided that I would like to seek ordination to the priesthood, not to make it a career, but where I might serve locally on a voluntary basis. My training over two years at Westcott House, Cambridge, was managed partly by weekly visits and partly by some periods of residence. In June 1978 I was ordained by the Bishop of London in St Paul's Cathedral and served as an assistant in various parishes until I took a retirement package in 2001. If redundancy had reared its head at Middlesex I then had two strings to my bow. For the record, after leaving Middlesex I became a parish priest in the Diocese of St Albans looking after two churches near Hitchin until retirement in 2008 at the age of 65. My working life has been perhaps an unusual mixture but by far the most significant watershed was my appointment at Enfield College in 1972. The *Damascus Road* has led me to interesting and challenging experiences as somebody else discovered 2000 years ago!

Now I am fully retired and, like my colleagues, full of memories of faces, events, graduations and examination boards. A colleague who retired a little before me said that the great benefit of going was never having to attend another examination board meeting. If I meditate on the concept of hell two things come to mind, one is Gatwick Airport in August, and the other is an eternal Examination Board! Come what may, I am thankful that I was appointed to Enfield College some forty-five years ago. My *Damascus Road* has had its ups and downs but it changed my life in ways I could not have imagined as a teenager. I hope that during those years that I was able to give something back.

31. The final chapter – making sense of it all

TOM BOURNER

At the start of this book we gave some context by taking a brief look at education more widely in England at the time when ECT was established (Chapter 1) and also the events leading up to its establishment (Chapter 2). The rest of the book contains an answer to the question 'what happened next?' presented in the form of personal experiences and reminiscences of twenty-eight people who taught at Enfield at some stage during its lifetime from 1962 to 1972. Some of these people had also been students at the college during part of that period.

The different accounts – delightfully disparate – have been written by individuals coming from different places who had different experiences at Enfield at different times during its eleven-year history. It would be surprising if the experiences of this group of different people were the same. For example, the experience of someone teaching in the engineering part of the college in 1963 is likely to have been quite different from that of someone teaching on the BASS degree in the early 1970s. It is also important to remember that the experiences recorded in this book took place half a century ago and memory can be selective, fill gaps and make interpretations.

The main aim of this chapter is to provide an account of Enfield College over its life, 1962-72 that is as compatible as possible with the different experiences recorded by the contributors to this book. It also looks at what was special or distinctive about ECT and expresses a view about its wider and longer-term impact.

Chapter 2 ended with the appointment of a new principal of the college, George Brosan, who had a distinctive philosophy of HE. That philosophy viewed the application of new knowledge as at least as important as the discovery of new knowledge and technological and vocational education as at least as intellectually demanding as academic education.

On taking up his position George Brosan was keen to appoint into senior positions capable people who would be sympathetic to his ideas about the application of knowledge and vocational HE and were knowledgeable about the development of HE. One of his earlier appointments was Eric Robinson, recruited initially to the post of Head of the Mathematics.

Eric Robinson has appeared in the majority of the accounts in this book so it is worth clarifying where he came from and where he was coming from.[38] He was born in 1927 and completed a Mathematics degree at London University, followed by an MSc by part-time study from Birkbeck College and a PGDip from the London's Institution of Education. He taught at technical colleges from the age of 22 quickly getting involved in the Association of Teachers in Technical Institutions (ATTI) and progressing to become its president. He was an active member of the Labour Party and remained a socialist all his life (he was vice-president of the *Socialist Education Association* from 1965 until his death in 2011).

By the late 1950s there was much criticism of university education. Criticisms from the right tended to emphasise growing over-specialisation of university education, which was no longer producing sufficient generalists able to apply their well-honed intellects to a broad range of responsible positions after graduating. Criticisms from the left included elitism, increasing disengagement from the society which provided the majority of university funding and reluctance to respond to society's need for a larger supply of graduates in technological fields to help raise the material wellbeing of the people of Britain.

The Labour Party had a long-standing Study Group on Education which played a significant role in Labour's policy-making on education. In the mid-1950s Richard Crossman was an influential[39] member this group and in 1957 he tabled a paper on the *problem* of the universities (Crossman, 1957). Crossman was most concerned about institutional discrimination which gave a middle-class child six times as good a chance of a university education as a working class child.

Crossman had clearly given much thought to the problem of the universities. In 1957 he submitted a paper to the Labour Party's Education Study Group in support of a memorandum from the Fabi-

[38] This chapter has benefited from access to a transcript of an interview with Eric Robinson in 2006 by Tom Steele for the book he co-authored with Richard Taylor (Taylor and Steele, 2011)

[39] He was a member of Labour's National Executive from 1952 to 1967.

an Society demanding a Royal Commission on the Universities. It demonstrated just how exercised Labour's privately educated leaders were on the subject of the universities...

> ... it created an 'Establishment' with a set of cultural values hostile to technology and applied science, and claiming a false sense of superiority. And this could not be allowed to stand in the way because the country needed a huge increase in technical literacy and improved status for the technologist. So it was necessary to 'shake our Arts courses loose from an obsolete classical humanism' and to challenge the dominance of elite institutions (ibid., p.5) Crossman further argued that the number of places in universities and institutes of technology must be increased 'even at the cost of "lowering standards".' (Taylor and Steele, 2011, p.71)

Crossman's paper led to a paper from the Study Group itself titled simply 'The Universities'. It called for:

> ... greater state control over universities; courses relevant to the community, especially in science and technology; expansion even at the cost of lowering standards; the abolition of fees; the establishment of a Royal Commission; an increase in working-class numbers and a reduction in specialization; and, finally, a reduction in the close connection of universities with public schools. (Taylor and Steele, 2011, p.71)

Afterwards, Crossman continued to meet with a small group to discuss higher education, which at times included Eric Robinson. (Taylor and Steele, 2011, p.71)

By the end of the 1950s, dissatisfaction with university education led to more insistent calls for a Royal Commission. There was concern in all parts of the political spectrum that university-led higher education was a restraining force on the modernisation of Britain. In November 1960 Conservative prime minister Harold Macmillan announced the appointment of a committee of enquiry under Lionel Robbins, head of the economics department at the London School of Economics of the University of London. It was set up in February 1961 to 'review the pattern of full-time higher education in Great Britain ...' According to Robbins it had 'the most ambitious terms of reference for HE to date.' (quoted in Taylor and Steele, 2011, p.72)

The Labour party responded to the establishment of the Robbins Committee by setting up a study group on higher education, chaired by Lord Taylor. Its membership included Tony Crosland and it took evidence from, amongst many others, Eric Robinson representing the ATTI. The Report of the Taylor Committee in 1962 accepted the arguments for the expansion of HE proposing the creation of forty-five new universities. This was not welcomed by the leadership of the ATTI which was concerned that the creation of a much larger university system would lead to the removal of HE from technical institutions into the new universities. HE in the technical institutions gave status to ATTI members and justified higher pay. The leaders of the ATTI were also concerned about a consequent loss of ATTI membership to the Association of University Teachers (AUT). 'This must have been a considerable worry to the ATTI as one of the results of giving university status to the CATS was that most of the teachers there joined the AUT and left the ATTI' (Sharp, p.51)

It concentrated the minds of the leadership of the ATTI to make the case for HE within the non-University colleges where the membership of the ATTI was based. Those leaders were Eric Robinson and Edward Britton (later, Sir Edward Britton) who were the ATTI president and general secretary respectively. They were both extremely able people; Robinson was the youngest-ever national president of the ATTI and Britton was a Cambridge educated mathematician who had already been national president of the National Union of Teachers (NUT) at the relatively young age of forty-seven. Under their leadership the membership of the ATTI had grown rapidly.

At that time HE in England was seen, particularly by those in more elevated positions in society, in terms of a hierarchy with Oxbridge at the top, then London and the redbrick universities, followed by colleges of advanced technology and specialist colleges with the HE in technical colleges at the bottom. The HE credibility of technical colleges was tainted by association with sub-degree teaching, non-qualification work and narrow vocational training for specific occupations. Another way of viewing this is as a series of concentric circles with Oxbridge at the centre extending outwards to the technical colleges at the ragged edge of the periphery. If the demand for HE rose then local techs could do more HE work and if the demand fell the decline would be felt most strongly in these marginal institutions:

> During the 1940s and 1950s 'university' was still commonly used as a synonym for higher education, and, if considered at all, further education and teacher training colleges were regarded as overspill institutions. These colleges had just expanded to meet the increased demand for places. (Sharp, 1987, p.4)

The Robbins Committee reported in 1963 recommending a large expansion of higher education in British universities including the creation of six new universities, the 'promotion' of CATS to university status and the transfer of teacher training from local authority college control to the universities. Its recommendations implied the transfer of HE work from FE/technical colleges to the universities that Robinson and Britton feared. The Robbins Report warned the area colleges that 'for reasons of economy of staff and equipment the work of university level will be confined to selected centres.' (Robbins, 1963, p.271). And of the regional colleges it said that some 'may follow the colleges of advanced technology and attain university status.' (Robbins, 1963, p.138). However, it did allow for the continuation of some 'overspill' role for HE by FE/technical colleges, particularly in the area of part-time HE (which was not part of the brief of the Robbins Committee). And it established a new Council for National Academic Awards to control developments outside of the universities.

Basically, the Robbins Committee adhered to the conventional hierarchical model of HE such that those colleges that modelled themselves on existing universities could be gradually promoted to the 'university club' as the expansion of HE materialised. The ratio of 'advanced' places (requiring A-level or A-level equivalent for entry) in 1964 in universities compared to non-university institutions was 55 to 45 and the Robbins proposals would have changed that to 88 to 12 (Godwin, 1998).

This rang alarm bells for several interested groups, the local authorities and the Ministry of Education as well as the ATTI; each had reason to preserve HE work outside of the universities. The local authorities valued HE in the local, area and regional colleges that met local needs for a highly qualified people in areas of particular importance to them, including local industry. The Ministry of Education had battled for years to persuade the universities to be more responsive to the needs of society as represented by the wishes of democratically-elected governments but the UGC buffer enabled the universities to pursue their own agenda. And, as we've seen, the ATTI had its own reasons for defending HE in the FE/technical colleges.

An unintended consequence of the Robbins Committee was to give a voice to other stakeholders of HE in Britain and create some new alliances and new forces within HE. One new alliance was between the ATTI, the Association of Education Committees (AEC) of local authorities and the DES. Each had a stake in preserving, if not expanding, HE in local authority institutions. The Robbins enquiry led to these advocates for HE in local authority institutions making common cause. Research for the Robbins Committee also, incidentally, had revealed how much HE had grown outside of the universities.

So long as the primary role of the local authority colleges was perceived to be to accommodate 'overspill' demand for HE from the universities they would be vulnerable as marginal providers of HE. The best way to defend HE in the local authority institutions was to develop an alternative narrative in which these institutions were not residual providers of HE but rather the constituents of a second sector of HE that was separate and different from that of the university 'sector'.

That narrative developed during 1963 and 1964 through conversations between individuals from organisations that had most at stake: Toby Weaver of the Ministry of Education, William Alexander (later 'Lord') of the Association of Education Committees of the local authorities, Ted Britton of the ATTI, and Eric Robinson, also of the ATTI and by then a senior figure at ECT which one of the colleges that would be much affected.

They constructed a picture of HE in the non-University sector colleges that could attract support for it. Instead of seeing technical institutions as marginal players in English HE, its ragged non-U edge, they developed the concept of a second sector of HE outside of the universities, with its own mission, values and history. In their alternative paradigm, the colleges that were not universities comprised a sector of higher education in its own right i.e. with an identity that was separate and different from the university 'sector'. In this they were helped by the fact that HE in technical colleges had expanded greatly in the 1950s and that expansion was particularly strong in technological fields and it was often focused on the local and regional needs for highly qualified people in areas of particular importance to a locality or region. They created a picture of a second sector that was inclusive, engaged with the local/regional communities, flexible and responsive to society's needs for more highly qualified technology experts. Moreover, it had realised this despite its shabby accommodation and relative neglect compared to the university sector.

In this story, it was the second sector that had been doing the heavy lifting in meeting the needs of society while most of the academics in universities had been pursuing knowledge for its own sake, or more cynically, for their own sakes. Once the notion of a second sector of HE had been born, it was possible to differentiate the two sectors in terms of privilege, exclusivity and responsiveness to the needs of society. And it was not difficult to construct a Cinderella version of this story by noticing the inferior conditions for working and studying in the second sector while the government had indulged the universities. This raised the question, if the second sector achieved so much despite its poor treatment compared to the more privileged university sector what could it not achieve if it received more support?

They argued that expansion of this alternative sector could meet the criticisms that were being levelled at university-led HE. Moreover, it would do so without the need to reform the universities which had been able to successfully resist change in the past. They offered a vision of an expanded second sector of HE in England that would be more open, flexible, engaged and responsive to the changing needs of society than the universities.

This was attractive to the Ministry of Education (renamed the 'Department of Education and Science' in 1964 by the incoming Labour government) which had battled for years to persuade the universities to be more responsive to the needs of the wider society. It was particularly attractive to Toby Weaver (later 'Sir') who was the senior civil servant who had produced reports for the Fabian Society on the need for reform of HE.

In 1964 a Labour government was elected and Tony Crosland was appointed Secretary of State for Education and Science. He set up an informal group led by his junior minister, Reg Prentice, which included both Robinson and Britton. The latter produced a paper for this group which proposed an HE system with a structure comprising an autonomous university sector and a separate 'public sector' of HE including technical colleges and teacher-training colleges, to be led by thirty polytechnics. It was accepted by the group and recommended to Tony Crosland. It formed the basis of Crosland's 1965 speech at Woolwich that established the binary system of HE in Britain.

Meanwhile Robinson as Head of Mathematics at ECT was soon acting as deputy to George Brosan. As we have seen, Brosan had his own ideas about HE at Enfield but these were, for the most part, compatible with Robinson's ideas and ECT became the site where those ideas could be tested out in practice.

The fullest expression of Robinson's ideas can be found in his 1968 book but here are seven elements that were particularly relevant to his impact at Enfield:

1. *Comprehensive.* Robinson thought the argument for comprehensive education at secondary school level also applied to education at the tertiary level. Against the highly selective system of HE in the early 1960s, he favoured a higher education system that was more open and inclusive. He was particularly keen to widen access to HE for students from working class homes that were hugely under-represented in higher education, particularly in the more prestigious universities.
2. *Student-centred.* He saw the primary purpose of HE institutions as meeting the educational needs of students at the tertiary level rather than the accumulation of new knowledge for its own sake. This meant recognising the vocational aspirations of students, particularly those from working class homes.
3. *Flexibility.* Further and Higher Education should be organised to enable easier transfer between subjects of study, levels of study, institutions and modes of study (particularly part-time and full-time). This is because students' circumstances change and the students themselves change. This belief in flexible FE and HE followed from a student-centred perspective and had

implications for relations between institutions, subjects and modes of study.

4. *Technical-rationalism.* Robinson placed much more weight on reason and critical discussion in reaching decisions than on tradition, recognised authority or established practice. He shared the technical-rational optimism of the 1950s that social problems could be fixed by the application of reason, knowledge and action.[40]
5. *Egalitarian.* Those in authority should be willing to answer to those they had authority over. Those in the higher echelons of organisations could learn from those at the lower levels of organisations with first-hand knowledge of problems.
6. *The value of youth.* Young people were less set in their ways as they have less invested in old beliefs and old practices. They usually had clearer ideas of how the world was changing and more energy and ambition to effect change. This meant that young people were particularly important in changing institutions and society more generally.
7. *Social engagement.* Institutions of HE could play important roles in their community and society more widely. It was possible to see the increasing specialisation and subject-centeredness (epitomised by the rise of single-subject Honours degrees) of universities in the 1950s as part of a retreat into ivory towers. There was a need for another kind of institution that placed value on engagement with the community and wider society.

All this may sound too good to be true and it was. Robinson did not always live up to his high aspirations or high ideals. When the going got tough, the ideal of critical discussion could degenerate into wheeling and dealing and horse-trading. It could also degenerate into *ad hominem* rancour. He had been a union leader and was used to negotiation and hard bargaining to get what he wanted. Robinson could be confrontational, cantankerous and political, in the pejorative sense of that word, in the service of his ideals.

---

[40] This was before the recognition of so-called 'wicked problems' (Rittel & Webber, 1973), reflective practice (Schon, 1988) and the demonizing of social engineering.

Brosan and Robinson shared many aspirations. For example, both favoured engagement with the world outside of HE institutions rather than ivory tower detachment, both supported interdisciplinarity in HE and both believed in technical-rational solutions to problems. In important ways, therefore, they were leading the new institution in the same direction.

However, there were also significant differences; Brosan did not share Robinson's socialist beliefs, while Robinson had a broader and more comprehensive vision of a new kind of HE system. Brosan was more autocratic and impulsive than Robinson who was more strategic and tactical. These differences meant they sometimes disagreed with each other and that disagreement could occasionally become acrimonious.

There was, however, one difference between Brosan and Robinson that was particularly productive for Enfield. Brosan knew best how local politics worked especially around education as he had been assistant Chief Education Officer for Middlesex the local authority for the college. Robinson, by contrast, had a better understanding of national educational politics and policy and the direction in which it was headed. He also had a better understanding of the Ministry of Education (and the Department of Education and Science which succeeded it) and its key figures, including Toby Weaver.

During the early years, 1962 and 1963, the main focus at ECT was on making the transition from being a local tech college to becoming a college of technology with a broader remit including a wider area of recruitment. This included developing more courses of HE in the form of London University external degrees.

Some innovation was possible immediately such as the establishment of a Learning Systems Unit to provide programmed learning support for students. The key development in those early very years, however, was the appointment of staff who would move the college in a new direction. Some of the appointments were of people with successful records in student politics. Many had a background in the social sciences. Given the academic profile of the college at the time which was concentrated on technical and technological subjects, and its new status as a college of technology, many were appointed in the name of 'liberal studies'.

The inclusion of liberal studies was a requirement for advanced courses in technology at that time. It was the way that technological subjects met the criticism of over-specialisation and demonstrated that they were providing a rounded higher education within the liberal education tradition. The appointment of social scientists aligned with Brosan's belief in HE focused on the application of knowledge because social sciences offered knowledge of the contexts within which new knowledge could be applied. From his perspective the social sciences provided *contextual* studies rather than *liberal* studies. From Robinson's perspective the appointment of social scientists provided an opportunity to bring into the college young people whose values resonated with his own. And by this time it was becoming clear that student demand was shifting from science and engineering (the main area of growth in the 1950s) towards the social sciences (Phillips, 1969).

By1964 ECT was ready for change; it was still mostly a local tech but it had big ideas and a disproportionate number of articulate young social scientists, some in surprisingly senior positions. 1964 was a momentous year for ECT for at least three reasons. First, the Labour Party won the general election, second, the CNAA was founded by Royal Charter in 1964 and, third, the Crick Report on Business Studies was published (Crick, 1964).

The success of the Labour Party in the1964 general election led to the adoption of a binary policy for HE, which assured the expansion of the non-University sector, including, of course, ECT. It is possible to overstate the significance of this election result, however, as it is now clear that the key members of the Conservative government also favoured a binary policy. According to a response to an enquiry from Toby Weaver about his position on the issue of the binary policy, Edward Boyle (Conservative Minister of Education, 1962-64, and Minister of State for Education and Science in 1964) responded:

> You are completely justified in your recollection that Quintin(Hogg) and I had concluded in favour of the binary policy before the 1964 election. (Boyle Papers, 11799/1 – quoted in Taylor and Steele, 2011, p.85)

There were, however, many people on the Conservative side who saw the binary policy as a way of protecting the traditional values of classical humanism within the universities from further attack or erosion; a binary policy introduced by the Conservative government would probably have been very different from that adopted by the Labour government.

The establishment of the CNAA in 1964 meant that Colleges of Technology could expand their degree-level work outside of the tutelage of universities with, at that time, their great respect for tradition and resistance to the development of courses in new vocational fields. At that time, according to (Pratt, 1997, p.11): 'Most colleges offered external London University degree courses, which their staff had no part in designing, planning or examining.'

The Crick Report of 1964 gave official approval to the development of undergraduate degree courses in Business Studies. The development of Business Studies was of considerable significance for the college for many reasons. First, it enabled ECT to expand. This meant that more new staff could be appointed, shifting power within the college further away from the more traditionalist engineering and technology.

Another reason that expansion into Business Studies was significant for ECT was that it offered a radical alternative to the continuing debate in higher education between the ideal of a broad liberal education versus subject-centred specialisation. The Business Studies degree envisaged the study of a range of academic disciplines for two years, providing breadth, followed by the study of a particular business specialisation (such as marketing, accounting or personnel). It thus combined the breadth of several different academic disciplines with the depth of specialisation in the final year.

Moreover, it combined academic study with vocational relevance. In theory, at least, the students would be applying the knowledge gained from academic studies in the lower levels of their course to vocational ends at the higher level. This turned the traditional university argument against narrow vocational training for a specific trade on its head. Advocates of the new Business Studies degree model criticised the over-specialisation of the single-subject Honours degree that had become dominant in universities as too narrow and offered instead a *broad* vocational course that prepared students for employment across the whole of industry, both private and public. This was not narrow vocationalism but broad vocationalism.

The new Business Studies degrees also turned the traditional hierarchy of academic values on its head. They placed academic subjects (in years 1 and 2) at the service of vocational relevance (in the final year). For those with a mindset that elevated 'academic education' above 'vocational training', this went against the natural order of things. Not all academic subject specialists at Enfield felt comfortable with this inversion of the established order of academic values, which helps to explain why there was so much acrimonious discussion in the development of the new courses.

The first course to be developed along these lines, the BA Business Studies, included a sandwich placement in the third year during which the students would gain work experience. The sandwich placement idea had been developed in the fields of engineering and technology by the old technical colleges. It engaged the students with the world outside of higher education, it provided a means of gaining first-hand knowledge about employment and industry and it enabled students to make their own assessment of the value of the academic subjects within the context of work. Most students on the Business Studies degree showed a marked increase in motivation for vocationally relevant study when they returned for their final year.

Undergraduate degrees in Business Studies were almost unknown in the universities of the mid-1960s and they proved popular. Consequently, recruitment was high, which provided the basis for significant expansion of the college. After the first-degree course in Business Studies was approved by the CNAA these courses became a distinctive feature of HE outside of the universities.

For students who had studied mathematics at A-level, the Mathematics for Business degree also expressed the new idea of a broad vocationalism; it gave access to employment across a wide range of occupations and organisations. This degree demonstrated that colleges in the public sector of HE could compete with universities in the recruitment of students even in traditional university subjects like mathematics if the courses were sufficiently applicable, applied and vocationally relevant.

Expansion of the college became an important way that Brosan and Robinson could realise their respective visions for HE at Enfield. Rather than trying to persuade and convert the relatively old staff who were employed at the college in 1962, at the time of its designation as a College of Technology, to their ideas of HE they were able to recruit new staff with values that were different from those embodied in the old technical college and staff who had strengths that could be used to grow the college in a different direction. Expansion of the college thus became an important part of changing the culture of the college from that of a technical college to that of a proto-polytechnic.

In 1965 Tony Crosland announced the binary policy for HE at Woolwich and in 1966 he announced that it would be implemented though the creation of polytechnics that would be formed by bringing together groups of colleges within each locality or region. It was proposed that Enfield would join with Hornsey College of Art and Hendon College of Technology to form a polytechnic. This gave another reason to pursue a policy of expansion at Enfield. The larger that Enfield was when it joined Hornsey and Hendon the less likely it would be that the values and culture of Enfield would be swamped by those of the two other colleges. This meant that, for those who cared about the values and culture of Enfield, growth was an imperative *before* the polytechnic was established.

Just as the 1950s had seen a shift in student demand in HE from the classics towards science and technology there was a shift in the 1960s in student demand towards the social sciences (Phillips, 1969). After the success of its development of degree-level work in Business Studies, especially the large Business Studies (sandwich) degree, it was clear that the social sciences offered scope for further expansion.

A large degree course in social sciences was proposed that would embody what could by now be recognised as Enfield's distinctive philosophy which included interdisciplinarity, social engagement through a period of work experience outside of the college, co-ordination of the different units of study in the development of a course, explicit attention to the philosophy of knowledge, comparatively open access (where interviews played a more important part relative to A-level results compared to most other HE institutions) and, by the final year, focus on the study of issues of social policy and/or vocational relevance rather than theory development per se. It would, for example, be the first social science degree in the country to include a period of supervised work experience i.e. a sandwich placement. The course was developed in the Enfield way i.e. by a lengthy period of critical and heated discussion where authority (cognitive and positional) played a relatively small role. The emergent course, the BA Social Science, was subject to much peer-review within the college, it passed CNAA scrutiny and it recruited well.

During 1967 Robinson was writing *The New Polytechnics: The People's Universities* (published in 1968). This book laid out a coherent philosophy, indeed blueprint, for the second sector of HE to meet the criticisms of university-based HE as it existed in the mid-1960s. In contrast to the vision of the Robbins Report which basically promised more of the same, the book provided a detailed account of a second sector of HE in Britain that would be more flexible, student-centred, socially-engaged and more focused on the application of knowledge than on the accumulation of new knowledge. It elaborated the ideas in Tony Crosland's Woolwich speech that announced the binary policy for HE and the subsequent announcement that the non-University sector would be led by the creation of polytechnics.

Meanwhile, another area of expansion at ECT was degree-level courses by part-time study. For the most part, part-time external degrees of London University were replaced by CNAA validated courses. In addition, entirely new part-time degrees were created where there was evidence of potential student demand. An early example, was the BA in Sociology of Education (the teachers' degree) where practicing teachers could top-up sub-degree or non-degree qualifications with degree-level study. And another important innovation was the part-time degree in Business Studies. This took the new concept of the Business Studies degree and developed it in ways that were suitable for part-time students. This was the first part-time Business Studies degree approved by the CNAA and is another illustration of the pioneering culture that had developed.

By the last years of the 1960s there seemed to be growing awareness outside of the college that something new and different was happening at Enfield. This was especially so after the publication in 1968 of Robinson's *New Polytechnics* which gave expression to ideas circulating within the college. It was a book that was very critical of traditional universities at the time and many people were naturally interested in what was going on at the college where Robinson was himself a leading light.

As the college got larger tension between courses and subjects became greater. An increase in size made it increasingly easy for staff to retreat from discussion about higher education, courses and the educational philosophy of the college into subject-centred groups and/or pursue their own research. The development of the CNAA proved a mixed blessing for Enfield's educational philosophy. On the one hand, it enabled the college to develop degree courses that were not external university degrees – so most of the new degrees embodied interdisciplinarity, engagement and application of knowledge. On the other hand, the CNAA was charged with validating degrees that were of comparable standard to those awarded by universities. The obvious way of ensuring that this was the case was to include a good proportion of university academics on CNAA visiting validation parties. Many key university academics who became involved in the CNAA were very supportive of the expansion of HE outside of universities as well as within them, but it also meant that the criteria of traditional universities would sometimes be applied in evaluating proposed courses. This strengthened subject-centred interests within the colleges. The establishment of staff academic credibility as measured in traditional university terms became an issue.

In the academic year 1969-70 Brosan left Enfield to become Director of the new North East London Polytechnic (NELP) and he then recruited Eric Robinson as his deputy. In his application (Brosan, not-dated) for this post he listed the achievements of ECT during his time as principal of which he was most proud, and this reveals much about his values and his philosophy of education while he was at Enfield. The achievements were listed under three headings:

1. The practical introduction of new educational ideas
2. The practical introduction of new organisational ideas
3. The practical introduction of a wide range of new courses

This is revealing as it confirms that he placed most value on the *application* of new ideas. The 'practical introduction of new ideas' can be disaggregated into testing out theoretical ideas in practice and the appliance of new knowledge, which reflect his background as a scientist and engineer.

He went on to explain that the educational ideas were in the areas of 'awareness of vocation, awareness of society, a problem-solving approach to teaching and a student-centred approach to teaching'. And he exemplified these with the introduction of interdisciplinary seminars, the construction of a new block for seminars and tutorials in which each member of staff would have their own room to conduct seminars and tutorials, personal tutorials based on the educational philosophy of the college, open-book and open-ended examinations, staff-study groups to think through new ideas and the use of technology (such as teaching machines) to support student learning.

Brosan elaborated on the practical introduction of new organisational ideas including the introduction of an elected academic board and an autonomous students' union which was rare in colleges in technology in those days. He also mentioned a 'unique' Faculty system with no departments but with each member of staff allocated to a course group. He went on to say that 'subject development is the responsibility of a subject head; but it is axiomatic that the interests of the course i.e. of the student are to take precedence over the interests of the subject.' And he mentioned additional student support services, including the establishment of a Programmed Instruction Centre and Higher Education Advisory Centre developed in partnership with the *Observer* newspaper.

Under the heading 'practical introduction of a wide range of new courses' he mentioned (*inter alia*):

- BSc Engineering (Hons and Ordinary) – CNAA
- BSc Mathematics for Business (Honours) – CNAA
- BA Business Studies (Honours) – CNAA
- BA Social Science (Honours) – CNAA
- BA Sociology of Education (Honours) – Part-time – CNAA
- BA Business Studies (Honours) - Part-time – CNAA
- A range of post-graduate Diplomas including those in Engineering Design, Social Work, Railway Mechanical Engineering and Highway and Traffic Engineering.

Brosan's departure led to the appointment of a new principal, John O'Neil with a far more conventional approach to education in the technical college tradition. More power was given to subject groups relative to courses. Meetings became shorter, more business-like and duller. The institution became more conservative. In terms of advanced further education, normal service was resumed.

However, the change in the culture and the leadership of ECT enabled more progress to be made in setting up Middlesex Polytechnic with Hendon College of Technology and Hornsey College of Art. It was easier for these colleges to do business with the new college leadership of Enfield which was less confrontational, less iconoclastic and less evangelical for a new kind of HE.

ECT ceased to exist at the end of 1972, becoming part of the newly-created Middlesex Polytechnic on 1 January 1973. The Director of the new polytechnic was appointed from outside of the constituent colleges and he again had a different view of HE. It was one much influenced by his experience of HE in the USA. It involved much greater student choice in the units of study that would make up the courses, it involved strengthening further the subject groups and it involved the erosion of interdisciplinarity, engagement and the reification of critical discussion that had characterised the high years of ECT. It was the end of an era at Enfield and the start of something quite different.

What was special or distinctive about ECT?

The life-course of ECT can be divided into three periods: its early years, 1962-63, its high years, 1964-69, and its late years, 1970-72. This section is focused on the high years of ECT as that was the time when it was most distinctive. At that time, ECT was very course-centred. It established an organisation structure that elevated courses above subjects because it prioritised the higher education of students above the accumulation of new subject-based knowledge and it was through the courses that that higher education was delivered. So its focus was on courses and course development. Courses were developed to meet the perceived needs of students and the perceived needs of the community and society more widely, including the application of new knowledge. The result was the development of a range of distinctive courses particularly in the fields of engineering, business studies and the social sciences, which together accounted for the large majority of the work of the college. Distinctive features of these courses included interdisciplinary studies, student engagement through work experience and a broad vocational relevance rather than narrow vocational training for specific occupations.

Some of the courses developed quite new ideas such as the replacement of 'liberal studies' by 'contextual studies' to support the application of new knowledge, the notion of academic subjects serving (and hence subservient to) vocational subjects and the development of part-time courses that were not simply full-time courses offered on the basis of part-time attendance.

The processes through which these courses were developed were also distinctive, at least compared to the way that courses had been prepared for university approval. Before the establishment of the CNAA it often meant simply trying to copy a university course on the basis of fewer resources in less suitable accommodation. The most distinctive element of the process of course development at ECT was the seemingly interminable discussion involved. The prevailing scepticism of university cultural values, authority and practices meant that each course had to be argued through from first principles, especially the principles of student advancement and social need and this was followed by very detailed planning. There was an absence of deference to universities, university models and university practices. That which was old and established had to justify itself in the same way as that which was new and untried. Arguably, the employment of a large number of philosophers at the college contributed to the argumentative nature of these discussions. There was quite a lot of informal staff development, taking place during the process of staff development, in the bar, within interdisciplinary seminars, through team teaching and by some staff sitting in on each others' classes.

The context in which the courses were developed was also distinctive. The most important aspect of that context was the ethos of ECT which was based on a set of dominant values and guiding beliefs. ECT, at least in its high years, had a set of values that underpinned course development, both the content and the processes. Critical discussion was valued as the basis for decisions and actions. Student-centeredness was valued above subject development and the accumulation of new subject-based knowledge. Action was valued in a way that reflected, intentionally or otherwise, MacMurray's philosophy that 'all meaningful knowledge is for the sake of action' (quoted in Weaver, 1994). Nothing and no-one was above criticism which fostered a sense of iconoclasm and meant that views of the youngest and most junior members of staff could prevail if they could make their case sufficiently forcefully. Youth was valued for its fresh ideas and energy. According to Eric Robinson in 1970:

> On the day I accepted an appointment to Enfield, I sought and obtained only one assurance – that the principal was willing to contemplate appointments of young people to the teaching staff at higher grades than they could normally obtain elsewhere. My belief in the value of employing young teachers was largely based on my experience at Brunel which included some research into the problems of improving curriculum and teaching methods. ... Much of the leadership in developing new degree courses at Enfield was shouldered by people who had only recently graduated themselves.[41]

Difference was valued at ECT even to the point of eccentricity. In order to test new ideas it was necessary to have those with contrary views, so even troublemakers were valued if they challenged conventional wisdom or the established order.

The culture of Enfield comprised also some dominant beliefs that influenced decisions and practices. One belief was that conflict can be creative – this helps to explain the tolerance of extended, and sometimes acrimonious, discussion. There was also a belief that there existed an alternative to the contemporary university conceptions of higher education. Another belief was that scholarship was not the same as research: good scholars did not have to be researchers and good scholarship was probably more important for effective teaching than research. From this followed the belief that that research excellence did not equate to teaching excellence. And there also was a belief in agency, that reason, knowledge and action can change, or at least influence, the status quo.

For most people, particularly those who got involved in course development, ECT was an exciting place to be. It offered a space for innovation and pioneering i.e. having new practical ideas and testing them out in action. It offered a high degree of personal and professional freedom. And it offered the opportunity to mix intellectual discussion with political intrigue – some staff excelled in the former, some in the latter and some used their freedom to steer clear of both.

---

41 See: http://studymore.org.uk/ssctim.htm

What was the larger significance of ECT?

The main aim of this last section is to offer an answer to the question, did ECT have an influence on the course of the development of HE in Britain and, if so, how? ECT was established in 1962 so the place to start is the nature of HE at that time.

In 1962 it was widely believed that HE in Britain was, for the most part, synonymous with university education, that the involvement of technical colleges and other FE colleges was at most peripheral and that such HE as took place in FE/technical colleges was only possible by association with a local university or the University of London External Programmes.[42] That sentence contains three assumptions and it is worth looking at each of them more closely.

University education was viewed as synonymous with higher education for several good reasons. First, the term 'higher education' was not in common use in Britain before WW2. Until then (and after) it was termed university-level education. Second, the 'higher' in higher education did not refer only to the fact that it was education 'on top of' secondary education, which would apply to all forms of tertiary education, but had connotations of morality and social status. Certainly the kind of university education advanced by Cardinal Newman or Benjamin Jowett at Oxford was intended to develop students morally and socially as well as intellectually. By tradition, it was universities that provided a proper higher education. It would not be an exaggeration to say that university education defined what was understood by higher education. From this perspective, real higher education was what took place in universities whereas that which took place in colleges outside of the universities was a kind of 'HE-lite', particularly if such HE was provided on the basis of part-time study. In other words, universities provided true higher education, which was of a superior kind to that available from FE/technical colleges. That is why, for most people, especially those who carried most weight, socially, politically and intellectually, the term higher education immediately brought mind university education.

Second, traditionally, the involvement of FE/technical colleges in HE had been only peripheral. It was peripheral in the sense that non-university colleges had contributed a small percentage of students

[42] Renamed 'University of London External System' in 2007.

engaged in degree-level study; the vast majority were believed to be in universities, certainly the vast majority of those engaged in full-time study. It was peripheral also because advanced further education was only a minority of the work of the technical and other FE colleges. Most of their work was at a lower level including recreational study, sometimes supported by the Workers Education Association, A-level work or its equivalent, and narrow vocational training for specific occupations, possibly involving manual employment.

Thirdly, degree-level work in local authority colleges was dependent on universities so that without the university sector there would be no non-University HE. Degree-level work in those colleges depended on the extension work of universities, particularly the extension work of the University of London External Programmes. It was the universities that designed and examined such degree-level courses as were available in local authority institutions. HE only existed in FE and technical colleges at all by the grace of the universities.

Together, these three beliefs were the foundations of the hierarchical view of HE centred on the most prestigious universities and extending outwards towards the kind of HE available within FE/technical colleges on the margins.

However, each of these beliefs could be challenged. First, the notion that universities provided the one true higher education did not stand up to scrutiny. The nature of university education, even the purpose of university education was, in fact, a much-contested issue. The main contest was between those who defined university education in terms of liberal education and those who defined it in terms of the advancement of knowledge. On one side were those who believed the main purpose of a university education was to develop the minds of the most intelligent young people of each generation to produce graduates with well-honed intellects which could be employed in any of a wide range of the most responsible positions in society. This reflected Newman's idea of a university education refracted through the influence of Jowett at Oxford. To realise its main goal it favoured a broad-based liberal education to produce well-rounded graduates. This belief found expression in Lindlay's establishment of 'Modern Greats' (Philosophy, Politics and Economics) at Oxford in the early twentieth century, the establishment of Keele University with its broad-based degrees in the mid-twentieth century and the establishment of new universities such as Sussex with interdisciplinary aspirations in the early 1960s.

On the other side, were those who saw the primary purpose of a university as the advancement of knowledge within recognised academic disciplines and the primary purpose of a university education as the preparation of young minds to be able to contribute to the advancement of such knowledge. It seemed clear that the most effective way of advancing the accumulation of knowledge was by academic specialisation. This view found expression in the adoption of the PhD by British universities after WW1; this elevated research training through research on a specialised topic to the pinnacle of higher education. Another manifestation was the growth of single-subject specialist Honours degrees after WW2. This was supported by the decline in student demand for classics-based HE and the rise in student demand for courses in science with its reductionist/specialisation approach to the advancement of knowledge.

Second, HE outside of the universities may have been peripheral until WW2 in that it constituted a small proportion of the total HE in the country but things had changed dramatically after the war. There had been large increase in demand for HE, particularly in science and technology, and the universities had resisted, through the UGC buffer, a larger expansion in student numbers. Consequently, there was a large 'overspill' demand that had been taken up by the technical colleges. It had grown much faster in the post-war period than the universities. So by the early 1960s the number of students, full-time and part-time, enrolled for degree-level study outside of the universities was comparable to the number within the universities themselves.

The belief that HE only existed in FE institutions at all because of the extension work of universities offering external degrees and examining them suggested that FE/technical colleges were incapable of designing and examining their own degree courses. This could be challenged by the experience of the colleges of advanced technology which, since the mid-1950s, had developed their own post-A-level Diploma courses which were scrutinised and validated by the National Council for Technical Awards. This showed that, at least in the field of technology, non-university institutions could design and examine degree-level courses. But advanced technology was still a minority interest for universities at the time and certainly far removed from the university education of Newman or Jowett, so whether FE/technical colleges could design and examine degree courses in fields distant from technology remained unproven.

In order to challenge the hierarchical model of HE, it was necessary to successfully refute each of the three beliefs on which it rested. While it was fairly easy to show that the first two were false, the third one, that technical colleges were not capable of developing degree courses, in a wide range of subject areas independently of universities, was at least plausible.

After 1962, Eric Robinson held a senior position at ECT which meant that he was the member of the group of proponents of the 'two sector' concept of HE who was actually in a position to test out in practice the ideas underpinning the concept of a non-University sector of HE as separate and different from the university sector.

Several contributors to this book have used the term 'Enfield experiment' and that was the way it sometimes felt to those who were teaching there. What was being tested by the experiment was nothing less than the new conception of a second sector of HE in Britain that was separate and different from the university sector and in particular that colleges of technology could design excellent courses of HE without continuing support and supervision by universities. The CNAA was established in 1964 and by the end of 1965 ECT had degree courses approved in a broad range of fields including engineering, business studies, mathematics and sociology of education. According to Robinson again:

> When I came to Enfield in September 1962 I expected to lead a small-scale but intensive educational experiment. The scale of the subsequent development was not anticipated.

The significance of the Enfield experiment in HE is that ECT did not seek to replicate university education in either of its two archetypal forms, broad-based liberal HE or specialised single-subject degrees. Instead, it sought to construct its degree courses from scratch. The Enfield experiment led to a myriad of innovations arising from building degree courses from first principles and creating a college environment in which they could succeed. Here are some examples drawn from the previous pages of this book:

- Testing out a new kind of vocationalism that was broad rather than narrow.
- Reconceptualising liberal studies as contextual studies and implementing interdisciplinarity through integrating studies.
- Social engagement of social science students through a period of work placement.
- Introduction of a college structure that made the subject groups subservient to the course groups.
- Programmed learning support for students
- Small group teaching of engineering students
- Testing out the Crick model of a degree-level course in business studies.
- Novel assessment methods

Some of these were less successful than others including, for example, seminar groups for engineering students. But the result of these innovations was a series of 'firsts' for the newly-conceived FE sector of HE. These included the first Business Studies degree to be approved by the CNAA, the first social science degree to include a period of work experience and the first Part-time degree in Business Studies to be approved by the CNAA.

ECT took the new concept of a second sector of HE that was based on different values and beliefs than those of the university sector and attempted to implement it in practice. It showed that it was possible for FE colleges to design and examine HE courses without regulation by a university. ECT provided 'proof of concept'.

The demonstration effect of this was significant for many colleges outside the universities. ECT provided evidence that FE colleges could stand on their own feet and need not be deferential to universities. More than that, ECT demonstrated that the CNAA would validate innovative courses and not just those that replicated university courses. This made it clear that the CNAA could be an instrument of liberation rather than a means of control. And it demonstrated that some of the HE myths of the 1950s and 1960s were false, such as the myth that FE colleges could not successfully provide courses of HE without regulation by universities and that academic freedom implies disengagement from society i.e. retreat into an ivory tower.

There were also two other significant consequences of ECT that stand out. It led to the production of the book, *The New Polytechnics: the Peoples Universities* by Robinson, which was very influential in the non-University sector of HE; there were probably few Directors of Polytechnics (or persons in senior positions in colleges who aspired to be a Director of Polytechnic) who did not read that book. For example, Derek Birley who became Director of N. Ireland Polytechnic (and, later, first Vice-Chancellor of the University of Ulster) said he knew nothing about the job until he read Robinson's book (Steele, 2018).

Finally, there was the effect of what has been termed 'The Enfield Diaspora'. After the high years at Enfield many of the more active players at ECT went on to influential posts in HE in Britain, including Directors of at least four polytechnics, three of whom became Vice-Chancellors of universities.[43]

HE in Britain was transformed in the second half of the twentieth century. At the start of the 1960s it was elitist, accounting for less than 5 per cent of school-leavers, unresponsive to the needs of society which was becoming more technology-based and it was desperately trying to cling on to the idea of broad-based liberal education intended to provide a well-rounded education for graduates who could apply their finely honed intellects in a wide range of responsible positions in society. The main concern of universities at that time was the battle between Newman's idea of a university education and the growth of specialised subject-centred Honours courses focused on narrow academic disciplines.

Fifty years later HE in Britain had expanded such that the age participation rate exceeded a third of school-leavers, courses of HE were available in subjects relevant to a large range of new learned professions, the privileged subjects had become the STEM subjects (science, technology, engineering and mathematics) and government funding for engagement (aka 'third leg' funding) had become a reality. In the early 1960s the large majority of university graduates became

[43] At a much more modest level the editors of this book made their own small contributions: Tony Crilly was involved with the development of City Polytechnic of Hong Kong and Tom's priority when he arrived at Brighton Polytechnic in 1980 was to establish a part-time degree in Business Studies and, later, the development of professional doctorates that owed much to thinking he first encountered at ECT.

teachers (in secondary or tertiary education) and 50 years later the large majority found employment across the other sectors of the economy.

It is possible to argue that ECT was a small North London (Ponders End) college with ideas above its station, unrealistic aspirations, even delusions of grandeur. It is also possible to argue that it made a significant contribution to the transformation of HE in Britain in the ensuing decades by providing proof of the concept of a second sector of higher education separate and different from universities and it demonstrated that it was possible for colleges that made up that sector to design and examine high quality HE without supervision by universities. Based on the accounts in this book, we think the balance of probabilities lies with the latter.

APPENDIX[44]

Post-war expressions of government concern about technical and technological education up to the 1962 start of Enfield College of Technology

1945: *Higher Technological Education* This is usually called the Percy Report and it recommended that some technical colleges offer courses at degree level.
1946: *Scientific Manpower* This is usually known as the Barlow Report. It recommended that Britain's universities double their output of scientists.
1947: *Advisory Council of Scientific Policy* (ACSP) was established.
1948: *Employment and Training Act 1948* This established the Youth Employment Service.
1948: Establishment of *National Advisory Council on Education for Industry and Commerce* (NACEIC)
1951: *Higher Technological Education* White Paper
1955: *National Council for Technological Awards* (NCTA) was established.
1956: *Technical Education* White paper which announced that selected technical colleges were to be 'upgraded' to Colleges of Advanced Technology.
1956: *Colleges of Advanced Technology (*CATs) established in Birmingham, Edinburgh (Herriot-Watt), London (Battersea) and Salford.
1957: *Colleges of Advanced Technology* (CATs) established in Bradford, Cardiff, London (Chelsea and Northampton Polytechnics) and Loughborough.
1957: 27 Regional colleges designated, mostly based on technical colleges.
1958: *Local Government Act 1958,* contained provisions relating to technical education.
1960: *College of Advanced Technology* established in Bristol.
1961: *Better Opportunities in Technical Education* White Paper
1962: *Education Act 1962* required local authorities to provide grants for living costs and tuition fees to students in universities and degree-level studies in technical institutions.
1962: Brunel at Uxbridge designated a *College of Advanced Technology.*
1962: *Enfield Technical College* becomes *Enfield College of Technology.*

[44] Most of the material for this Appendix came from Gillard D (2011) *Education in England: a brief history* www.educationengland.org.uk/history and Tight, M. (2009) *The Development of Higher Education in the UK since 1945*, Maidenhead: Open University Press.

REFERENCES

Arnold, M. 1869. *Culture and Anarchy: An Essay in Political and Social Criticism*. Oxford: Project Gutenberg.

Ashby E. 1958. *Technology and the academics; an essay on universities and the scientific revolution.* London: Macmillan.

Ashby E. 1974. *Adapting universities to a technological society*. London: Jossey-Bass.

Baillie, R. 1996. 'Long Memory Processes and Fractional Integration in Econometrics', *Journal of Econometrics*, 73: 5-59.

Baillie, R. and McMahon, P. 1989. *The Foreign Exchange Market: Theory and Econometric Evidence*. Cambridge University Press.

Baillie, R., Lippens R. and McMahon, P. 1983. 'Testing Rational Expectations and Efficiency in the Foreign Exchange Market', *Econometrica*, 51: 553-563.

Bandura, A. 1997. *Self-efficacy: The exercise of control*. London: Macmillan.

Barnett, R. 1994. *The limits of competence: knowledge, higher education and society*. London: Open University Press.

Binswanger, H., and Landell-Mills, P. 2016. *The World Bank's strategy for reducing poverty and hunger: a report to the development community*. Washington DC: World Bank.

Bourner, T. and Rospigliosi, A. 2008. 'Forty years on: long-term change in the first destinations of graduates', *Higher Education Review*, 41(1): 36-59.

Bourner, T. 2008. 'The fully-functioning university'. *Higher Education Review*, 40(2): 26-45.

Bourner, T. and Crilly, T. 1981. 'Mathematics Graduates in the Labour Market', *International Journal of Mathematical Education in Science and Technology*, 13(2): 227-239.

Bourner, T. and Hindmarch, A. 1981. 'CNAA Business Studies Degrees 1971-75', *Business Education*, 74-83.

Bourner, T., Greener, S. and Rospigliosi, A. 2011. 'Graduate employability and the propensity to learn in employment: a new vocationalism', *Higher Education Review*, 433: 5-30.

Bourner, T., Heath, L. and Rospigliosi, A. 2014. 'Research as a transferable skill', *Higher Education Review*, 46(2): 20-45.

Bourner, T., Reynolds, A., Hamed, M. and Barnett, R. 1991. *Part-time Students and their Experience of Higher Education*. London: Open University Press with the Society for Research into Higher Education.

Box, G. E. P. and Jenkins, G. M. 1970. *Time Series Analysis, Forecasting and Control.* San Francisco: Holden Day.

Brosan, G. undated. Application form for the position of Director of North East London Polytechnic. George Brosan Archives in Library of East London University.

Brown, R. G. 1962. *Smoothing, Forecasting and Prediction of Discrete Time Series*. Holden day, San Francisco.

Burgess, T. 1964. *A Guide to English Schools*. Middlesex: Pelican.

Butterfield, H. 1962. *The universities and education today*. London: Taylor and Francis.

Carr, J. and Roberts, A. 1998. 'Sparks Flying. The History of the Enfield Campus of Middlesex University', *North Circular*, (11.6.1998). (Republished in study handbooks, and student introductions to Enfield from 1998 until 2008, when the Enfield campus closed).

Clark, G. 2008. *A farewell to alms: a brief economic history of the world.* Princeton University Press.

Clarke, A. 2001. 'The Joy of Maths' in *Greetings, Carbon-Based Bipeds!: Collected Essays, 1934-1998.*

Committee on Higher Education 1963. *Higher Education: Report of the Committee appointed by the Prime Minister ('The Robbins Report')*. London: HMSO.

Cowling, A. J. 1998. 'Knowing versus Doing: Academic and Vocational Education for Informatics in the UK'. In *International Symposium on Computer Employment and Education. Available at: http://www. dcs. shef. ac. uk/~ajc/seteach/knowdo. pdf. [Accessed 28/03/2017].*

Crick, W. F. 1964. *A Higher Award in Business Studies: report of the advisory sub-committee on a Higher Award in Business Studies*. London: HMSO.

Crilly, T. and Millward, S. 1988. 'Sums of powers of integers: A general method', *Mathematical Gazette*, 72: 205–207. http://www.jstor.org/stable/3618252.

Crilly T. and Millward. S. 1992. 'An optimisation problem for triangles', *Mathematical Gazette*, 76: 345–350. http://www.jstor.org/stable/3618370.

Crosland, S. 1982. *Tony Crosland.* London: Jonathan Cape, Penguin Random House.

Crossman, R. 1957. 'Some notes on elite education with special reference to the Problem of Universities', Re211/Oct 1957, Labour Party Study Group on Education Minutes, National Museum of Labour History.

Deaton, A. 2006. 'The Great Escape: A Review of Robert Fogel's *The Escape from Hunger and Premature Death, 1700-2100'*, *Journal of Economic Literature*, 44(1): 106-114.

Deaton, A. 2013. *The great escape: health, wealth, and the origins of inequality*. Princeton University Press.

Doyal, L. 1974. 'Interdisciplinary studies in higher education', *Higher Education Quarterly,* 28(4): 470-87.

Earle, J., Moran C., and Ward-Perkins, Z. 2016. *The Econocracy: The perils of leaving economics to the experts*. Manchester University Press.

Edgerton, D. 1996. 'The 'White Heat' revisited: the British government and technology in the 1960s', *Twentieth Century British History*, *71*: 53-82.

Elton, L. 1992. 'Research, Teaching and Scholarship in an Expanding Higher Education System', *Higher Education Quarterly*, 46(3): 252-268.

Fogel, R. W. 2004. *The escape from hunger and premature death, 1700-2100: Europe, America, and the Third World.* Vol. 38. Cambridge University Press.

Ford, J. 1970. *Social Class and the Comprehensive School.* Routledge and Kegan Paul.

Gardner, H. 1983. *Frames of mind: The theory of multiple intelligences.* New York: Basics.

Gibson, M. 1998. *A history of Kingston University*. Kingston University Press.

Gilbert, D. 2006. *Stumbling on happiness*. New York: Random House.

Gillard D, 2011. *Education in England: a brief history*. www.educationengland.org.uk/history

Godwin, C. 1998. The origin of the binary system. *History of Education, 27*(2): 171-191

Gott, B. and Crothall, H. 1915. *Secondary Schools and Technical Institutes in the Administrative County of Middlesex*. Middlesex County Council.

Gott, B. and Maples, E. 1907. *Higher education in the administrative County of Middlesex.* Middlesex County Council.

Grattan-Guinness, I. and Holliman P. 1983. 'Undergraduate mathematics for the blind: Report on a case study', *Mathematical Gazette*, 67: 77–89, http://www.jstor.org/stable/3616876.

Hale, E. 1964. *Report of the Committee on university teaching methods*. University Grants Commission, HMSO.

Hammarling, S. 1970. *Latent Roots and Latent Vectors*. Bristol: Adam Hilger. (Also published by The University of Toronto Press. http://eprints.ma.man.ac. uk/1021/).

Healey, M. and Jenkins, A. 2009. *Developing undergraduate research and enquiry*. York: Higher Education Academy

Healey, M., Jenkins, A. and Lea, J. 2014. *Developing research-based curricula in college-based higher education*. York: Higher Education Academy

Hindmarch, A., Atchison, M. and Marke, R. 1977. *Accounting: An Introduction.* London: Macmillan 1977.

Humboldt, W. v. [1810] 1970. 'On the Spirit and Organisational Framework of Intellectual Institutions in Berlin', *Minerva* 8: 242-267.

Hutchins, R. and Adler, M. 1969. *The Great Ideas Today*. Chicago: Encyclopaedia Britannica.

Kerr, C. 1991. *The Great Transformation in Higher Education: 1960-1980.* Albany: State University of New York Press.

Kivinen, O., Hedman, J. and Kaipainen, P. 2007. 'From elite university to mass higher education: educational expansion, equality of opportunity and returns to university education', *Acta Sociologica* 50: 231–247.

Knowles, E. 2010. *How to Read a Word.* Oxford University Press.

Lipsey, R. and Archibald, G. 1967. *An introduction to a mathematical treatment of economics*. London: Weidenfeld and Nicholson.

Lipsey, R. and Lancaster, K. 1956. 'The General Theory of Second Best', *Review of Economic Studies*, 24(1): 11–32.

McAdams, D. 1993. *The Stories We Live: Personal Myths And The Making Of The Self.* New York: Guildford Press.

Millican J. and Bourner T. 2014. *Learning to Make a Difference: Student Community Engagement and the Higher Education Curriculum.* Leicester: National Institute for Adult and Continuing Education.

Ministry of Education *15 to 18: A report of the Central Advisory Council for Education England* (*'Crowther Report'*) 1959. London: HMSO.

Ministry of Education: *The New Secondary Education.* Ministry of Education Pamphlet No. 9, 1947. London: HMSO.

Mokyr, J. 2011. *The Lever of Riches: Technological Creativity and Economic Progress.* Oxford University Press.

Newman, J. 1873. *The Idea of a University*. London: Holt, Rinehart and Winston.

Ormerod, P. 1994. *The Death of Economics*. London: Faber and Faber.

Phillips, C. M. 1969. *Changes in subject choice at school and university.* London: Weidenfeld and Nicolson.

Pratt, J. 1997. *The Polytechnic Experiment: 1965-1992*. Buckingham: Open University Press.

Rawls, J. [1971] 1999. *A Theory of Justice*. Cambridge, Mass.: Harvard University Press.

Rittel H., and Webber M. 1973. 'Dilemmas in a General Theory of Planning', *Policy Sciences,* 4: 155–169.

Robbins, L. 1963. *Higher Education: Report of the Committee appointed by the Prime Minister under the chairmanship of Lord Robbins, 1961-1963.* London: HMSO.

Roberts, A. 2002- *Science, Society and Creativity at Middlesex University.* http://studymore.org.uk/ssctim.htm

Robinson, E. E. 1968. *The New Polytechnics: The People's Universities.* Harmondsworth: Penguin Press.

Roser, M. 2017 - 'Life Expectancy', *Published online at OurWorldInData.org.* Retrieved from: 'https://ourworldindata.org/life-expectancy' [Online Resource].

Safire, W. 1997. *Watching My Language:: Adventures in the Word Trade*. Random House.

Schön, D. A. 2002. 'From technical rationality to reflection-in-action', In *Supporting Life-long learning,* (M. Cartright, M. Edwards, R. Reeve, Editors, London: Routledge ,pp. 40-61,

Sharp, P. 1987. *The Creation of the Local Authority Sector of Higher Education.* Lewes: Falmer Press.

Shattock, M. 1994. *The UGC and the Management of British Universities*. Surrey: Society for Research into Higher Education and Open University Press.

Simpson, R. 1983. *How the PhD Came to Britain. A Century of Struggle for Postgraduate Education. SRHE Monograph 54*. Surrey: Society for Research into Higher Education.

Snow, C. 1963. The Two Cultures: and A Second Look. Cambridge University Press.

Spiegel, M. 1963.*Advanced Calculus*. New York; Schaum.

Steele, T. 2018. Transcript of an interview with Eric Robinson in 2006 (for Richard Taylor and Tom Steele).

Tarnas, R. 1993. *The passion of the Western mind: Understanding the ideas that have shaped our world view*. New York: Ballantine Books.

Taylor, R. and Steele, T. 2011. *British Labour and Higher Education, 1945 to 2000: Ideologies, Policies and Practice*. London: Bloomsbury Publishing.

Tight, M. 2009. *The Development of Higher Education in the UK since 1945*. Maidenhead: Open University Press.

Trow, M. 1974. 'Problems in the Transition from Elite to Mass Higher Education'. In *Policies for Higher Education: Conference on Future Structures of Post-Secondary Education*, Organisation for Economic Co-operation and Development, Paris: OECD.

Walkington, H. 2015. *Students as researchers: Supporting undergraduate research in the disciplines in higher education.* York: Higher Education Academy

Weaver, T. 1994. 'Knowledge alone gets you nowhere', *Capability*, 1(1): 6-12.

Wells, H. G. 1915. Boon: *The Mind of the Race, The Wild Asses of the Devil, and The Last Trump*. George H. Doran Company.

Printed in Poland
by Amazon Fulfillment
Poland Sp. z o.o., Wrocław